Migrating Raptors of the World

Migrating Raptors of the World

THEIR ECOLOGY & CONSERVATION

KEITH L. BILDSTEIN

COMSTOCK PUBLISHING ASSOCIATES

a division of

CORNELL UNIVERSITY PRESS

Ithaca & London

First published 2006 by Cornell University Press

Printed in the United States of America

Library of Congress Cataloging-in-Publication Data

Bildstein, Keith L.
  Migrating raptors of the world : their ecology and conservation / Keith L. Bildstein.
    p. cm.
  Includes bibliographical references and index.
  ISBN-13: 978-0-8014-4179-0 (cloth : alk. paper)
  ISBN-10: 0-8014-4179-X (cloth : alk. paper)
  1. Birds of prey—Migration. I. Title.
  QL677.78.B55 2006
  598.9—dc22   2006014457

Cornell University Press strives to use environmentally responsible suppliers and materials to the fullest extent possible in the publishing of its books. Such materials include vegetable-based, low-VOC inks and acid-free papers that are recycled, totally chlorine-free, or partly composed of nonwood fibers. For further information, visit our website at www.cornellpress.cornell.edu.

Cloth printing   10 9 8 7 6 5 4 3 2 1

*For Mr. Sarkis Acopian, whose
visionary support for raptor-migration science
and conservation at Hawk Mountain Sanctuary
has provided a new generation of conservation
scientists with the tools needed to protect
the world's migratory birds of prey*

CONTENTS

PREFACE

I grew up in the meadowlands of northern New Jersey, just outside New York City, and the first raptor I ever saw was a Cooper's Hawk (scientific names are in the appendix). I was fourteen at the time, and the bird in question was targeting my father's prize homing pigeons. The in-flight pursuits I watched, which typically lasted less than 10 seconds, changed my life. I wanted to know more about birds of prey, and I wanted to know more as quickly as possible. I have spent much of my life realizing the first of these twin ambitions. The second, knowing more as quickly as possible, has proved to be more elusive. *Migrating Raptors of the World: Their Ecology and Conservation* summarizes much of what I have managed to learn.

Birds of prey, or raptors—the hawks, eagles, and falcons of the world—are a diverse group of approximately 300 species of charismatic predatory birds about which much has been written. The subjects of numerous technical accounts and popular treatments, raptors are as well portrayed in the avian literature as is any group of birds. Literally hundreds of books have been written about their behavior, ecology, conservation, identification, and interactions with humans. So is another book about raptors necessary? I believe so. Despite the enormous amount of literature, recent advances in our understanding of raptor biology, particularly our understanding of their short- and long-distance movements, have created a gap in the literature that this book is intended to help fill.

The most recent book on raptor-migration science, Paul Kerlinger's *Flight Strategies of Migrating Hawks*, purposely ignored "much of the hawk migration literature based on counts of hawks at particular locations," as well as most "conservation/management-oriented materials," while focusing on the results of "basic research" (Kerlinger 1989). Its predecessors, including Donald Heintzelman's *Autumn Hawk Flights* (1975), *A Guide to Hawkwatching in North America* (1979) (updated in 2004), and *The Migrations of Hawks* (1986), do admirable jobs presenting information on the movements of raptors at single sites and along flyways in North and Central America, as well as summarizing much of that region's technical literature. My own atlas of raptor migration, *Raptor Watch: A Global Directory of Raptor Migration Watchsites,* coauthored with Jorje Zalles (Zalles and Bildstein 2000), details the global geography of raptor migration and conservation pressure points, but offers little in the way of raptor-migration science. Although all of these books have contributed much to the raptor literature, no previous book combines an up-to-date balanced overview of the principal aspects of raptor-migration science and conservation, together with a detailed global geography of the phenomenon. This, then, is the purpose of this book.

Each year at least 183 species of raptors—62 percent of all birds of prey—undertake seasonal migrations. Although some individuals travel fewer than 100 kilometers, millions regularly undertake long-distance, and in many cases intercontinental, migratory journeys. Unlike smaller birds that fly chiefly by night using flapping flight, raptors are largely solar-powered migrants that fly by day, and often while soaring. Many, including Ospreys, harriers, and falcons, often migrate across broad fronts; whereas others, including many hawks and most eagles, concentrate their movements along established migration corridors. Overall, the long-distance movements of raptors represent the most spectacular migrations of land-based predators on earth.

Most birds of prey avoid extended over-water flights because of the general lack of soaring conditions there. Many European breeders, for example, avoid lengthy Mediterranean passages by funneling through the Iberian Peninsula and crossing into West Africa at the Strait of Gibraltar at the western end of the Mediterranean. Others island hop across the central Mediterranean via the Italian peninsula, Sicily, and the Maltese archipelago. Still others fly southeast across the Balkans and along the western shore of the Black Sea before entering the Middle East via the Bosporus and Dardanelles at the eastern end of the Mediterranean, there to be joined by trans-Caucasus migrants from easternmost Europe and Asian migrants from as far away as Eastern Siberia. Altogether, 43 species of Asian and European raptors funnel through the Middle East each spring and autumn, making the region one of the most important migratory corridors in the world. Six species, the Black Kite, Western Honey Buzzard, Levant Sparrowhawk, Steppe Buzzard, Lesser Spotted Eagle, and Steppe Eagle, compose the bulk of the visible flight. Although the species composition and timing of the flight differ in Mesoamerica and Southeast Asia, similar large-scale movements occur there as well. Smaller-scale movements occur elsewhere across the globe.

Imagination, ideas, criticism, and controls—all essential aspects of scientific inquiry (Alerstam 1990)—have been applied to studies of raptor migration for some time. Intensive and extensive studies, including visual counts at traditional watchsites, trapping and banding, and satellite, radio, and radar tracking of migrants, have combined to increase our understanding of raptor migration globally. Most recently, expanded efforts in the tropics are challenging many of our ideas regarding the "rules" by which migrating raptors travel. *Migrating Raptors of the World: Their Ecology and Conservation* analyzes and summarizes both benchmark and recent findings in raptor-migration science and conservation in ways that should be of value to both professional biologists and interested laypeople. Largely up-to-date through early 2005, the work is designed to stimulate additional efforts.

Credit for this book resides in many places. Michele Pilzer, Kyle McCarty, Kristen Naimoli, and several dozen Hawk Mountain Sanctuary interns carefully read and critiqued most or all of the manuscript. I thank them for their thoughtful criticisms, many of which helped clarify my writing. Several colleagues, including Mike Collopy, David Bird, George Cox, and Ted Davis reviewed one or more chapters. Artist Tony Geiger constructed the many maps and figures that grace the work. Photographer extraordinaire Fernando Barrios contributed photographs of birds of prey at the Strait of Gibraltar, and Visual Resources for Ornithology (VIREO) supplied a series of images of many additional migrants from elsewhere in the world. Cornell University Press, and in particular Peter J. Prescott, who first suggested the book, Lou Robinson, Katherine R. Lentz, and Candace Akins patiently shepherded my amblings throughout the effort. Cathi Reinfelder patiently copy edited the work.

A series of visits to Hawk Mountain Sanctuary in the late 1960s led me to a career in raptor-migration science and, eventually, to work in raptor conservation. More recently, that same organization and its board of directors have provided the professional environment within which to plan, undertake, and complete this manuscript. The Sanctuary's Julian Hill Library in raptor biology and conservation helped broaden my perspective considerably. I am especially indebted to Mr. Sarkis Acopian whose many gifts to Hawk Mountain Sanctuary have fostered an intellectual climate for work in raptor-migration science and conservation.

Finally, much of what follows draws heavily upon the many productive conversations and correspondences I have had with peers during the past thirty-five years. Among the many individuals who have helped refine my thoughts are Bea Arroyo, Marc Bechard, David Bird, Bill Clark, Mike Collopy, Miguel Ferrer, Laurie Goodrich, the late Frances Hamerstrom, Donald Heintzelman, Steve Hoffman, Mike McGrady, Bernd Meyburg, Juan Jose Negro, Ian Newton, Jemima Parry-Jones, Rob Simmons, John Smallwood, Jeff Smith, John-Marc Thiollay, Martin Wikelski, Reuven Yosef, and Jorje Zalles. The interpretations presented below are mine, however, and any imbalances or faults are mine as well.

KEITH L. BILDSTEIN

Hawk Mountain Sanctuary, Pennsylvania USA

Migrating Raptors of the World

—1—

The Phenomenon of Raptor Migration

Migration is not only an intensely interesting proceeding in itself,
but a function fraught with importance in the history of avian life.
Charles Dixon, 1897

Migration—the seasonal, directed movements organisms undertake while traveling back and forth between their "breeding grounds" and "wintering areas"—occurs in almost all forms of life, plant and animal, large and small, and most of what is in between. Aquatic creatures from algae to Green Turtles to Blue Whales do it, as do land-based organisms from Monarch butterflies to birds, reindeer, and humans. (Terms in italics are defined in the Glossary. Scientific names of all organisms appear in the Appendix.)

As organisms respond to seasonal shifts in the kinds and amounts of light, temperature, and food available to them, many of them migrate as conditions deteriorate locally. Although widespread across the tree of life, migration is

1

not uniformly distributed. More than any other group of organisms, birds have thoroughly adopted and adapted to a migratory lifestyle and, via long-distance movements, have extended migration to its planetary extreme. About 4000 of the world's 10,000 species of birds migrate on a regular basis, and many do so across extraordinary distances. Arctic Terns shuttle 30,000 to 40,000 kilometers (km) between their Arctic breeding grounds and Antarctic wintering areas each year, Red Knots undertake annual roundtrips of anywhere from 5000 to 32,000 km, and insect-sized Ruby-throated Hummingbirds commute 6000 km between Canada and Central America. Overall, long-distance migration defines birds behaviorally in much the same way feathers define them anatomically.

Included among thousands of avian migrants are about 200 species of diurnal birds of prey, or raptors. Members of the suborder Falconides (hawks, eagles, falcons, and *Old World* vultures) and the subfamily Cathartinae (*New World* vultures), raptors comprise a diverse assemblage of about 300 species of predatory birds. Found on many oceanic islands and on all continents except Antarctica, raptors are one of the most broadly distributed groups of all birds. Predators and scavengers, raptors possess numerous adaptations for finding and eating other animals, including keen vision, hooked beaks, and large, sharp talons. Many are generalist predators, a few of which, including "avivorous," or bird-eating species like the Peregrine Falcon, take hundreds of species of prey. Others, including the Snail Kite, are dietary specialists that take only a few species of prey. The availability of food that many raptors prey on changes seasonally, particularly at high latitudes, and especially among raptors that feed heavily on swarming insects, hibernating mammals, and migratory birds. Nevertheless, high latitudes provide longer hours of daylight and flushes of both abundant and vulnerable prey each summer, and many temperate and subarctic regions host dense populations of breeding birds of prey.

Each spring and autumn tens of millions of these and other birds of prey set off on long journeys that carry them across six continents. Together, their travels represent the most spectacular movements of land-based predators on earth. Liberated via long-distance migration from single habitats that "imprison" many mammalian predators, raptors are able to build substantial populations by shuttling between alternatingly available prey bases on geographically disjunct breeding areas and wintering grounds.

Unlike many birds that migrate principally at night, raptors travel almost entirely by day, many along well-established corridors. Raptors often flock on migration, and about 20 species regularly travel in huge groups of hundreds to thousands of individuals. Although their often-conspicuous flights have been known to small groups of peoples for millennia—Asiatic falconers, for example, have been trapping migrating birds of prey at least since 4000 B.C.—for most people, including avian biologists, the phenomenon of raptor migration is a recently discovered part of the natural world.

Indeed, the now widely celebrated transequatorial movements of the Broad-winged Hawk, eastern North America's most abundant and most mobile migratory bird of prey, were unknown to most naturalists well into the 1880s, and the now popular sport of hawkwatching was not "invented" until the early 1930s. The last half of the twentieth century changed all of that. Today, the likelihood of seeing large numbers of migrating raptors regularly attracts thousands of hawkwatchers to well-established raptor-migration watchsites such as Elat, Israel; Falsterbo, Sweden; Tarifa, Spain; Kenting, Taiwan; Cape May, New Jersey; and Hawk Mountain, Pennsylvania. And, except perhaps for waterfowl and shorebirds, the often convoluted migration choreographies of migratory raptors are as well known today as those of any group of birds.

Raptors in general and migratory raptors in particular include some of the most widely distributed of all land-based vertebrates. The ranges of 19 of the world's 22 species of *complete migrants* encompass at least two continents. Seven species of raptors, including the White-tailed Sea Eagle, Northern Harrier, Northern Goshawk, Rough-legged Hawk (aka Rough-legged Buzzard), Golden Eagle, Merlin, and Gyrfalcon, occur in both the Old and the New World, and two truly cosmopolitan species, the Osprey and the Peregrine Falcon, range across all continents except Antarctica. A handful of migrants, including the Turkey Vulture, Osprey, Swallow-tailed Kite, Snail Kite, and Peregrine Falcon, breed in both the northern and southern temperate zones, as well as in the tropics.

The enormous distributional ranges of many migratory raptors result in some of the longest land-based migratory journeys of any birds. Swainson's Hawks that breed in northern North America and that overwinter in temperate South America, and Steppe Buzzards that breed in northern Eurasia and that overwinter in southern Africa, undertake annual roundtrip migrations of more than 15,000 km. Overall, 38 species of migratory birds of prey, or 19 percent of all known migrants, commute at least 3000 kilometers a year.

Like other groups of birds, raptors migrate largely along north-south, latitudinal gradients (Figure 1). Not surprisingly, the Northern Hemisphere, which has 15 times as much land between 30° and 80° as does the Southern

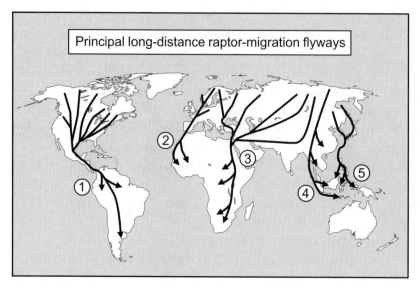

Figure 1. The world's principal raptor-migration flyways, including (1) the Trans-American Flyway, (2) the Western European–West African Flyway, (3) the Eurasian–East African Flyway, (4) the East–Asian Continental Flyway, and (5) the East–Asian Oceanic Flyway. (See Chapter 7 for details.)

Hemisphere, has many more migratory raptors. Asia alone has 66 species, and North America and Europe have 33 and 38 species, respectively. Australia, by comparison, has only 11 (Figure 2).

Many raptor migrants undertake transequatorial journeys. Others travel long distances between high and low latitudes entirely within either the Northern or Southern Hemisphere. Overall, the result of such latitudinal movements shifts the global center of raptor populations, as well as that of raptor diversity, toward the tropics during northern winter.

Movements of as few as several kilometers up and down mountain slopes allow migrants to reap the same climatic benefits as do latitudinal movements of hundreds and, sometimes, even thousands of kilometers latitudinally, and several species of raptors are *altitudinal migrants* that breed in mountainous areas and over-winter in the surrounding lowlands. Tropical and subtropical species of raptors, which are decidedly less exposed to seasonal fluctuations in temperature, often migrate in response to seasonal shifts in precipitation, some toward and others away from rains during the breeding season depending on their foraging ecology.

Raptors are relatively large-bodied, lightly *wing-loaded* birds, and many are capable of extended soaring flight. *Soaring* is an especially efficient form

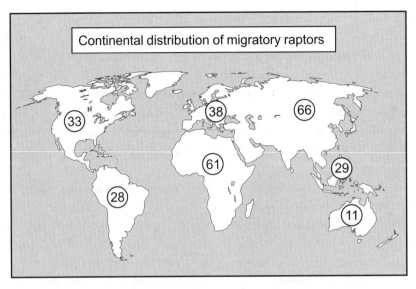

Figure 2. Continental distributions of complete and partial migratory raptors. The Pacific Islands, including New Guinea, are considered separately from mainland Asia and Australia. Northern Hemisphere breeders boost the numbers of migrants in Africa, South America, and the Pacific Islands.

of transport, during and outside of long-distance migration, and, with the exception of seabirds, swifts, and swallows, many raptors spend more time flying than do most other species of birds. Although it is believed that soaring flight initially developed in raptors to reduce the costs of searching for prey (and carcasses), many species of birds of prey soar more often during migration than at other times of the year, and almost all truly long-distance migratory raptors, including North America's Broad-winged and Swainson's hawks, Eurasia's Steppe Buzzard and Steppe Eagle, and East Asia's Chinese Sparrowhawk, depend on soaring flight to complete their lengthy journeys. Raptors differ considerably in their flight "anatomy," and the extent to which individuals soar on migration—as opposed to using powered flapping flight—depends not only on the weather but also on body type.

Raptors often migrate across broad fronts, particularly at the beginnings and ends of their migratory journeys. Even so, many birds of prey aggregate along well-established and seemingly traditional corridors, particularly at *migration bottlenecks* including the tips of peninsulas and other habitat discontinuities, as well as at low latitudes, as migrants build in numbers. Most raptors hesitate or refuse to cross water bodies of greater than 25 kilometers, and many are reluctant to fly across exceptionally high mountain barriers. In the

Old World, water avoidance is best seen in the European-African migration system where many migrants circumnavigate the Mediterranean and Black seas, concentrating their passage at places such as the Strait of Gibraltar at the western end of the Mediterranean, and at the Bosporus, the narrow strait between the northeastern Mediterranean and the southwestern Black Sea. In the New World, water avoidance is best seen along the Mesoamerican Land Corridor that many migrants traveling between North and South America use to circumnavigate the Gulf of Mexico and Caribbean Sea (see Figure 1 and Chapter 7).

In Europe and Asia, most formidable mountain ranges, including the Pyrenees, Alps, Greater Caucasus, and Tibetan Plateau, are largely aligned along east-west axes, and Old World migrants approaching such barriers frequently follow circuitous routes around them. In the New World, where most mountain ranges, including the Cascades, Rockies, Appalachians, and Andes, are aligned largely north-to-south, many New World migrants employ mountain ranges as *leading lines* along which they *slope soar* for short and long distances (see Chapter 4).

Like the long-distance movements of other species of birds, raptor migration ultimately is driven by seasonal fluctuations in food availability. Because many of their prey estivate in summer, hibernate or hide under the snow in winter, or migrate seasonally, migratory raptors evacuate their breeding ranges when food becomes scarce and return only when sufficient prey are available once again. Despite this single, overriding force, modes of migration vary enormously across and, sometimes, even within populations. This diversity occurs for many reasons, including differences in continental and local geography, ecology, flight mechanics, and population densities, as well as the age and sex of the individuals involved.

Entirely tropical raptors are far less likely to migrate than are species whose populations lie largely outside of the tropics; and entirely nontropical species are more migratory still (Figure 3). The same is true among populations within species whose ranges extend across large latitudinal gradients. Consider, for example, the Eurasian Buzzard, a raptor that breeds from 35° N to 65° N across much of Eurasia. Northernmost populations of the species consist entirely of long-distance migrants, many of which overwinter in southern Africa, whereas southernmost populations are largely, if not entirely, sedentary. Populations in the middle of the latitudinal gradient exhibit a mixed pattern with some individuals migrating and others remaining sedentary.

Prey availability plays a major role in determining such latitudinal trends. Temperate-zone species that feed principally on homeotherms, or "warm-

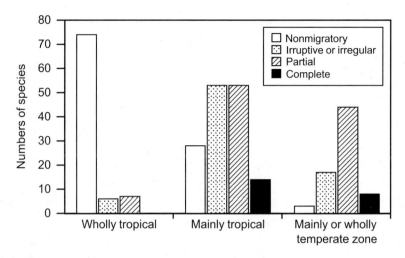

Figure 3. Migration characteristics of wholly tropical, mainly tropical, and mainly or wholly temperate-zone raptors.

blooded" animals such as birds and mammals, are far less migratory than are those that feed on "cold-blooded" poikilotherms such as insects, fishes, reptiles, and amphibians. Because of this and other species differences, one-third of all raptors do not migrate at all, presumably because they are able to locate sufficient prey locally year-round.

Migratory raptors differ enormously in distances traveled and in tactics employed. Some, like the Amur Falcon of easternmost Asia, migrate more than 10,000 kilometers, across 70° of latitude and 70° of longitude, between nesting areas in Russia and China and wintering areas in southern Africa. Others, including Short-tailed Hawks in Florida, migrate fewer than several hundred kilometers across several degrees of latitude. Many raptors with large distributions, including Red-tailed Hawks in the New World and Eurasian Sparrowhawks in the Old World, employ mixed strategies in which some individuals are regular migrants whereas others are largely sedentary. Others, including those that feed on arctic and subarctic species including voles, lemmings, Snowshoe Hares, and Ruffed Grouse, whose populations fluctuate through boom-and-bust cycles interannually, are nomadic, migrating in some years, but not in others.

The diversity of raptor migration has led specialists to classify species as complete, partial, or irruptive or local migrants. According to this scheme, *complete migrants* are species in which at least 90 percent of all individuals shuttle seasonally between separate breeding and nonbreeding areas; *partial*

Table 1. *Migration tendencies of the world's 307 species of raptors*

Migration type	Number of species	% of all raptors	% of all migrants
Nonmigratory	105	34%	—
Migratory	202	66%	—
Irruptive and local	76	25%	38%
Partial	104	34%	52%
Complete	22	7%	11%

migrants are species in which fewer than 90 percent of all individuals migrate; and *irruptive* and *local migrants* are species whose movements occur more sporadically and, typically, over shorter distances than do those of complete and partial migrants. As is true for most groups of birds, partial migrants are by far the most common "type" of migratory raptor, and complete migrants are the least common (Table 1).

Both as a group and as individuals, complete migrants appear to have embraced the more extreme aspects of raptor migration. Every one of the 22 species in this category migrates at least 3000 kilometers one way, and all but three are transequatorial migrants. All complete migrants sometimes coalesce into flocks while migrating, and half of these are known to do so regularly. More than one in four regularly travel in supersized flocks consisting of thousands of birds. All but two migrate at least short distances over water, and 10 regularly undertake water crossings of at least 100 kilometers. Partial migrants are far more varied in their migratory habits.

Although many broad patterns underlie the various tactics employed by migratory birds of prey, the specific migration ecology and geography of each species of migratory raptor is unique (see Chapter 8). Details regarding the migration tendencies and characteristics of the world's 202 species of migratory raptors are depicted in Table 2.

In the chapters that follow I detail the origins and evolution of raptor migration (Chapter 2), the methods that have been used to study the phenomenon (Chapter 3), the flight mechanics and general flight strategies of migratory raptors (Chapter 4), the orientation and navigational systems used by migrants (Chapter 5), and the ecology (Chapter 6) and geography (Chapter 7) of raptor migration. I then detail the migrations of eight of the world's great raptor migrants (Chapter 8) and characterize twelve of the world's great migration watchsites (Chapter 9). I finish with an overview of the conservation status of migratory raptors (Chapter 10) that describes the causes and

Table 2. *Characteristics of complete, partial, and irruptive or local raptor migrants*

Species	Long-distance migrant[a]	Trans-equatorial migrant[b]	Rains migrant[c]	Altitudinal migrant[d]	Maximum flock size[e]	Maximum distance traveled over water
Complete migrants						
Osprey	Yes	Yes			>50	>100 km
Western Honey Buzzard	Yes	Yes			>**1000**	>100 km
Mississippi Kite	Yes	Yes			>**100**	
Short-toed Snake Eagle	Yes		Yes		>10	<25 km
Pallid Harrier	Yes				<10	<25 km
Pied Harrier	Yes				<10	<100 km
Montagu's Harrier	Yes	Yes			<10	>100 km
Levant Sparrowhawk	Yes				>**1000**	<100 km
Chinese Sparrowhawk	Yes	Yes			>**100**	>100 km
Grey-faced Buzzard	Yes	Yes			>**1000**	>100 km
Broad-winged Hawk	Yes	Yes			>**1000**	<25 km
Swainson's Hawk	Yes	Yes			>**1000**	<25 km
Rough-legged Hawk	Yes				>**10**	<100 km
Lesser Spotted Eagle	Yes	Yes			<10	<100 km
Greater Spotted Eagle	Yes				<10	<100 km
Steppe Eagle	Yes	Yes	Yes		<10	
Lesser Kestrel	Yes	Yes			>**1000**	>100 km
Red-footed Falcon	Yes	Yes-			>**1000**	>100 km
Amur Falcon	Yes	Yes			>**1000**	>100 km
Eleonora's Falcon	Yes	Yes			>**10**	>100 km
Sooty Falcon	Yes	Yes			<10	>100 km
Northern Hobby	Yes	Yes	Yes		<**100**	<100 km
Partial migrants						
Turkey Vulture	Yes	Yes			>**1000**	<25 km
Black Vulture				Yes	>**10**	
African Cuckoo Hawk			Yes			
Jerdon's Baza						
Pacific Baza			Yes			
Black Baza				Yes	<**100**	
Crested Honey Buzzard	Yes	Yes			>**100**	<**100 km**
Swallow-tailed Kite	Yes	Yes		Yes	>**100**	<100 km
Black-shouldered Kite			Yes			
White-tailed Kite						
Scissor-tailed Kite			Yes		<50	
Snail Kite					>**10**	
Plumbeous Kite					>**100**	
Red Kite					<10	<100 km
Black Kite	Yes	Yes	Yes	Yes	>**1000**	<100 km

Species	Long-distance migrant[a]	Trans-equatorial migrant[b]	Rains migrant[c]	Altitudinal migrant[d]	Maximum flock size[e]	Maximum distance traveled over water
Whistling Kite			Yes		>100	
Brahminy Kite			Yes	Yes	>10	<25 km
Pallas's Fish Eagle					<10	
White-tailed Sea Eagle						<100 km
Bald Eagle					<10	<100 km
Steller's Sea Eagle						<100 km
Lesser Fishing Eagle				Yes		
Palmnut Vulture			Yes			
Bearded Vulture				Yes	<10	
Egyptian Vulture				Yes	<10	<25 km
African White-backed Vulture			Yes			
Indian White-backed Vulture					**<100**	
Himalayan Griffon			Yes		<10	
Eurasian Griffon						
Cinereous Vulture				Yes		<25 km
Lappet-Faced Vulture			Yes			
Beaudouin's Snake Eagle						
Black-breasted Snake Eagle						
Western Marsh Harrier	Yes				<10	>100 km
African Marsh Harrier						
Eastern Marsh Harrier						
Pacific Marsh Harrier						
Long-winged Harrier						
Spotted Harrier			Yes			<100 km
Black Harrier			Yes	Yes		
Northern Harrier	Yes				<10	>100 km
Cinereous Harrier				Yes		<25 km
African Harrier Hawk			Yes			
Dark Chanting Goshawk						
Pale Chanting Goshawk						
Gabar Goshawk						
Grey-bellied Goshawk						
Shikra			Yes			
Australasian Goshawk				Yes		<100 km
Japanese Sparrowhawk	Yes	Yes			**>100**	<100 km
Besra				Yes		
Ovambo Sparrowhawk			Yes			
Eurasian Sparrowhawk	Yes			Yes	<10	<100 km

Species	Long-distance migrant[a]	Trans-equatorial migrant[b]	Rains migrant[c]	Altitudinal migrant[d]	Maximum flock size[e]	Maximum distance traveled over water
Sharp-shinned Hawk	Yes			Yes	<10	<25 km
Cooper's Hawk				Yes	<10	<25 km
Bicolored Hawk				Yes		
Chilean Hawk						
Northern Goshawk				Yes		<25 km
Grasshopper Buzzard			Yes			
White-eyed Buzzard						
Common Black Hawk						
Savanna Hawk						
Harris' Hawk						
Black-chested Buzzard Eagle						
Grey Hawk						
Red-Shouldered Hawk					<10	<25 km
Short-tailed Hawk					<10	
White-throated Hawk				Yes		
White-tailed Hawk					<10	
Red-backed Hawk						
Zone-tailed Hawk					<10	
Red-tailed Hawk					>10	<25 km
Eurasian Buzzard	Yes	Yes		Yes	>**1000**	<25 km
Mountain Buzzard						
Long-legged Buzzard	Yes				<10	
Upland Buzzard						
Ferruginous Hawk					<10	
Red-necked Buzzard			Yes		<10	
Indian Black Eagle						
Imperial Eagle						
Wahlberg's Eagle					<10	
Golden Eagle	Yes					<100 km
Verreaux's Eagle						<25 km
Bonelli's Eagle					<10	<25 km
Booted Eagle	Yes	Yes			>10	<25 km
Rufous-bellied Eagle						
Chimango Caracara						<25 km
Common Kestrel			Yes		<100	<100 km
Australian Kestrel			Yes	Yes	<10	<100 km
American Kestrel					<10	<100 km
Fox Kestrel			Yes			
Grey Kestrel			Yes			

Species	Long-distance migrant[a]	Trans-equatorial migrant[b]	Rains migrant[c]	Altitudinal migrant[d]	Maximum flock size[e]	Maximum distance traveled over water
Red-necked Falcon			Yes			
Aplomado Falcon				Yes		<25 km
Merlin	Yes			Yes	<10	>100 km
Oriental Hobby					<10	<25 km
Australian Hobby				Yes		<100 km
New Zealand Falcon				Yes		<100 km
Brown Falcon					<10	<100 km
Lanner Falcon			Yes	Yes		
Saker Falcon	Yes					<100 km
Gyrfalcon						>100 km
Prairie Falcon				Yes		
Peregrine Falcon	Yes	Yes				>100 km

Irruptive and local migrants

Species	Long-distance migrant[a]	Trans-equatorial migrant[b]	Rains migrant[c]	Altitudinal migrant[d]	Maximum flock size[e]	Maximum distance traveled over water
Lesser Yellow-headed Vulture						
Greater Yellow-headed Vulture						
King Vulture						
California Condor					<10	
Andean Condor						
Hook-billed Kite				Yes		
Square-tailed Kite						
Black-Breasted Buzzard						
Bat Hawk						
Australian Black-shouldered Kite					<100	
Letter-winged Kite			Yes		<100	
Double-toothed Kite						
Rufous-thighed Kite						
White-bellied Sea Eagle						<25 km
African Fish Eagle			Yes			
Hooded Vulture			Yes			
Long-billed Vulture				Yes		
Rüppell's Griffon				Yes		<25 km
Cape Griffon						
Red-Headed Vulture				Yes		
Brown Snake Eagle			Yes			
East African Snake Eagle						
Banded Snake Eagle			Yes			
Bateleur			Yes			
Crested Serpent Eagle						

Species	Long-distance migrant[a]	Trans-equatorial migrant[b]	Rains migrant[c]	Altitudinal migrant[d]	Maximum flock size[e]	Maximum distance traveled over water
Madagascar Marsh Harrier						
Lizard Buzzard						
Eastern Chanting Goshawk						
Crested Goshawk						
African Goshawk			Yes			
African Little Sparrowhawk			Yes			
Collared Sparrowhawk						
Rufous-breasted Sparrowhawk				Yes		
Black Sparrowhawk						
Red Goshawk						
Crane Hawk						
White-necked Hawk						
Mantled Hawk						
Great Black Hawk						
Black-collared Hawk						
Black Solitary Eagle						
Crowned Solitary Eagle						
Roadside Hawk						
White-rumped Hawk						
Puna Hawk				Yes		
Hawaiian Hawk						
Rufous-tailed Hawk						
Madagascar Buzzard						
Augur Buzzard					<10	
Jackal Buzzard						
Harpy Eagle						
Tawny Eagle			Yes			
Gurney's Eagle						
Wedge-tailed Eagle						
Little Eagle				Yes		
Ayres' Hawk Eagle			Yes			
Long-crested Eagle						
Changeable Hawk Eagle						
Mountain Hawk Eagle				Yes		
Black Hawk Eagle						
Ornate Hawk Eagle				Yes		
Secretarybird						
Carunculated Caracara						
Mountain Caracara						

Table 2, continued

Species	Long-distance migrant[a]	Trans-equatorial migrant[b]	Rains migrant[c]	Altitudinal migrant[d]	Maximum flock size[e]	Maximum distance traveled over water
Striated Caracara						
Crested Caracara						
Yellow-headed Caracara						
Collared Falconet				Yes		
Pied Falconet				Yes		
Greater Kestrel						
Bat Falcon						
Orange-breasted Falcon						
African Hobby					<10	
Grey Falcon						
Black Falcon			Yes			
Laggar Falcon						

Sources: Characteristics are based on largely Kerlinger (1989) and Zalles and Bildstein (2000), as updated by the literature.
[a] Long-distance migrants are those in which at least 20% of all individuals migrate >1500 kilometers one way.
[b] Transequatorial migrants are long-distance migrants at least 20% of whose populations migrate across the equator.
[c] Rains migrants are species that regularly migrate in response to seasonal rains.
[d] Altitudinal migrants are species in which at least some populations are known to migrate from high-altitude breeding areas to lower areas during the nonbreeding season.
[e] Species whose maximum known flock sizes are in bold regularly migrate in flocks, all others with maximum flock sizes listed do so occasionally.

consequences of raptor declines historically and discusses ways of avoiding such declines in the future.

Understanding why, where, when, and how raptors migrate is key to protecting these important sentinels of ecosystem change. This book is a step in that direction.

—2—

Origins and Evolution of Raptor Migration

Nothing in biology makes sense except in the light of evolution.
Theodosius Dobzhansky, 1973

Raptors have been migrating for a very long time.
    With evidence of bird migration dating from the Cretaceous period of the Mesozoic era more than 65 million years ago, long-distance movements are thought to be an ancient and, possibly, ancestral avian trait (Berthold 2001). The occurrence of recognizably "modern" birds of prey in the early Eocene of England (Feduccia 1996), together with the fact that many living species regularly undertake long-distance seasonal movements, suggest that birds of prey have been migrating for as long as 40 million years (Table 3). The devil, however, is in the details of evolutionary study, and the evolution of raptor migration is no exception to this rule.

Long-distance migration defines birds behaviorally almost as well as feathers define them anatomically. And perhaps not surprisingly, investigations into the origins of bird migration, like those of feathers, are both rich and colorful (Dixon 1895; Clarke 1912; Dorst 1962; Baker 1978). Today, the evolution of bird migration, particularly that of intercontinental migration systems, continues to enjoy the attention of many ornithologists (Rappole 1995). This is true not only because migration itself is inherently important to many species of birds but also because its complexity offers exciting challenges to those who study it. The evolution of migration can only be inferred from the fossil record, and even then only when information about paleoclimates and the ancient juxtapositions of continental landmasses is reasonably available. Also, it is now clear that many behavioral patterns, including long-distance migration, can appear and disappear rapidly in species, making their occurrence particularly difficult to track over evolutionary time. Nevertheless, growing knowledge of the timing and geography of existing systems of raptor migration (Zalles and Bildstein 2000), together with laboratory studies of the genetics of migration (Berthold 1999, 2001), provide a framework for understanding the origins of the phenomenon.

Overall, raptor migration is best thought of as a remarkably flexible, behavioral response to a series of both extrinsic and intrinsic factors that include continental geography, climate, and the seasonal availability of food resources, together with the population dynamics and flight mechanics of the birds themselves. This chapter outlines the history of hypotheses regarding the evolution of avian migration and develops a working model that explains the origins and occurrence of the phenomenon in raptors.

Ultimately, the origins and occurrences of raptor migration reflect those of bird migration in general, and many of the examples and references that follow involve species that are not birds of prey.

Historical Hypotheses

Although most theories of the origins of bird migration differ considerably in detail, all assume the presence of sedentary ancestral populations. All of the theories also assume that something initially motivated birds to begin moving, that the ensuing migrations improved the individual fitness of the birds involved, and that natural selection is responsible for spreading and maintaining the trait. Most of the theories also suggest that migration developed on several, if not many, separate occasions and that it continues to do so today (Gauthreaux 1982; Rappole 1995).

Early theories of bird migration focused on how long-term historical events—mainly geographic, climatic, or both—initially induced birds to migrate. The north-south movements of birds across the Sahara Desert, for example, were thought to have evolved in response to the large-scale desertification of what was formerly a much greener northern Africa; whereas trans–Indian Ocean movements between peninsular India and the island of Madagascar were thought to echo the ancient juxtaposition of those two now widely separated landmasses (Dorst 1962). Continental drift, in particular, was used by many theorists to explain how once locally *nomadic* species had evolved into increasingly migratory ones as the continents on which they lived slowly drifted apart over long periods of time (Wolfson 1948). Although theories involving continental drift were criticized immediately for their faulty chronology (many of the families of birds involved had not yet evolved at the time the continents in question were slowly separating [Amadon 1948]) and are now discredited, such ideas were once widespread. Unfortunately, continental-drift hypotheses continue to be presented as gospel in many introductory biology texts.

A second early idea concerning bird migration was its static and all-but-irreversible nature. Existing north-south biases in temperate-zone migrations, for example, were thought to have become "fixed in place" following their presumed development on the heels of Pleistocene glacial retreats more than 10,000 years ago. Today, however, most scientists believe that migration is a dynamic phenomenon that responds to environmental change via natural selection and that current ecological circumstances, rather than events in the distant past, are largely responsible for the occurrence and maintenance of the migratory movements of today's birds, including modern raptors (Berthold 1999, 2001; Rappole 1995).

Another historic bone of contention in studies of avian migration has been its geographic origin. Today, almost all long-distance bird migration occurs along a north-south or latitudinal axis, and the same is true for most raptor migration (see Figure 1). Over the years, many migration theorists have argued in favor of either a "northern" (i.e., temperate zone) or "southern" (i.e., tropical) origin of these migration systems, suggesting that the systems evolved when sedentary ancestral populations developed migratory habits when individuals began to migrate either into and out of new breeding areas (the southern origins model) or into and out of new nonbreeding areas (the northern origins model). Although this dispute remains an active field of inquiry, and although there is good reason to believe that because of greater levels of avian diversity in the tropics bird migration has evolved more frequently there than elsewhere (Rappole 1995; Berthold 2001), the comprehensive theory presented below suggests that migratory tendencies have evolved, and continue to evolve, in species across latitudes, and that whether or not migration develops within a population has far more to do with local ecological conditions and regional geographic possibilities than with latitudinal proclivities.

A Comprehensive Theory for the Evolution and Maintenance of Raptor Migration

As useful as previous explanations for the evolution of bird migration have been, no theory has managed to provide general explanations for the variety of migration strategies seen within and among species of birds, nor has any been able to explain the rapidity with which many species of birds are able to switch between sedentary versus migratory strategies. Peter Berthold has recently tackled this problem, and his solution, which builds on the work of George W. Cox, is the most inclusive and satisfying explanation offered to date (Cox 1968, 1985; Berthold 1999).

Berthold began studying the evolution of bird migration after learning about a rapid and dramatic shift in the migratory habits of central European populations of an Old World warbler called the Blackcap. The species, which occurs throughout much of Europe, is a relatively large, grayish, and sometimes migratory songbird, with a distinctive black cap. As is true of several other European songbirds, Blackcaps from the United Kingdom and western Europe typically migrate southwest each autumn and overwinter mainly in western Mediterranean landscapes. On the other hand, individuals from central and eastern Europe migrate south or southeast and overwinter mainly in the central and eastern Mediterranean. Thus, when a Blackcap that had been banded as a breeder in Austria turned up in Ireland in 1961, it was thought that the individual was accidentally disoriented and lost. Shortly thereafter, however, additional Austrian breeders and their progeny began adopting this new migration habit, and an accidental mishap on the part of a single individual no longer seemed plausible.

Intrigued by the rapidity of the directional shift and wanting to learn more, Berthold captured 40 Austrian Blackcaps and tested the preferred direction of their migrations in the lab. Once caged, the birds directed their autumnal movements at the northwest side of their cages, in the direction of the new wintering areas in Great Britain, rather than to the south in the direction of the population's traditional wintering areas in the central Mediterranean. Offspring of the tested birds also directed their movements toward the northwest. In contrast, "control" birds from a German population directed their movements to the south. Berthold interpreted his results as indicating that the shift in the preferred orientation direction had become genetically fixed within the Austrian population during the 30 years that Blackcaps had first been reported overwintering in Great Britain.

Presumably, due to normal variation in the migration orientation, small numbers of Blackcaps had reached Ireland and England before but had failed to survive the winter there. That began to change, however, following the Second World War as winter bird feeding became more widespread in the region and as milder winters became more common there. Once this happened, the stage was set for the evolution of the new migration habit via natural selection.

Since these early trials, Berthold has conducted two-way selection experiments on captive, partially migratory blackcaps from southern France in which he and coworkers have been able to artificially select for both complete migratory behavior and complete sedentary behavior in as few as three to six generations (Berthold 2001). The results of his experiments have led Berthold to propose that many populations of birds possess the genetic variability needed for natural selection to shift their migratory habits as rapidly as changing environmental circumstances merit and that flexibility in migration is the rule rather than the exception. And indeed, most avian migrants, including most migratory raptors, are *partial migrants* rather than *complete migrants,* suggesting not only that migration is a flexible avian trait but also that flexibility in migration has been and continues to be an important factor in the success of many species of birds.

The genetic basis for migratory behavior described by Berthold suggests that birds have genes for sedentary and migratory behavior and that these genes, when partly expressed at the population level, produce partial migration in the species. Berthold's work also confirms what many have known for some time: that most of the major features of raptor migration, including the timing, direction taken, distance traveled, and orientation methods used, are transmitted genetically and act according to the principles of microevolution.

Berthold's genetic-based theory also allows us to model how migratory raptors can evolve from sedentary ancestors. Consider, for example, a hypothetical sedentary population of raptors living in an aseasonal or slightly seasonal environment. So long as sedentary young in the population survive and reproduce as well as the dispersing young, the population will remain sedentary (Cox 1985; Berthold 1999; Bell 2000). Furthermore, if the number of young that survive to reproductive age equals the number of adults that die each year, the population size will remain stable. On the other hand, if the number of young that survive exceeds the number of adults that die, the population will grow. If the population increases to the point that resources in the environment become limiting and individuals increasingly compete for those resources, selection will favor *dispersal* if dispersants are more likely to survive and reproduce than nondispersants. Also, because within-species competition is likely to favor experienced adults over inexperienced young in situations such as these, juveniles

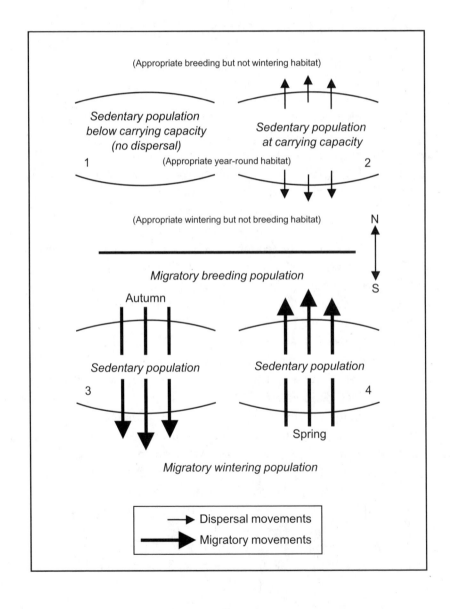

rather than adults are more likely to adopt a dispersal strategy. And indeed, a growing number of empirical studies indicate that post–breeding-season dispersal is far more common in young raptors than in adults.

At least initially, selection should favor juvenile dispersal into similar, reasonably aseasonal habitats close to the species' breeding range. However, if the population continues to grow and spread, dispersing juveniles eventually will be forced to occupy more distant and, presumably, less-similar habitats, some of which may be more seasonal (i.e., suitable at certain times of the year but not at others). At this point, natural selection will favor a strategy in which dispersants into seasonal habitats will remain there for part of the year but move to other locations at other times of the year (i.e., they will become migratory). Once this occurs, the former sedentary species becomes a partial migrant.

When such a series of events plays out against latitudinal gradients in the degree of habitat seasonality, *leapfrog migration,* in which migratory individuals breed at higher latitudes than sedentary individuals and overwinter at lower latitudes, often results (Figure 4) (see Chapters 7 and 8, respectively, for details and examples of this type of migration pattern). Overall, this line of reasoning, which draws heavily on George Cox's earlier models for the evolution of migration behavior (1968, 1985), places the origins of raptor migration squarely upon the shoulders of competition for limited resources.

Figure 4. Diagrammatic representation of events involved in the origins and development of leapfrog migration. (1) An initial sedentary population of raptors remains sedentary, so long as its numbers remain below carrying capacity. (2) Once a sedentary population reaches or exceeds its regional carrying capacity, recently fledged young from the population begin to disperse into surrounding areas. In the Northern Hemisphere, young that disperse north encounter increasingly seasonal habitats that may be appropriate for breeding but not for overwintering; whereas those that disperse south encounter habitats that may be appropriate for overwintering but not for breeding. (3, 4) Individuals that initially disperse south fail to establish breeding populations and either remain there as nonbreeders or, eventually, travel north and attempt to breed there. Individuals that initially disperse north, move south as conditions deteriorate in autumn and continue traveling until they reach less-densely settled habitats south of established sedentary populations. These individuals, should they reverse the journey in spring in response to postdispersal *philopatry,* can evolve into migratory populations that seasonally leapfrog over preexisting sedentary populations. When gene flow is sufficient among sedentary and migratory populations, the different groups can act as reciprocal "source and sink" populations (*sensu* Pulliam 1988) as conditions that favor one strategy (i.e., migratory versus sedentary behavior) over the other wax and wane. On the other hand, if gene flow is minimal or nonexistent, the two populations eventually may speciate.

In addition to the "intrinsic" population-growth model described above, migration behavior also can evolve in sedentary populations when environmental conditions "extrinsic" to the population shift from aseasonal to seasonal in all or parts of a species' range to the extent that migratory behavior is selected for in the absence of increased within-species competition. Note that the reverse situations—population decline due to factors other than declining ecological resources or ecological conditions becoming less seasonal— would be expected to reduce and possibly extinguish migration in a population. On the other hand, partial migration would be expected when both sedentary individuals and migratory individuals in the population were reasonably successful, and complete migration would be expected when sedentary individuals were continually less successful than migratory individuals.

Large numbers of raptors are difficult to maintain in captivity, and, not surprisingly, most experimental evidence for the genetic basis of their migration, including Berthold's, is inferred from work on smaller birds, particularly songbirds. There is one important exception, however. In the 1930s, German ornithologist Rudolf Drost conducted a series of "displacement" experiments involving migrating adult and juvenile Eurasian Sparrowhawks (Drost 1938). The work provides one of the earliest and best examples of how genetics and learning together play important roles in determining migration geography in raptors. Eurasian Sparrowhawks are smallish bird-eating *accipiters*—a species larger than a Sharp-shinned Hawk but smaller than a Cooper's Hawk—that occur throughout Europe and across much of northern Asia. Northern populations of sparrowhawks are migratory, and large numbers of Scandinavian breeders migrate along the shorelines of the Baltic and North Seas each autumn en route to wintering areas in southwestern Europe. Drost trapped and banded several hundred of these migrants on Helgoland, a tiny island on the North Sea coast of Germany. The birds were captured at the banding station in a series of gigantic funnel traps called "fyke nets" as they sought cover and prey in trees that had been planted there to attract migrating songbirds. All of the sparrowhawks were aged and banded, and 209 of them were transported 600 kilometers (410 miles) east-southeast to eastern Poland where they were released. A second, control group of sparrowhawks was held and subsequently released at the capture site on Helgoland.

Recaptures of several dozen control birds indicated that sparrowhawks captured and released in Helgoland migrated southwest and spent the winter in the Netherlands, Belgium, northwestern France, and, in one instance, Portugal. Thirty-six of the displaced individuals also were recaptured in winter. Displaced juveniles continued to move southwest, and most were recaptured in central Europe, east-southeast of the population's traditional wintering areas. On the other hand, displaced adults redirected their movements west upon being released in Poland, and most of their recoveries were substantially closer to the population's "targeted" wintering ground. Drost's results, which are similar to those of displacement experiments involving Eurasian Starlings and Hooded Crows (Matthews 1968), suggest that naïve, first-autumn raptors possess genetic instructions regarding directional orientation but lack the navigational skills needed to correct their course if displaced by weather (see Chapters 6 and 7). Experienced adults, on the other hand, apparently are able to make midcourse corrections and reestablish themselves relative to their intended destinations.

Displacement experiments similar to Drost's have yet to be performed on other species of raptors, but observations of wind-drifted and storm-deflected migrants suggest that natural displacements such as these also are more likely to affect juvenile than adult raptors, suggesting that learning, as well as genetics, plays an important role in the development and maintenance of migration patterns (Mueller and Berger 1967a, b; Kerlinger 1989; Maransky and Bildstein 2001).

The theory of the evolution and control of bird migration outlined above posits that partial migration maintains sufficient genetic variability in most species of migratory raptors so that as conditions change, natural selection can track the changes and populations can respond appropriately (Helbig 2003). Several examples of such changes involving Merlins, Sharp-shinned Hawks, and Bald Eagles, support this idea.

Merlins

The Merlin is a compact, circumboreal falcon that breeds in forested and open habitats across much of northern North America, Europe, and Asia. There are 9 subspecies worldwide, some of which are more migratory than others. Overall, the species is considered a partial migrant. In the early part of the twentieth century, one of the three North American subspecies, a pale gray prairie form known as the Richardson's Merlin, began to expand the northern limits of its *wintering range* from Colorado and Wyoming into southwestern Canada. Reports of the expansion place overwintering Merlins in Saskatchewan, Canada, in 1922, and in Alberta, Canada, in 1948. The expansion, which continued well into the second half of the twentieth century, was especially apparent in urban areas, with Christmas Bird Counts suggesting substantial increases in several of Canada's prairie cities from the late

1950s into the early 1980s. By 1970, Richardson's Merlins not only were overwintering in cities but were beginning to breed there as well (Plate 1) (Warkentin et al. 1990). Since then, nonmigratory populations of "city" Merlins have appeared in numerous urban areas throughout southern Canada and the northern United States.

Several factors appear to have played a role in this shift from migratory to nonmigratory behavior. First, the initial northward expansion of the Merlin's wintering range coincided with the regional expansion of the species' predominant urban prey, the House Sparrow, an Old World species that had been introduced into North America in the 1850s and had spread into the American West in the early part of the twentieth century (Lowther and Cink 1992; Sodhi and Oliphant 1993; Sodhi et al. 1993). It seems likely that increased prey availability, including both House Sparrows and Cedar Waxwings—the latter being attracted to urban areas by ornamental trees—contributed substantially to the Merlin's wintering farther north. A second factor, declining human persecution throughout the period (in the 1930s Richardson's Merlin was still characterized as "never allowing [humans] to come within gunshot range") also may have played a role by allowing the species to take advantage of this new source of urban prey (Bent 1938, 88; Bildstein 2001).

Sharp-shinned Hawks

Sharpies or sharpshins, as they are sometimes called, are small, largely migratory, woodland raptors that breed across most of forested Canada and the United States. Like Merlins, Sharp-shinned Hawks were once described as vicious bird killers, and the species was heavily persecuted throughout much of the eastern part of its range into the 1960s. Sharpies were particularly vulnerable to shooting during migration when large numbers concentrate along traditional flyways. This, together with the misuse of organochlorine pesticides in the 1940s through 1960s, combined to reduce the species numbers throughout much of eastern North America in the mid-twentieth century. Fortunately, the widespread use of *DDT* was banned in Canada and the United States in 1971 and 1972, respectively, and the sharpshin received full protection under the Migratory Bird Treaty Act in 1972. Not surprisingly, populations of Sharpies began to rebound in eastern North America shortly thereafter (Henny 1977; Bednarz et al. 1990; Bildstein 2001).

The species' secretive nature makes it difficult to find and study during the breeding season, and populations of sharpshins are best monitored during autumn and spring when large numbers of migrants concentrate along major *migration corridors* and at *migration bottlenecks*. Thus, when counts of Sharp-shinned Hawks reported at hawkwatches in the northeastern United States began to decline in the 1980s, concerns were raised about the species' status. Initial reports of the decline suggested somewhat benign explanations, including the possibility that the species had reached its natural carrying capacity in the region following a period of explosive population growth in the 1970s. However, as the hawkwatch counts continued to decline into the late 1980s and early 1990s, more ominous explanations were advanced, including pesticides, acid precipitation and its impact on the sharpshin's songbird prey base, and the loss of forested nesting habitat. Because the reduction was especially acute at coastal watchsites where juveniles were known to dominate the flight, several observers suggested that reproductive success had declined. By the early 1990s, many conservationists were suggesting that eastern populations of Sharp-shinned Hawks were in so-called free fall. Oddly enough, declines were not reported at hawkwatches west of the Great Lakes.

As it turned out, none of the explanations mentioned above was correct. Rather than reflecting a shift in population numbers overall, declines in the counts of sharpshins at eastern hawkwatches reflected a shift in the species' migration behavior, for at the same time that numbers of migrating sharpshins were declining at hawkcounts throughout much of southern New England and the Mid-Atlantic states, their numbers were increasing on early-winter Christmas Bird Counts north of the hawkwatches (Figure 5).

The northward shift in wintering areas appears to be due to a phenomenon migration biologists refer to as *short-stopping*. First-year migrants appear particularly inclined to short-stopping, which occurs when food availability increases along the migratory route and individuals stop or slow their migratory movements to take advantage of it. For Sharp-shinned Hawks, the food in question appears to have been increased numbers of backyard birds. Sharpshins rank above domestic cats as the most frequently seen predator at backyard bird feeders (Dunn and Tessaglia 1994), and increases in bird feeding throughout the northeastern United States and eastern Canada during the last quarter of the twentieth century and a series of especially warm winters beginning in the 1980s and continuing into the 1990s, coupled with reduced human persecution, appear to have induced the shift (Plate 2) (Bildstein and Meyer 2000; Duncan 1996; Viverette et al. 1996). Intriguingly, observations suggest that numbers of Sharp-shinned Hawks at bird feeders in the northeastern United States decline after December. And it remains possible that some sharpshins may simply delay their movements until after the first of the year. Either way, this species' rapid response to changing environ-

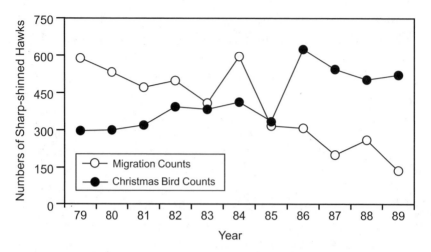

Figure 5. Relationships between numbers of migrating Sharp-shinned Hawks counted per 10 hours of observation at Cape May Point, New Jersey, and numbers of Sharp-shinned Hawks seen per 100,000 party-hours of effort on Christmas Bird Counts in northeastern North America, 1979–1989, as regional populations of the species began to change their migratory habitats by short-stopping at bird feeders in the northeastern United States and southeastern Canada. Note the reciprocal relationship in numbers seen. (Based on data in Viverette et al. 1996)

mental conditions provides another example of how quickly migration habits can shift when conditions merit.

Bald Eagles

A third example of how quickly raptors can change their migration behavior habits involves the Bald Eagle. Bald Eagles are large, typically fish-eating raptors that breed in and near aquatic habitats throughout much of Canada and the United States. Individuals evacuate northern and, particularly, interior portions of their range each autumn as temperatures decline and waterways freeze, and they move to more coastal and southerly areas. In the late 1930s, eagles breeding in the Mackenzie River Basin in the Canadian northwest began overwintering in the Flathead Lake region in and around Glacier National Park, northwestern Montana, where large numbers of individuals fed on the region's landlocked Kokanee Salmon during that species' spawning runs.

Counts indicate that the numbers of Bald Eagles overwintering in and around Flathead Lake grew from 37 in 1935 to more than 600 in 1981. The population collapsed precipitously to 25 individuals in 1989, when salmon numbers crashed because of competition with recently introduced Opossum Shrimp. Alternatives to salmon were not available in the area, and wintering eagles apparently dispersed to more adequate wintering areas following the salmon decline at Flathead Lake (Spencer et al. 1991; McClelland et al. 1994). The ephemeral nature of this important migration stopover site and winter destination provides additional evidence of just how flexible raptor migration patterns are.

A Speculative Prehistoric Record

Based on the arguments and examples presented above, it is possible to envision a scenario for the prehistoric origins and evolution of raptor migration.

Assuming that the first migrating raptors evolved from sedentary ancestral stock, the initial question becomes "when did migration first appear in raptors?" One possibility is that migration evolved contemporaneously with raptors themselves. Another is that conditions were not appropriate for raptor migration when raptors first evolved, and that the evolution of raptor migration followed that of raptors, themselves, by some time.

The scenario for the development of raptor migration offered below is based on the fossil record for birds of prey, and the paleoclimates, ecoregions, and continental geography that the ancestors of modern raptors faced. I assume that past and present taxa resemble each other ecologically and that past and present ecological conditions have affected the likelihood of raptor migration similarly (Wing et al. 1992). Unfortunately, knowledge of the distant past declines precipitously with time, and the evolutionary tale I tell is both simple and speculative. Even so, the scenario that follows links evolutionary change to specific ecological events, and as such provides a useful working hypothesis for future investigations.

My reconstruction begins with the origins of raptor-like predatory birds in the early Cenozoic, the so-called era of recent life. Raptors first appear in the fossil record in Europe in the early Eocene, approximately 50 to 55 million years ago (MYA). The first truly recognizable accipitrid "hawk," *Messelastur gratulator* (most fossil birds lack common names), makes its appearance in Germany in the middle Eocene, approximately 10 million years later. The oldest buteo-like raptor appears in the middle Oligocene of France, 10 million years after that. The first modern genus, *Pandion*—the one to which the modern-day Osprey belongs—makes its appearance in the Oligocene of Egypt shortly thereafter (see Table 3) (Feduccia 1996).

Table 3. *A hypothetical history of the evolution and occurrence of raptor migration during the Tertiary and Quaternary periods of Cenozoic Era.*

Geologic time	Significant ecological and evolutionary events
Tertiary period	
Paleocene epoch (55–65 MYA)	*The age of ancient recent life.* Sea levels fall. Subtropical climates extend beyond the Arctic Circle. Deciduous forests cover the poles. Insects diversify. Mammals and birds begin to radiate. There is no evidence of raptors.
Eocene epoch (34–55 MYA)	*The dawn of recent life.* The world begins to warm. Tropical forests extend beyond the Arctic and Antarctic circles. Mammals continue to diversify and spread. Recognizable primates first appear in the fossil record. Raptor-like falconiforms first appear in the fossil record in the early Eocene of Europe. *Messelastur gratulator*, a small bird of prey the size of a Sharp-shinned Hawk, is described from the middle Eocene of Germany. By the beginning of the late Eocene, approximately 40 MYA, temperatures peak, the world cools, and tropical vegetation begins to withdraw toward the Equator. It is at this time (35–40 MYA) that long-distance raptor migration most likely first develops and spreads.
Oligocene epoch (23–34 MYA)	*The age of slightly recent life.* The world continues to cool and becomes more seasonal. Glaciers form in Antarctica. India collides with Asia, broad-leaved deciduous forests appear for the first time. Recognizable passerines (songbirds) appear in the fossil record. The first fossils of accipiter-like hawks appear in Australia, and those of falcons appear in France. A paleo-osprey (*Pandion* sp.) appears in the Old World Oligocene of Egypt, and buteos (*Buteo* spp.) first occur in the fossil record. Long-distance raptor migration probably is well underway, although the geography of paleomigration systems differs considerably from those of today.
Miocene epoch (5–23 MYA)	*The age of less recent life.* In the early to middle parts of the epoch, the world warms and becomes drier. Inland seas decrease in size and new land bridges form. Mammalian diversity peaks. A new habitat type, thorn-scrub develops, and modern mammalian insectivores differentiate. A falcon-like raptor *Badiostes patagonicus* appears in Argentina. By the late Miocene, the world again begins to cool and continues to dry. Another new habitat type, grassland savanna, develops in temperate North and South America. This seasonal habitat, which today is used by many migratory raptors, almost certainly permits and promotes the development and spread of long-distance raptor migration. Paleo-ospreys first appear in the New World in California and Florida.

Table 3, continued

Geologic time	Significant ecological and evolutionary events
Pliocene epoch (1.8–5 MYA)	*The age of more recent life.* The world continues to cool and dry, and climates begin to resemble those of today. Modern geography, ice caps, and prehistoric humans appear. Expansive tropical grasslands develop in Africa, Australia, and South America. The Isthmus of Panama, connecting North and South America, forms approximately 2.5 MYA. Modern migration systems begin to take shape.
Quaternary period	
Pleistocene epoch (0.01–1.8 MYA)	*The age of most recent life.* Climates alternate between ice ages and warmer, interglacial periods. Temperate- and tropical-zone habitats alternately shrink and expand, latitudinally. Neanderthal man appears. Most species of modern birds emerge. Falcons, including the modern Australian Kestrel, the Brown Falcon, and the Peregrine Falcon occur in the fossil record of Australia for the first time. Many modern migration systems are in place, although they shift in response to glacial expansions and retractions. The appearance and disappearance of glaciers and the temperate zone habitats they cover affects the population sizes of many species of migratory raptors.
Holocene epoch (0–0.01 MYA)	*The age of completely recent life.* A warm, interglacial extension of the Pleistocene. Human civilization develops. Modern systems of raptor migration, including the principal flyways described in chapter 7, continue to shift in light of climate and landscape change, some of which results from human actions.

Sources: Principal sources include Olson 1985; Behrensmeyer et al. 1992; Janis 1993; Olsen 1995; Feduccia 1996.
MYA = million years ago.

Based on this information, and assuming that the fossil record for raptors reasonably reflects their actual appearances, raptor migration could have developed no earlier than the early Eocene, or 50 to 55 MYA. The world, however, was much warmer and considerably less seasonal in the early Eocene than it is today, and sea levels were much higher. At the time, Europe was far more island-like, and subtropical forests extended well beyond the Arctic Circle. Although raptors may have made short-distance, nomadic movements under these conditions, the epoch's relatively aseasonal climates are not likely to have fostered the extensive long-distance latitudinal movements typical of today's transequatorial migrants. The late Eocene and Oligocene worlds that followed, however, were substantially cooler and far more seasonal than those of the early Eocene. This, together with coincidental equatorial retreats of high- and midlatitude subtropical and tropical forests, would have created ideal climatic and habitat conditions for the evolution of long-distance movements (see Table 3).

The early Miocene (18–23 MYA) that followed was warmer and far drier as well, and although its warmer temperatures potentially reduced the need for long-distance, latitudinal migration, its drier climates reduced the sizes of inland seas, creating new land bridges within and among continental plates (Janis 1993). The bridges, in turn, should have increased the likelihood of intercontinental movements by land-based migrants (see Chapters 4 and 7). By the start of the late Miocene (5–10 MYA), the warming trend had reversed, and cooler, drier climates latitudinally compressed subtropical and tropical rainforests equator-ward, creating a new habitat type: temperate-zone savannas. Today, such seasonally productive grasslands provide wintering habitat for many raptors, including insect-dependent, long-distance transequatorial migrants. Cooling and drying continued throughout the relatively brief, three-million-year Pliocene that followed, almost certainly increasing the likelihood of long-distance migration, and the creation of the Isthmus of Panama during this epoch 2.5 MYA provided an important intercontinental land-bridge connection between North and South America for transequatorial migrants.

The glacial-interglacial Pleistocene that followed further increased the likelihood of long-distance latitudinal movements, most likely to the point of their historic maximum. The current Holocene, which began 10,000 years ago, and is considered by many to be but a brief interglacial episode, has resulted in conditions in which populations of slightly more than 40 percent of all raptors are partial or complete migrants, a percentage that is typical of birds in general (Berthold 2001).

In sum, the fossil and climatic records indicate opportunities for long-distance raptor migration as far back as the late Eocene (35–40 MYA). That one of the most migratory genera of all modern raptors, *Pandion* (Osprey), appears in the fossil records in both the Old World Oligocene and the New World Miocene, all but certainly establishes the occurrence of at least some form of raptor migration 15 MYA. The open habitats that emerged in the drier and more seasonal Miocene (5–10 MYA) and expanded in the Pliocene (1.8–5 MYA), created ecological circumstances that, today, foster long-distance migration in many raptors. It is seems reasonable to assume that the same occurred in those epochs as well. If this scenario is correct, modern raptors are typical of most groups of modern birds in having adopted migratory strategies relatively soon after they, themselves, evolved (Alerstam 1990; Berthold 2001).

Synthesis and Conclusions

1. Migration evolves in sedentary populations of raptors when habitats change so that they are no longer capable of supporting overwintering populations or when populations increase to the point that recently fledged young are forced to disperse into areas that provide inadequate year-round habitats.

2. Migratory populations of raptors can coexist with sedentary populations, so long as individuals within both populations are reasonably successful. In such instances, partial migration develops and is maintained.

3. Complete migration in a species occurs when sedentary populations become unsuccessful to the point of decline and extirpation, whereas migratory populations do not, and when populations of the latter do not act as sources for new sedentary populations.

4. Migratory populations revert to sedentary populations when conditions on the breeding grounds permit successful overwintering and when the cost of migration selects against individuals that engage in it.

5. Due to both behavioral flexibility and rapid evolutionary change, shifts in migratory tendencies can appear and disappear in raptors within decades.

6. Many aspects of raptor migration—including its genetic basis and the relative numbers of nonmigratory, partially migratory, and completely migratory species—reflect those of birds in general.

—3—

History of Raptor-Migration Studies

There is indeed no such thing as "the" scientific method.
Sir Peter Medawar, 1984

Raptors and their migrations have intrigued humanity for thousands of years. An innate curiosity for the birds themselves, the development and practice of falconry, an urgent need to protect many species of raptors, and, most recently, an array of high-tech tools to study them, all have shaped the history of raptor-migration science. As is true in much of ornithology, armies of dedicated amateurs, working shoulder to shoulder with professional biologists, have made, and continue to make, important contributions to the field. This chapter traces the history of raptor-migration studies, describes the many approaches that have been taken, and shows how each factor has contributed to what is now known about the long-distance movements of birds of prey.

Counts of Visible Migrants at Watchsites

One of the oldest, if not the oldest, written references to raptor migration is an Old Testament admonition to Job (39:26): "Doth the hawk fly by her wisdom, and stretch her wings toward the south?" In the New World, Mayan-like Huastecs were reenacting the flights of soaring migrants from atop 100-foot poles in Gulf Coast Mexico in pre-Colombian times (Wilkerson 1980). And peoples along other major migration corridors and flyways certainly must have recognized the predictable seasonal appearances and disappearances of large flocks of migrating raptors. Serious studies of migrating raptors date at least to the early thirteenth century when the great Holy Roman Emperor Friedrich II of Hohenstaufen (1194–1250), writing in *De arte venandi cum avibus* (The Art of Falconry), became the first of many to describe a direct link between raptor migration and weather: "We notice also that when a favorable wind sweeps up, whether by day or by night, migrating birds generally hasten to take advantage of it, and even neglect food and sleep for this important purpose" (quoted in Wood and Fyfe 1943).

By the middle of the sixteenth century, Spanish historian Gonzalo Fernández de Oviedo y Valdés was describing large-scale movements of raptors in the Caribbean: "Every yeare there pass from the end of Cuba infinite numbers of diverse sorts of Birds, which come from the North of the Firme Land, and crosse over the Alacrain Islands and Cuba, and flye over the Gulfe Southwards. I have seen them passe over Darien and Nombre de Dios and Panama in divers yeares, in the Firme Land; so many that they cover the Skie; and this passage or march continueth a moneth or more about the Moneth of March. . . . The lowest are the Eaglets and the Eagles, and all seeme Birds of prey of many kinds and plumes" (Baughman 1947, 304).

About the same time, French zoologist Pierre Belon was describing similar migrations of Black Kites over the Bosporus in Istanbul, Turkey: "[I]f they had continued for a fortnight in the same strength as on that day, we could surely have said that they were in greater number than all men living on the earth, [and that] they seem to pass in this way as thick as ants, and so do continue for many days" (Nisbet and Smout 1957).

In the late 1700s, massive movements of migrating Broad-winged Hawks were reported in Colonial North American newspapers (Goldman 1970).

Despite these observations, the study of raptor migration remained an ornithological backwater well into the late 1800s, when 2x–4x field glasses and, soon after, 7x–10x prismatic binoculars came into widespread use among birdwatchers (Kastner 1986). This "revolution" in field equipment allowed observers to "see" the high-flying, soaring-bird component of raptor migration and, almost immediately, ornithologists and birders began documenting their observations.

In the initial rush to publication, several of the earliest contributions misidentified the migrants they were watching, most likely because modern field guides were not yet available. Most of the errors involved transposing the identities of locally conspicuous and frequently encountered species for seldom-seen, long-distance migrants. In the northeastern United States, for example, high-flying Broad-winged Hawks were sometimes misidentified as Red-tailed Hawks, whereas in Mexico and Argentina, high-flying Swainson's Hawks were sometimes misidentified as White-tailed Hawks (cf. Merriam 1877; Hudson 1920; Wetmore 1943). The 1934 publication of Roger Tory Peterson's popular *Field Guide to the Birds* helped correct the situation almost immediately.

Misidentifications aside, by the mid-1880s, ornithologists were reporting "immense clusters" of migrating raptors in southern New England. In 1911, ornithologist Frank Burns devoted 16 pages of a 180-page monograph on Broad-winged Hawks to migration in the species, a bird that only several decades earlier had been thought to be sedentary. Properly equipped, nature lovers flocked to hawkwatching, particularly in eastern North America where migrants concentrated along the Atlantic Coast. By the late 1920s, both the timing and the geography of raptor migration, as well as its association with local and regional weather patterns, was well established in the Mid-Atlantic region (Trowbridge 1895; Burns 1911; Ferguson and Ferguson 1922; see Robbins 1975 and Heintzelman 1986 for additional details).

Serious hawk counts from this era date from 1886 when, aided by field glasses, C. C. Trowbridge (1895) began monitoring the southbound movements of birds of prey near New Haven, Connecticut. Typical of those who followed, Trowbridge kept meticulous daily records that documented the numbers of individuals of each species seen, along with aspects of their flight behavior. Trowbridge was the earliest to assess the impact of northwesterly winds on the numbers of birds seen, as well as the first to recognize the role that the region's east-west coastline plays in concentrating southbound migrants. The earliest of what would become a genre, Trowbridge's benchmark contributions established standardized visual counts along major corridors as an effective technique in the study of raptor migration.

A second spurt in the field occurred in the 1920s to 1930s when raptor conservationists attempted to reverse the increasing assault of raptor persecution. Most raptorial birds were considered vermin at the time, even by birdwatchers and conservationists, and large numbers of hawks, eagles, and falcons were being shot along traditional flyways. Premiere "shooting galleries" included Cape May Point, New Jersey, where a recent prohibition on targeting Northern Flickers had focused the fuselage at Sharp-shinned Hawks and other raptors, and Hawk Mountain, Pennsylvania, where a new $5 bounty on Northern Goshawks fostered a "shoot-first-and-identify-later" mentality (Bildstein 2001). Landmark counting and anti-shooting campaigns were initiated at both of these sites in the early 1930s (Broun 1935; Allen and Peterson 1936).

Initially designed to document the magnitude of the overall flight and to halt the carnage associated with it, additional values associated with full-season counts at migration hotspots quickly became apparent. A 39-bird flight of Golden Eagles at Hawk Mountain in 1934, for example, led to the discovery of a previously unrecognized but significant eastern corridor for this species. The arrival of 1,250 visitors at the Hawk Mountain Sanctuary in the autumn of 1935 led to the realization that concentrated raptor migration could be used to introduce the general public to these normally secretive birds (Broun 1949).

Hawkwatching, both as science and conservation and as recreation, continued to expand in mid-twentieth-century North America. At first, the growth occurred primarily along major migration corridors and bottlenecks in the northeastern United States. Eventually it expanded throughout most of the country. Systematic, regionwide counts were established in several areas in the 1950s, and a conference on hawkwatching in 1974 in Syracuse, New York, led to the formation of the Hawk Migration Association of North America (HMANA). HMANA began to standardize counts at watchsites shortly after, and by 1999, North American hawkwatchers had reported counts from more than 1800 watchsites, 60 of which had been active for more than a decade (Robbins 1975; McCarty et al. 2000).

The development of hawkwatching had a similar history in Europe, particularly in the Mediterranean region where widespread shooting and trapping inspired conservation efforts similar to those in North America (Table 4). Count activities increased in the Middle East in the 1980s as a result of concerns about bird-aircraft collisions. In eastern Asia, worries about shooting and trapping helped increase count activities there in the 1990s. As a result, close to 400 migration watchsites now exist in 89 countries on six continents. More than 110 of these hawkwatches count at least 10,000 raptors annually, 18 sites count at least 100,000 raptors, and 3 of the sites—Veracruz River-of-Raptors in Gulf Coast Mexico, the Kéköldi Indigenous Reserve in

Box 1. Serendipity in Raptor-Migration Science and Conservation

Serendipity, the propensity for making accidental but useful discoveries, or of being in the right place at the right time, has played a major role in science, including the discoveries of meiosis, penicillin, and cellular immunity. One of the best examples of serendipity in raptor-migration science involves Hawk Mountain Sanctuary's counts of Bald Eagles and other raptors in mid-twentieth-century North America.

Hawk Mountain Sanctuary was founded in 1934 by conservationist Rosalie Edge. Raptors were considered vermin at the time, and many were being slaughtered during migration along major migration corridors, including the central Appalachian Mountain ridge in eastern Pennsylvania that includes Hawk Mountain. Edge hired ornithologist Maurice Broun to post and patrol the new wildlife refuge and asked him to start counting the numbers of raptors he was protecting. The migration counts that Broun began on 30 September 1934 initially served to document the magnitude of the flight and to build financial support for the conservation effort. However, it quickly became apparent to Broun and Edge that a series of annual counts at Hawk Mountain would allow the Sanctuary to monitor regional populations of raptors, and within several years of initiating the count in 1934, migration counts from the North Lookout became the Sanctuary's primary field effort (Broun 1935, 1939).

This set the stage for serendipity: the use of the counts in documenting the impact that synthetic organochlorine pesticides had on raptor populations in northeastern North America. Although it is now clear that the misuse of DDT and other organochlorine pesticides in mid-twentieth-century North America deleteriously affected populations of many species of birds including many raptors, this was not the case in the 1930s. The potential for an impact had been mentioned in the late 1940s shortly after the new "wonder" pesticides had come into widespread use and regional populations of many species of birds "apparently" began to decline, but documenting the relationship proved difficult because of the lack of pre–DDT-Era population data for the birds in question.

The situation changed in the early 1950s when Maurice Broun started commenting on substantial declines in the numbers of migrating juvenile Bald Eagles seen at Hawk Mountain (Broun 1952). The declines, which had begun in the late 1940s and initially involved only first-year birds, suggested a drop in reproductive success in the species. The downward trend continued, and by the mid-1950s, ratios of juvenile-to-adult Bald Eagles at Hawk Mountain were less than half of what they had been in the 1930s. In 1962, conservationist Rachel Carson used the then-25-year series of Sanctuary counts to support her arguments for the impact of organochlorine pesticides on the reproductive success of birds of prey in her book *Silent Spring* (Carson 1962; Bildstein 1998).

The Sanctuary's long-term counts, which now span eight decades, have proved useful not only in tracking declines in ratios of juvenile-to-adult Bald Eagles but also in documenting delayed declines in the total numbers of eagles counted at the site and in documenting rebounds in these two demographic parameters following bans on the widespread use of DDT in the early 1970s (Figure 6).

Hawk Mountain Sanctuary's long-term counts also helped track DDT-Era declines and post–DDT-Era rebounds in populations of other species, including Sharp-shinned Hawks, Cooper's Hawks, and Peregrine Falcons, highlighting the counts' value in long-term ecological monitoring, something that was not envisioned when they were started in 1934 (Broun 1949; Bildstein 2001). Serendipity indeed.

Caribbean-slope Costa Rica, and Elat in southern Israel—count more than one million migrants annually (Figure 7) (Bijlsma 1987; Bildstein et al. 1993; Shirihai et al. 2000; Zalles and Bildstein 2000). Many active hawk-watches are organized and run by trained volunteers who provide important, high-quality, low-cost count data to scientists and conservationists.

Because raptors are normally secretive and thus difficult to survey and monitor, counts at migration watchsites can help track the status of regional and, sometimes, continental populations of birds of prey. This is particularly so when counts are used in conjunction with banding efforts and satellite tracking that help delineate the geographic sources and destinations of the migrants. Information from geographic networks of hawkwatches is useful in this regard, especially when counts extend over many years. Recent analyses suggest that migration counts can be useful even when the numbers of individual birds are small. At Hawk Mountain Sanctuary, for example, where, until recently, fewer than 100 Bald Eagles and 50 Peregrine Falcons have been counted each autumn, long-term trends of both of these species clearly

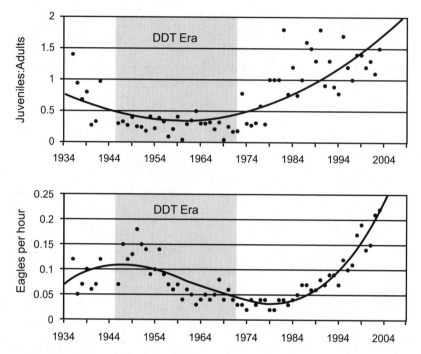

Figure 6. Long-term shifts in the ratio of juvenile-to-adult Bald Eagles at Hawk Mountain Sanctuary, Pennsylvania, 1934–2003 (above), together with long-term shifts in annual rates of passage of Bald Eagles at the site during the same period (below). (Hawk Mountain Sanctuary database)

tracked DDT-Era (i.e., 1945–1972) declines in the mid-twentieth century, as well as subsequent post–DDT-Era rebounds in the 1970s through 1990s (Bildstein 1998).

Although counts frequently vary considerably among years because of annual differences in the weather and other factors, a growing body of evidence suggests that over the long haul, numbers of raptors reported at migration watchsites typically reflect the long-term status of the source populations (Newton 1979; Bildstein 1998; Hoffman et al. 2002). For example, Tadoussac Bird Observatory (TBS), Quebec, Canada, and Hawk Mountain Sanctuary (HMS), Pennsylvania, USA, are along the Appalachian Mountain Flyway of eastern North America, and both record movements of about 17,000 raptors annually. Tadoussac is approximately 930 km northwest of Hawk Mountain, however, and annual variation in the numbers of two "northern" migrants—Northern Goshawk and Rough-legged Hawk—are lower there than at Hawk Mountain, presumably because in most years large-scale

Table 4. *Migration watchsites that have grown largely from conservation efforts*

Name	History
Hawk Mountain Sanctuary Pennsylvania, U.S.A.	Hawk Mountain Sanctuary (HMS) was founded in 1934 by Rosalie Edge to stop the slaughter of migrants atop a major promontory on the Kittatinny Ridge in the central Appalachian Mountains of eastern Pennsylvania. Today, Hawk Mountain Sanctuary Association is the largest and oldest member-based raptor conservation organization in the world. The Sanctuary maintains the longest and most complete record of raptor migration in existence (Bildstein and Compton 2000).
Cape May Point New Jersey, U.S.A.	The National Audubon Society began detailed migration counts at Cape May Point in 1931. Most shooting at the site was eliminated in the mid-1930s with the creation of the Whitmer Stone Wildlife Sanctuary, largely as a result of protests by the National Audubon Society. New Jersey Audubon has monitored autumn raptor migration at the site since 1976 (Allen and Peterson 1936).
Hawk Ridge Minnesota, U.S.A.	Raptor shooting was reported in the area in the mid- to late 1940s. P. B. Hofslund and other members of the Duluth Bird Club began sporadic counts at the site at the western end of Lake Superior in 1951. Consistent coverage was initiated in 1972 when, with funds from the Nature Conservancy, Hawk Ridge Nature Reserve was established in suburban Duluth. Counts are managed by the Duluth Audubon Society (Hofslund 1966).
Organbidexka Col Libre France	Since 1980, Organbidexka Pass, which is believed to be the most important raptor migration bottleneck in the western Pyrenees, has been a *col libre,* or "shooting free zone." In the late 1990s, there were more than 6000 shooting blinds along 200 km of ridges of the Atlantic Pyrenees. Although most shooters target passerines and pigeons, raptors, too, often are killed. Organbidexka Col Libre of Bayonne, France, monitors the movements of raptors at the site (Devisse 2000).

Name	History
Straits of Messina Sicily	In the late 1970s, raptors and storks were being shot from dozens of multiperson concrete bunkers in the Peloritani Mountains of eastern Sicily in spite of regional and national prohibitions. Raptor-conservation protest camps were initiated in the region in 1981, and counts of both migrants and numbers of shots heard started in 1984. By the late 1990s, many shooting bunkers had been abandoned. Shooting continued on the Calabrian (mainland) side of the Straits as recently as 2002 (Giordano et al. 1998).
Buskett Gardens Malta	A bird sanctuary in the central Mediterranean since 1932, Buskett Gardens is regularly used as a roosting site by migrating raptors. Although a "200-m" safety area extends around the approximately 30-ha forested site, shooting continues in the area. Movements of raptors have been monitored at the site since 1976. The Maltese Ornithological Society compiles count data from the site (Fenech 1992; Sammut and Bonavia 2004).
Batumi Georgia	Large numbers of sparrow hawks have been shot or trapped for falconry for a long time in Georgia, particularly along the western Black Sea coast where trans-Caucasus migrants concentrate in large numbers. By the late 1990s Georgian law "protected" migrants from such actions. Unfortunately, enforcement remained spotty in many areas. The Georgian Center for the Conservation of Wildlife began monitoring the movements of raptors and conducting education programs near Batumi, western Georgia, in autumn 2000 (van Maanen et al. 2001).
Kenting Park Taiwan	Raptors had been shot at roosting sites in and around Manchou, near Kenting, southernmost Taiwan for some time. By the late 1980s interest in hawkwatching in the region had grown, and official counts were underway. Counts are conducted by the Raptor Research Group of Taiwan and maintained by the Chinese Wild Bird Federation. Former shooters serve as tour guides for hawkwatchers (Lin and Severinghaus 1998).

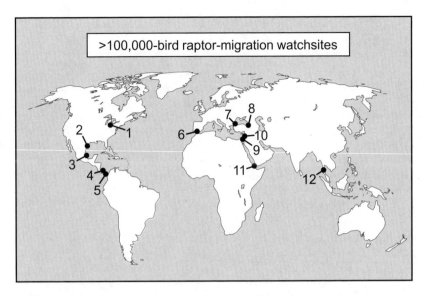

Figure 7. Raptor-migration watchsites that regularly count 100,000 or more raptors annually. (1) Lake Erie Metropark, Michigan; (2) Corpus Christi Hawk Watch, Texas; (3) Veracruz River-of-Raptors, Mexico; (4) Kéköldi Indigenous Reserve, Costa Rica; (5) Ancon Hill, Panama; (6) Tarifa, Spain; (7) Bosporus, Turkey; (8) Borçka, Turkey; (9) Elat, Israel; (10) Northern Valley's, Israel; (11) Bab el Mandeb strait, Djibouti; and (12) Chumphon, Thailand. Three of the watchsites—Veracruz River-of-Raptors, Kéköldi Indigenous Reserve, and Elat—record more than one million migrants annually. (See Chapter 9 and Zalles and Bildstein 2000 for details)

movements of these species occur largely north of Hawk Mountain. On the other hand, Hawk Mountain draws migrants from a considerably greater geographic area than does Tadoussac, and because birds breeding close to one another are more likely to show synchronous fluctuations in breeding success than are those breeding across large geographic regions, annual variation in counts of other migrants at the two sites tend to be lower at Hawk Mountain (Table 5).

Counts at migration watchsites typically consist of timed records of the numbers of raptors seen traveling in prolonged, unidirectional flight along the region's *principal axis of migration.* Most watchsites record counts hourly and most begin counting shortly after dawn and continue until dusk. Full-season watchsites begin their watches at or about the time that the earliest migrants begin their movements and continue to count on a daily basis, weather permitting, until almost all of the latest migrants have passed

Table 5. *Annual variation in raptor migration counts at Tadoussac Bird Observatory and Hawk Mountain Sanctuary, 1993–2001*

| | Coefficient of Variation (%)[a] | |
Species	Tadoussac Bird Observatory	Hawk Mountain Sanctuary
Osprey	44	20
Bald Eagle	50	22
Northern Harrier	40	38
Sharp-shinned Hawk	29	23
Northern Goshawk	30	61
Broad-winged Hawk	54	52
Red-tailed Hawk	47	27
Rough-legged Hawk	52	56
Golden Eagle	39	18
American Kestrel	33	24
Merlin	37	31
Peregrine Falcon	35	28

Source: M. Bélisle and J. Ibarzabal, Tadoussac Bird Observatory, unpubl. ms.
[a] The coefficient of variation (CV) is the standard deviation of each species' annual mean expressed as a percentage of that mean. Larger CVs indicate greater annual variation around the mean. Because CVs take into account the different magnitudes of species means, it is possible to compare them both across and within species.

through the region. Hawk Mountain Sanctuary at 40° N, for example, begins its official count on 15 August and continues the count through 15 December.

To reduce biases associated with annual differences in count effort, data are usually standardized prior to analysis. Standardization involves several procedures. In most instances, raw counts are converted to numbers of raptors seen per hour of observation, and the counts themselves are typically truncated on a species-by-species basis to the time period in days when 95 percent of the species' passage occurs. Long-term trends can be unduly influenced by exceptionally high single-day or single-season counts, and observers often *log-transform* their counts to reduce the impact of this potential bias. Most analyses assume that whereas weather can affect the magnitude and detectability of migrants at particular sites, such effects are likely to be random and, as such, not likely to affect long-term trends, other than to make such trends more difficult to detect. An additional statistical concern, positive autocorrelation, which involves the likely correlation of sequential counts in a time series resulting from population persistence across years, is often tested for during analysis and dealt with statistically thereafter. Overall, such techniques substantially increase the validity of resulting analyses of migration counts in determining long-term population trends (Bednarz et al. 1990; Dunn and Hussell 1995; Hoffman and Smith 2003).

Counts at migration watchsites can be used to study aspects of migration behavior and ecology, including flocking and soaring dynamics, speed of travel, intra- and interspecies interactions, roosting and feeding, energy management and habitat use en route, and site and weather effects. The counts also are useful for introducing students and the general public to the whys and wherefores of raptor biology and conservation.

Counts of visible migrants at watchsites are not perfect. Even short-term counts are biased toward low-flying individuals and by observer fatigue, and long-term counts can be compromised by improved optics and shifts in count protocols. In addition, because most hawkwatches are along major flyways, count results tend to reflect the narrow- and not necessarily broad-frontal movements of migrating raptors (see Chapter 4). That said, statistical treatments of migration-count data continue to improve, and preliminary evaluations suggest that counts at traditional hawkwatches are likely to provide important information on raptor migration and population status for some time (Haugh 1972; Bednarz and Kerlinger 1989; Kerlinger 1989; Titus et al. 1990; Bildstein 1998).

Trapping and Banding

In addition to counting at watchsites, trapping and banding efforts have a long history of use in studies of raptor migration. Indeed, humans have been trapping raptors for at least 6000 years. Historically, birds of prey have been caught for predator control, for their feathers and other body parts, for pets, and to be trained for falconry. Although humans have finessed and modified traps to catch raptors for all of these reasons, falconers have provided most of the devices that scientists and conservationists currently use to capture birds of prey.

Falconry—the art of training hawks to hunt with humans—developed in the deserts of central Asia some 4000 years ago. Incessant tinkering since then has produced a multitude of traps that, when properly deployed, capture their targets unharmed and are easily reset for additional captures. Falconers quickly discovered that one of the best times to trap birds of prey was during migration when large numbers of individuals concentrated along well-established flyways, and most devices they developed are well suited to studies of raptor migration (see Bub 1978 and Meredith 1999 for details). The ability to trap large numbers of migratory raptors for "science" set the stage for a major advance in one aspect of raptor-migration studies: raptor banding.

Although scientists had trapped raptors to secure specimens for museum collections and for anatomical and food-habits studies for hundreds of years, it was not until the end of the nineteenth century that live-trapping of raptors to study their migrations began in earnest. A Danish school teacher, Hans Christian Cornelius Mortensen, is credited with being the first to recognize the value of banding large numbers of individual birds with uniquely numbered return-addressed aluminum bands. Mortensen pioneered the technique in the autumn of 1899 when he attached handmade, numbered leg bands to 165 Eurasian Starlings that he had trapped in Viborg, Denmark, and announced his activities in several European journals. The following year, he reported that two of his birds had died in Viborg during the autumn in which they were banded, that two others had been seen 60 kilometers (km) southeast the following spring, and that four banded individuals had bred in Viborg that summer (Jespersen and Tåning 1950). Word of Mortensen's successes spread rapidly, and the newly established marking technique underwent a period of exponential growth among amateur and professional ornithologists.

A paper detailing the migratory movements of Rough-legged Buzzards banded as nestlings and as outbound migrants in Sweden and Lapland appeared in the *Journal für Ornithology* in 1913–14 (see Thompson 1926), and several papers describing the movements of other species of raptors were published shortly after. Government banding offices opened in the United States in 1920 and in Canada in 1922, and by 1935 more than 4000 raptors of 17 species had been banded in North America. Remarkably, 11 percent of these birds already had been "recovered" after being shot, mainly as a result of widespread predator control (Lincoln 1936). Scientific banding has continued to grow, particularly in North America and Europe. By the end of the twentieth century, more than a million raptors had been banded in North America alone, and an additional 145,000 had been "ringed" in England,

Scotland, and Ireland (Table 6). Although many birds of prey are banded as nestlings, many others, including most accipiters, are trapped during migration at well-established banding stations along major migration corridors and bottlenecks. At most stations, raptors are caught by teams of field workers who operate multiple devices from small huts or blinds (Figures 8 and 9). Most modern traps attract their quarry with living, dead, or mechanical lures representing potential prey or, in a few instances, natural enemies such as owls (Jacobs 1996). The idiosyncratic nature of trapping and the fact that species of raptors differ considerably in their "trap-ability" has given birth to an almost infinite number of devices, including walk-in and fall-in traps, spring-powered bow-nets, cannon- and rocket-powered nets, static and dynamic vertical nets, snares, and all possible combinations therein (Table 7).

Migrating raptors have been trapped and banded at hundreds of locations, several of which have taken trapping and banding to their extreme. One of the oldest raptor banding establishments in North America, Cedar Grove Ornithological Station in southeastern Wisconsin, typifies the intensity of the work that sometimes occurs at such sites. Close to 1000 raptors were caught at Cedar Grove between 1936 and 1949, and more than 10,000 have been trapped there since. Trapping occurs at five venues spread across a series of forest openings within 200 meters of Lake Michigan. Dho-gazas, bow nets, and stationary nets usually are worked in combination. Caged and tethered House Sparrows, European Starlings, and Rock Pigeons are used as lures (Bub 1978).

Other active New World banding stations include Cape May Point, New Jersey, where banding has been underway since 1967, and where more than 27,000 Sharp-shinned Hawks, alone, were trapped during the first 16 years of banding; Hawk Ridge on Lake Superior in northern Minnesota, where more than 85,000 raptors, representing 23 species, were trapped in 1972–2001; HawkWatch International banding stations in the Goshute Mountains of northeastern Nevada (41,361 raptors in 1980–2001), and in the Manzano and Sandia mountains of central New Mexico (13,511 raptors in 1985–2001); and Golden Gate Raptor Observatory, at the mouth of San Francisco Bay (15,698 raptors in 1983–2000). Notable Old World banding sites include Chokpak Pass in southern Kazakhstan (5,246 raptors in 1966–1997), and Elat, Israel (>16,000 in 1982–2001) (Hoffman et al. 2002; D. Evans, pers. comm.; A. Fish, pers. comm.; Y. N. Grachev and E. I. Gavrilov, pers. comm.; R. Yosef, pers. comm.).

Table 6. *Numbers of raptors banded and numbers subsequently encountered in Canada and the United States, 1955–2000[a]; and in Ireland and the United Kingdom, 1909–2000[b]*

	Canada and the United States		Ireland and the United Kingdom	
	Number banded	Number subsequently encountered (% banded)	Number banded	Number subsequently encountered (% banded)
Black Vulture	2936	403 (14%)		
Turkey Vulture	1775	169 (10%)		
Osprey	34,714	2474 (7%)	1640	133 (8%)
Western Honey Buzzard		0	62	0
Hook-billed Kite	4			
Swallow-tailed Kite	200	1 (<1%)		
White-tailed Kite	644	24 (4%)		
Snail Kite	2451	20 (1%)		
Mississippi Kite	1037	12 (1%)		
Red Kite			1861	112 (6%)
White-tailed Sea Eagle			88	4 (5%)
Bald Eagle	26,622	3404 (13%)		
Northern Harrier	18,966	620 (3%)	7763	412 (5%)
Montagu's Harrier			480	42 (9%)
Western Marsh Harrier			1585	60 (4%)
Eurasian Sparrowhawk			39,696	3,978 (10%)
Sharp-shinned Hawk	341,718	4018 (1%)		
Cooper's Hawk	68,606	1948 (3%)		
Northern Goshawk	21,363	816 (4%)	4190	156 (4%)
Common Black Hawk	43	1 (2%)		

Species				
Harris' Hawk	3870	122 (3%)		
Grey Hawk	248	13 (5%)		
Red-shouldered Hawk	13,072	723 (6%)		
Roadside Hawk	18	0		
Broad-winged Hawk	7036	188 (3%)		
Short-tailed Hawk	16	1 (6%)		
Swainson's Hawk	17,865	729 (4%)		
White-tailed Hawk	164	1 (<1)		
Zone-tailed Hawk	35	4 (11%)		
Red-tailed Hawk	133,770	6987 (5%)		
Eurasian Buzzard			10,415	739 (7%)
Ferruginous Hawk	19,026	648 (3%)		
Rough-legged Hawk	4,424	213 (5%)		
Golden Eagle	8,111	734 (9%)	1,030	49 (5%)
Crested Caracara	383	14 (4%)		
American Kestrel	213,050	3,808 (2%)	52,146	4,541 (9%)
Common Kestrel			15,048	926 (6%)
Merlin	26,308	674 (3%)		
Aplomado Falcon	417	1 (<1%)		
Northern Hobby			1,453	42 (3%)
Gyrfalcon	1,571	20 (1%)		
Peregrine Falcon	36,569	2,413 (7%)	7,628	656 (9%)
Prairie Falcon	15,608	715 (5%)		
Number of species	34		15	
All species	1,022,640	31,917 (3%)	145,085	11,850 (8%)

[a] Bird Banding Lab, Patuxent Wildlife Research Center, United States Geological Survey, Laurel, Maryland.
[b] Clark et al. 2002.

Figure 8. Set mist nets at a raptor banding station in Elat, Israel. (Photo by the author)

Figure 9. A bow net being set at a raptor banding station in Elat, Israel. Note the trappers' hide at the edge of the field. (Photo by the author)

Table 7. *Traps used to capture migratory raptors*[a]

Bal-chatri. The Bal-chatri is an ancient snaring device developed by falconers in East India to capture small accipiters and falcons. The original construction consisted of a small conical cage (the name, *bal-chatri*, means a "small umbrella") of 15 to 20 split sticks strapped together with twine, to which were attached several dozen upright slip-nooses made from horsehair. The trap is baited with two or more small birds or mammals, depending on the species of raptor sought. The modern equivalent is constructed of metal hardware cloth or caging, festooned with mono-filament slip nooses. Trap diameters range from about 25 to 50 cm, with noose diameters ranging from 4 to 12 cm. The trap is usually weighted down with iron rods on the base to prevent it from being carried off by ensnared birds. North American ornithologists have been using Bal-chatris to capture raptors since the 1940s. Tossed from slow-moving vehicles, this small trap is particularly effective for catching American Kestrels perch-hunting from roadside utility lines. Bottom-less variants of the Bal-chatri are sometimes placed in nests with nestlings to capture parental adults (Bub 1978; Berger and Mueller 1959).

Bow net. Modern clam-shaped bow nets are pairs of semicircular pieces of metal covered with loose netting that are connected at their bases with self-closing, torsion-spring hinges. Most are 1 to 2 meters across. The trap is set by firmly attaching one of the semicircular sides to the ground and latching the other directly on top of it. A lure is placed at the center of the hinged end. When a raptor is attracted to the lure, the trap is sprung-closed remotely by the person working it, either electronically or mechanically, or by the movements of the attacking raptor itself. The original, ancient Chinese torsion mechanism consisted of a wooden bow (hence the name bow net) strung with twisted animal sinew or "bow string," that was pulled taut by a crossbar trigger mechanism, which, when released, untwisted the sinew, pulling the upper net frame to the ground. Bow nets take considerable patience and practice to operate, and a misused bow net can seriously injure or kill a raptor (Bub 1978).

Dho-gaza. Dho-gazas have long been used by falconers in Arabia, Persia, and Japan. Most are square or rectangular, and are 5 to 8 feet on a side. Dho-gazas are break-away net-traps in which loosely attached, light-weight netting is hung vertically between two bamboo, metal, or fiberglass poles. Raptors are lured to the set by caged bait or by tethered live owls or stuffed owls placed in front of or behind the net. When a raptor flies into the net, it pulls the fall-away netting from its loose attachments and becomes entangled within it. The bander then rushes to the tangled mass and removes the bird from it. Dho-gazas work best when their nets are placed in front of appropriate backdrops and are thus nearly invisible to the approaching bird (Bub 1978; Clark 1981).

Mist net. Stationary mist nets (*kasumi-ami* in Japanese) were perfected for bird trap-ping in Japan in the late 1800s. Originally made of cotton or silk thread, modern mist nets are constructed of black nylon. Most are 6 meters long and 3 meters high. The delicate, light-weight nets, which "disappear" visually against most backgrounds, are used both with and without mechanical or live tethered lures. Unlike dho-gazas, mist nets are firmly suspended end-to-end from bamboo, metal, or fiberglass poles, typically in parallel or angled arrays. Nets are placed in areas that are likely to attract feeding migrants, and in many instances raptors are at-

Table 7, continued

tracted to the nets by already-captured passerines. Small accipiters and falcons are trapped using this technique (Bub 1978).

Cannon and rocket netting. Cannon and rocket netting is used to capture relatively large, scavenging birds of prey. Cannon and rocket nets often exceed 5 meters in length and typically require two or more people to operate. Projectiles fired from a series of two or more cannons or rockets are used to propel a gathered net over baited birds. Most trap sites are baited with carcasses for several days in advance of being set, and a single firing can capture several individuals. Sometimes used to capture raptors for satellite tracking, cannon and rocket nets are not usually used at migration banding stations (Bub 1978).

[a]Detailed histories of the many ingenuous techniques and devices that falconers have used to capture raptors can be found in Bub (1978) and Meredith (1999).

Marking is another important procedure associated with trapping. Marking birds in ways that allow them to be identified in the field as individuals without recapture increases the rate at which information about their movements can be gathered. One of the most primitive ways of marking raptors is to create a small "window" in the feathers of the wing or tail by clipping away portions of the vanes of a number of adjacent flight feathers, or by dying or painting groups of flight feathers. Imping, a marking technique adapted from falconry, involves gluing previously molted and subsequently dyed feathers from the species in question into the clipped shaft of an individual's existing flight feather. More permanent marking methods include attaching a conspicuous wing tag or affixing one or more colored leg bands, which often are lettered or numbered for individual identification. Marking schemes, which should be tested for negative impacts prior to use, work best when major efforts are spent trying to resight individuals.

Color marking has been used to test the extent to which migrants "adhere" to ridges while traveling along well-established migration corridors (E. Ruelas, pers. comm.), the extent to which raptors "water-cross" versus "backtrack" at peninsular bottlenecks (M. Fuller, pers. comm.), and the extent of among-year, winter home-range site-fidelity in migrants (C. and S. Robertson, pers. comm.). Young and Kochert (1987) provide an excellent review of color marking and its uses in the field of raptor biology.

In addition to banding and color marking, migrants also are trapped to attach radio and satellite tags (see "Tracking with Telemetry" below), as well as to age, sex, and measure individuals, and to assess feather molt, external and internal parasite loads, and the physical condition and health of the birds, including the amount of subcutaneous fat they are traveling with (Giron Pendleton et al. 1987; Kerlinger 1989).

Trappers and banders are well networked, and their protocols tend to be similar. Many details, however, including the kinds of lures (e.g., mechanical versus live) and trapping devices used, as well as the species that are trapped, differ considerably among banding stations (Clark 1985a; Hoffman et al. 2002).

Tracking with Telemetry

Telemetry, which is ancient Greek for "distance measuring," involves catching and tagging individual raptors with signaling devices and remotely "following" or tracking their movements. Conventional VHF (very-high frequency) radio tracking uses small radios to signal the locations and short-distance movements of individual birds, whereas UHF (ultra-high frequency) satellite tracking uses equally small transponders, together with an array of satellites, to locate and monitor long-distance movements of individual birds. Both techniques have contributed substantially to studies of raptor migration.

Because the flight mechanics of birds are relatively fragile, signaling devices, which are attached as close to the bird's center of gravity as possible, usually weigh no more than 3 percent of the individual's body mass. Most devices are attached as "backpacks" or "fanny packs." A few have been glued directly to the skin of birds or sewn onto the quills of their tail feathers. Most attachments are designed to deteriorate over time so that the attached tag eventually will fall free of the bird. Detection ranges of VHF radio tags are affected by battery size (solar or chemical), antenna length, vegetative cover, and local terrain. In most cases, radio tags are not detectable with ground receivers at distances of more than 5 to 15 km.

Detecting tags from fixed-winged aircraft and helicopters is another matter entirely. In southern England, for example, where researchers tracked dispersal in young Eurasian Buzzards from fixed-wing aircraft while traveling along transects spaced at 40-km intervals, a few birds were detected at up to 80 km (Kenward et al. 2000). Even so, the utility of radio tracking in studies of long-distance migration is limited.

Satellite tracking, which extends detection ranges radically, can be used to track migrants that undertake intercontinental and even transoceanic journeys. Developed at the U. S. Army's Applied Physics Laboratory in Maryland in the early 1980s, the technique now includes the use of 20–35 gram, solar-powered, platform transmitter terminals (PTTs) that are capable of transmitting locations for several years. Unlike conventional battery-powered units in which power usage typically limits signaling to 50 to 100 locations per year, solar-powered units are capable of delivering hundreds or even thousands of locations annually, enabling researchers to track an individual's movements within, as well as across, days (Seegar et al. 1996).

First tested in the autumn of 1984 on Bald Eagles, satellite tracking has been used to monitor the movements of one or more individuals of at least 27 species of relatively large-bodied raptors (Table 8). Used in conjunction with the French–U. S. Argos-Tiros satellites, the system, theoretically, can provide locations of ±150 meters (m) across the surface of the earth. Even so, locations for moving targets such as migrating raptors often fall within the range of ±2 km. Recently developed global positioning system (GPS) receivers have increased locational accuracy to ±20 m.

A principal drawback to satellite tracking is its expense. The general rule of thumb is that it costs about $4,500 per year, per bird for the PTT and satellite tracking time. Not surprisingly, most studies that use this technology manage to track only a handful of birds. Notable exceptions include a collaborative study of North American Ospreys that tracked 117 birds (M. Martell and P. Nye, pers. comm.) and a study of Alaskan Golden Eagles that tracked 51 individuals (C. McIntyre, pers. comm.). Although large sample sizes are needed to assess the extent of migration variability within species, satellite-tracking studies of even one or two birds have yielded important insights. The range of Greater Spotted Eagles wintering in Africa has been extended 1500 km south based on satellite tracks of two individuals that overwintered in South Luangwa National Park, Zambia (Meyburg and Meyburg 2002). And satellite tracks of a single Lesser Spotted Eagle indicate that the bird, which detoured some 500 km to avoid a water crossing at the southern tip of the Sinai Peninsula in northwestern Egypt as a first-autumn migrant in 1997, followed the same circuitous route in 1998 on its second outbound migration (Meyburg et al. 2002).

Although still in its infancy, satellite telemetry offers the holy grail of raptor-migration studies: the opportunity to follow an individual raptor on a daily and even hourly basis, throughout its migrations. As miniaturization proceeds—the smallest raptors capable of carrying existing units must have a body mass of at least 500 grams—and costs decline, this space-age technology will continue to grow in importance.

Table 8. *Raptors whose movements have been studied using satellite tracking*

Species	Breeding region	Source
Turkey Vulture	New Jersey	Place et al. 2001
	California	P. Bloom, pers. comm.
	Pennsylvania	J. Mandel, pers. comm.
	Canada	S. Houston, pers. comm.
Osprey	Sweden	Kjellén et al. 1997
	North America	Martell et al. 1998
	Western Mediterranean	R. Triay, pers. comm.
	Scotland	R. Dennis, pers. comm.
	Germany	Meyburg and Meyburg 2002
Madagascar Fish Eagle	Madagascar	Rafanomezantsoa et al. 2002
Swallow-tailed Kite	Southeastern United States	K. Meyer, pers. comm.
White-tailed Sea Eagle	Germany	Meyburg et al. 1994
	Eastern Russia	Ueta et al. 1998
Bald Eagle	Alaska	Fuller et al. 1995
	Canada, Michigan	Grubb et al. 1994
	Washington	J. Watson, pers. comm.
Steller's Sea Eagle	Eastern Russia	Meyburg and Lobkov 1994
		Ueta et al. 2000
Western Honey Buzzard	Germany	Meyburg and Meyburg 2002
Crested Honey Buzzard	Japan	H. Higuchi, pers. comm.
Eurasian Griffon	Israel	O. Bahat, pers. comm.
	Spain	Berthold et al. 1991
		Griesinger et al. 1992
Egyptian Vulture	France and Bulgaria	Meyburg and Meyburg 2002
Bearded Vulture	Republic of Georgia	A. Gavashelishvili, pers. comm.
Short-toed Snake Eagle	France	Meyburg et al. 1998
Northern Goshawk	Western United States	J. Smith, pers. comm.
Broad-winged Hawk	Eastern and central United States	Haines et al. 2003
White-throated Hawk	Argentina	V. Sympson, pers. comm.

Table 8, continued

Species	Breeding region	Source
Swainson's Hawk	Western North America	Fuller et al. 1998
	Minnesota	Martell et al. 1998
Red-tailed Hawk	Western United States	J. Smith, pers. comm.
Lesser Spotted Eagle	Germany	Meyburg et al. 1995a
Greater Spotted Eagle	Germany	Meyburg et al. 1995b
	Poland	Meyburg and Meyburg 2002
Steppe Eagle	Central Asia	Meyburg and Meyburg 2002
Imperial Eagle	Hungary	Meyburg et al. 1995c
	Eastern Russia	Ueta and Ryabtsev 2001
Wahlberg's Eagle	Namibia and South Africa	Meyburg et al. 1995d
Bonelli's Eagle	Spain	M. Alacántra, pers. comm.
Golden Eagle	Quebec	Brodeur et al. 1996
	Alaska	C. McIntyre, pers. comm.
Harpy Eagle	Venezuela and Panama	Alvarez-Cordero 1996
Prairie Falcon	Idaho	K. Steenhof, pers. comm.
Saker Falcon	Central Russia	Eastham 1998
	Mongolia	Potapov et al. 2001
Peregrine Falcon	Alaska	Britten et al. 1999
	North America	Fuller et al. 1998
	Ontario and Quebec	M. Gahbauer, pers. comm.
	Greenland	K. Burnham, pers. comm.

pers. comm. = personal communication.

Stable Isotopes

Isotopes are forms or types of individual elements that differ in the number of neutrons (but not protons) in their nuclei and, thus, have different atomic masses and different nuclear properties but retain identical chemical properties. The element hydrogen, for example, which ordinarily has a single proton and no neutron in its nucleus (^1H), also occurs rarely as deuterium (^2H), an isotopic form that has one neutron and one proton in its nucleus. A third manufactured isotopic form, tritium (^{3}H), which has two neutrons and one proton in its nucleus, does not occur naturally.

One potentially powerful technique for studying raptor migration uses geographic variations in relative occurrences of naturally occurring rare and common stable isotopes in the feathers of captured migrants to determine an individual's breeding and overwintering areas. Deuterium (^{2}H), for example, which occurs naturally in rainfall and is ingested by birds and subsequently deposited into growing feathers, varies with latitude relative to typical isotopic hydrogen (^{1}H) across much of North America. Because many migrating raptors grow new feathers prior to migration, it is possible to determine the approximate general latitude of origin of individuals by assessing the ratio ^{2}H: ^{1}H in single body feathers.

Isotopes of carbon, sulfur, and strontium also vary geographically, albeit in slightly different ways. The rare isotope of sulfur (^{34}S), for example, is more common in marine ecosystems than in terrestrial ecosystems, making it possible to distinguish migrants that have fed on coastal versus inland prey. Simultaneous analyses of isotopes of several elements increase the accuracy of the technique considerably, enabling researchers who trap and sample the feathers of migrants to determine the degree to which populations of widespread species are structured geographically. Such results can play important roles in conservation by allowing workers to focus protection efforts on truly at-risk populations of birds (Hobson 2002).

Investigators already have used isotopic hydrogen to investigate the birthplace latitudes of juvenile Cooper's Hawks migrating through the Florida Keys in autumn (Meehan et al. 2001). Studies examining the latitudinal birthplaces of other species of raptors migrating through the Keys also are underway (C. Lott, pers. comm.). In addition, stable isotope analysis has been used to uncover *chain migration* in hatch-year Sharp-shinned Hawks in the American West (Smith et al. 2003). Although the technique remains in the early stages of development, the use of stable-isotopes has enormous potential for use in studies of raptor migration.

Radar Ornithology

Radar, or radiolocation, uses reflected radio waves to detect the range, direction of travel, and speed of moving objects. Originally developed for the military in the 1930s, radar has been used to study bird migration since the 1940s (Eastwood 1967). Systematic studies of raptor migration using this technique date from the mid-1970s, when radio waves were used to detect birds migrating at the Strait of Gibraltar in southern Spain, and in southern Ontario, Canada. High-resolution marine surveillance radar, which is both inexpensive relative to other radars and portable, has been used to detect movements of raptors that are too distant to be seen with binoculars and telescopes. Vertical fixed-beam radar, which also is relatively portable, has been used to determine flight altitudes of migrating birds of prey. Tracking radar, which "locks on" individual targets and follows their images moving across a screen, has been used together with simultaneous visual observations to determine the speeds and altitudes of individual raptors.

Doppler weather-surveillance radar, which also measures the velocity of "targets" moving to or from the radar antenna, recently has been installed at 150 stations across the United States. The imagery from this new network, whose beams blanket much of the United States, enables researchers to assess the geographic tracks of small streams of migrants up to 110 km from each station (Eastwood 1967; Able 1985; Kerlinger 1989; Gauthreaux et al. 2001). Although radar ornithology has been used only episodically to date, the technique has considerable potential in raptor-migration science. Radar already has played an important role in explaining the so-called *noonday lull* in migrating Broad-winged Hawks (Kerlinger and Gauthreaux 1985a), as well as in determining the extent of nocturnal migration in Levant Sparrowhawks in the Middle East (Stark and Liechti 1993). In the first instance, radar demonstrated that broadwings soar higher and, therefore, are more difficult to see at and around midday, and in the second it confirmed substantial night-time flight in this completely migratory, *flocking* migrant.

Radar ornithology's greatest limitations are its cost, the development of skills needed to interpret radar imagery, and the frequent need for coincidental visual observations to identify the species being tracked. As the technology improves and limitations are reduced, the role of radar ornithology in raptor-migration science will increase substantially. Despite its limitations, the use of radar in quantifying the large-scale movements of raptors and other soaring migrants relative to the flight paths of commercial and military aircraft already has saved lives.

Modeling

The complexities of raptor migration offer formidable challenges for migration scientists, and many researchers employ simple models to test how various external and internal factors affect the migratory behavior of birds of prey. Verbal, graphical, and mathematical models distill complex ecological and behavioral events by focusing attention on presumably important environmental interactions, and thereby enable researchers to test various theories regarding migration systems and migrant behavior. Simulation models allow researchers to modify the extent and effects of input variables and to ask and answer "what if" questions of migration systems and their migrants (Odum 1993).

Migration scientists have used aerodynamic models to determine how idealized soaring migrants should interact with thermals and other atmospheric features to best fuel their migratory journeys, and then have compared theoretical predictions of the occurrence of supposed advantageous behavior with that employed by real migrants in the field (Spaar and Bruderer 1997). Others have used energetics models to test the possibility of long-distance migration devoid of feeding (Smith et al. 1986) as well as tradeoffs associated with the use of different feeding strategies en route (Candler and Kennedy 1995). Advances in computer software continue to facilitate the use of mathematical models, suggesting that this versatile tool will someday play an expanded role in raptor-migration science.

Synthesis and Conclusions

1. Many methods, both old and new, have been used to study raptor migration.
2. Hawkwatches along major migration corridors and bottlenecks, together with trapping and banding stations, are the most frequently used means by which scientists study raptor migration. Many count sites and banding stations are operated by trained volunteers, which substantially reduce the cost of their operations.
3. Most hawkwatches and banding stations are in the northern temperate zone, particularly eastern North America, Western Europe, and the Middle East, and much remains to be learned about raptor migration elsewhere in the world (see Chapter 7).
4. New technology, including conventional and satellite tracking, stable isotopes, and radar, complements established long-term migration-count and banding efforts.
5. Satellite tracking allows researchers to follow individual long-distance migrants across the surface of the globe. This technology, though expensive, is experiencing explosive growth in raptor-migration science.

6. No one study technique or method is a substitute for another. All offer complementary and potentially rich sources of information, and none is without its limitations. Not surprisingly raptor-migration scientists usually employ a variety of methods to answer questions of interest in their discipline.

—4—

Flight Strategies

The answer, my friend, is blowin' in the wind,
the answer is blowin' in the wind.
Bob Dylan, 1962

To migrate successfully, raptors need to accomplish three things. First, they need to locate appropriate wintering areas on their outbound journeys and return to appropriate breeding areas on their return migrations. Second, they need to time their migrations to coincide with appropriate climatic and ecological conditions, both en route and at their intended destinations. And third, they need to complete their *outbound* and *return migrations* in a condition that leaves them physically fit and capable of successfully overwintering and reproducing.

As might be expected, different species of raptors face different challenges in reaching these goals, and many differ widely in their responses. There are, however, common threads to successful "flight strategies" during migration, and this chapter focuses on several of them, including how atmospheric considerations affect raptor migration and how flight mechanics affect flight behavior. How raptors manage to locate appropriate wintering areas and breeding grounds is covered in Chapter 5, and the timing of raptor migration is covered in Chapters 6 and 7.

Atmospheric Considerations

Earth's atmosphere provides raptors with three indispensable ingredients for successful long-distance migration: (1) oxygen for metabolic processes, (2) a gaseous medium in which to generate lift during flapping and gliding flight, and (3) vertical wind or updrafts to generate additional lift for soaring flight. A fourth atmospheric component, horizontal wind, can either help or hinder migrants.

Air Pressure and Flight Altitudes

Although the atmosphere extends approximately 120 kilometers (km) above the surface of the earth, the bulk of its mass is within 5 km of the ground. Within this narrow band of dense air, most "weather," including *thermals, deflection updrafts,* and horizontal winds, occur, and it is here that temperatures and oxygen pressures are most like those at the earth's surface. It is also where most raptors migrate.

Visual observations at hawkwatches indicate that many raptors migrate within several hundred meters of the surrounding landscape. Radar and following migrants in fixed-wing aircraft indicate that many others travel long distances at heights that make them impossible for observers to see from the ground.

Radar in particular has provided important insights into the altitudes at which raptors migrate. American raptor migration specialist Paul Kerlinger has used this technique to assess the altitudes at which raptors migrate at several sites in the United States. Radar tracks of spring migrants in eastern New York State indicate that many migrants, including Ospreys, Northern Harriers, Northern Goshawks, Sharp-shinned Hawks, Cooper's Hawks, Broad-winged Hawks, Red-shouldered Hawks, and American Kestrels, typically migrate between tree-top level and about 1500 meters (m) above the ground, that species averages range from 740 to 840 m, or about a half-mile high, and that more than 80 percent of migrants travel within 1000 m of the ground. A study involving many of the same migrants in Gulf Coast Texas produced similar results (Kerlinger et al. 1985; Kerlinger and Gauthreaux 1985a, b), as did one in southern Israel, where the upper limit of the flight was 2000 m, and where more than 90 percent of the migrants flew within 1000 m of the ground (Spaar 1995). Intriguingly, Levant Sparrowhawks—one of only a handful of raptors known to migrate at night as well as by day—migrated at up to 3000 m during evening flights in the same area (Spaar et al. 1998). On the other hand, all but one of ten species of raptors migrating above a forested valley in east-central Alaska, near the beginnings and ends of their migrations, flew at mean altitudes lower than 150 m—the single exception being the Golden Eagle which averaged 230 m. This is probably because they were searching for food, which is typical of migrants near the starts and finishes of their journeys (Cooper and Ritchie 1995).

This said, raptors also are known to travel at significantly greater altitudes. Turkey Vultures, Broad-winged Hawks, and Swainson's Hawks followed in fixed-winged aircraft in Panama, for example, migrated at 4000 to 5000 m (or about 3 miles) above the ground (Smith 1985a). And Bald Eagles migrating across Canada and the western United States regularly reached altitudes of up to 4,500 m (Harmata 2002). Old World Vultures sometimes travel at even greater heights. Radio-tracked Eurasian Griffons soar at up to 10,000 m (Bögel 1990), and a Rüppell's Griffon that struck a commercial airliner above Ivory Coast, West Africa, was traveling at an altitude of 11,300 m, about 7 miles high (Laybourne 1974).

High-altitude flight in bitterly cold, thin air is both physiologically and aerodynamically challenging for raptors. One problem associated with this type of flight is that "normal," or low-altitude, hemoglobin cannot capture, transport, and release oxygen effectively in thin air. Unlike most birds, Rüppell's Griffons produce four forms of hemoglobin, two of which function effectively at low partial pressures of oxygen encountered at high altitudes, and two of which function best at lower altitudes (Hiebl and Braunitzer 1988). It is not known whether Eurasian Griffons and other high-flying migratory raptors possess the same adaptation, although it seems likely that they do.

Updrafts and Soaring Behavior

Because the heights at which most raptors migrate are where most weather occurs, meteorological phenomena are of considerable significance to the migrants. *Updrafts,* or vertical winds, provide numerous opportunities for low-cost soaring flight and almost always assist migrants during their travels.

Thermals. Thermals are isolated pockets of warm, rising air that form when different surfaces in landscapes receive and absorb different amounts of sunlight, or solar radiation. Dark surfaces have low reflectivity indexes, or surface *albedos,* than do light colored surfaces, and as such absorb more solar radiation than the latter. Dry surfaces, including rocky outcrops and parched fields, warm more quickly than do "evaporatively cooled" wet surfaces including water and live vegetation. In hilly terrain, surfaces that are oriented perpendicular to incoming solar radiation—east-facing mountain slopes in the morning and west-facing slopes in the afternoon, for example—warm more quickly than do shaded and less-perpendicular surfaces.

Land-based thermals typically require sunlight to sustain them. Thus, the strongest and largest thermals usually occur on bright, sunny days between midmorning and midday, after the sun is high enough to differentially warm the landscape and create thermals but before strong afternoon horizontal winds begin to tear them apart. Because land-based thermals are fueled by sunlight, they are stronger in summer than in winter in the temperate zone and are stronger overall in the tropics. Also, because the sun rises more vertically (and quickly) in the tropics, thermals form earlier in the morning there than in other areas. Thermals often are capped with cumulus clouds, which form when the warm rising air begins to cool and water droplets begin to form.

Thermals are most useful to migrants when they are wide enough for raptors to circle within them and strong enough to allow individuals to soar high enough so that they can glide to the next thermal.

Land-based thermals routinely reach heights of more than 2000 m outside of the tropics, and higher still within them. Although the diameters of some thermals exceed 1000 m, most in the temperate zone range in size from several meters to several hundred meters. Stronger thermals tend to be taller and wider than weaker thermals. *Thermal strength* (i.e., the speed at which air rises within the thermal) varies predictably within each individual cell and decreases significantly both with height and with distance from the center of the cell. Not surprisingly, raptors that soar within thermals typically seek out the cores of the vortices and circle within them, and typically leave thermals before reaching the top (Pennycuick 1983; Kerlinger 1989).

Although most thermals form individually and are isolated from one another, *thermal streets,* or linear arrays of thermals aligned with the prevailing wind or with shorelines, are sometimes created during periods of intense solar radiation, particularly in the tropics. The locations of thermal streets often are apparent by the linear arrays of clouds that form above them. Under certain circumstances, particularly large and powerful thermal updrafts can extend for hundreds of kilometers. When such formations are aligned along

Figure 10. Cumulus clouds, including a coastal cloud street aligned parallel to the wind at that height, over the lowlands of south-central Cuba. When the photograph was taken in late October 2002, the surface temperature of the land was greater than that of the adjacent Caribbean Sea. A sea breeze keeps the coast free of clouds. (Photo by the author)

the *principal axis of migration* in the region, migrants are able to soar linearly within them in much the same way as they *slope soar* along similarly aligned deflection updrafts that form above mountain ridges (Smith 1985a; Kerlinger 1989).

Most thermals form over land, which explains why banks of cumulus clouds often dissipate along coastlines (Figure 10). Oceanic or *sea thermals* also occur, however, and they, too, play a critical role in shaping the migration geography of long-distance raptor migration. Sea thermals regularly form in tropical and subtropical oceans and seas between 5° and 30° north and south of the equator that are dominated by easterly *trade winds*. Within these latitude belts, predominant northeasterly winds in the Northern Hemisphere and predominantly southeasterly winds in the Southern Hemisphere, blow relatively cool, subtropical surface air toward the equator. As they do, the increasingly warmer surface waters of the equatorial zone heat the cooler air, producing bands of sea thermals (Augstein 1980). Because the temperature differential between the cooler trade winds and the warmer sea exists both day and night, sea thermals occur 24 hours a day (Pennycuick 1983).

The existence of predictable oceanic updrafts allows several species of seabirds, including the Magnificent Frigatebird, to engage in long-distance, multiday foraging flights (Heiling et al. 2003). Sea thermals also allow Chinese Sparrowhawks, Grey-faced Buzzards, and other migratory raptors to soar hundreds of kilometers over water along the East-Asian Oceanic Flyway each autumn and spring (see Figure 1; Chapters 7 and 8), and they make it possible for the Amur Falcon to undertake the longest overwater passage of any migratory raptor, a seemingly implausible 4000-km outbound passage across the Indian Ocean between India and East Africa (see Chapters 7 and 8) (Bildstein and Zalles 2005).

It is difficult to overstate the extent to which thermals, both land- and sea-based, affect long-distance raptor migration. Every one of the world's 22 species of complete migrants (see Table 1) soars within thermals at least occasionally when migrating, and more than half of these species—including the Western Honey Buzzard, Mississippi Kite, Grey-faced Buzzard, Chinese Sparrowhawk, Broad-winged Hawk, Swainson's Hawk, Lesser Spotted Eagle, and Greater Spotted Eagle—depend on this type of flight to complete their long-distance journeys (Kerlinger 1989; Ferguson-Lees and Christie 2001; Chapter 8).

One of the most thorough studies of *thermal soaring* in raptors was conducted by Swiss ornithologist Reto Spaar. Spaar and his coworkers radar-tracked the individual flight paths of more than 2000 raptors migrating above the Arava Valley (aka Wadi Araba) and the Negev Desert of Israel during several springs and autumns in the early 1990s (Spaar 1995, 1997; Spaar and Bruderer 1996; Spaar et al. 1998). Soaring conditions and flight behavior varied predictably over the course of each day. Most of the migrants, which included several species of harriers, Western Honey Buzzards, Steppe Buzzards, and Steppe Eagles, began each day migrating in relatively weak thermals that usually formed within several hours of sunrise. On most days, climbing rates increased through the morning before peaking at a little over 3 meters per second (msec^{-1}) (or about 7 miles per hour [mph]) by late morning, and began to decrease by late afternoon. Overall, climbing rates for individual species averaged from 1.5 to 2.1 msec^{-1} (or about 3.5 to 5.0 mph). Steppe Eagles climbed at rates of up to 5 msec^{-1} in strong midday thermals.

Migrants flew higher when their climbing rates were higher, suggesting that they were able to determine the strengths of thermals they were in, and they remained in stronger thermals longer than in weaker ones. Observations of individuals circling as few as once or twice in weak thermals before gliding in the direction of another updraft suggest that the birds were able to determine the strength of a thermal quickly and that they actively searched for stronger ones.

When gliding and soaring between thermals, Steppe Eagles traveled at speeds that averaged 12 msec⁻¹ (30 mph), and that sometimes reached 20 msec⁻¹ (45 mph). Gliding speeds were positively correlated with intrathermal climbing rates, and were 1 msec⁻¹ faster in tail winds than at other times. The higher temperatures and quicker surface warming rates of the Arava Valley produced stronger thermals there than in the Negev highlands. Migrants soaring above the valley floor often climbed to 2000 m, whereas those traveling across the highlands rarely exceeded 1000 m. On very sunny days, the characteristic pattern of individual migrants alternating between *circle soaring* in thermals and directed, straight-line gliding between thermals was replaced with directed, straight-line soaring as birds made use of larger-scale thermals and thermal streets.

Within- and between-species comparisons of two of the most numerous soaring migrants at the site, Steppe Buzzards (Plate 3) and Western Honey Buzzards (Plate 4), led Spaar to conclude that at least for these two migrants, the behavior of the two species was more similar under similar weather conditions than was the behavior of each species under different weather conditions. That said, Spaar did record consistent species differences in the flight behavior of several of the raptors he watched. Steppe Eagles, for example, whose wingspans are 40 percent greater than those of Western Honey Buzzards (Ferguson-Lees and Christie 2001), rarely soared in the weak early-morning and late afternoon thermals, whereas Western Honey Buzzards regularly did. Larger raptors tend to have larger minimal turning radiuses than do smaller birds (Table 9), and weaker early and late-day thermals have smaller diameters than stronger midday thermals, and the difference in flight behavior between these two species most likely reflects the difference in their size (Kerlinger 1989; Spaar 1995, 1997; Spaar and Bruderer 1996).

My own observations of migrants reveal similar body-size affects. In southern Israel, small Levant Sparrowhawks circling in thermals together with larger Steppe Buzzards pivoted more tightly and climbed at greater rates. And the same relationship repeated itself among migrating Broad-winged Hawks, Swainson's Hawks, and Turkey Vultures soaring together in thermals in Costa Rica and Panama. The smallest of the three, the Broad-winged Hawk, turned in tighter circles and climbed more rapidly than the intermediate-sized Swainson's Hawk, which, in turn, circled more tightly and climbed more rap-

Table 9. *Wingspans and characteristics of circle soaring in some raptors*

Species	Wingspan (mm)[a]	Circling radius (m)
Black Vulture[b]	147	17, 24
Turkey Vulture[c]	170	13
Lappet-faced Vulture[d]	270	15
Indian White-backed Vulture[e]	203	40–50
Sharp-shinned Hawk[f]	56	6–12
Broad-winged Hawk[g]	84	15

[a]All wingspan values are from Ferguson-Lees and Christie 2001.
[b]Pennycuick 1983
[c]MacCready 1976
[d]Pennycuick 1971
[e]Hankin 1913
[f]Welch 1975
[g]Cochran 1972.

idly than the larger Turkey Vulture. That smaller migrants outperform larger migrants in their use of weaker thermals has important implications for the daily distances covered by different species (Kerlinger 1989).

Deflection updrafts. In addition to soaring in thermals, raptors also soar in *deflection updrafts,* which occur when horizontal winds strike surface discontinuities, including mountains, buildings, and tall vegetation, and are deflected up and over them. As is true of thermals, deflection updrafts can be too small or too weak for migrants to soar on. They also can be too turbulent for migrants. Many deflection updrafts, however, create ideal soaring conditions, and at such times large numbers of migrants are attracted to them. Deflection updrafts rarely extend more than 300 m to 400 m above the surrounding landscape, and migrants that soar within them often are more visible to observers on the ground than are migrants soaring in thermals. Mountain ridges, gorges, cliffs, and elevated coastlines often provide the best sources of deflection updrafts.

Deflection updrafts are an important source of flight energy for many species of migratory raptors. New World migrants use them in the Appalachians of eastern North America, the Rockies of western North America, the Sierra Madre Oriental of eastern Mexico, the Talamanca Mountains of Costa Rica, and the Andes of northwestern South America. Old World migrants use them in the Alps of Switzerland and France, the Tien Shan and Hindu Kush of central Asia, and the southern Himalayas of Nepal and India,

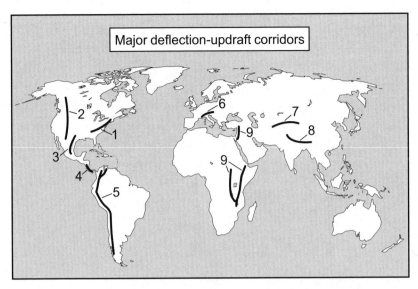

Figure 11. Locations of major mountain ranges and escarpments used as sources of deflection updrafts: (1) the Appalachian Mountains, (2) the Rocky Mountains, (3) the Sierra Madre Oriental, (4) the Talamanca Mountains, (5) the Andes, (6) the Alps, (7) the Tien Shan and Hindu Kush, (8) the southern Himalayas, and (9) the escarpments of the Great Rift Valley of East Africa and the Middle East.

as well as along the escarpments of the Great Rift Valley of East Africa and the Middle East (Zalles and Bildstein 2000) (Figure 11).

Migrants use deflection updrafts three ways: (1) by alternately *circle soaring* within them and then gliding to the next updraft along the region's *principal axis of migration,* (2) by straight-line, *slope soaring* when mountain ridges produce linear arrays of updrafts that parallel the principal axis of migration, and (3) by soaring at great altitudes in *lee waves* created by deflection updrafts. The latter are standing, or stationary waves that form on the lee, or downwind, sides of mountain ranges under specific conditions of wind and temperature. Although lee waves sometimes extend to 10,000 m above the mountains that create them, most form at 2000 to 3000 m above the landscape. Lee waves are thought to help raptors cross the 14-km wide Strait of Gibraltar between southern Spain and Morocco (Evans and Lathbury 1973).

In some situations, including near the beginnings of their migrations when migrants are more likely to be deflected from a preferred direction of travel by local conditions (see Chapter 7), individuals sometimes slope soar within deflection updrafts for relatively short distances, even when doing so

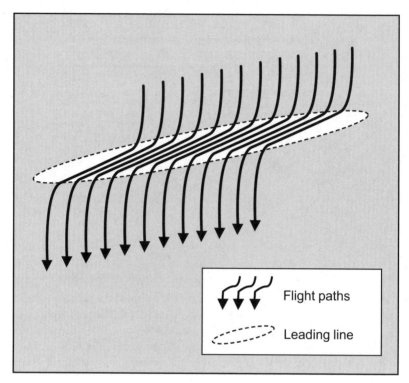

Figure 12. The effect of a leading line on the flight paths of migrating raptors. In this example, deflection updrafts along a mountain ridge create the attraction. Note both the deflecting and concentrating effects of the leading line and that most migrants remain on the line for relatively short distances.

may take them off course. When this happens, migrants are said to be following a *leading line*, or *Leitlinie* in German.

As originally detailed by Geyr von Schweppenburg (1963), leading lines are narrow and relatively long geographical and topographical features that intersect with the principal axis of migration in a region, and whose properties attract migrants and induce individuals to change their direction of travel so as to follow them. In addition to mountain ridges and associated deflection updrafts, leading lines include rivers and associated riparian areas, which often attract and concentrate large numbers of potential prey for migrants (Figure 12).

Leading lines differ from *diversion lines,* such as land-water interfaces and lowlands adjacent to high mountain ranges, along which migrants concentrate not because they are attracted to them but because they are trying to avoid what lies beyond them (Figure 13). Migrants will follow diversion lines

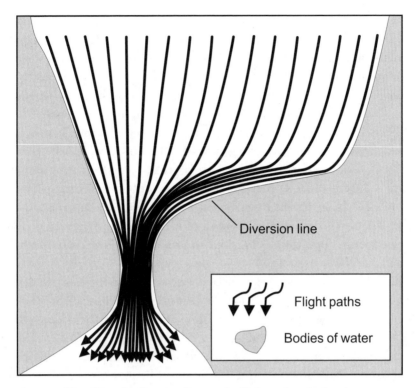

Figure 13. The effect of a diversion line on the flight paths of migrating raptors. Note both the deflecting and concentrating effects of the diversion line, that migrants remain on the line for differing amounts of time, and that concentrations build toward a bottleneck.

for hundreds of miles or more, far longer than most leading lines, even to the point of reversing their direction of travel along peninsulas and erratic forest-desert edges (see Chapter 7 for examples). By comparison, leading lines typically divert migrants for much shorter distances, sometimes for as few as several kilometers (see Figure 12). Because of their substantial regional and sometimes continentwide effect in diverting and concentrating large numbers of migrants along narrow flight lines, diversion lines frequently are associated with *migration bottlenecks,* such as the Strait of Gibraltar and the Bosporus at the western and eastern ends of the Mediterranean Sea, respectively.

The northeast-to-southwest oriented Central Appalachian Mountains of eastern Pennsylvania form one of the better known leading lines for migrating raptors. Autumn *cold fronts,* which typically pass through the region at four- to five-day intervals, approach the Appalachian's even-topped "corduroy ridges" at right angles, and their northwest winds are deflected up and over them. The result is a series of parallel leading lines of deflection updrafts for outbound migrants. Kittatinny Ridge, the southeasternmost mountain in the region, creates the strongest leading line in the area (Van Fleet 2001), possibly because it offers the last opportunity for southbound migrants to slope soar there. Adherence to this particular leading line appears to be considerable, with as many as 95 percent of all migrants traveling along it continuing to do so after reaching a 1.3-km (0.8-mile) wide Lehigh River "water gap" or break in the ridgeline (Klem et al. 1985a). Even so, simultaneous counts at multiple sites along the Kittatinny suggest that many migrants seen along the ridge remain on it for several kilometers to several dozen kilometers, rather than for most of its 400-km length, even on days when excellent opportunities for slope soaring prevail (Frey 1940; Heintzelman 1982; Hawk et al. 2002).

Several factors, including the species involved, the strength of the deflection updrafts being produced, and the coincidental occurrence of off-ridge thermals, are known to affect the extent to which mountain ridges such as the Kittatinny function as leading lines. Migrants that pass through eastern Pennsylvania in August and September, for example, thermal soar more and slope soar less than do later migrants, apparently because of the availability of strong late-summer thermals then. And whereas watchsites in the region typically record their best late-season (i.e., October–November) flights during periods of strong northwest winds, strong early season (August–September) flights are most common on days when strong thermals form and winds are light or variable, or on days when northeasterly tail winds prevail. For example, the largest single-day count in the 72-year history of Hawk Mountain Sanctuary, the oldest watchsite on the Kittatinny, occurred on a somewhat cloudy day (14 September 1978) with east-northeasterly winds, during which more than 20,000 migrants were counted crossing the ridge on a broad front on weak tail winds—apparently in pursuit of thermals—rather than slope soaring along it (Nagy 1979).

Another good example of seasonal shifts in the use of leading lines by raptors involves the flight behavior of Red-tailed Hawks at Hawk Mountain Sanctuary. A long-term analysis of the species' flight at the site indicates that passage rates peak during the two days following the passage of a cold front (Allen et al. 1996). At such times, clear skies and moderating temperatures create ideal conditions for the formation of thermal updrafts, and coincidental northwest winds produce abundant deflection updrafts, which suggests that Red-tailed Hawks are more likely to migrate when opportunities for soaring flight increase. But the story does not end there. Southbound Red-tailed Hawks migrate through eastern Pennsylvania from late summer through early winter each year, and August and September cold fronts bear little resemblance to those that pass through the region in November and December. A 1997 study of Red-tailed Hawk migration at the site reveals that early season cold fronts enhance red-tail movements principally by creating opportunities for cross-ridge thermal soaring, whereas late-season fronts do so by creating opportunities for ridge-line slope soaring (Maransky et al. 1997).

Taken as a whole, these and other studies suggest that leading lines are best thought of as linear patches of favorable habitats and atmospheric conditions along which migrants concentrate for brief periods while taking advantage of local flight, feeding, or roosting conditions rather than as long-distance "highways in the sky."

Horizontal winds. Depending on their alignment with the principal axis of migration in the region, horizontal winds can help or hinder the passage of migrating raptors. *Tail winds,* or winds that are aligned with the preferred direction of travel, help migrants by "pushing" them forward. *Head winds,* or winds aligned against the preferred direction of travel, hinder migrants by "pushing" them backward. *Crosswinds,* or winds that intersect the preferred direction of travel at perpendicular and near perpendicular angles, can hinder migrants by shifting the intended direction of travel via a phenomenon known as *wind drift.* Winds vary locally and regionally, often in predictable ways, and field evidence suggests that migrants often alter their flight behavior to take advantage of favorable winds as well as to reduce the costs of unfavorable winds.

Everything else being equal, wind speed increases with height. Thus it is not surprising that raptors migrating into strong head winds fly lower and those migrating with strong tail winds fly higher than those migrating in light or variable winds. Similarly, raptors migrating in coastal areas tend to fly lower than those migrating along inland corridors, presumably to reduce the risk of being blown out to sea. This is particularly true of raptors about to undertake water crossings in crosswinds (Evans and Lathbury 1973; Kerlinger 1984, 1989; Inoue 1993) (see Chapter 7 for details).

The direction, force, and regularity of a region's prevailing winds change with latitude. Overall, prevailing winds are westerly between 30° and 60° of latitude north and south of the equator, and easterly north and south of these two belts. Latitudinal shifts in the directions of prevailing winds are reliable enough that during the age of sail, explorers used them to complete transatlantic journeys by sailing east from Europe to North America at 5° to 30° north in easterly trade winds, and by returning to the Old World at 30° to 60° north in temperate zone westerlies.

The predictable nature of these large-scale latitudinal belts of easterly and westerly winds is brought about by two phenomena: (1) the differential heating of the earth's surface by the sun and (2) the so-called *Coriolis force,* which is caused by inertia and the earth's spinning on a north-south axis.

The differential heating of the earth's surface means that temperatures are higher and thermals are stronger near the equator than they are poleward. As warm air rises near the equator, it is replaced by relatively cooler surface air from the north and south. The warm rising air, in turn, cools as it ascends through the atmosphere and begins to spread poleward. Eventually, the twin streams of high-level air cool sufficiently and descend to the surface at approximately 30° north and south of the equator. They then turn toward the equator as surface airstreams. As they do, the earth's daily rotation "deflects" these winds to the right in the Northern Hemisphere and to the left in the Southern Hemisphere, via the so-called Coriolis force. Because the air is southbound in the Northern Hemisphere and northbound in the Southern Hemisphere, the deflection is westward in both hemispheres, resulting in parallel bands of easterly trade winds 5° to 30° north and south of the equator. The mechanism for this circulation was first detailed by mid-eighteenth-century London Barrister George Hadley, and the conveyer-like belts of circulating air are known as Hadley cells. Additional Hadley cells operating at 30° to 60° north and south of the equator push surface air poleward rather than equatorially. The Coriolis force again deflects these surface parcels to the right in the Northern Hemisphere and to the left in the Southern Hemisphere, which, because the air masses are moving poleward, means eastward in both hemispheres. This, in turn, creates the so-called mid-latitude westerlies, two regions of predominant winds 30° to 60° north and south of the equator.

The breeding and wintering areas of most migratory raptors are aligned along north-south axes, and the existence of latitudinal bands of alternating westerly and easterly predominant winds presents a migration challenge for species prone to wind drift. This is particularly true for long-distance, trans-equatorial migrants whose outbound and return movements traverse several of these bands. Although wind drift can occur at any stage of migration, field evidence suggests that it is most likely to occur early rather than later in migration, and that migrants are most likely to compensate for wind-drift displacement toward the end of their migrations. Some biologists have suggested that migrants purposefully allow themselves to be wind drifted when doing so allows them to complete their journeys more quickly and at a lower cost than by delaying flights during periods of crosswinds or by correcting for them continually en route (Alerstam 1990) (see Chapter 5 for details).

Such behavior, which is called *adaptive wind drift,* likely explains the circuitous "elliptical" roundtrip journeys of several long-distance migrants whose outbound journeys in autumn initially are influenced by temperate-zone westerlies and whose return journeys in spring initially are influenced by trade-wind easterlies. In North America, for example, large numbers of Broad-winged Hawks breeding in eastern Canada and the northeastern United States are drifted southeast in autumn along flight-lines that sometimes take them east of the Appalachian Mountains, whereas in spring the same individuals, which are drifted west by easterlies in Mexico and south Texas, migrate northwest of the Appalachians along the southern shorelines of Lakes Erie and Ontario (Kerlinger 1989). In the Old World, Pallid Harriers from eastern Europe migrate south to their sub-Saharan wintering grounds through Turkey and the Middle East while circumventing the eastern Mediterranean, but they return to their breeding grounds along a more western central Mediterranean route via Sicily, southern Italy, and the Balkans (Corso and Cardelli 2004). Within the Middle East, outbound Steppe Eagles fly south along the Arabian Peninsula east of the Red Sea before crossing into Africa, whereas return migrants fly north through Egypt west of the Red Sea, before turning east at Sinai (Meyburg et al. 2003). And in Asia, outbound Amur Falcons breeding in northeastern China and easternmost Russia travel to Bangladesh and eastern India along flight-lines east of the Tibetan Plateau, and from there across the Indian subcontinent and the Indian Ocean into East Africa, but they return to their breeding grounds via East Africa, the Arabian Peninsula and central Asia northwest of the Tibetan Plateau (Ferguson-Lees and Christie 2001) (see Chapters 7 and 9 for details).

Observations also suggest that naïve juvenile migrants are more prone to wind drift than are experienced adults. Satellite trackings of adult and juvenile Ospreys and Western Honey Buzzards migrating between nesting areas in northern Europe and wintering grounds in Africa, for example, indicate that first-year migrants are wind drifted in strong crosswinds, whereas adults compensate and are drifted only one-third as much (Thorup et al. 2003). Similarly, coastal flights of Sharp-shinned Hawks in eastern North America are dominated overwhelmingly by juveniles, whereas inland flights are not, presumably because juveniles are more prone to be drifted by the region's prevailing northwest winds (Mueller and Berger 1967a, 1967b; Viverette et al. 1996). The fact that large numbers of juvenile Broad-winged Hawks over-winter in peninsular Florida, far north of the species' principal overwintering areas in Central and South America and substantially east of the species' typical North American migration route, suggests that first-year migrants in this species, too, are more likely to be blown off course than are more experienced adults (Tabb 1973). Intriguingly, juvenile Sharp-shinned Hawks banded on migration along a coastal flyway in New Jersey often are recaptured migrating along inland routes in later years (Clark 1985a), and juvenile Broad-winged Hawks banded while overwintering in Florida have been recovered as adults in southern Mexico and Guatemala along the species' principal migration corridor (Tabb 1979).

Flocking

Field evidence suggests that almost all species of migratory raptors *flock* (i.e., join together in groups) at least occasionally while migrating. Most migratory flocks are small single- and mixed-species groups of a couple to a dozen or so birds, and most occur along major flyways, migration bottlenecks, and other points of concentration (Table 10). Most last for several minutes to less than an hour, and most appear to be little more than avian traffic jams that result when many birds travel in the same direction at the same place at the same time.

In addition to such small-scale opportunistic *flocking*, several species of rap-

Table 10. *Flocking behavior of raptors during outbound migration in central New York State, 1978–1979*

Species	N	% in flocks	Maximum number in flock	Flocked with other species
Osprey	26	19	2	Yes (Broad-winged Hawk)
Northern Harrier	22	18	2	Yes (Broad-winged Hawk)
Sharp-shinned Hawk	271	34	3	Yes (Broad-winged Hawk)
Cooper's Hawk	10	0	—	No
Northern Goshawk	15	7	1	Yes (Sharp-shinned Hawk)
Broad-winged Hawk	1130	88	115	Yes (Sharp-shinned Hawk)
Red-shouldered Hawk	27	44	3	Yes (Red-tailed Hawk)
Red-tailed Hawk	382	43	9	Yes (Sharp-shinned Hawk)
American Kestrel	86	25	6	Yes (Sharp-shinned Hawk)

Source: Adapted from Kerlinger et al. 1985.

Table 11. *Species of super-flocking migrants and maximum flock sizes reported*

Species	Migration flyway	Maximum flock size reported
Turkey Vulture	Trans-American	> 50,000
Western Honey Buzzard	Eurasian–East African	> 5,000
Swallow-tailed Kite	Trans–American	> 100
Mississippi Kite	Trans–American	> 1,000
Black Kite	Eurasian–East African	> 1,000
Grey-faced Buzzard	East–Asian Oceanic	> 1,000
Levant Sparrowhawk	Eurasian–East African	> 5,000
Chinese Sparrowhawk	East-Asian Oceanic	> 10,000
Japanese Sparrowhawk	East-Asian Oceanic	> 100
Broad-winged Hawk	Trans-American	> 50,000
Swainson's Hawk	Trans–American	> 50,000
Steppe Buzzard	Eurasian–East African	> 5,000
Lesser Spotted Eagle	Eurasian–East African	> 100
Steppe Eagle	Eurasian–East African	> 100
Lesser Kestrel	Eurasian–East African	> 1,000
Red-footed Falcon	Eurasian–East African	> 1,000
Amur Falcon	Trans-Indian Ocean	> 1,000
Northern Hobby	Eurasian–East African	> 100

tors flock on a regular basis and on a much larger scale. In these raptors, flocking appears to be an essential aspect of successful migration. A few species of *super-flocking migrants* predictably coalesce into groups of hundreds to tens of thousands of birds that, once formed, can remain together for days or even weeks (Table 11). All but one of 18 known super-flocking migrants are long-distance, transequatorial travelers (Levant Sparrowhawk is not transequatorial), and most super-flocks form in and around the tropics. North America's Broad-winged Hawk is a well-studied example of this type of obligate flocking.

Broad-winged Hawks, or broadwings, begin coalescing into small groups of several birds to several hundreds of birds almost as soon as they initiate their migrations across eastern Canada and the northeastern United States. A few of these flocks—particularly those diverted by the northern shorelines of the Great Lakes—number in the tens of thousands (Heintzelman 1975; Zalles and Bildstein 2000). Flocks of broadwings are so typical that hawkwatchers have developed a special term for them: *kettles* (Box 2).

Most of North America's approximately two million Broad-winged Hawks overwinter in the Neotropics, and by the time their flight has reached

Box 2. The Use and Origins of Several Hawkwatching Terms

Among hawkwatchers, the term **kettle** refers to a group of raptors wheeling or circling in a thermal (Heintzelman 1975). Raptors in kettles are sometimes said to be **"kettling."** Both of these terms, which came into widespread use in the mid-twentieth-century, owe their origins to a boulder-field at the foot of Hawk Mountain Sanctuary.

The lowlands that surround the Sanctuary in the central Appalachian Mountains of eastern Pennsylvania were settled by German immigrants in the first half of the nineteenth century. The settlers, known as Pennsylvania Germans, called the rocky, bowl-shaped depression immediately southeast of Hawk Mountain "der kessel," which in the Pennsylvania-German vernacular means "a hollow enclosed by hills or mountains" (Stine 1989). By the early 1900s, English-speaking settlers and, shortly after, hawkwatchers at Hawk Mountain Sanctuary, were referring to the prominent landscape feature, which is visible from the Sanctuary's lookouts, as "The Kettle" (Edge 1941). The barren, rocky valley floor, above which thermals regularly form, is a literal hotbed for soaring migrants at the site, and Sanctuary interpreters use the name of this landscape feature to help visitors locate flocks of Broad-winged Hawks that often circle above it.

Although I have been unable to determine when the phrase "look at the flock of Broad-winged Hawks circling over the Kettle" was shortened to "look at the kettle of broadwings" or "look at the kettling broadwings," by the late 1950s, biologists were describing circling flocks of broadwings, both at Hawk Mountain and elsewhere in the world, as kettles, and the two neologisms, *kettle* and *kettling,* had become part of the hawkwatcher's lexicon (Hofslund 1966; Brown and Amadon 1968; Nagy 1970; Fingerhood 2001). Today, the terms often are used not just for flocking broadwings but for all raptors (Kerlinger 1989).

Another pair of hawkwatching terms, **stream** and **streaming,** are used to describe the unidirectional and often linear head-to-tail flocks of migrants that glide and soar between isolated thermals, as well as within thermal streets. The terms most likely are derived from the image of long and narrow, unidirectional flocks of raptors, which call to mind water coursing along streambeds. When such linear flocks consist of thousands of individuals, they frequently are called **rivers of raptors,** a term Horace Loftin (1963) used to describe the flowing, multithousand bird flocks of Turkey Vultures he observed migrating through Panama.

Group leaders use the term **glass,** as in "the eagle is three *glasses* above the top of the hill to your right," to direct hawkwachers to a point in the sky where migrants can be seen. Among birdwatchers, *glass* is shorthand for binoculars. In the example above, the hawkwatchers are being told to look for the eagle three binocular fields of view above the hill on their right. The use of the term in hawkwatching dates at least as far back as 1936, when Robert Porter Allen and Roger Tory Peterson described a flight of Turkey Vultures at Cape May Point, New Jersey, as passing so high that the birds "could scarcely be discerned without a glass" (Allen and Peterson 1936).

southern Mexico, flocks have swelled substantially, with some groups exceeding fifty thousand birds. Except for several minutes of flight in early morning and late afternoon when birds are departing from and returning to their roosts, all but a few broadwings migrate in large flocks for at least several weeks. Although such flocks are no longer surprising, early observations of similar events appear to have baffled observers. Legendary late-nineteenth- to early twentieth-century American ornithologist Frank Chapman, for example, once described a springtime passage of what were probably Broad-winged Hawks in the Sierra Madre Oriental of Veracruz, Mexico, as resembling "a swarm of bees circl[ing] about and among each other in a most remarkable and confusing fashion" that "in spite of their wheeling . . . passed rapidly northward and were soon out of sight" (Chapman 1916).

Although few measurements have been made of the flight behavior of migrants in supersized flocks, researchers have attempted to explain why such flocks exist. One hypothesis posits that traveling in large flocks allows migrants to find thermals more quickly than when traveling alone, thereby reducing the cost of migration by increasing the percentage of time spent in soaring flight (Kerlinger 1989). A second hypothesis suggests that large flocks form because inexperienced juveniles cluster around and follow more experienced adults (Thake 1980). A third suggests that social attractions are not involved at all, and that large groups are the consequence of crowded flyways and the patchy distribution of thermals (i.e., birds aggregate in large flocks simply because that is where the updrafts are) (Smith 1985a). The first two hypotheses, which are not mutually exclusive, suggest that flocking improves the chances of birds successfully completing their migrations; the third does not (Liechti et al. 1996). I discuss evidence for each below.

Advantages of Flocking

The idea that migrants might be attracted to one another because traveling in flocks helps individuals find and use updrafts more efficiently has been around for some time (Kerlinger 1989). Powered as opposed to soaring flight is expensive. Most estimates place the metabolic cost of flapping flight at well over 10 times that of resting metabolism, or about 50 to 120 watts per kilogram. (Assuming this to be true, a Red-tailed Hawk in flapping flight consumes energy at about the same rate as a bright incandescent light bulb.) On the other hand, soaring flight is only about 2.5 times as costly as resting metabolism, making it less then 25 percent as expensive as flapping flight (Kerlinger 1989). Soaring flight also may help migrants save energy by lowering their resting metabolism. There are two reasons to believe that this is so. First, species that regularly soar on migration tend to be less active than other species, and less active species tend to have lower rates of metabolism overall. And second, resting metabolism is influenced by microclimate, and birds that face high thermoregulatory costs have higher basal metabolic rates overall. Raptors that regularly soar on migration spend more time in sunlit pockets of warm, rising air than do flapping migrants, and it is reasonable to assume they have lower rates of resting metabolism as a result (Weathers 1979; Wasser 1986; McNabb 2002; Lindström and Klassen 2003).

Consider, for example, the energetic consequences of soaring behavior for Broad-winged Hawks:

> Aeronautic equations developed by British ornithologist Colin Penny-cuick, together with information on the general metabolic demands of broadwings and their overall levels of activity, make it possible to esti-mate the amount of energy an individual broadwing saves by soaring en route to South America each autumn. By [these] calculations, [seden-tary] broadwings burn about 65 to 75 calories a day, both during the breeding season and on the wintering grounds. Assuming that the same bird flies all the way from southern Canada to central Brazil at its most efficient air speed (i.e., 50–55 kph [30–35 mph]), it would need to travel two to three hours a day to complete its journey of 4,000 to 5,000 miles in two months. Migration using powered flight almost

doubles the bird's metabolic needs each and every day of the flight. The broadwing using this method needs to find more food in less time, and in unfamiliar territory, than it does on either its breeding or wintering grounds.

On the other hand, assuming the bird uses soaring rather than powered flight to complete 80% of its migration—which seems reasonable given what is known about the species' flight behavior en route—the bird's metabolic needs increase by only about 20%, which while not inconsequential, can be met. (Bildstein 1999, 94–95)

North American hawkwatchers have known for some time that flock size in broadwings is related to the magnitude of the day's flight. At Hawk Mountain Sanctuary, for example, on days in which 100 or so broadwings are counted, flocks range in size of from several birds to several dozens of birds, whereas on days in which a thousand or so broadwings are counted, flocks range in size from several dozens of birds to several hundred birds. Observations in the Neotropics suggest that the same thing also happens there, albeit at a much larger magnitude.

Observations at a watchsite in Caribbean-slope Costa Rica at the Kéköldi Indigenous Reserve at approximately 10° N, where the broadwing flight exceeds 500,000 birds annually, indicate that broadwing flocks swell enormously on high-magnitude flight days and that flocks of >10,000 birds are far more common on days when ≥25,000 broadwings are counted than on days when fewer migrants pass.

A recent study of the flight behavior of broadwings at the Kéköldi hawkwatch tested the extent to which flock size influences soaring behavior in the species. Sherbrooke University students Vincent Careau and Jean-François Therrien tracked more than 2000 soaring broadwings for 30 seconds each while recording the number of times each bird flapped, as well as whether it was traveling within a flock and, if so, flock size. On average, broadwings flapped their wings fewer than five times during each 30-second observation compared with the 70 to 80 flaps that would be expected during powered flight. Moreover, individuals in flocks flapped significantly less than those that traveled alone, and individuals in larger flocks flapped significantly less than those traveling in smaller flocks even when flock size exceeded 1000 birds (Figure 14). Overall, these observations suggest that Broad-winged Hawks soar more efficiently when flying in flocks than when flying alone and that soaring efficiency increases with flock size. However, the apparent benefits of flocking behavior for broadwings do not end there.

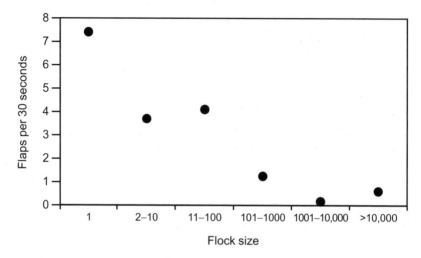

Figure 14. Flapping rates of migrating Broad-winged Hawks as a function of flock size at the Kéköldi Indigenous Reserve watchsite in Costa Rica. (Data from V. Careau and J.-F. Therrien)

A two-year study of broadwing flocking behavior at Hawk Mountain Sanctuary indicates that adult Broad-winged Hawks are significantly more likely to fly in flocks than are juveniles (78 percent of all individuals versus 62 percent), and that adult Broad-winged Hawks are more likely to fly in larger flocks. The study also showed that when adults and juveniles *streamed* together in mixed-age flocks between thermals, adults were more likely than juveniles to be in the leading half of the flock. Taken together, these findings suggest that juveniles have fewer flocking skills than adults and, thus, are more likely to follow adults into flocks than vice versa (Maransky and Bildstein 2001). Following experienced adults probably assists juveniles in two ways: (1) by helping them in finding thermals faster and (2) by helping them stay on track and find appropriate wintering areas (Liechti et al. 1996).

Although similar studies do not exist for other species of raptors, observations indicate that White Storks soar more efficiently when traveling in large flocks than when traveling alone (Liechti et al. 1996), and it seems reasonable to assume that the flocking benefits detailed for Broad-winged Hawks apply to other species of raptors as well.

Taken as a whole, the field evidence above suggests that flocking benefits migrants in at least two ways: first by enhancing their ability to find good soaring space, and second by helping inexperienced migrants locate appropriate wintering areas. The evidence also suggests that the formation of very large flocks enhances the extent of the first benefit and that inexperienced juveniles probably benefit from flocking more than adults.

Finally, there is no evidence to suggest that super-flocking is simply the result of crowding along major migration corridors. And indeed, there is substantial evidence to the contrary. Most super-flocking migrants, including Western Honey Buzzards, Chinese Sparrowhawks, Levant Sparrowhawks, and Broad-winged Hawks, have precisely timed migrations in which most of each year's flight passes within a week or two, and, sometimes, within a single day, whereas nonflocking migrants have far more protracted flights (Leshem and Yom-Tov 1996; Bildstein 1999; Shirihai et al. 2000; Zalles and Bildstein 2000). This, together with the facts that super-flocking migrants begin assembling into flocks almost as soon as they begin to migrate and that they travel in flocks of increasing size long before they reach significant bottlenecks, suggests that the birds themselves rather than narrow migration passageways create the enormous flocks in which they migrate.

Potential Disadvantages of Flocking

That said, super-flocking is not without its downside, particularly when birds travel in mixed-species groupings. Although individuals in single-species flocks rarely collide, species differences in flight mechanics create conditions for numerous "near-misses" as well as collisions within mixed-species flocks. The problem is especially obvious at watchsites along major bottlenecks in Latin America and the Middle East.

In Mexico and Central America, migrants traveling in enormous mixed-species flocks dominated by Turkey Vultures, Swainson's Hawks, and Broad-winged Hawks sort themselves by species when streaming between thermals or when flying unidirectionally within large thermal streets. In such situations, agile and buoyant Broad-winged Hawks stream above the somewhat less buoyant Swainson's Hawks, which, in turn, stream above the even less buoyant Turkey Vultures. Decidedly less numerous Ospreys, Mississippi Kites, and Peregrine Falcons also pass in well-formed, single-species subgroups, most often at the perimeters of the main flight-line. Even so, when large, mixed-species streams of migrants spiral together in multidirectional kettles, near-misses and collisions occur at higher frequencies than in single-species flocks. The same phenomenon repeats itself in southern Israel when migrating Levant Sparrowhawks and Steppe Buzzards commingle in mixed-species flocks. When soaring individuals do collide, most use flapping flight to right themselves and to regain their position within the flock.

Other potential downsides of flocking behavior include the threat of interspecies predation and its potential to spread contagious diseases (Klem et al. 1985b), as well as the amount of prey robbery within and between species that feed aerially while migrating (Pienaar 1996). Traveling in large flocks also may affect where raptors roost at night and, in turn, their habitat needs. On the other hand, roosting in large numbers can reduce the potential impact of night-time predation on individual birds. Migrating in large flocks also restricts the timing of migration, which, in turn, may result in individuals migrating earlier than their body condition merits. The relative costs of these and other potential negative effects of super-flocking have yet to be investigated.

Wing Shape and Flight Behavior

Longtime student of animal movement Klaus Schmidt-Nielson (1972) once quipped that "flight has the potential of being the most energetically costly form of animal locomotion." Although this is true theoretically, natural selection has shaped both the flight mechanics and flight behavior of birds over the course of millions of years, and today modern birds, including raptors, are remarkably efficient flying machines. This section discusses how wing shape and flight behavior together help improve aerodynamic performance and reduce the metabolic costs of sustained migratory flight. Empirical data are available for only a few species, and this summary focuses mainly on theoretical considerations. Raptor migration biologist Paul Kerlinger (1989), avian flight specialist Colin Pennycuick (1969, 1972), and animal locomotion expert R. McNeill Alexander (2003) all have written extensively on this subject and what follows draws heavily on their work.

As mentioned earlier, cross-country thermal soaring substantially reduces the energetic costs of long-distance flight. One might expect, therefore, that most, if not all, species of raptors would soar extensively on migration. But this is not so. Although super-flocking migrants regularly soar while migrating and although all species of raptors soar at least occasionally on migration, several species of migrants frequently employ powered flapping flight en route, and most migrants typically alternate between the two flight types. At least three phenomena contribute to the less-than-consistent use of soaring flight.

First, parts of many migration routes and corridors lack dependable soaring opportunities, and birds have little choice but to use more expensive flapping flight at such times. Second, smaller-bodied migrants often need to travel at higher speeds than soaring allows. This is because smaller birds, which have higher metabolic rates than larger birds, are living life in the "metabolic fast lane." Their higher rates of resting metabolism allow them to build large fat reserves quickly but also require them to migrate quickly before their reserves run out. As a result, smaller migrants tend to be high-energy "time minimizers" en route, whereas larger species tend to be lower-speed "energy minimizers." Third, a raptor's wings are shaped by many selective forces, including nonmigratory foraging flight and predator avoidance, and because of this not all raptors have wings that are particularly well suited for soaring. Most soaring migrants, for example, are species whose foraging behavior depends heavily on soaring flight and whose risk of predation is little compromised by their inability to engage in high-speed flapping flight.

The amount of time a migrant spends soaring on migration, as well as the type of soaring its employs, can be seen in several aerodynamic aspects of its wings. Species that depend heavily on thermal soaring, for example, tend to have proportionately larger wings than other migrants. Proportionately larger wings result in lighter *wing loading,* which allows a bird to fly more slowly without stalling. This, in turn, enables a migrant to circle more tightly in thermals, thereby increasing the efficiency of its cross-country flight. Another characteristic feature of thermal-soaring migrants is *wing slotting,* a condition in which the tips of the outermost flight feathers are separated both horizontally and vertically when the wings are outstretched, creating the appearance of "fingered" wings. The roughly parallel series of aerodynamic surfaces that results from this configuration substantially reduces *drag* near the wingtips of slow-flying, soaring migrants, thereby increasing their flight efficiency (Kerlinger 1989; Tucker 1993; Alexander 2003). Although both of these characteristics are valuable during low-speed soaring flight, large wing surfaces and wing slotting often compromise the energetic efficiency of other types of flight including high-speed soaring and gliding, high-speed prey-pursuit flight, and continuous flapping flight. As a result, the wings of nonsoaring migrants differ considerably from those of soaring migrants. Overall, the wing shapes of migratory raptors differ enough among species that most field guides use the differences as important field marks.

Raptor-migration specialists recognize five generalized groupings of wing shape within the anatomical spectrum: (1) kites, (2) harriers and osprey, (3) accipiters, (4) buteos and eagles, and (5) falcons. Kites and falcons have relatively long and slender, so-called high-*aspect-ratio* wings that feature pointed tips. Harriers and ospreys also have relatively long and slender, high-aspect-ratio wings, but the tips of their wings are rounder than those of kites and falcons, and usually have wing slotting. Most, but not all, accipiters have relatively short, rounded wings with some wing slotting. Buteos and eagles tend to have large and somewhat oversized, broad wings, often with considerable wing slotting.

Efficient, high-speed *linear soaring* and gliding, including slope soaring, soaring in large thermal streets, and soaring over water, requires wings with relatively high-aspect ratios and high wing loading. Migrants such as Chinese Sparrowhawks, Grey-faced Buzzards, and Amur Falcons that depend on this type of soaring flight to complete their journeys tend to have relatively smaller and more pointed wings than do thermal-soaring migrants.

Raptors that depend on powered flight to complete much of their journey, including Ospreys, harriers, most small accipiters, and most falcons, employ a variety of flapping styles. Osprey and harriers, for example, typically intersperse relatively lengthy bouts of slope- and thermal soaring with those of flapping flight. Accipiters, on the other hand, usually employ undulating flapping flight, which also is called intermittent gliding and flapping flight, during which relatively short bursts of flapping flight alternate with similarly brief periods of linear soaring or, more typically, gliding. The "flap-flap-sail . . . flap-flap-sail" pattern that results is also used at times by thermal soaring migrants when they are forced to fly long distances among well-spaced updrafts. Falcons, most of which at least occasionally soar on migration, often engage in prolonged bouts of high-speed flapping flight en route, particularly during periods of weather that ground most other migrants.

Like many birds, raptors exhibit remarkable wing dexterity, and they are able to reconfigure the shape and relative position of their wings depending on local flight conditions. Peregrine Falcons, for example, usually hyperextend their wings to the point of wing slotting when circling in small thermals, and harriers tend to flatten their otherwise *dihedral* flight profile under the same circumstances. Ospreys, which also circle-soar in thermals on relatively flattened, fully outstretched and slotted wings, quickly reassume their characteristic M-shaped flight profile when *flex gliding* and when linear soaring at higher speeds. Other migrants, too, reconfigure their wings as conditions merit, and although many birdwatchers think of the flight profiles of raptors as being set in stone, careful observations indicate that most migrants

constantly refine their flight configurations while traveling, presumably to reduce the energetic costs of their potentially expensive journeys.

Nocturnal Flight

Although birds of prey often are characterized as quintessential diurnal migrants (Brown and Amadon 1968; Newton 1979; Heintzelman 1986), a
growing body of field evidence suggests that many migrate both night and
day. Species that are most likely to migrate nocturnally include (1) those
that engage in inconsiderable flapping flight while migrating, (2) those that
migrate long distances over water, and (3) small-bodied, high-energy time
minimizers that complete their journeys as quickly as possible. Obligate
nocturnal travelers include Chinese Sparrowhawks and Grey-faced Buzzards
migrating between Japan and the Philippines via the Ryukyu Islands and
Taiwan, Amur Falcons crossing the Indian Ocean between India and East
Africa, and Merlins traveling across the North Atlantic between Iceland and
Great Britain, all of which undertake over-water journeys of at least 450 km.
Other species that migrate nocturnally over water include Peregrine Falcons
that short-cut across the Atlantic Ocean while traveling south along the
Eastern Seaboard of North America and then cross the Caribbean Sea be-
tween the Greater Antilles and South America (Cochran 1985; Holroyd and
Duxbury 1999), Ospreys that fly out over the Atlantic Ocean between Scotland and southern Europe and cross the Mediterranean Sea between southern Europe and North Africa (R. Dennis and B. Meyburg, pers. comm.),
and Northern Harriers that cross the mouth of Delaware Bay between Cape
May Point, New Jersey, and Cape Henlopen, Delaware, at night (Russell
1991).

Most over-water migrants appear to time their flights to coincide with sea
thermals or tail winds. Both conditions reduce energy costs en route, and the
latter reduces the amount of time spent over water without the opportunity
to seek cover should conditions merit. Tail winds appear to be critically important. Beaman and Galea (1974), for example, noted that large numbers of
harriers and falcons frequently made landfall on Malta in the central
Mediterranean in early morning when strong head winds forced them to seek
shelter after flying through the night in unfavorable circumstances. Others
have reported similar groundings on other islands. Nocturnal migration also
occurs among land-based migrants. Evening flights of migrating Turkey Vultures have been reported in Texas (Tabor and McAllister 1988) and in

Colombia (M. Echeverry, pers. comm.), and Levant Sparrowhawks regularly migrate into the night in the Middle East (Stark and Liechti 1993).

Extreme Weather

Most raptors time their migrations to take advantage of prevailing climatic conditions in the regions through which they travel. Many, however, migrate through major tropical and subtropical cyclone zones, and cyclonic storms and other forms of extreme weather, including heavy rains, can significantly disrupt the regional geography, timing, and ultimate success of both short- and long-distance migratory movements. Hurricanes passing through eastern North America, for example, are known both to delay flights and to shift, longitudinally, the principal passageways of migrants. Five days of rainy weather on 17–21 September 1938, coinciding with the coastal passage of the "Great Hurricane" of that year, stalled and compressed the southbound movements of Broad-winged Hawks at Hawk Mountain Sanctuary for almost a week, after which an unprecedented five-day passage of more than 10,000 individuals, representing more than 95 percent of that season's total flight, was counted at the Sanctuary's North Lookout (Broun 1939). In 1961, a record-breaking flight of 70,000 broadwings at Hawk Cliff, Ontario, on 16 September followed Hurricane Carla's movement through the middle of the Great Lakes region on 13–14 September. And in 1999, a record-shattering flight of 500,000 broadwings on 17 September at Lake Erie Metropark, at the western end of the lake, followed the passage of Hurricane Dennis east of the Great Lakes in early September 1999 as well as the more coastal passage of Hurricane Floyd in mid-September. Farther south, Crouse and Keith (1999) reported a record-high one-day migration count of more than 60 Ospreys in a single hour on Hispaniola, together with that island's first report of a Swallow-tailed Kite, on 28 August 1999, as Hurricane Dennis crossed the Bahamas to the northwest. Finally, a satellite-tracked Peregrine Falcon flying from Hispaniola toward Venezuela in late October 1998 returned to that island, having completed more than 80 percent of its 650-km over-water passage, after encountering southerly head winds associated with the passage of category 5 Hurricane Mitch (Holroyd and Duxbury 1999).

Reports of how migrants behave within hurricanes are rare, not only because cyclonic storms are relatively uncommon and unpredictable but also because field work is difficult and dangerous at such times. One eye-witness account that does exist indicates why raptors attempt to avoid such events: an

Osprey "caught" near the center of a hurricane in central Florida was said to have "vanished" into clouds while attempting to fly south into hurricane-force head winds (Sutton 1945).

Synthesis and Conclusions

1. Atmospheric structure, climate, and weather play major roles in determining the flight strategies of raptors.

2. Most raptors migrating over land fly within 1000 meters of the surrounding landscape. Migration altitudes over large bodies of water are as yet unstudied.

3. All raptors soar (i.e., gain lift while flying on outstretched wings in updrafts) at least occasionally while migrating.

4. Soaring flight saves raptors considerable energy during their migrations, and many long-distance migrants depend on soaring to complete their journeys.

5. Raptors soar in isolated thermals, thermal streets, deflection updrafts, and lee waves over land, as well as in sea thermals over tropical and subtropical oceans.

6. Horizontal winds can both help and hinder migrating raptors.

7. Many long-distance migrants flock when migrating. Raptors flying in large flocks tend to soar more efficiently than those flying alone or in smaller flocks.

8. Selective forces both within and outside the migration period affect the wing structure and flight mechanics of migratory raptors.

9. Most raptors migrate entirely by day. Some species, however, also migrate at night, and a few species depend on nocturnal movements to complete their migrations.

10. Tropical cyclones and other forms of extreme weather can disrupt the regional geography, timing, and ultimate success of raptor movements.

—5—

Orientation and Navigation

Students of bird migration have generally assumed
that birds head straight toward their goal.
Donald R. Griffin and Raymond J. Houk, 1948

W e know a great deal more about *why* raptors migrate
than about *how* they manage to do so. Ornithologists
investigating how birds orient and navigate during their long-distance movements typically have done so experimentally. Some investigators have used
"displacement experiments," procedures in which individuals are gathered up
at some point during their migrations, transported to a distant site, released,
and subsequently tracked to see if they are capable of correcting their displacement. Others have mapped presumed migration-intention movements
in captive individuals. Still others have tested the homing abilities of trained
pigeons (Alerstam 1990; Berthold 2001).

Because of both finances and logistics—big birds tend to be both more expensive and more difficult to keep in captivity in large numbers—most orientation and navigation research has been done with relatively small and easy-to-keep seed-eating songbirds and domestic pigeons. As a result, except for a single displacement experiment involving Eurasian Sparrowhawks (see Chapter 1), experimental approaches to orientation and navigation are lacking for raptors, and most ideas regarding their way-finding behavior during migration have been inferred from the results of experiments involving other species of birds. Nevertheless, observations at migration watchsites, together with banding returns and satellite tracking, suggest that the navigational skills of raptors are similar to those of other long-distant migrants, and it seems reasonable to assume that the factors underlying their abilities are similar as well.

This chapter reviews what is known about orientation and navigation in birds in general and suggests how this information applies to migratory raptors.

Orientation and Navigation

To successfully complete long-distance, goal-oriented journeys, migratory birds need to be able to do two things: (1) orient themselves and (2) navigate during their travels. *Orientation* is the ability to maintain a specific geographic direction across an external grid on a curved surface, such as the longitudinal and latitudinal gridwork that cartographers use to plot locations on the surface of the earth. Simply put, to be able to orient themselves, migrants need to know north from south and east from west. *Navigation,* on the other hand, is the ability to move toward a goal while reorienting en route and, equally important, to know the distance between one's current location and the appointed goal.

Perhaps the easiest way to distinguish the significance of these two essential aspects of successful long-distance migration is to imagine a situation in which someone is "lost" in the woods and wants to get out as quickly as possible. The use of a magnetic compass or, for that matter, any orientation device that allows a person to travel in a constant direction, is of little value by itself, particularly if one uses it to travel deeper into the woods and away from the nearest way out. Only when a person also has an accurate "map" of the area and knows their location—as well as the location of their intended goal—on it, does the compass become a useful tool for navigating oneself out of the woods.

Maps are essential for successful long-distance human travel. European navigators, for example, "discovered" the New World fewer than 20 years after the first star map and Ptolemy's *Geography,* the first printed world map, were published in the 1470s (Snyder 1993). Maps appear to be equally important for migratory birds. But recognizing that map-and-compass navigation is critical for successful long-distance travel in migratory raptors is one thing; describing the types of "compasses" and "maps" that birds actually use is another matter entirely.

A growing body of both field and laboratory evidence suggests that birds use one or more of three environmental cues to orient themselves while traveling long distances. The cues include the sun, the stars, and the earth's magnetic field. The "solar" compass was the first to be discovered. Working in the late 1940s, German behaviorist Gustav Kramer noticed that in the months when they would otherwise be migrating, captive Eurasian Starlings hopped and flitted about their cages more often than at other times of the year, a phenomenon that one of Kramer's colleagues had called *Zugunruhe* (German for *migratory restlessness*) several years earlier. Kramer noted that the migratory restlessness he observed was far more frequent on sunny than on overcast days and that most of the hopping and fluttering was aimed in the direction the birds would normally migrate along. Kramer's observations led him to propose that the birds were using the sun's location in the sky to appropriately orient themselves. To test this idea, Kramer performed a series of experiments in which he used mirrors to shift the "direction" of the sun that the birds saw and confirmed his suspicion (Kramer 1952). The results of additional experiments, in which the starling's normal day-night cycles were "time-shifted" 6 or 12 hours with artificial light, so that the birds could no longer use the sun's relative position in the sky to orient correctly, indicated that the birds were using an internal 24-hour clock, together with the sun's horizontal position in the sky, or azimuth, to orient themselves.

Many species of birds, however, migrate at night, and within a few years of Kramer's discoveries, other scientists looked to see if these so-called nocturnal migrants were using individual stars or constellations of stars as cues for orientation and navigation. American behavioral ecologist Steven Emlen conducted a series of unusual "laboratory" experiments to test this possibility. Emlen placed captive Indigo Buntings in a planetarium in which he shifted and reconfigured nighttime skies in ways that demonstrated that the birds used stars to orient themselves during migration. He also discovered that the birds were able to do so only if they had been exposed to the natural movements of the constellations as juveniles (Emlen 1967).

Earth's magnetic field provides a reliable reference for both direction and location, and by the 1960s, experiments with caged individuals of several species added this planetary feature to the list of compass cues. Subsequent attempts to determine how birds detect and correctly interpret the earth's magnetic fields suggest that at least some species use magnetically sensitive photo-pigments for directional orientation, and that precise arrangements of tiny magnetite crystals (Fe_3O_4) within individual cells enable birds to sense magnetic anomalies and declinational differences in the earth's magnetic field, along with its polarity, thereby allowing them to create "magnetic maps" of the landscapes they migrate across (Able 1995).

Most recently, a growing consensus has suggested that migrants use multiple sources of information, including celestial and magnetic cues, along with polarized light and, possibly, regionally specific predominant wind patterns, to orient themselves during long-distance travel. Explanations for navigational maps, however, remain more elusive. Work involving pigeons in Italy suggests that under certain conditions, olfaction can play a major role in helping birds map their current locations relative to their geographic goal. Whether the same holds for long-distance migrants remains unclear. Indeed, the point to which birds use true navigation, as opposed to simple *compass orientation,* to locate their wintering areas and breeding grounds is still an open question, with some researchers suggesting that the former may come into play only near the end of long-distance travel, when its value in pinpointing an individual's exact breeding and wintering areas might become critical (Able 1995; Berthold 2001).

Evidence for Orientation and Navigation in Raptors

Most of the scant evidence we have for navigational ability in raptors comes in the form of band-recovery data and resightings of individually marked birds. For species that have been banded in large numbers, there is evidence that many individuals, particularly males, return to the same nest site or within several nesting territories of where they have bred in previous years (Newton 1979). The phenomenon of breeding-site fidelity, which is well studied in several populations of Ospreys and Peregrine Falcons (Poole 1989; Ratcliffe 1993), apparently occurs in many species of raptors, including long-distance, transequatorial migrants such as Broad-winged Hawks, Swainson's Hawks, Northern Hobbies, and Lesser Kestrels (Matray 1974; Fiucznski 1978; England et al. 1997; Serrano et al. 2001).

Although *winter-site* fidelity is decidedly less well studied than *breeding-site* fidelity, it too appears to occur. Examples include individual Rough-legged Hawks wintering on the same home ranges in California (Garrison and Bloom 1993), and migrant American Kestrels doing the same in southern Florida (Tabb 1977).

Additional support for multidirectional navigation in raptors comes from direct observations of thousands of migrants traveling along some of the world's most heavily used migration corridors. North America's most abundant complete migrant, the Broad-winged Hawk, provides the archetypal example. Each year millions of Broad-winged Hawks migrate from northern temperate zone breeding grounds centered in southern Ontario to wintering areas stretching from southern Mesoamerica into northern and central South America. The 5000- to 8000-mile one-way journey is far from unidirectional. Eastern populations of Broad-winged Hawks begin their outbound migrations along a roughly southwesterly (240°) arc that transports them from southeastern Canada and the northeastern United States to the Gulf Coast of southern Texas. Once there, the flight is redirected approximately 60° to the east, thereafter following a roughly 180°, southerly course toward coastal Veracruz, Mexico, before shifting another 60° east and following a southeasterly course into northern Central America. By the time the flight has reached western Panama, outbound Broad-winged Hawks are flying directly east toward Colombia in northwestern South America. Once the flight reaches Colombia, the birds disperse across an arc of 180° en route to individual wintering areas across Colombia, Ecuador, Venezuela, and elsewhere in South America (Figure 15). This decidedly circuitous land-based journey, which circumnavigates the Gulf of Mexico and Caribbean Sea, and enables the birds to soar on land-based thermals en route, presumably presents a fair share of navigational challenges, particularly for juveniles attempting their first long-distance migration.

In addition to these and other direct observations of the principal flight-lines of populations of long-distance migrants, the movements of single satellite-tracked birds reveal that individuals sometimes use all-but-identical paths on successive outbound and return migrations (Figure 16) as well as on successive outbound routes in sequential years (Figure 17) (Meyburg et al. 1996, 2000, 2002). Although such observations provide little evidence for the mechanisms involved, taken as a whole they strongly suggest that raptors are capable of navigating and orienting during long-distance movements.

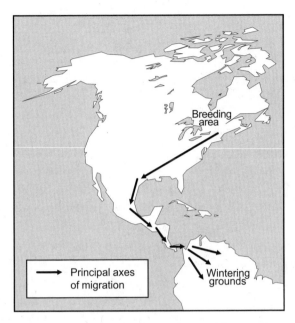

Figure 15. Principal axes of migration used by Broad-winged Hawks at various points during outbound migration. Note the many changes in direction during the journey.

Navigational Challenges

In addition to evidence indicating that many raptors are capable of navigating long distances along established flight-lines, there also is evidence that many individuals, and in particular juveniles, have problems doing so. Although many factors contribute to navigational mistakes, *crosswinds* appear to be particularly important. As opposed to *tail winds,* which propel migrants in the preferred direction of travel, and *head winds,* which hold them back, crosswinds tend to misdirect migrants rather than speeding or slowing their rates of travel.

The impact of so-called *wind drift* on raptor migration has been known for some time. In 1902 C. C. Trowbridge suggested that wind drift was responsible for the passage of enormous streams of migrants on the coastlines of southern New England each autumn. As Trowbridge put it, "Hawks drift with the wind when soaring, and as they soar continually, their movements during migrations are largely dependent on the direction of the wind" (1902,

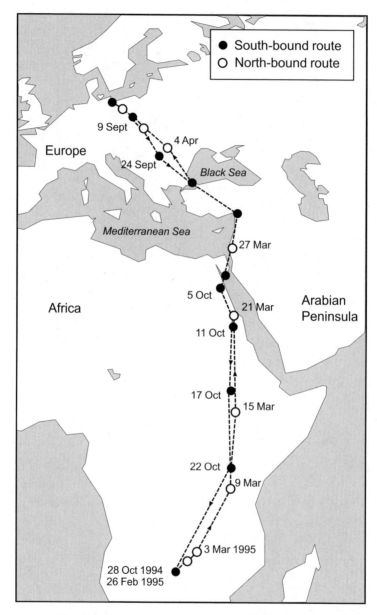

Figure 16. Outbound and return movements of an adult Lesser Spotted Eagle between its breeding grounds in northern Germany and its wintering area in Zambia, 1994–1995. Note the similarity between outbound and return routes (after Meyburg et al. 1995a).

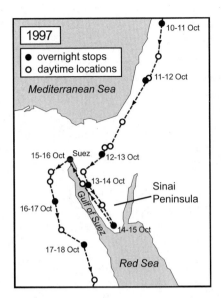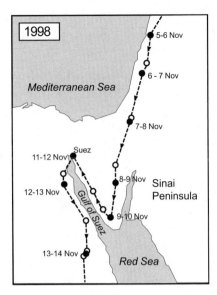

Figure 17. Outbound movements of a Lesser Spotted Eagle through the Middle East in successive years. Note the similar detours taken by the bird in the Sinai Peninsula in 1997 and again in 1998 (after Meyburg et al. 2002).

737). He went on to suggest that northwesterly crosswinds, which entered the region on the heels of cold fronts, pushed the otherwise southwest-bound migrants southeast and up against the region's largely east–west Atlantic Coast diversion line, which served to concentrate the movements of the hydrophobic birds westward into coastal New Jersey (Trowbridge 1902). The phenomenon, which was expanded by Allen and Peterson in 1936, and again by Mueller and Berger in 1967b, has since been used to explain concentrated raptor flight-lines in many parts of the world.

Age-related differences in vulnerability to wind drift are especially well studied in eastern North America, where flights of the two most common migrants, Sharp-shinned Hawk and Broad-winged Hawk, provide several examples of the phenomenon (see Chapter 4).

What eventually happens to significantly wind-drifted raptors remains unclear. Along the eastern seaboard of North America, many land-based migrants that have been wind drifted face formidable over-water barriers when reaching the tips of coastal peninsulas in southern Nova Scotia (80 km to Maine), New Jersey (26 km to Delaware), Virginia (24 km to Cape Henry), and Florida (>140 km to Cuba). In such cases, the migrants have three choices: (1) stop migrating and overwinter where they are, (2) continue mi-

grating and set out for the nearest land to the south, or (3) continue migrating but retrace their steps and follow the inland coastline of the peninsula
northward before turning "south" again once they reach the mainland. Although migrants often delay their decisions for up to several days at such apparent cul-de-sacs, few, if any, stop migrating. Juvenile Broad-winged Hawks,
for example, often are seen soaring to great heights before taking off across
such barriers. Even so, few are reported at the southern termini of their supposed over-water passages, and many are later seen retracing their movements
north along the peninsula they had earlier departed from.

Observations of broad-wing movements at the straits of Florida between
the Florida Keys and Cuba appear typical in this regard. In some years, as
many as 10,000 migrants, at least 90 percent of which are juveniles, reach the
southern tip of the Florida peninsula. Although most apparently remain in
southern Florida or turn back and retrace their movements off the peninsula,
a few island-hop across the Florida Keys toward northwestern Cuba. At least
some that continue farther south make landfall in the Dry Tortugas 95 km
west of Key West, where individuals have been seen making futile attempts to
leave the island, only to return again and again and, eventually, starving.
Others fall into the straits and drown during attempted passages (Hagar
1988; Hoffman and Darrow 1992). Still others successfully navigate the
straits and overwinter in the West Indies. The latter, presumably, providing
ancestral stock for the five nonmigratory races of broadwings scattered across
the region's archipelago (Ferguson-Lees and Christie 2001).

Most migratory raptors apparently recognize the threat of being blown out
to sea on crosswinds. Birds of prey fly lower in coastal areas when crosswinds
prevail than at other times, and many are reluctant to attempt over-water
passage in such winds (Kerlinger and Gauthreaux 1984; Finlayson 1992).
Some of the best evidence for "decision making" on the part of migrants
prone to potentially devastating wind drift comes from observations of outbound Black Kites about to cross the 14-km-wide Strait of Gibraltar between
southern Spain and northern Morocco. Lightly wing loaded, buoyant, and
prone to wind drift, Black Kites adopt tactics to reduce the possibility of
being blown into the Atlantic. In autumn, when strong *Poniente,* or westerly
winds, prevail, most kites either cross in the early morning before the daily
winds have built or much later in the evening after the winds have subsided.
During *Levante,* or easterly winds, which pose the threat of pushing the birds
in the open Atlantic, most individuals attempt their crossing farther east
along the Strait and much closer to the Rock of Gibraltar, apparently in anticipation of being wind drifted westward during their flight. At such times,

light and variable winds enhance the rate of passage, and even then individuals quickly reverse course and return to Spain if crosswinds begin to push them toward open water at the western end of the Strait. During extended periods of strong easterlies, Black Kite numbers increase in the region as individual migrants wait for a week or more for more favorable conditions before attempting to cross. At such times, flocks of hundreds of birds can be seen "kiting" into easterly crosswinds while waiting for the winds to drop. In spring, when westerly winds prevail at the site, wind-drifted kites returning from Africa make landfall near the eastern end of the Strait, with many individuals reaching the coastline in labored flapping flight and barely above the waves (Finlayson 1992). Radar studies of outbound migrants in eastern Canada revealed similarly extensive impacts of wind drift on migration flight-lines north of the Great Lakes (Richardson 1975).

Despite its potential importance in influencing the migration geography of migrants—or perhaps because of it—wind drift has become a somewhat contentious and controversial aspect of raptor-migration science. At least one researcher has suggested that most so-called wind drift actually results from migrants flying closer to the ground in crosswinds and being more visible to counters then rather than from wind drift per se (Murray 1964), whereas others have objected strenuously to this explanation (Mueller and Berger 1967). Finally, a study at Hawk Mountain Sanctuary suggests that American Kestrels, Merlins, and Peregrine Falcons actually take advantage of strong crosswinds and the mountain updrafts they create along this important leading line and are more likely to migrate during these wind conditions than at other times (Allen et al. 1996).

Adaptive Wind Drift

Although in most instances it appears that wind drift results in misorientation and is costly to migrants, in some circumstances birds purposefully allow themselves to be drifted, both to speed their rates of travel and to reduce the overall costs of long-distance migration. Raptors that migrate short distances tend to have the luxury of restricting their movements to periods of favorable weather, and many appear to do so. Raptors that migrate long distances, however, often cannot afford to be delayed by the weather and because of this, long-distance migrants frequently undertake movements in suboptimal weather, including crosswinds. Migration specialist Thomas Alerstam (1990) has suggested that at such times many long-distance migrants engage in *adaptive wind drift* in which travel time is maximized and distance to the goal reduced as far as possible given the prevailing winds that are encountered during different stages of the journey. According to Alerstam, adaptive wind drift is more likely during the early stages of migration than later on when birds are nearing their intended destinations and need to compensate for earlier wind drift. Adaptive wind drift helps migrants in three ways: (1) they complete their journeys more quickly, (2) they move through inhospitable habitats faster, and (3) wind drift places them as close to their goal as possible throughout the journey. The latter means that if particularly unfavorable weather interrupts the flight completely and migrants are forced to expand precious metabolic fuel while waiting for conditions to improve, the remaining portion of the journey, which may need to be completed on reduced fat reserves, is as short as possible.

Elliptical migrations (see Chapters 4 and 6 for details) provide some of the strongest support for adaptive wind drift. In such circumstances, outbound migrants initially drifted east in predominant temperate westerlies, compensate by flying westward farther south, whereas returning migrants initially drifted westward in tropical easterlies, subsequently compensate by flying eastward farther north.

Adaptive or not, wind-drifted birds often need to redirect their movements at the ends of their journeys to reach their goals. Forty percent of 7779 migrants reported on spring migration at Cedar Grove, Wisconsin, in 1953–1957 and 1962–1964, for example, were seen flying south rather than north, presumably having overshot their intended breeding grounds (Mueller and Berger 1969). Even more remarkable is the direction of prominent flight-line at the Parc du Bic hawkwatch on the Gaspé Peninsula of southern Quebec. Almost all spring migrants—there is no concentrated migration at the site in autumn—are counted traveling southwest, rather than northeast, along the shoreline of the 50-km wide St. Lawrence Seaway, presumably backtracking to shorter water crossings at the base of the peninsula to the west. Perhaps the most remarkable aspect of such observations is not that sizeable numbers of migrants are drifted off course in crosswinds, but that the drifted birds are capable of eventually recognizing their predicaments and are able to reorient themselves in an attempt to reach their intended destinations.

A Working Model for Raptor Navigation

Drost's (1938) displacement experiments with Eurasian Sparrowhawks (Chapter 2) demonstrate that first-time migrants, although lacking true navigational skills, are programmed to orient their movements in a predetermined direction for proscribed distances. Although arguably crude and susceptible to wind drift, this innate orientation ability places many, if not most, juveniles in the right place at the right time, allowing them to follow adults en route and to take advantage of the navigational skills of these far more experienced birds. This may be the case even when juveniles begin their migrations before adults since the former tend to migrate more slowly than the latter.

The extent to which juvenile Broad-winged Hawks follow adults under such circumstances was studied at Hawk Mountain Sanctuary in September 1996 and 1997 (Maransky and Bildstein 2001). Adult broadwings were significantly more likely to migrate in flocks than were first-year birds (78% versus 62%), and whereas juvenile flocks averaged 2.0 birds, adult and mixed-aged flocks averaged 4.5 and 4.7 birds, respectively. This suggests that juveniles were more likely to join adults en route than vice versa. Adults were the first, or "lead," birds in 80 percent of mixed-species flocks, even though they made up only 68 percent of all birds seen in such flocks. Taken as a whole, these results indicate that first-year Broad-winged Hawks regularly follow experienced adults. Following behavior probably helps juveniles in three ways. First, it makes long-distance navigation easier. Second, it helps juveniles find thermals and updrafts more quickly. And third, it increases the likelihood of juveniles finding safe roosting areas as evening approaches.

Whether or not similar following behavior occurs in other species awaits additional study, but the notion of cultural transmission, or transgenerational imitation of various aspects of migratory behavior, seems likely. Evolutionary biologist Richard Dawkins (1976) has coined the term *meme* (from the ancient Greek *mime* [or mimic]) to describe this kind of information exchange. Memes are believed to evolve in much the same way as genes, by natural selection, with cultures that best improve an individual's chances of survival and reproduction thriving and spreading, and those that do not withering and dying. Memetic transfer is likely to be particularly important in long-distance migrants that follow complicated migration routes, such as the Broad-winged Hawks that travel between North and South America each spring and autumn (see Figure 15). In such cases, a combination of migrating in a fixed direction, orientation "genes," leading lines, and an innate tendency to flock during migration together could position an individual within an appropriate stream of migrants early on, after which navigational memes could help direct "knowledgeable" flocks the rest of the way. That most long-distance migrants travel in large groups where cultural transmission would be possible lends support to this idea.

It is not clear how much easier it is for novice migrants that already have completed a successful outbound migration to navigate back to their intended breeding grounds on their first return journey, particularly when the return journey is part of a *loop* (or *elliptical*) *migration* route. Having completed at least one round-trip journey, however, experienced migrants should be able to use their knowledge of local and regional landmarks on future migrations, presumably reducing both the costs and risks of making these movements.

Synthesis and Conclusions

1. Raptors need to be able to both *orient* and *navigate* to complete their long-distance migrations. Exactly how they manage to do so remains unclear.
2. Because raptors are poor candidates for experiments in orientation and navigation, most of what we "know" about their skills in these areas is based on extrapolations from field and laboratory experiments involving other groups of birds.
3. Such experiments show that diurnal migrants use the sun and that nocturnal migrants use the stars to orient their movements, that some species also use internal magnetic cues, and that most migratory birds depend on more than one type of compass to orient themselves.
4. Band recoveries and, more recently, satellite tracking indicate that raptors are capable of precise navigation.
5. First-time migrants may use a simple direction-and-distance system that places them in the right place at the right time to take advantage of the practiced navigational skills of experienced migrants to complete their journeys.
6. Experienced migrants may rely on local and regional landmarks to retrace earlier migrations.

—6—

The Ecology of Migratory Raptors

Ecology is a new name for a very old subject . . . natural history.

Charles Elton, 1927

Raptors are inseparably connected to and shaped by the environments in which they live. The biology of these connections and the reactions they produce is called "ecology." Ecology is complicated enough when the species involved is a nonmigrant; when the species in question migrates, it is even more so. Migratory raptors, for example, need to succeed in at least three different environments: their breeding grounds, their wintering areas, and the area or areas through which they migrate. As a result, their populations often are limited by conditions in more than one part of the world (Newton 2004). In a way, migratory raptors are moving targets for raptors ecologists, and knowledge of their natural histories has lagged far behind that of their sedentary kin.

This chapter reviews the ways in which migratory raptors successfully interact with their environments, not only when migrating but also when they are breeding and overwintering. The focus is on raptor ecology from the viewpoint of the birds: how they find the resources needed to survive, how they avoid becoming a resource for other organisms, and how, in turn, this affects their distributions and abundances.

Migration Ecology

Despite the opportunities it creates, long-distance migration challenges raptors in many ways. Compared with the home ranges that birds of prey breed and overwinter in, the ecological neighborhoods across which they migrate are truly enormous. Most birds of prey travel through a series of different ecosystems en route to their seasonal destinations, and juveniles, at least, face entirely new circumstances daily on their initial outbound migrations in autumn and, in many instances, on their return journeys in spring as well. Deciding how best to use and acquire available energy resources, avoid potential predators, parasites, and disastrous weather, and locate appropriate roosting sites each evening are decidedly more difficult under changing and novel circumstances than in more familiar terrain. Raptors meet these ecological challenges in several ways.

Many migratory birds of prey, including species that are not social outside of migration, fly and roost in groups while migrating, most likely because doing so enhances flight performance and roost-site selection and allows the birds to locate their intended destinations via the "institutional memory" of the group members. Many, if not most, migrants engage in *hyperphagia* prior to migration, eating excessively as they attempt to lay down fat to help fuel their journeys. Many raptors replace worn flight feathers before migrating, presumably to enhance their aerodynamic performance en route. And almost all raptors suspend molt while migrating, both because feather gaps impede flight performance and because growing new feathers is energetically costly. At least two species of long-distance migrants, the Steppe Buzzard and the Swainson's Hawk, spend so much time migrating and so little time on the breeding and wintering grounds that it takes them more than a year to replace all of their flight feathers (Schmutz 1992; Herremans 2000).

Energy and Water Resources for Migration

Raptors fuel their migratory movements three ways: by building fat reserves prior to migration and, subsequently, burning fat en route; by feeding regularly on migration; and by soaring on thermals and mountain updrafts. Although most species use all three sources of energy, many depend disproportionately on one or two of these "fuels" to complete their migrations.

Fat Reserves

Fat is the fuel of choice for most avian migrants. Numerous small songbirds, for example, are known to double their lean body mass prior to migration, and many others are known to regularly interrupt their flights and replenish fat stores en route (Blem 1980).

The phenomenon of premigratory fattening has not been studied in detail in raptors, and the extent to which it occurs has been inferred almost entirely from examinations of individuals captured while migrating (e.g., Harden 1993; Gorney and Yom-Tov 1994; Yosef et al. 2003; Delong and Hoffman 2004). Available data suggest that the fat stores of migratory raptors rarely exceed 20 percent of their lean body mass. Overall, researchers have found that juveniles have lower fat stores than adults, and that females tend to carry more fat on their return migrations than on their outbound flights. Most likely, the former reflects the fact that juveniles are less efficient predators and migrants than are adults (Ueta and Higuchi 2002; Yosef et al. 2003), and the latter that natural selection favors females who arrive on their breeding grounds with sufficient fat to produce viable eggs (Newton 1979; Delong and Hoffman 2004).

Juvenile Red-tailed Hawks trapped on migration in southern Wisconsin early in the season had less subcutaneous fat than those trapped later on, either because in being from more northerly breeding areas they had initiated their migrations sooner after fledging than later migrants and had not laid down as much fat overall, because they had traveled farther than later migrants had and had burned more fat en route, or both (Geller and Temple 1983).

One problem with studies involving trapped migrants is the likelihood of a sampling bias. Raptors trapped during migration almost always are lured with food, and it seems reasonable to assume that food-stressed birds are more likely to be captured than are their less-hungry counterparts (Gorney and Yom-Tov 1994). As a result, the stored-fat values reported in these studies likely represent the lower end of the amounts that are carried by most migrants. And indeed, one could argue that the fact that many investigators have had difficulties capturing long-distance transequatorial migrants near the midpoints of their migrations suggests that most raptors are carrying sufficient fat at this point in their journey and are not "fuel stressed." That said, any "condition bias" that does exist is likely to operate equally across species, ages, and genders of raptors, and the age and gender differences reported above probably reflect real differences in fat storage among these categories of birds of prey.

Feeding Regularly en Route

Many raptors, particularly those that travel alone and that migrate short distances, regularly feed en route (Niles et al. 1996). Some individuals apparently feed daily, others do so episodically and opportunistically when weather conditions preclude efficient migration, and others still do so only when they encounter areas of abundant and easily available prey while traveling to their destinations. Studies involving satellite-tracked raptors indicate that many species begin their migrations slowly, increase their speeds as they approach and pass the midpoints of their journeys, and slow down again as they approach their destinations (Meyburg et al. 1995a; Fuller et al. 1998; Hake et al. 2003). Presumably, such differences reflect differences in the likelihood of feeding en route, with individuals hunting more when starting out in an effort to build fat reserves for the journey and again toward the end of their migrations, either to avoid metabolizing protein as fat stores are depleted or to sample prey availability on potential wintering areas.

Some species apparently time their migrations to take advantage of migratory prey en route. Peregrine Falcons, which fuel their migrations by feeding while migrating (Cochran 1975), typically interrupt their journeys for a week or more to feed at traditional *stopover sites* that predictably host seasonal concentrations of migrating shorebirds, waterfowl, and other waterbirds (Dekker 1980; Busche et al. 1998; Lank et al 2003). The impact of peregrine predation in these situations is such that researchers have suggested that prey species sometimes shift their migrations in an attempt to decouple them from those of the falcons (Lank et al. 2003). Other largely avivorous accipiters, including the Sharp-shinned Hawk in North America and the Eurasian Sparrowhawk in northern Europe, apparently time and position their migrations to tap the concentrated movements of their songbird prey (Rosenfield and Evans 1980; Newton 1986; McCanch 1997).

Many raptors, including Black Kites, Broad-winged Hawks, Merlins, and American Kestrels, regularly hunt swarming insects while migrating, some of which are migrating themselves (Bahat 1985; Shelley and Benz 1985; Nicoletti 1997). Others, including numerous accipiters and buteos, regularly prey on birds and mammals, either before or after their daily movements or throughout the day during periods of poor weather (Gorney and Yom-Tov 1994; Yosef 1996). In Israel, Egyptian Vultures interrupt their migrations to feed at garbage dumps and on roadkills (Yosef 1996). Ospreys, which often fuel their migrations by feeding en route, frequently carry prey while traveling, usually with the fish held tightly in both feet and oriented head-first in the most aerodynamic fashion (Shelley and Benz 1985; Finlayson 1992).

Feeding rates can vary considerably within species, with individuals migrating longer distances being more likely to stop and refuel en route than those migrating shorter distances (Candler and Kennedy 1995), and individuals with greater fat stores being less likely to feed than those with smaller reserves (Kjellén et al. 2001). And overall, feeding appears to be far more common immediately before and after long-distance travel across inhospitable landscapes, such as deserts and large bodies of water, than at other times (Yosef 1996).

Soaring Flight

Many raptors, particularly those that migrate long distances, depend heavily on energy efficient soaring flight to complete their migrations (see Chapters 4 and 8 for general and specific details, respectively). Almost all transequatorial and most complete long-distance migrants, including Western Honey Buzzards, Mississippi Kites, Chinese Sparrowhawks, Grey-faced Buzzards, Broad-winged Hawks, Swainson's Hawks, Lesser Spotted Eagles, Steppe Eagles, Lesser Kestrels, Red-footed Falcons, Amur Falcons, and Northern Hobbies, are super-flocking, *obligate soaring migrants* that time their migrations so that the overwhelming majority of the flight passes any one site in fewer than two weeks (Leshem and Yom-Tov 1996; Porras-Peñaranda et al. 2004). Several of these so-called *calendar migrants,* including the Amur Falcon and the Swainson's Hawk, stop over in relatively small groups and feed for up to a month or more early in their migrations before massing into truly enormous flocks and flying, presumably without feeding, for most of the remainder of their journeys (Ali and Ripley 1978; Smith et al. 1986 [but see Kirkley 1991]; Johnson et al. 1987) (see Chapter 8). Others, including Broad-winged Hawks and Steppe Buzzards, either lay down considerable fat stores prior to migration or feed episodically and opportunistically on superabundant insects while migrating (Gorney and Yom-Tov 1994; Shelley and Benz 1985; Brett 1995).

The efficiencies of soaring flight notwithstanding, raptors that depend heavily on this source of energy to complete their migrations often reach their destinations in a weakened state. For example, many of the Turkey Vultures and Swainson's Hawks that migrate between breeding sites in North America and wintering areas in South America arrive at the latter in late autumn fat-depleted and at barely 70 percent of their typical body mass. Most, however, quickly regain body condition and are able to lay down fat needed for the return journey well in advance of their departures the following spring (Kirk and Gosler 1994; Goldstein et al. 1999a).

Water Needs

It is usually assumed that migrants, including raptors, secure sufficient water when traveling long distances via fat metabolism, a process that results in the production of so-called metabolic water (Berthold 2001). Even so, many raptors, including Western Honey Buzzards, Black Kites, Steppe Buzzards, Short-toed Snake Eagles, and Lesser Spotted Eagles, have been observed drinking at migratory stopover sites, most notably in Africa and the Middle East (Dupuy 1969; Clark and Gorney 1987; Yosef 1996). Some appear to be especially dependent on drinking water while migrating, even to the point of using brackish and saltwater sources. Such individuals avoid salt poisoning by excreting excess salt via paired salt glands located above their eyes. The glands, which occur in many species of raptors and serve mainly to reduce salt loads resulting from the consumption of desiccated prey, are capable of concentrating and dumping salt at rates that enable migrants to drink seawater-strength saltwater without ill effect (Cade and Greenwald 1966; Shoemaker 1972).

Timing of Migration

Many factors, including age, gender, and flocking, as well as the extent of feeding en route, affect the timing of raptor migration.

Flocking versus Nonflocking Migrants

The timing of peak migration is decidedly more acute and temporally more predictable in super-flocking migrants than in species that migrate alone or that flock episodically. At Hawk Mountain Sanctuary, for example, half of all Broad-winged Hawks—the only obligate flocking migrant at the site—typically pass within 8 days each autumn, whereas the site's nonflocking migrants take 16 to 39 days to do so (see Table 17, page 180), and the same appears to be true for flocking versus nonflocking migrants in Israel (Leshem and Yom-Tov 1996). Presumably, flocking species, which benefit by traveling in large groups (see Chapter 4), time their flights to increase the likelihood of doing so, whereas nonflocking species do not. And indeed, the latter, many of which feed regularly on migration, most likely "space" their movements temporally and spatially to reduce competition while traveling.

Outbound versus Return Migration

Numerous factors affect the timing of outbound migration. Many adults replace some or all of their flight feathers prior to autumn migration and then suspend molt during their movements, presumably to increase flight performance while traveling. Males and females tend to time their postbreeding molts differently, and their departure schedules typically reflect this. Bird-eating raptors that depend on migrating birds to fuel their migrations typically time their movements to coincide with those of their prey. And species that use soaring flight, particularly those that depend on late-summer, early-autumn thermals in the temperate zone, need to time their departures to harness this phenomenon (see Chapter 4). Finally, regardless of how they fuel their journeys overall, almost all raptors need to build at least modest fat stores prior to migration, and an individual's ability to lay down this fuel can affect its departure schedule (Morton and Pereyra 1994). In addition to all of this, departure dates for return migration in reproductively active individuals may be affected by the so-called urge to reproduce.

In many species of birds, including many raptors, rates of travel differ considerably during outbound and return migration. In most, but not all of these species, the return journey is more rapid than the outbound passage (Berthold 2001). One possible explanation for this is that outbound migration occurs in autumn after prey populations have reproduced and are relatively available, whereas return migration occurs in spring before prey have reproduced, and because of this outbound migrants are more likely to fuel their journeys while feeding en route than are return migrants, and, as a result, travel more slowly (O'Reilly and Wingfield 1995). Another possibility is that outbound migration includes large numbers of inexperienced—and typically slower—juvenile migrants, whereas return migration involves only experienced birds that tend to migrate faster than first-time migrants.

One factor that does not affect the faster rate of travel in spring is the so-called urge to reproduce. It makes little sense for raptors to migrate at anything other their optimal rate of travel given their physical state, weather conditions, and prey availability en route (Izhaki and Maitav 1998), and there is no indication that reproductive urges induce them to do otherwise. A forced march back to the breeding grounds in spring is counterproductive, particularly when arrival there in appropriate body condition is so important for territorial establishment and breeding and when, in most circumstances, an earlier departure from the winter grounds is likely to allow migrants to arrive earlier on the breeding grounds in appropriate condition. And indeed, whereas satellite tracking indicates that many raptors, including Steppe Eagles (Ellis et al. 2001), complete their return journeys more quickly than their outbound migrations, the reverse is true in other raptors, including White-tailed Sea Eagles (Ueta et al. 1998), Swainson's Hawks (Fuller et al. 1998), and Wahlberg's Eagles (Meyburg et al.1995b).

Age and Gender Differences

Ornithologists have known for some time that within species, individuals of different ages and genders often differ in their migration schedules (Nice 1937). The phenomenon has been widely studied in raptors, particularly in species whose plumages allow individuals to be aged or sexed in the field (Table 12). Evidence has been collected in a number of ways, but most has come from direct observations at migration watchsites and banding stations and, more recently, from studies of satellite-tracked birds (Ueta et al. 2000). Unfortunately, few universal patterns have emerged. In 1989, Paul Kerlinger cited six different hypotheses in attempting to explain *differential migration* and overwintering behavior in raptors and was forced to admit that "the picture for differential timing by sex is not clear," and furthermore, that in autumn, at least, "there is no predominant trend in whether adults precede immatures or vice versa." The same remains largely true today (see Table 12; Mueller et al. 2000).

Some researchers have argued that adult males, which do most of the hunting on the breeding grounds and therefore have a better knowledge of the prey base there than do females, should extend their stays there and depart from these areas later in autumn and return to them earlier in spring than their mates. Others have suggested that males should return to the breeding grounds earlier than females because they are under intense selection pressure to acquire the best nesting territories. And indeed many, but not all, observations of sex-dependent differences in outbound and return migration support these views (see Table 12).

Table 12. *Species exhibiting differential timing of migration*

Migration type Timing difference	Species	Reference (method)[a]
Outbound		
Males precede females	Northern Harrier (juveniles)	Bildstein et al. 1984 (BM)
	Eurasian Sparrowhawk	Moritz and Vauk 1976 (BM)
	Peregrine Falcon	Hunt et al. 1975 (BM)
Females precede males	Western Honey Buzzard (?)	Hake et al. 2003 (ST)
	Western Marsh Harrier	Kjellén 1992 (VC)
	Northern Harrier	Broun 1949 (VC), Haugh 1972 (VC), Kjellén 1992 (VC)
	Eurasian Sparrowhawk	Kjellén 1992 (VC)
	Sharp-shinned Hawk	Rosenfield and Evans 1980 (BM), Duncan 1982 (BM), Mueller et al. 2000 (BM)
	Cooper's Hawk	Hoffman 1985 (BM),
	Cooper's Hawk (juveniles)	Mueller et al. 2000 (BM)
	Common Kestrel	Kjellén 1992 (VC)
	American Kestrel	Stotz and Goodrich 1989 (VC), Mueller et al. 2000 (BM)
	Merlin	Clark 1985b (BM), Kjellén 1992 (VC), Mueller et al. 2000 (BM)
Adults precede juveniles	Osprey	Newton 1979, Kjellén 1992 (VC)
	Western Honey Buzzard	Kjellén 1992 (VC), Hake et al. 2003 (ST)
	Northern Harrier	Kjellén 1992 (VC)
	Black Kite	Schifferli 1967 (VC)
	Rough-legged Hawk (Buzzard)	Kjellén 1992 (VC)
	Steppe Buzzard	Broekhuysen and Siegfried 1970 (WG), Kjellén 1992 (VC)
	Golden Eagle	Hoffman 1985 (VC)
	Northern Hobby	Kjellén 1992 (VC)
	Peregrine Falcon	Hunt et al.1975 (BM), Ward and Berry 1972 (BM), Kjellén 1992 (VC)

Migration type Timing difference	Species	Reference (method)[a]
Juveniles precede adults	Red Kite	Kjellén 1992 (VC)
	Western Marsh Harrier	Kjellén 1992 (VC)
	Northern Harrier	Broun 1949 (VC), Haugh 1972 (VC), Bildstein et al. 1984 (VC), Mueller et al. 2000 (BM)
	Eurasian Sparrowhawk	Moritz and Vauk 1976 (BM), Kjellén 1992 (VC)
	Sharp-shinned Hawk	Broun 1949 (VC), Mueller and Berger 1967a (BM), Mueller et al. 2000 (BM)
	Cooper's Hawk	Broun 1949 (VC), Hoffman 1985 (BM), Mueller et al. 2000 (BM)
	Northern Goshawk	Mueller et al.1977 (BM), Kjellén 1992 (VC), Mueller et al. 2000 (BM)
	Red-shouldered Hawk	Mueller et al. 2000 (BM)
	Red-tailed Hawk	Haugh 1972 (VC), Mueller et al. 2000 (BM) Geller and Temple 1983 (BM)
	American Kestrel	Haugh 1972 (VC), Mueller et al. 2000 (BM)
	Merlin	Mueller et al. 2000 (BM)
Return		
Males precede females	Bald Eagle	Harmata 1984 (BG, BM)[a]
	Red Kite	Brown and Amadon 1968
	Northern Harrier	Hamerstrom 1969 (BG), Haugh 1972 (VC), Bernis 1980 (VC)
	Montagu's Harrier	Robinson 1950 (BG)
	Pied Harrier	Brown and Amadon 1968
	Sharp-shinned Hawk (adults)	Mueller et al. 2003 (BM)

Table 12, continued

Migration type Timing difference	Species	Reference (method)[a]
	American Kestrel	Willoughby and Cade 1964 (BG), Smith et al.1972 (BG)
	Merlin	Newton et al.1978 (BG), Clark 1985b (BM)
	Gyrfalcon	Platt 1976 (BG)
Females precede males	Eurasian Sparrowhawk (juveniles)	Newton 1975 (BG), Moritz and Vauk 1976 (BM)
	Sharp-shinned Hawk (juveniles)	Mueller et al. 2003 (BM)
	Cooper's Hawk (juveniles)	Mueller et al. 2003 (BM)
	American Kestrel	Haugh 1972 (VC)
	Prairie Falcon	Enderson 1964 (BG)
	Peregrine Falcon	Mearns 1982 (BG)
Adults precede juveniles	Steller's Sea Eagle	Ueta and Higuchi 2002 (ST)
	Egyptian Vulture	Brown and Amadon 1968 (BG?)
	Northern Harrier	Haugh 1972 (VC), Mueller et al. 2003 (BM)
	Levant Sparrowhawk	Yosef et al. 2003 (BM)
	Sharp-shinned Hawk	Haugh 1972 (VC)
	Sharp-shinned Hawk (males only)	Mueller et al. 2003 (BM)
	Cooper's Hawk	Mueller et al. 2003 (BM)
	Northern Goshawk	Haugh 1972 (VC)
	Broad-winged Hawk	Haugh 1972 (VC), Matray 1974 (BG), Kerlinger and Gauthreaux 1985b (VC)
	Red-tailed Hawk	Haugh 1972 (VC), Mueller et al. 2003 (BM)
	Peregrine Falcon	Haugh 1972 (VC)

Source: Updated from Kerlinger 1989, 341–342.
[a]BG = arrival on breeding grounds; BM = banding during migration; ST = tracked by satellite; VC = visual count during migration; WG = shift in age or sex ratio on wintering grounds.

In terms of age-related differences, many researchers have suggested that inexperienced juveniles should follow rather than proceed adults on their first outbound migrations (see Chapter 6). But although this makes intuitive sense in terms of the relative navigational skills of the two age classes and although in many species juveniles do follow adults during the formers' initial outbound movements, in many other species, where adults remain on the breeding grounds and molt prior to migration, the reverse is true (see Table 12). Another potential reason for age-related differences in migration timing is that juveniles and adults often follow different routes on autumn migration. In Western Europe, for example, most juvenile Western Honey Buzzards fly directly across the Mediterranean Sea to wintering grounds in Africa, whereas adults tend to circumnavigate the water barrier (Schmid 2000; Hake et al. 2003). And in eastern North America, juvenile Sharp-shinned Hawks migrate principally along the Atlantic seaboard, whereas most adults migrate inland (Clark 1985a). In both instances, the difference is best attributed to inexperience on the part of first-time, juvenile migrants.

Another factor complicating age-related differences in migration timing is that adults often overwinter closer to their breeding grounds than do juveniles, possibly because doing so allows them to return to these areas earlier in spring (Mueller et al. 1977; Kjellén 1990). In some species, including the Northern Goshawk and the Rough-legged Hawk, males over-winter farther from their breeding areas than do females, whereas in many others the reverse is true. The first situation is often attributed to behavioral dominance or to climate, with smaller males either being outcompeted by larger females for the closer and presumably preferred wintering areas (Clark 1985a) or being less able to tolerate the ferocity of northern winters (Olson and Arsenault 2000); whereas the second situation is believed to result from males attempting to remain as close as possible to the breeding territories so that they are better able to reestablish them in the spring (Myers 1981).

Unlike outbound migration in autumn, there is considerable evidence for adults preceding juveniles during return migration in spring, and no evidence for the reverse (see Table 12). Why? Whereas adults are under strong selective pressure to return as early as reasonably possible to their breeding grounds (see above), individuals born during the previous season, which in many species do not breed until their third calendar year of life, are not (see below). Even so, the extent to which adult precedence in spring is due to age-related differences in navigational or flight efficiencies remains largely unstudied, and it, too, may play a significant role.

Delayed Return Migration by Juveniles

It has been known for some time that juveniles and subadults in many mi-gratory species "over-summer" on their winter quarters for one or more breeding seasons before undertaking their first return migration (Thomson 1926). Several researchers have suggested that the phenomenon is related to molt, with juveniles remaining on their wintering grounds so that they may molt during periods of reduced competition with adults and, therefore, be in better flight condition on their initial return migration. Others have sug-gested that delayed return migration is related to the cost of migration itself, particularly in species with *delayed maturation* or in which the likelihood of successful breeding during the second year is low (Poole 1989; Yosef and Alon 1997; Nebel et al. 2002). *Delayed return migration* occurs in a number of migratory raptors (Table 13), suggesting that it is of considerable ecologi-cal significance within the group. The phenomenon is best known in migra-tory populations of Ospreys. In the Afrotropics, over-summering juveniles from breeding populations in Europe move into apparently preferred habi-tats occupied by overwintering adults as soon as the latter depart for their breeding grounds in the spring (Prévost 1982 in Poole 1989). Similar shifts are thought to occur in the Neotropics. These observations, together with the fact that in sedentary populations of raptors the juveniles often disperse from their breeding grounds and remain dispersed for a year or more (e.g., Walls et al. 1999; Ferrer 2001) (Table 14), suggest that delayed return migration in juvenile raptors functions largely to reduce intraspecies competition with more experienced and, presumably, competitively superior adults at a time when juveniles are unlikely to breed anyway.

Insect Eating on the Wintering Grounds

Insects, particularly swarming insects such as termites and locusts, play major roles in the ecology of migratory raptors (Plates 5 and 6). A number of rap-tors, including Swainson's Hawks, Steppe Eagles, American Kestrels, Red-footed Falcons, Sooty Falcons, and Eleonora's Falcons, feed mainly on verte-brates, including birds and mammals, during the breeding season but switch to feeding largely on insects on the wintering grounds (England et al. 1997; Ferguson-Lees and Christie 2001). Unlike many migratory raptors whose movements simply track a "mobile climate regime" (*sensu* Nakazawa et al. 2004), and its associated resources and who basically feed on the same type of

Table 13. *Species in which delayed return migration by juveniles is known to occur*

Species	Comment	Reference
Osprey	Many British juveniles remain in Africa or wander no farther north than the Mediterranean region in their second year.	Martin 1992
	Many, if not most, juveniles remain in Central and South America or the Caribbean basin throughout their second year.	Brown and Amadon 1968
Western Honey Buzzard	Many juveniles remain in Africa throughout their second year.	Ferguson-Lees and Christie 2001
Crested Honey Buzzard	Many juveniles are believed to remain in southern Asia throughout their second year.	Ferguson-Lees and Christie 2001
Red Kite	Many western European juveniles remain in Iberia throughout their second year.	Brown and Amadon 1968; Ferguson-Lees and Christie 2001
Black Kite	Many, if not most, central European juveniles remain in northwest Africa, Spain, or France throughout their second year.	Cramp and Simmons 1980
Egyptian Vulture	Many juveniles remain in Africa at least throughout their second year (but see Yosef and Alon 1997).	Verner 1909; Mundy et al. 1992
Western Marsh Harrier	Many European juveniles return to breeding areas, but others wander considerably, with Danish, Dutch, and German birds recovered in Britain in April through September of their second year.	Cramp and Simmons 1980
Montagu's Harrier	Some European juveniles remain in their winter quarters, including Africa, throughout their second year.	Mead 1973; Morel and Roux 1966
Lesser Kestrel	Many juveniles apparently remain in Africa throughout their second year.	Ferguson-Lees and Christie 2001
Peregrine Falcon	At least some Arctic Alaskan juveniles probably remain south on their wintering grounds throughout their second year.	Cade 1960

Plate 1. Recently fledged Merlins in suburban Saskatchewan, Canada. The species began breeding and overwintering in suburban habitats in parts of its North American range in the mid-twentieth century. (Photo by Lynn Oliphant)

Plate 2. Sharp-shinned Hawk at a backyard bird feeder. Sharp-shinned Hawks, which feed on small birds attracted to bird feeders, recently have changed their migratory habits in eastern North America to take advantage of this new food resource. (Photo by H. P. Smith, Jr./VIREO)

Plate 3. Soaring Steppe Eagle. This species is a common soaring migrant above the deserts of the Middle East. (Photo by H. and J. Eriksen/VIREO)

Plate 4. Western Honey Buzzard, another common soaring migrant above the deserts of the Middle East. (Photo by W. S. Clark/VIREO)

Plate 5. Desert Locust. (Photo by Reuven Yosef)

Plate 6. Desert Locusts near Elat, southern Israel, during an outbreak in the autumn of 2004. This often-swarming species, which ranges across much of northern Africa, the Arabian Peninsula, and south-central Asia as far east as central India, is an important winter prey item for a number of Old World migrants, including Levant Sparrowhawks, Montagu's Harriers, and Lesser Kestrels. (Photo by Reuven Yosef)

Plate 7. A Black Kite attacked by a gull over the Strait of Gibraltar as the former attempts to reach southern Spain. (Photo by F. Barrios)

Plate 8. A Booted Eagle drying off along the Spanish coastline after having been driven into the waters of the Strait of Gibraltar by gulls. In spring, Yellow-legged gulls nesting in the area regularly harass low-flying migrants whenever the latter approach the former's breeding colonies. (Photo by F. Barrios)

Plate 9. North American Turkey Vulture, *septentrionalis* subspecies. (Photo by A. Morris/VIREO)

Plate 10. Turkey Vultures of the *meridionalis* subspecies traveling south to overwintering areas in central and northern South America. (Photo by N. G. Smith/VIREO)

Plate 11. Hawk shooters near Buskett Gardens, Malta. (Photo by the Maltese Ornithological Society/Hawk Mountain Sanctuary archives)

Plate 12. Western Honey Buzzard, shot near Buskett Gardens, Malta. Hundreds of migrating raptors are shot on the Maltese archipelago in the central Mediterranean each spring and autumn. (Photo by the Maltese Ornithological Society/Hawk Mountain Sanctuary archives)

Plate 13. An Amur Falcon on its wintering grounds in South Africa. The species undertakes the longest water crossing of any migratory raptor. Note the bird's long wings, which extend well beyond the tip of its tail. (Photo by W. Tarboton/ VIREO)

Plate 14. A Short-toed Snake Eagle after colliding with a high-tension power line. Power lines close to migratory bottlenecks, such as this one in southern Spain near the Strait of Gibraltar, pose a particular threat to migrants. (Photo by F. Barrios)

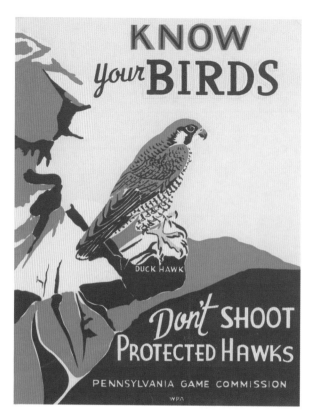

Plate 15. Pennsylvania Game Commission "Know your birds" poster from the 1930s.

Plate 16. Note that whereas both posters caution against shooting "protected hawks," the poster depicting the Northern Goshawk indicates that this species is "unprotected."

Table 14. *Species in which juveniles, but not adults, disperse from breeding areas in nonmigratory populations*

Type migrant	Species	Percentage of all species in this category
Complete	None	
Partial	Brahminy Kite, Palmnut Vulture, African White-backed Vulture, Eurasian Griffon, Pale Chanting Goshawk, Gabar Goshawk, White-tailed Hawk, Eurasian Buzzard, Mountain Buzzard, Wahlberg's Eagle, Verreaux's Eagle, Bonelli's Eagle, Australian Hobby, New Zealand Falcon, Brown Falcon, Peregrine Falcon	15%
Irruptive or local migrant	White-bellied Sea Eagle, African Fish Eagle, Hooded Vulture, Himalayan Griffon, Cape Griffon, Brown Snake Eagle, Bateleur, Crested Serpent Eagle, Madagascar Marsh Harrier, Crested Goshawk, Collared Sparrowhawk, Rufous-breasted Sparrowhawk, Black Sparrowhawk, Hawaiin Hawk, Rufous-tailed Hawk, Augur Buzzard, Jackal Buzzard, Tawny Eagle, Gurney's Eagle, Wedge-tailed Eagle, Changeable Hawk Eagle, Mountain Hawk Eagle, Greater Kestrel, Bat Falcon, Black Falcon	33%
Nonmigratory	Madagascar Cuckoo Hawk, Grey-headed Hawk, Long-tailed Buzzard, Barred Honey Buzzard, Pearl Kite, Madagascar Fish Eagle, Greater Fishing Eagle, Sulawesi Goshawk, Chestnut-flanked Sparrowhawk, Frances's Sparrowhawk, Variable Goshawk, Black-mantled Goshawk, Pied Goshawk, New Caledonia Sparrowhawk, Fiji Goshawk, Moluccan Goshawk, Slaty-backed Goshawk, Grey-headed Goshawk, Rufous-necked Sparrowhawk, New Britain Sparrowhawk, Madagascar Sparrowhawk, Henst's Goshawk, New Guinea Eagle, Spanish Imperial Eagle, African Hawk Eagle, Martial Eagle, Black-and-white Hawk Eagle, Cassin's Hawk Eagle, Blyth's Hawk Eagle, Javan Hawk Eagle, Sulawesi Hawk Eagle, Philippine Hawk Eagle, Wallace's Hawk Eagle, Crowned Hawk Eagle	32%

Sources: Based on Ferguson-Lees and Christie 2001 and other references.

prey year-round, the species mentioned above shift their niches substantially and feed on decidedly different types of prey at different times of the year. Most raptors that depend on insects in winter begin to shift their diets toward them in late summer on or near the breeding grounds and long before they reach their wintering areas, typically in response to the availability of late-summer swarming insects that are easily tracked and cropped by both adults and recently fledged juveniles, which by that time are no longer "tied" to their nests.

Migrants that depend on swarming insects on the wintering grounds typically travel long distances to find them (Newton 1998) (Chapter 8). All six of the world's complete migrants (Mississippi Kite, Swainson's Hawk, Red-footed Falcon, Amur Falcon, Sooty Falcon, and Eleonora's Falcon) (see Table 2) that breed entirely north of the equator and overwinter almost entirely south of it, for example, are principally insectivorous outside of the breeding season.

Breeding Ecology of Migrants

We know more about the breeding ecology of raptors than about any other aspect of their ecology (Newton 1979), and there are many indications that the breeding biology of migrants differs from that of sedentary species in a number of important ways. The percentage of raptors that are migratory increases with latitude (Kerlinger 1989), and, overall, migratory raptors tend to breed in more seasonal habitats than do sedentary birds of prey. The result is that during the breeding season, migratory populations encounter more temporally acute pulses of prey availability than do sedentary populations, providing them with a greater peak in prey abundance but also restricting prey abundance and, often, sufficiency, to much shorter time periods. As a result, migrants tend to have briefer breeding seasons than nonmigrants and often breed at higher densities. Seasonally abundant prey, particularly small mammals and small birds, are usually more important in the breeding-season diets of migrants than in those of sedentary species, and, overall, migrants are more likely to breed in open habitats than in forests, presumably because the former tend to offer greater flushes of seasonal prey than the latter. Furthermore, when migrants do breed in forests, they are more likely to do so in deciduous than coniferous woodlands, either because the former offer more suitable seasonal prey than the latter or because the former are less likely to be inhabited by nonmigrants (van Manen 2004).

Most migratory raptors are partial migrants and in many instances migratory and nonmigratory individuals from the same species nest side-by-side. Most researchers assume that under such circumstances, migrants and non-migrants nest assortatively (i.e., that migrants pair with migrants and that nonmigrants pair with nonmigrants) and, furthermore, that migrants nest later than nonmigrants. The extent to which both of these phenomenon occur, however, remains a largely unstudied topic, as is the degree to which the shorter breeding season of migrants affects clutch size and nesting success. Comparative studies of migratory and sedentary individuals breeding in the same population of partial migrants are likely to yield important insights in these areas.

Wintering Ecology of Migrants

Migratory raptors have been relatively little studied in winter, in part because they are no longer "attached" to a nest site and therefore are far more mobile and in part because many raptors overwinter in the tropics where field ornithologists are few and where most field work is focused on local species. Although the increased mobility that raptors have in winter sometimes brings them together both at large roosting assemblages (Moreau 1972; Newton 1976) and at superabundant food resources (Lack 1946; Sherrod et al. 1976; Prévost 1982 in Poole 1989), their increased freedom of movement also makes them more difficult to study for long periods. The extent of this mobility has becoming increasingly evident as a result of satellite tracking.

Three Lesser Spotted Eagles that bred in Germany and that overwintered in East Africa, for example, ranged across regions of between 11,000 to 25,000 km^2 (4000–10,000 mile^2), or areas about the size of the state of New Jersey (Meyburg et al. 1995a). The birds did so most likely while feeding on swarming termites in the shifting *Intertropical Convergence Zone* (ITCZ; see Chapter 7 for details regarding this climatic phenomenon). Even more impressive is the nomadic overwintering behavior of a Wahlberg's Eagle that bred in Namibia in southwest Africa and overwintered 3500 km (2200 miles) north in west-central Africa. The bird spent the first six weeks on its "wintering grounds" ranging across an enormous 60,000-km^2 (23,000 mile^2) West Virginia–sized area that included parts of Cameroon, Nigeria, and Chad, before "settling down" into a far smaller 5000-km^2 (1900-mile^2) area of savanna in northern Nigeria during the austral winter of 1994 (Meyburg et al. 1995b). Other species of satellite-tracked raptors, including Ospreys, which are far less nomadic in winter (Kjellén et al. 1997), show considerable interyear site fidelity to individual home ranges (Prévost 1982 in Poole 1989), as do American Kestrels overwintering in Florida (Layne 1982).

One thing that is certain about overwintering raptors is that local distributions are largely determined by food availability (Newton 1998). Most northern breeders overwintering within or south of the tropics do so either in coastal and inland wetlands (e.g., Turkey Vulture, Osprey, Western Marsh Harrier, Peregrine Falcon, etc.) or in open grasslands and savannas (e.g., Mississippi Kite, Swallow-tailed Kite, Levant Sparrowhawk, Swainson's Hawk, Steppe Buzzard, Steppe Eagle, Red-footed Falcon, Amur Falcon), seasonal habitats in which the benefits of year-round site fidelity are few and, consequently, densities of year-round residents are often quite low, and in which northern-winter flushes of productivity provide ideal feeding conditions for northern migrants (Alerstam 1990). Examples of such habitats include savannas and grasslands in East Africa, where overwintering populations of more than a dozen migrants feed on rain-season–related insect and rodent outbreaks (Auburn 1994; Newton 1998), and those of West Africa, where migrants congregate along dry-season fire lines to feed on locusts and grasshoppers (Thiollay 1971). In addition, migratory raptors that overwinter in forested habitats tend to do so along forest edges and in second-growth woodlands, rather than in large, undisturbed forested tracts.

There is no evidence that nonmigratory species competitively exclude migrants from undisturbed forests, or that predation risks are greater in large wooded areas than in other habitats (Newton 1995), and it seems likely that migratory raptors choose more open and disturbed habitats either because the latter are more similar to those they inhabit during the breeding season or because flushes of seasonally abundant prey are more readily available there, or both (Karr 1976). Whatever the reason, the arrival of large numbers of migratory species in open and semi-open habitats can significantly affect regional patterns of species diversity. The expansive grasslands and savannas of the Great Rift Valley of East Africa, for example, host larger numbers of raptors than adjacent tropical rainforests, a phenomenon that has important consequences for raptor conservation in the region. East Africa's wide-open spaces, and in particular some of its more productive farmland areas, also host nonbreeding populations of short-distance, intra-African migrants (Brown 1970). Perhaps not surprisingly, both types of migrants arrive at or near the beginning of the region's short rainy season, at the peak of prey availability. Remarkably enough, when the timing of the rainy season shifts among years, so does the arrival of the migrants, despite the fact that the latter includes an array of "ecologically very different species" (Smeenk 1974).

Populations of migratory raptors fluctuate across the landscape far more than those of resident species, reinforcing the notion that migrants are more mobile than breeding birds and, therefore, are better able to track and respond to local outbreaks of prey and regularly congregate to feed upon them (Brown 1970). The same pattern appears to hold across open habitats in South America where, as in Africa, the numerical bulk of intercontinental migrants appears to concentrate in winter (Jamarillo 1993; Kirk and Gosler 1994; Bildstein 2004). Overall, the picture is one of disproportionate use of seasonally or sporadically productive tropical, subtropical, and temperate open habitats by mobile predators, which in most instances are able to successfully track and subsequently "crop" outbreaks of seasonally superabundant prey across large geographic areas.

That said, it is important to remember that most species of migratory raptors have decidedly smaller species wintering areas than breeding ranges, and that in some species the difference is considerable. The African wintering ranges of at least three species of Eurasian migrants, the Short-toed Snake Eagle, Red-footed Falcon, and Northern Hobby are less than one-third the size of their breeding ranges, for example (Newton 1995). And the same is true of the South American wintering areas of at least two species of North American migrants, the Mississippi Kite and Swainson's Hawk. This, together with the fact that many of the areas used by overwintering raptors also host large numbers of intracontinental, short-distance migrants, as well as many resident species, has led some to suggest that overwintering migrants might compete both among and within species for food and other resources.

Competition among and between migratory and resident species was much in evidence in the farmlands of south-central Ohio when I studied raptors there for four winters in the 1970s (Bildstein 1987). In winter, the region's open-habitat raptor community is dominated by four species: Northern Harriers, Red-tailed Hawks, Rough-legged Hawks, and American Kestrels. Northern Harriers and Rough-legged Hawks are exclusively winter visitors in the region, whereas populations of Red-tailed Hawks and American Kestrels include both year-round residents and winter visitors. My estimates indicate that raptor numbers more than doubled on the site in winter, at the very same time that episodic snow cover reduced the availability of the small mammal prey base that all four principal species feed heavily on. All four species differ significantly in habitat use and hunting behavior, which led previous researchers to conclude that niche segregation reduced or even eliminated interspecies competition within the feeding guild (Craighead and Craighead 1956), something that was definitely not true in south-central Ohio.

Although individuals of all four species frequently hunted close together, sometimes to the extent that members of each species hunted the same field at the same time, and whereas many of these instances passed without obvious interaction, many of these juxtapositions resulted in increasingly predictable interspecies interactions. Most interactions involved a member of one species displacing a member of another species or its own, either from a hunting perch or from the air space over the field. Many of the interactions were subtle, with one bird leaving its perch or the air space when the second bird was still more than 200 meters away. And, indeed, on many occasions I did not see a second bird until after the first bird had departed. Although in such instances the departure of the first bird may have precipitated the arrival of the second as opposed to vice versa, the two were "interacting" nevertheless.

Overall, I recorded what I interpreted to be 172 overt instances of aggressive behavior during the course of the four-winter study or a rate of about one encounter for every four hours in the field. During 80 percent of these interactions, neither of the participants possessed prey. Most of the "prey less" encounters were directed at perched birds, and in most cases the perched bird was displaced. Smaller species were more likely to be the aggressor in interspecies interactions that did not involve prey than vice versa. When such interactions were successful, the approaching bird typically hunted in the area after the perched bird left. When they were unsuccessful, the approaching bird almost always left the area. Harriers and Rough-legged Hawks most frequently initiated such encounters.

Every time a harrier successfully displaced a Rough-legged Hawk the harrier subsequently hunted in the area. And every time they were unsuccessful the harrier left the area, presumably to hunt elsewhere. Interactions begun by Rough-legged Hawks differed from those initiated by harriers in being brief high-speed aerial pursuits, rather than the prolonged bouts of repeated diving. Rough-legged Hawks always succeeded in displacing the harriers they approached and always remained in the area after the encounters. Overall, these differences appear to reflect the different motivations of the two species. Rough-legged Hawks, which are approximately twice as massive as harriers, were attempting to determine if the harriers they approached possessed prey. Harriers, on the other hand, were trying to chase Rough-legged Hawks from areas in which they, themselves, wanted to hunt. The reason for the latter became apparent when I watched the two species interact when the harrier was feeding on or carrying prey.

Harriers, which were approached and chased by other raptors 28 times, or

33 percent of the time that I saw them with food, were the most frequent victims of prey robbery. Nineteen of the attempted piracies were made by Rough-legged Hawks or Red-tailed Hawks; the remainder were made by other harriers. Whether individual harriers suffered substantially as a result of this piratical behavior is not known. That they actively avoided hunting near Rough-legged Hawks, the most common interspecies pirate, and may have been forced into suboptimal feeding areas as a result, suggests that they were. Indeed, it seems likely that the successful perpetration of several robberies in rapid succession, especially during periods of severe weather, could significantly compromise a harrier's energy reserves. Harrier densities were relatively high in the area, and whether or not competition with larger raptors limited their numbers regionally is not clear. Nor is it clear if the numbers of Rough-legged Hawks, a species that was regularly pursued and sometimes pirated by larger Red-tailed Hawks, were, in turn, limited by the latter. American Kestrels, which by far were the smallest open-habitat raptors in the area, typically were not harassed by the three larger species, probably because they fed on less profitable insects rather than vertebrates whenever temperatures rose above freezing and the latter became active, and because they tended to hunt close to active farm buildings and other human-dominated landscapes, habitats the three larger species tended to avoid.

Consistent and strategic piracy, such as that reported above is known in only a few species of raptors, including, perhaps most notably, Bald Eagles, which regularly take prey from Ospreys, Ferruginous Hawks, Red-tailed Hawks, and Rough-legged Hawks, as well as other Bald Eagles (Prévost 1979; Fischer 1985; Jorde and Lingle 1988). Nevertheless, prey robbery has been observed on numerous occasions among migrants, both at stopover sites and en route (Woffinden 1986), as well as on the wintering grounds (Meinertzhagen 1959; Clark 1975; Temeles and Wellicome 1992; Pienaar 1996). Overall, it appears to occur most frequently in areas where several or more species of migrants aggregate around abundant or superabundant prey, particularly if the site also hosts large numbers of resident raptors. Although the ecological significance of such interactions remains largely unstudied, evidence involving Turkey Vultures in Central and South America indicates that it can be significant.

Each year, more than two million migratory Turkey Vultures from western North America pour into wintering areas that stretch from southern Central America into northern South America (Smith 1980; Porras-Peñaranda et al. 2004) (see Chapter 8 for details). The migrants involved are members of the *meridionalis* subspecies of the Turkey Vulture; the local residents belong to the smaller-bodied *ruficollis* subspecies. At close range and in good light, *ruficollis* is easily distinguished from *meridionalis* by their conspicuous yellow to whitish-green nape bands and crown patches, which the former lack (Ferguson-Lees and Christie 2001). In the seasonal Llanos wetlands of central Venezuela, where interactions between the migrant and resident Turkey Vultures were studied for three winters in the early 1990s, migrants dominated and bullied residents at carcasses, so much so that when migrants were present many residents shifted from seemingly preferred open areas to feeding in gallery forests along rivers. In addition, whereas the body condition of migrants improved during the winter dry season that of the residents declined, and even though carrion appeared to be abundant throughout the time of co-occurrence, residents did not begin breeding until the migrants had left. Taken as a whole, these observations indicate substantial competition between migrants and residents, at least in this part of Venezuela (Kirk and Currall 1994; Kirk and Gosler 1994). The same appears to be true along the Caribbean coast of northern Colombia, where the annual arrival of migratory Turkey Vultures boosts local populations sevenfold, and where *meridionalis* similarly dominates and displaces *ruficollis*. That the migrants are able to hold their own against local populations of Black Vultures, something the smaller resident Turkey Vultures apparently are not capable of, allows the migrants to exploit a wider range of food resources, including garbage dumps, which are dominated by Black Vultures at other times of the year (Koester 1982).

Synthesis and Conclusions

1. Migratory raptors are affected by ecological conditions in more than one part of the world (i.e., their breeding grounds, wintering areas, and the areas through which they migrate). Because of this, their ecology often is more complicated than that of sedentary species.
2. Migratory raptors fuel their migrations in three ways: first by laying down fat prior to migration and using fat to fuel their movements, second by feeding en route, and third by extracting energy from the atmosphere and using energy-efficient soaring flight to complete their journeys. Most raptors use all three to help fuel their migrations, with many depending heavily on two of the three to complete their migratory journeys.
3. Raptors flock more on migration than at other times of the year, most likely because flocking helps soaring migrants find thermals more ef-

fectively and because flocking helps experienced migrants find appropriate roosting sites and wintering areas.

4. Obligate flocking migrants synchronize their migrations more than nonflocking migrants, presumably to enhance the benefits of flocking.

5. Raptors time their outbound and return migrations based on many factors, including molt, body condition, the amount of available solar radiation for soaring, and the migrations of their avian prey.

6. In spring, the urge to reproduce plays a role in the timing of departure from the wintering grounds but not in the speed of migration.

7. Sex- and age-related differences in migration timing are widespread in raptors. General patterns include earlier return migration by adult males than by adult females and earlier return migration by adults, overall, than by juveniles.

8. Many juvenile raptors, particularly those belonging to species with delayed maturation, postpone returning to prospective breeding grounds for a year or more, most likely to reduce competition with adults.

9. The breeding season of migrants is often shorter than that of nonmigrants.

10. Many long-distance migrants that feed on small vertebrates while breeding switch to feeding on swarming insects on the wintering grounds.

11. Migrants tend to be more nomadic on their wintering grounds than on their breeding grounds.

12. The wintering ranges of most species of migrants are decidedly smaller than their breeding ranges, and competition for food, both among migrants and between migrants and local resident species, can be intense on the wintering grounds.

—7—

Migration Geography

Migration does not always follow straight lines,
but often finds its goal by an indirect path.
A. Landsborough Thomson, 1926

Many factors shape the geography of raptor migration. Significant extrinsic forces include seasonality in prey availability, the distribution and juxtaposition of the world's continental landmasses and oceanic islands, and the global patterns of predominant regional winds. Intrinsic factors include the flight mechanics and metabolic rates of the birds. This chapter reviews the basic principles and processes that determine the routes, directions, and distances traveled by outbound and returning migratory raptors and describes and characterizes the world's five principal migration flyways (see Figure 1) and the migrants that use them.

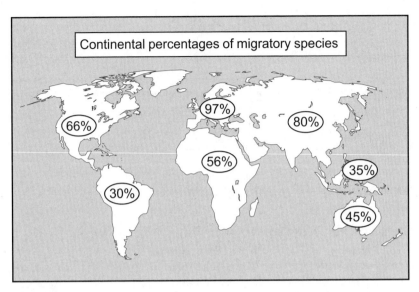

Figure 18. Percentages of partial and complete migrants in continental and regional raptor communities.

Seasonality and Global Geography

As is true for other birds, the tendency to migrate in raptors increases with increased seasonality on the breeding grounds (Kerlinger 1989; Berthold 2001). Thus, most species of raptors are sedentary at low latitudes, whereas most are migratory at higher latitudes. This is particularly true in the Northern Hemisphere, where large continental landmasses enhance the likelihood of significant seasonal shifts in both weather and prey availability (Kerlinger 1989; Helbig 2003) (Figure 18). Raptors breeding at high latitudes migrate largely along north-south axes, either from high latitudes to low latitudes in the same hemisphere, from high latitudes toward equatorial regions in both hemispheres, or from high latitudes in the Northern Hemisphere to equatorial and temperate regions in the Southern Hemisphere. Species with large geographic distributions, such as the Turkey Vulture, Osprey, Eurasian Buzzard, and Peregrine Falcon, often exhibit two or more of these patterns (Table 15).

There is no evidence that high-latitude Southern Hemisphere breeders migrate to equatorial and temperate regions in the Northern Hemisphere. And this is true among species that are long-distance migrants in similar situations in the Northern Hemisphere. It is not clear why this is so. One possibility is that because there is far less land at high latitudes in the Southern versus the

Table 15. *Geographic examples of largely north-to-south outbound movements of migratory raptors that breed in the temperate zone*

Species	Continental movements
Migrate from high to low latitudes in the Northern Hemisphere	
Turkey Vulture	Within eastern North America
Pallas Fish Eagle	Within Asia
Bald Eagle	Within North America
Cooper's Hawk	Within North America
Red-tailed Hawk	Within North America
Golden Eagle	Within Northern Hemisphere
Merlin	Within Europe and Asia
Migrate from high to low latitudes in the Southern Hemisphere	
Bicolored Hawk	Within South America
White-throated Hawk	Within South America
Red-backed Hawk	Within South America
Migrate from high latitudes in the Northern Hemisphere to equatorial regions	
Turkey Vulture	Western North America to neotropical Central and South America
Western Honey Buzzard	Europe and western Asia to tropical and subtropical Africa
Grey-faced Buzzard	Northeast Asia to South East Asia and Pacific Islands
Montagu's Harrier	Eastern Europe and western Asia to equatorial Asia and Africa
Steppe Eagle	Eastern Europe and northcentral Asia to equatorial Asia and Africa
Migrate from high latitudes in the Northern Hemisphere to the Southern Hemisphere	
Swainson's Hawk	North American to temperate South America
Red-footed Falcon ·	Eastern Europe and northcentral Asia to equatorial and temperate Africa
Amur Falcon	Northeastern Asia to equatorial and temperate Asia
Eleonora's Falcon	Mediterranean Europe and Asia to Madagascar
Northern Hobby	Europe to equatorial and temperate Africa

Northern Hemisphere, and because much of this landmass has a maritime rather than continental climate, both the opportunity and need for long-distance migration are reduced. Another possibility is that raptors breeding at high latitudes in the Southern Hemisphere do migrate transequatorially, but that their movements have yet to be discovered by raptor biologists.

Migration along latitudinal (i.e., north-south) axes is particularly charac-

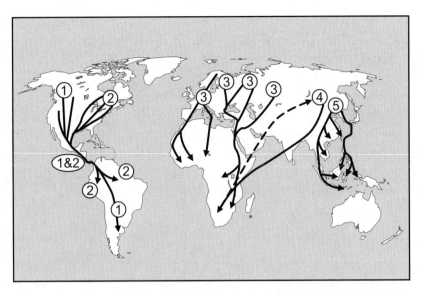

Figure 19. Long-distance outbound migration routes of (1) Swainson's Hawks, (2) Broad-winged Hawks, (3) Western Honey Buzzards, (4) Amur Falcons, and (5) Chinese Sparrowhawks. Note the elliptical outbound and return routes (dashed line) taken by Amur Falcons.

teristic of the world's 22 species of long-distance migrants, all but one of which (Osprey), breed entirely in the Northern Hemisphere, and 16 of which are transequatorial migrants (Figure 19). Many mid- to high-latitude migratory nesters have longitudinally expansive breeding ranges, and nine, including two complete migrants (Osprey and Rough-legged Hawk) and seven partial migrants (White-tailed Sea Eagle, Northern Harrier, Northern Goshawk, Golden Eagle, Merlin, Gyrfalcon, and Peregrine Falcon), are circumboreal species that breed in both the Old and New Worlds.

Fifty-seven percent (72 of 126) of the world's complete and partial migratory raptors are loath to cross bodies of water greater than 25 kilometers (km), and all but one of the world's principal migration flyways consist of series of largely overland corridors that allow migrants to avoid long-distance, over-water journeys. The only exception to this is the East Asian Oceanic Flyway (see Figure 1), which is dominated by species that use seasonal monsoonal winds, persistent trade winds, and sea thermals to complete their outbound and return movements.

Continental and oceanic landmasses, which together cover 29 percent of the earth's surface, are unevenly distributed across the globe. Seventy-two percent of all land is in the Northern Hemisphere, and 75 percent of that occurs in the Old World. In addition, excepting Antarctica, continental land-masses extend far closer "poleward" in the Northern Hemisphere than in the Southern Hemisphere, and 94 percent of all high-latitude land (i.e., land found more than 40° N or S) occurs in the Northern Hemisphere. Thus it is not surprising that 82 percent or 18 of 22 of the world's complete migrants breed principally or exclusively in Europe, Asia, or both and that all 22 species breed principally or entirely in the Northern Hemisphere. On the other hand, the breeding ranges of many partial migrants extend well into the Southern Hemisphere, and several partial migrants occur exclusively in the Southern Hemisphere, particularly in southern South America.

Water-Crossing Behavior

For most raptors, traveling over water is energetically more costly and poten-tially more dangerous than traveling over land. This is particularly so for fac-ultative and obligate soaring migrants. As a result, many raptors avoid even short water crossings whenever possible. Indeed, 55 percent of all complete migrants and 96 percent of all partial migrants rarely, if ever, undertake water crossings of 100 km or more; and 27 percent and 77 percent, respectively, rarely make crossings of as little as 25 km (see Table 2).

Even so, several raptor migrants regularly undertake long-distance, over-water journeys during their long-distance movements. Sea thermals, which facilitate low-cost, oceanic travel in small-bodied, powered-flight migrants traveling among subtropical and tropical islands and continental landmasses, are routinely used by several species, most notably the 150- to 200-gram Chi-nese Sparrowhawk and the 95- to 190-gram Amur Falcon (see Chapters 4 and 8 for details). Oceanic thermals, however, are restricted to the twin trade wind zones 30° to 5° N and S of the equator, and the presence of large land-masses for breeding and wintering at or near the beginnings and ends of these potential oceanic routes is limited globally. As a result, truly oceanic migra-tion remains an exceptional form of raptor migration. Additional species that regularly migrate long distances (i.e., >100 km) over water include Ospreys, Red-footed Falcons, Merlins, and Peregrine Falcons, all of which are capable of sustained powered flight.

Raptors flying over large expanses of water risk being "blown out to sea" by strong crosswinds. Consequently most raptors that migrate over water do so within the confines of the world's great seas, including the Mediterranean and Caribbean, or along Oceanic archipelagos. Exceptions include Amur Fal-cons that travel up to 2000 km across the Indian Ocean between peninsular

India and East Africa on outbound migration; Merlins that shuttle 800 km above the North Atlantic between breeding grounds in Iceland and wintering areas in Great Britain and Europe each spring and autumn; and New World Peregrine Falcons that regularly shortcut hundreds of kilometers across the temperate and tropical Atlantic between North and South America each autumn (Cochran 1985; Ferguson-Lees and Christie 2001).

Notwithstanding such movements, there are numerous examples of raptors spending considerable time and effort to avoid even relatively short overwater passages. Many migrants use peninsulas to reduce the amount of overwater travel. Well reported New World examples of this *peninsular effect* include Cape May Point in southern New Jersey at the mouth of Delaware Bay, 18 km north of Cape Henlopen, Delaware; Kiptopeke, Virginia, at the southern tip of the Delmarva Peninsula at the 22-km mouth of the Chesapeake Bay; and southernmost peninsular Florida and the Florida Keys along the 100-km-wide Straits of Florida. Old World examples include Falsterbo, southwestern Sweden, 25 km from eastern Denmark; Tarifa and the Rock of Gibraltar in southernmost Iberia, 14 km across the Strait of Gibraltar from northern Morocco; Cape Rachado, Malaysia, 22 km via the Strait of Malacca from Sumatra (Zalles and Bildstein 2000); and the 35-km long Sadamisaki Peninsula on Shikoku Island in southern Japan (Inoue 1993) (Figure 20). In such instances, most migrants travel the length of a peninsula before making an over-water crossing. Presumably the reverse (i.e., making landfall on a peninsula as opposed to departing from one) also occurs.

In addition to using peninsulas to shorten over-water travel, many migrants, including those traveling across broad fronts, *island hop* along oceanic archipelagos and continental islands in apparent attempts to reduce the costs and risks of over-water travel. New World examples of island hopping include flights of accipiters and falcons along the Florida Keys at the southern tip of Florida, north of the Florida Straits, and along the Sabana-Camaguey Archipelago in Cuba, south of the straits; and flights of Ospreys, Merlins, and Peregrine Falcons, along the Greater and Lesser Antilles of the West Indies. Old World examples include Rough-legged Hawks island hopping across the Bay of Bothnia, between eastern Sweden and western Finland; and Chinese Sparrowhawks and Grey-faced Buzzards island hopping from Korea through southern archipelago Japan, the Ryu Kyu Islands, and Taiwan to the Philippines, a mostly over-water journey spanning 25° of latitude, or about 2500 kilometers (Zalles and Bildstein 2000).

Observations at Cape May Point along the Atlantic coast of southern New Jersey, Whitefish Point at the eastern end of Lake Superior in northern

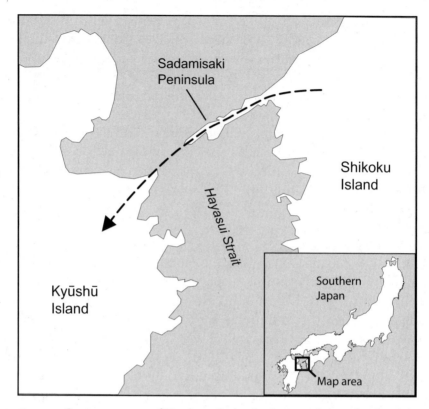

Figure 20. Over-water route of Northern Goshawks, Japanese Sparrowhawks, and Eurasian Sparrowhawks traveling across Hayasui Strait from Shikoku Island to Kyūshū Island, Japan. The "peninsular effect" of the flight reduces the length of the over-water flight from 50 km to 20 km.

Michigan (Kerlinger 1984, 1985), and the Strait of Gibraltar between southern Iberia and northern Morocco (Evans and Lathbury 1973; Finlayson 1992) provide examples of the extent to which migrating raptors modify their behavior to reduce the energetic costs and physical hazards of over-water travel.

Southbound raptors reaching Cape May Point in autumn face several options: They can continue south over water across 18-km-wide Delaware Bay to Cape Henlopen, Delaware; they can retreat more than 100 km over land northwest along the northern edge of the bay and make a less-than-2-km-wide river crossing at its headwaters on the Delaware River; or they can hedge their bets and backtrack part of the way and cross a narrower portion of the bay short of the river. Returning migrants reaching Whitefish Point in spring face either an 18- to 27-km crossing of Lake Superior depending on the direction of the flight or a circuitous detour of more than 120 km. Observations at the two sites suggest that (1) many individuals backtrack rather than undertake water crossings and (2) the likelihood of water crossings depends both on the weather and on the species involved. Obligate soaring species, for example, are far less likely to shortcut across water than are species that regularly engage in powered flight while migrating. Thus, whereas Turkey Vultures and Broad-winged Hawks crossed the two bodies of water on fewer than one-third of their approaches, Sharp-shinned Hawks and American Kestrels did so most of the time. Not surprisingly, widely distributed, broad-frontal migrants including Ospreys, Northern Harriers, and Peregrine Falcons, were most likely to continue over water, and they crossed on more than 90 percent of their approaches (Kerlinger 1985). Species that were the least likely to attempt over-water passage also were more likely to abort crossings and return to the shoreline than were species that regularly attempted crossings.

During most over-water flights, migrants flapped continually or intermittently flapped and glided en route. Three of 14 Peregrine Falcons appeared to engage in energetically efficient *dynamic soaring* (*sensu* Pennycuick 1972) while crossing. Although some individuals soared to great heights before attempting to cross, most flew relatively low over the water, often within 5 meters of the surface.

Observations of more than 7000 Sharp-shinned Hawks demonstrated that this species was more likely to undertake water crossings in light rather than strong winds and at higher rather than lower altitudes, both of which appear typical of most raptors. Sharp-shinned Hawks also were less likely to cross during cross winds than during head winds. And in fact, they rarely attempted passage in cross winds greater than 5 meters/second (11 mph), and those that did clearly tacked into the wind while doing so. Finally, sharpshins rarely crossed during periods of low visibility regardless of the wind.

Observations along the 14-km-wide Strait of Gibraltar corroborate these findings (Evans and Lathbury 1973; Finlayson 1992). Almost all of the 150,000 or so raptors that pass through this major migration bottleneck between Western Europe and West Africa each autumn do so either along an approximately 20-km-long windswept stretch of Spanish coastline between Punta Marroqui, Tarifa, and Punta del Carnero, Algeciras, or from the Rock of Gibraltar several kilometers to the east.

Nineteen species regularly migrate at the Strait of Gibraltar. In general, easterly (or Levante) crosswinds tend to forestall passage at the site, most likely because they increase the energetic cost of the trip as well as the likelihood of an individual being blown out to sea. Although migrants do cross in light rain, individuals rarely depart in heavy fog, and birds encountering fog over the Strait almost always abort their passage and return to shore.

Western Honey Buzzards—the most powerful flapping flyers among soaring migrants at the site—are less likely to be held back by crosswinds than are more lightly wing-loaded and far more buoyant Black Kites, which are typically grounded at such times. And, whereas many Western Honey Buzzards cross the Strait immediately upon reaching it, regardless of the wind, Black Kites that reach the Strait after midmorning on windy days typically spend the rest of the day and subsequent night roosting in Spain only to cross the next morning before daytime winds build. During periods of particularly persistent Levante winds, thousands of these soaring migrants have been known to spend a week or more alternately "kiting" into the wind by day and roosting in agricultural fields by night, waiting for the winds to abate. Although a few opportunistically hunt and scavenge for food at such times, most apparently feed little during such delays. Short-toed Snake Eagles and Booted Eagles also seem reluctant to cross at such times, and their numbers, too, tend to build in the area during adverse winds, as do the numbers of Eurasian Griffons, the largest obligate soaring migrant at the site.

Eurasian Griffons are ideally suited to short- and intermediate-distance soaring flight and, indeed, are masters of the technique. The species, however, is incapable of sustained flapping flight, and their reluctance to cross the Strait of Gibraltar under all but ideal soaring conditions is not without reason. Loathe to cross during strong levante crosswinds, Eurasian Griffons wait in Spain for weeks for better weather, and, indeed, many of the individuals that mass at the Strait never cross. When they do cross, most do so within two hours of noon, typically on warm days with light winds and, almost always, after having soared to great heights along the coast. Many of the birds, most of which are dispersing juveniles, cross in flocks of dozens to hundreds of individuals. Presumably, the vast majority successfully complete the overwater passages. There are many records, however, of griffons drowning in the Strait while attempting to cross in autumn, and in spring, griffons can be seen resting for hours after making landfall on the beaches near Tarifa, having reached the shoreline in apparently exhausting flapping flight within a few meters of the surface. Some even "land" in the surf and wade to shore.

And, as if the winds were not trouble enough, in spring Yellow-legged Gulls breeding along the Spanish coast regularly harass low-flying migrants that have the accidentally approached the former's breeding colonies. Although most of these interactions are brief, protracted engagements can result in struggling migrants being driven into the sea, where many drown (Plates 7 and 8).

At the other extreme, so-called broad-frontal migrants that regularly employ flapping flight rarely hesitate to cross the Strait. Three species of harriers, the Marsh, Hen, and Montagu's, readily cross in all but the strongest Levante winds, typically individually, along a wider stretch of the Strait and often at great heights. And the same appears to be true of Ospreys, Eurasian Sparrowhawks, Common Kestrels, Lesser Kestrels, and Northern Hobbies.

Viewed in their entirety, these observations suggest that a raptor's reluctance to fly over water has at least as much to do with the chance of being blown out to sea, or being physically incapable of sustained flapping flight, as with any attempt to minimize the energetic costs of its migratory journey overall.

Island Raptors

Despite the fact that most species of migratory birds of prey are reluctant to cross even narrow stretches of water, 50 species—or one in six species of all raptors—are insular forms that occur only on islands. Many island species are not closely related to raptors that regularly travel long distances over water, and the details of the colonization events that led to their existence are largely unexplored. No insular raptor is a complete or partial migrant, and only four are known to be irregular or local migrants. Migratory behavior is a rapidly evolving and readily reversible trait in birds, however (see Chapter 2), and it is well known that most island-restricted birds, particularly those on small islands, lose their migratory habits quickly, sometimes even before evolving into new species. Thus, the paucity of migratory behavior among island-restricted raptors is not unexpected. Nevertheless, migratory raptors would appear to be better equipped to fly long distances over water than sedentary raptors, and the question then becomes "to what extent has migration played a direct role in the formation of island-restricted species of raptors?"

To answer this question, one needs to recognize that there are different kinds of islands and that one must distinguish among them when trying to explain the origins of the raptors that inhabit them. *Oceanic islands,* which are formed from volcanic activity or coral reefs, have never been attached to the mainland. The mid-Pacific Hawaiian Islands, the most remote archipelago in the world, are an example of this island type, as are the tropical Galapagos Islands off the coast of Ecuador and the Lesser Antilles in the western Caribbean. *Continental islands,* on the other hand, were formerly portions of continents that subsequently split from the mainland. Cuba, the British Isles, Madagascar, and New Zealand are examples of this island type. Archipelagos are groups of near-adjacent islands that can be oceanic, continental, or of mixed origin (Newton 2003).

The theory of island biogeography suggests that islands that are relatively large and those that are relatively close to continents or to other islands will host larger numbers of species than will islands that are smaller and more remote (Mac Arthur and Wilson 1968). The theory also suggests that true island-endemic species—as opposed to continental species that also occur on islands—are more likely to occur on islands that are large enough to permit viable populations of ancestral stock to speciate and remote enough to forestall regular gene flow from mainland landmasses. These principles appear to hold for most species of island raptors.

Madagascar, a large continental island close to mainland Africa and its associated smaller islands, for example, is inhabited by 16 species of raptors, including 4 migrants and 11 island endemics. On the other hand, New Zealand, a group of two large and many smaller continental islands that is currently far from any other continental landmass, has only two species of raptors, one of which is endemic. Similarly, in the New World, Cuba, a large continental island in the Greater Antilles close to North America, has 16 species of raptors, including 9 migrants and 1 or, possibly, 2 endemics, whereas Puerto Rico, a smaller island in the same archipelago but farther from the mainland, has only 9 species, all of which possibly migrate, and no endemics.

Migration-Dosing Speciation

The phenomenon of *migration-dosing speciation* also appears to apply to island raptors. Each year, a small proportion of the world's more than 15 million migratory raptors is displaced from its principal migration route, either by ordinary wind drift, exceptional and episodic weather systems, including tropical cyclonic storms and El Niño events, or failed navigation systems. These so-called *vagrants,* or lost raptors, face one of four scenarios: (1) they die while lost on migration; (2) they reach an inappropriate wintering area and die shortly thereafter; (3) they survive in a new wintering area, reorient themselves in spring, and return to their traditional breeding areas; or (4) along with other misguided individuals from the same species, they reach a new wintering area and survive there but fail to initiate return movements the following spring. They eventually breed in isolation in the new area, and, subsequently, diverge sufficiently from their ancestral stock to form a new species. This fourth series of events is migration-dosing speciation (Bildstein and Zalles 2005).

Migratory raptors are likely candidates for migration-dosing speciation for several reasons. Most feed on "nutritionally substitutable" prey, making it easy for them to shift their diets to new prey bases. Many are soaring migrants that are vulnerable to disorientation via wind drift. And many migrate in large groups, thereby significantly increasing the likelihood of simultaneous vagrancy. Transequatorial migrants, in particular, would appear to be likely ancestral stock for such events given their obligate flocking behavior, relatively large populations (see Figure 39), and the fact that they episodically encounter tropical storms and associated hurricane-strength winds in regions through which they travel.

The most striking example of apparent migration-dosing speciation in raptors involves the accipiters of the South Pacific. Nineteen of the world's 50 members of the genus *Accipiter* occur on the islands of Melanesia in and around New Guinea and in Australia. The likely origins of most of these forms appears to be tied to the seasonal long-distance, over-water migrations of hundreds of thousands of super-flocking Chinese Sparrowhawks, a migratory accipiter that irregularly but predictably "doses" the region's oceanic and continental landmasses. In most years Chinese Sparrowhawks complete their outbound journeys from breeding areas in northeastern Asia to overwintering areas in the Philippines and Indonesia aided by monsoonal northwesterly winds, and their return journeys aided by easterly trade winds. Their migrations, however, carry the birds across a tropical cyclone belt in which episodic typhoons can misdirect and displace them downwind, as well as into a region where, during the springs of El Niño events, strong westerly winds replace the typical easterly trade winds. Climatic conditions such as these provide the backdrop for episodic, but inevitable, pulses of misdirected outbound movements in which flocks of Chinese Sparrowhawks are blown downwind onto islands in the region from which westbound return migration the following spring is compromised by significant headwinds. Such doses of vagrants provide seed stock for regional endemics.

Other examples of island endemics that most likely resulted from migration-dosing speciation include the Gundlach's Hawk of Cuba, which appears to be derived from the migratory Cooper's Hawk, and the Galapagos Hawk and the Hawaiian Hawk, both which are most likely derived from the migratory Swainson's Hawk (Riesing et al. 2003). All of this is not to say that every island endemic has been derived via migration dosing, and indeed, many insular raptors have no close migratory relative. Nevertheless, the dosing potential of migratory raptors appears to have played a significant role in seeding the world's oceanic and continental islands with many endemic species. The extent to which the same process may result in non-migratory continental forms, as some have implied (Snow 1978), remains to be investigated in detail.

Leapfrog and Chain Migration

Two important contrasting geographic patterns of migration have been long recognized in birds, including migratory raptors (Holmgren and Lundberg 1993). *Leapfrog migration* occurs when migratory populations that breed at high latitudes migrate substantially farther than and in fact "leap over" non-migratory or migratory populations breeding at lower latitudes, thereby reversing their latitudinal relationships between seasons. *Chain migration* occurs when migratory populations that breed at higher latitudes migrate approximately the same distance as those that breed at lower latitudes, thereby maintaining their latitudinal relationship between seasons.

Although leapfrog migration is known in many kinds of birds, some of the best examples come from partially migratory raptors, many of which breed across broad latitudinal gradients in the northern temperate zone. The Eurasian Buzzard, a widespread and well-studied *Buteo* that breeds across most of Europe and much of Asia, from 35° to 65° north, is a classic example of a leapfrog migrant. Buzzards are long-distance complete migrants at and near the northern limits of their range, short- or intermediate-distance partial migrants immediately to the south, and largely sedentary in southern portions of their range (Ferguson-Lees and Christie 2001). In Europe, for example, Eurasian Buzzards breeding in eastern Finland migrate more than 10,000 km to southern Africa each autumn, whereas Danish breeders travel no farther than southern France, and British, French, and Spanish buzzards are largely sedentary (Alerstam 1990). The same migration pattern occurs among populations in the Far East, with Siberian breeders leapfrogging over partially migratory and sedentary populations in Japan en route to wintering areas in Southeast Asia (Ferguson-Lees and Christie 2001). Additional examples of leapfrog migration involve Turkey Vultures in western North America (Palmer 1988), Egyptian Vultures in southern Europe and northern Africa (Mundy et al. 1992), Northern Harriers in North America (Palmer 1988), Western Marsh Harriers in Europe (Brown et al. 1982), Eurasian Sparrowhawks in Europe (Ferguson-Lees and Christie 2001), Wahlberg's Eagles (*Aquila wahlbergi*) in southern Africa (Steyn 1982), Common Kestrels in western Europe (Wallin et al. 1987), American Kestrels in North America (Smallwood and Bird 2002), and Peregrine Falcons in North America and, most likely, throughout much of their range elsewhere (Palmer 1988; Ferguson Lees and Christie 2001).

Individuals from more northern populations usually begin their outbound movements before conspecifics that breed farther south, presumably because autumn begins earlier at higher latitudes than at lower latitudes. Although northern populations most often consist of individuals that are larger than their southern counterparts, the reverse also can be true, and it is unclear whether or not leapfrog migration contributes to size differences among populations within individual species of raptors (Kerlinger 1989). It is likely that raptors engage in leapfrog migration because competition on the wintering grounds typically favors those with prior access to a territory, and more northern populations would be forced to migrate beyond areas already occupied by less migratory southern populations (Holmgren and Lundberg 1993). Exceptions to this rule occur when southern populations migrate in advance of northern populations thereby facilitating chain migration, which is what happens among juvenile Sharp-shinned Hawks in parts of the American West (Smith et al. 2003) and in Ospreys in southern Florida (Martell et al. 2004).

Elliptical or Loop Migration

Raptors often follow different routes during their outbound and return migrations. In many instances the differences reflect climatic or other external events, including prey availability, that favor different passages at different times of the year. In other cases the differences may result from *adaptive wind drift* (see Chapter 4 for details), a situation in which birds allow themselves to be wind-drifted early in their journeys to increase their rates of passage and later compensate for such drift near the end of their migrations (Alerstam 1990; Berthold 2001). In some instances outbound and subsequent return migrations are clockwise, in others they counterclockwise.

One well-studied example of *elliptical migration* involves the outbound and return migrations of Broad-winged Hawks in North America. Enormous, multithousand bird flocks of this species regularly funnel north and south along the Mesoamerican Land Corridor from southernmost Texas to northwestern Colombia each spring and autumn, as they shuttle back and forth between wintering areas in Central and South America, and breeding areas in North America. North of southern Texas, however, the Broad-winged Hawk flight traces an elliptical path, in which outbound migrants in autumn fly south considerably farther east than do returning migrants flying north in spring. As a result, many of the Broad-winged Hawks that pass Hawk Mountain Sanctuary and other hawkwatches in the Central Appalachian Mountains of eastern Pennsylvania on outbound migration in autumn find themselves migrating hundreds of miles west of these sites during return migration in spring. As a result, whereas Hawk Mountain Sanctuary records autumn counts of between 5000 and 10,000 Broad-winged Hawks each year, it records only several hundreds of birds in spring. Conversely, watchsites along the southern shorelines of Lake Erie and Lake Ontario northwest of the Sanctuary record large broadwing flights in spring, but small movements in autumn. The decidedly elliptical route taken by broadwings results from the region's prevailing winds, which are easterly below 35° north and westerly above it, together with the species propensity for adaptive wind drift (see Chapter 4 for details). Simply put, autumn outbound migrants from the core of the species breeding grounds in eastern Canada allow themselves to be pushed eastward through New England and the Mid-Atlantic states by the region's prevailing westerly winds, only to redirect their flight westward to circumnavigate the Gulf of Mexico farther south. In spring, the same birds allow themselves to drift westward through northern Mexico by the region's prevailing easterly winds, only to redirect their flight eastward once they have reached the largely insurmountable water barriers of Great Lakes Erie and Ontario farther north.

Another well-studied example of elliptical migration involves the clockwise route taken by land-based soaring migrants that circumnavigate the Red Sea each autumn and spring. Outbound migrants, including Steppe Buzzards and Steppe Eagles follow a course east of the Red Sea and enter Africa via the Bab el Mandeb strait—the "gate of tears" in Arabic—at the southern end of the Arabian Peninsula; returning birds follow a more westerly course along the Eastern Desert of Egypt, crossing into the Middle East at the Sinai Peninsula at the northern end of the Red Sea (Figure 21). Presumably, the route results from adaptive wind drift and the birds' reluctance to cross the Red Sea at all but its narrowest points (Yosef and Alon 1997; Shirihai et al. 2000). Another Old World example of elliptical migration involves Black Kites breeding in Switzerland and Short-toed Snake Eagles breeding in northwestern Italy. Both migrate to Africa via the Iberian Peninsula and the Strait of Gibraltar at the western end of the Mediterranean, but return to their breeding grounds via the Sicilian Channel, Sicily, and Italy, in the cen-

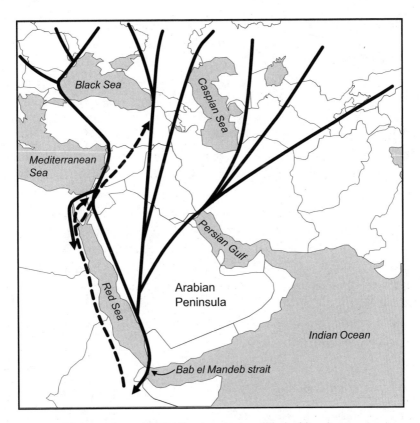

Figure 21. Major outbound (solid lines) and return (dashed lines) migration corridors in Middle East portions of the Eurasian–East African Flyway. Return routes that differ significantly from outbound routes are indicated with dashed lines. Note the many deflection lines caused by the region's bodies of water and the elliptical route of migrants around the Red Sea.

tral Mediterranean (Schifferli 1967; Agostini et al. 2002a). Additional "Mediterranean" examples of elliptical migration involve Pallid Harriers and Red-footed Falcons, both of which travel chiefly through the eastern Mediterranean, on outbound migration but return along more westerly routes that cross the central part of the Sea (Forsman 1999; Corso and Cardelli 2004).

The most spectacular loop migration is the 7000- to 12,000-km elliptical journey undertaken by the Amur Falcon, a species that breeds in northeastern Asia and overwinters in southern Africa. The outbound track involves southerly movements that take the birds along the eastern edge of the Tibetan Plateau, followed by southwesterly and then westerly treks across both the Indian peninsula and Indian Ocean, with landfall occurring in equatorial East Africa. The return track has the birds traveling north through East Africa and, thereafter, northeast across the Arabian Peninsula, and from there across central Asia north of the Tibetan Plateau and on to Amurland in northeastern Asia (see Chapter 8 for details). Other elliptical migrations in Asia include those of Chinese Sparrowhawks and Grey-faced Buzzards, both of which island hop in large numbers on outbound migration across Japan, Taiwan, and the Philippines each autumn, but return to their breeding grounds in spring via mainland China rather than Japan (McClure 1998), and White-tailed Sea Eagles from eastern Siberia that migrate to and from wintering areas on the northern Japanese island of Hokkaido via a circuitous 5400-km (3400-mile) route that involves a complete circumnavigation of the 1,530,000 km^2 (590,000 mile^2) Sea of Okhotsk (Ueta et al 1998).

Elliptical migration is a common and widespread phenomenon in raptor migration. Although adaptive wind drift and predominant winds help to explain at least some of the circularity in routes taken, the phenomenon remains a poorly understood and often underappreciated aspect of raptor-migration geography.

Temperate versus Tropical Migration

With few notable exceptions, almost all of what we know about raptor migration is based on observations of migrants in the northern temperate zone, and particularly, in North America, Europe, and the Middle East, a not surprising phenomenon given that most hawkwatches and raptor biologists are in these parts of the world (Broun 1949; Harwood 1975, 1985; Heintzelman 1975, 1986; Kerlinger 1989; Shirihai et al. 2000; Bildstein and Klem 2001). Nevertheless, more than half of all long-distance migrants, as well as numerous short- and intermediate-distance migrants, are transequatorial travelers that spend substantial amounts of time migrating to, within, and, in a few instances, across the tropical regions of the world. Studies of their movements are the new frontier of raptor-migration science.

Several circumstances suggest that raptors might behave differently in tropical regions than in temperate regions. Most of the world's principal migration flyways include tropical bottlenecks, points at which long-distance transequatorial migrants assemble in numbers far greater than in temperate areas. Solar energy is more available in the tropics than in the temperate zone, and thermals are decidedly stronger and more readily available to soaring migrants there. Finally, the trade wind zone stretching from 5° to 30° north and south of the equator permits migrants to travel long distances over water on sea thermals there. Although much remains to be learned about how raptors migrate in the tropics, what is known suggests that migrants behave differently there than in the temperate zone. The information comes from two sources: observations at recently initiated migration watchsites in the region and satellite tracking of transequatorial migrants.

It has been known for some time that flock size increases appreciably toward the equator, particularly among soaring migrants (Bildstein and Zalles 2001). Only recently, however, have biologists recognized a relationship between increased flock size and decreased wing flapping, and thus a link between flock size and energy expenditure en route (see Chapter 4 for details). The impact of this relationship on individual migrants has yet to be studied in detail, but one of its obvious consequences, a substantial increase in flight efficiency, may explain how many long-distance migrants manage to complete their transequatorial journeys while feeding little, if at all, during the journey.

Increased solar radiation, too, contributes significantly to increased migration efficiency in the tropics. Thermal streets are far more common in tropical regions, and their relative abundance there increases the likelihood of *linear soaring* (Smith 1985a). Increased linear soaring, together with the confluence of regional corridors into continental and intercontinental flyways, produce enormous rivers of raptors that characterize many tropical hawkwatches (Loftin 1963; Sutton and Sutton 1999) (Figures 22 and 23). Another factor enhancing raptor migration in the tropics is that the sun rises and sets more vertically there. This means that thermals form earlier in the morning and last later in the day, which, in turn, means that soaring migrants can begin migrating earlier in the day and continue to migrate later in the afternoon. And indeed, this is precisely what happens at the Kéköldi Indigenous Reserve in coastal Costa Rica where soaring migrants, including Turkey Vultures, Broad-winged Hawks, and Swainson's Hawks, typically begin their flights within an hour of sunrise. Turkey Vultures, in particular, start early in the day, usually at first light, while soaring in weak but persistent, near-shore thermals created when the warm shallow waters of the Caribbean heat the cooler air above, and then move inland later in the day as the rising sun warms coastal beaches and adjacent lowlands farther inland. On most days, raptor migration continues until about an hour before sunset.

Another significant difference between tropical and temperate zone migration is that rain affects migration less in the tropics than in higher latitudes. At most temperate zone hawkwatches, for example, soaring migrants often

Figure 22. Small portions of mixed flocks of Turkey Vultures, Broad-winged Hawks, and Swainson's Hawks at the Kéköldi Indigenous Reserve, Costa Rica. (Photo by the author)

Figure 23. Mixed flocks at Ancon Hill, Panama. Multithousand bird flocks such as these typify movements of obligate soaring migrants in the tropics. (Photo by the author)

suspend movements during periods of light rains, and heavy rains almost always forestall the flight. In Costa Rica, on the other hand, light rains pose little, if any, noticeable impediment to long-distance migrants, and isolated bands of heavier rains are often bypassed by flocks that shift direction and circumnavigate them. Although heavy and extensive rains sometimes force migrants to interrupt their flight and roost during the day (see Smith 1985b), many continue to migrate even on heavily overcast, rainy days when soaring conditions were marginal and forward progress was slowed to rates of less than 5 km an hour (Bildstein and Saborío 2000). This, together with other differences mentioned above, may explain why migrants travel faster in the tropics than in the temperate zone. North American Swainson's Hawks and Peregrine Falcons tracked by satellite on outbound and return migrations to and from wintering areas in Central and South America, for example, increased their daily rates of travel by 35 percent and 10 percent, respectively, when traveling through the tropics compared with the temperate zone (Fuller et al. 1998). Although it is unclear if the birds did so by extending the duration of their daily flights or by flying more rapidly in stronger thermals, the observations above suggest that shifts in both aspects of flight behavior may have been involved.

Intratropical Migration

Seasonal change in day length is minimal in the tropics. At the equator, every day of the year is exactly twelve hours long, as is every night. Days do lengthen and shorten seasonally within the tropics as one moves away from the equator, but not as much as in the temperate zone. Seasonal temperature fluctuations in the tropics are modest as well, with daytime highs typically peaking at about 29°C (85°F) year-round and day-to-night shifts being greater than seasonal ones overall. On the other hand, rainfall is often seasonal in the region, sometimes remarkably so. Biologists have known for some time that seasonal differences in rainfall affect tropical plants and animals in much the same way as seasonal shifts in temperature affect temperate zone counterparts, and tropical raptors are no exception to this rule.

Most tropical raptors are sedentary, stay-at-home species that time their breeding activities to take advantage of seasonal fluctuations in prey availability; others, however, migrate within the tropics, typically among regions that exhibit pronounced wet-dry cycles. The latter comprise a small group of several dozen raptors known as *intratropical migrants*. Distances traveled within the tropics often are modest, and in many instances the species involved appear to be partial rather than complete migrants. Consequently, for many intratropical migrants, the movements produce a shift in the center of species abundance without substantially changing the perimeter of the species' range. Because of this, the phenomenon can be difficult to study. Nevertheless, several patterns are beginning to emerge, particularly among a group of African migrants whose movements appear to be closely tied to those of the *Intertropical Convergence Zone* (ITCZ), a latitudinal band of heavy rains that wavers seasonally north and south across the world's tropical regions.

Between 5° north and 5° south, the heated and moist northeast and southeast trade winds converge in a Hadley cell to form a low-pressure equatorial region sailors call the "doldrums" because of general windlessness. With few winds and high solar radiation, convective activity within the ITCZ is both intensive and extensive, with moisture-laden clouds forming continually to create all-but-daily midday rains, making the region one of the wettest places on earth. This band of profound precipitation straddles the tropics year-round. This so-called meteorological equator shifts northward in boreal summer and southward in the winter, creating a series of rainy seasons across more than 20° of tropical latitudes. The cell's effect on intratropical migrants is best known in the Afrotropics, where many of the world's 39 species of *rains migrants* occur (see Table 2).

Rains migrants there include the African Cuckoo Hawk, a small and rather secretive kite that moves north in July and September on the heels of the retreating ITCZ in West Africa; the Black-shouldered Kite, a pointed-winged raptor that migrates to avoid the rains; and the African Swallow-tailed Kite, a somewhat nomadic species, that in equatorial West Africa moves north into the sub-Saharan Sahel to breed *during* the rains. In the New World, the Snail Kite—a wetland specialist that feeds mainly on apple snails (*Pomacea* spp.), and whose migrations and seminomadic movements are closely tied to both water depth and hydrological periods—also migrates within the tropics in response to the shifting in the ITCZ. Shifts in the location of the meteorological equator also affect the movements of longer-distance, transtropical migrants, several of which, apparently, time and direct their flights to take advantage of the belt's convective thermals (Auburn 1994).

Although much remains to be learned about intratopical migration, what is known suggests that raptors in the tropics, as elsewhere, are driven principally by food availability and the limitations of their own, intrinsic flight mechanics.

Altitudinal Migration

Altitudinal migration consists of relatively short-distance movements between areas of high and low altitudes, usually along mountain slopes. Such movements occur because in most places temperatures decrease at a rate of approximately 0.7°C per 100 meters in elevation up to about 10 kilometers above sea level (Whiteman 2000). Species inhabiting exceptionally high-mountain plateaus and mountain ranges—including Egyptian Vultures, Indian White-backed Vultures, Long-billed Vultures, and Lesser Fishing Eagles in the Himalayas, and Cinereous Harriers and Aplomado Falcons in the Andes (Ferguson-Lees and Christie 2001)—are prone to this type of migratory movement. Because the distances involved tend to be short and because the movements often are coupled with longer latitudinal migrations, altitudinal migration is decidedly less well-understood than its latitudinal counterpart. Nevertheless, at least 32 species of partial migrants and 13 species of irruptive or irregular migrants are believed to be altitudinal migrants within portions of their ranges, and two neotropical raptors, the Grey-headed Kite and White-breasted Hawk, which are not known to migrate otherwise, are thought to migrate altitudinally (see Table 2).

Broad-Front versus Narrow-Front or Corridor Migration

Most birds of prey are territorial and dispersed on their breeding areas, and some are so even on their wintering grounds. As a result, many begin their migrations in parallel across a wide front, with individual birds moving as singletons rather than in flocks (Bednarz and Kerlinger 1989) in what is called *broad-front migration.* The extent to which such movements coalesce into more concentrated, *narrow-front migration* depends on several factors, including overall distances traveled and regional geography, and the flight mechanics and the feeding and social behavior of the birds themselves. Under most circumstances, combinations of these factors produce predictable species- and geographic-specific regional migration routes and corridors that in some instances coalesce into major flyways.

Everything else being equal, raptors that migrate short distances are more likely to travel principally across broad fronts than are those that migrate long distances. Most likely this is because shorter journeys provide less time for individuals to coalesce into flight-streams than longer journeys, and because short-distance migrants are less likely to encounter leading or diversion lines en route than are long-distance migrants. Also, many short-distance migrants complete their journeys using flapping flight, presumably because they are able to store sufficient fat to do so. Doing so reduces both travel time and wind drift en route, both of which, in turn, reduce the likelihood of corridor travel.

Although the migrations of all raptors appear to be affected by regional geography, obligate soaring migrants in particular are prone to *canalization* (*sensu* Berthold 2001) by mountain ranges, water barriers, and abrupt habitat discontinuities. As a result, long-distance soaring migrants, including Turkey Vultures and many kites, buteos, eagles, and, in a few cases, accipiters, are known to coalesce by the dozens to hundreds in high-latitude regional corridors and in low-latitude intercontinental flyways by the thousands to tens of thousands, most likely because doing so enhances their energy efficiency en route. As a result of increasing coalescence en route, narrow-front migration is particularly common in the tropics, even among species that often migrate across broad fronts elsewhere. Ospreys, for example, which characteristically migrate alone or in small flocks in the temperate zone (Ferguson-Lees and Christie 2001), congregate in larger numbers along traditional corridors in the New World tropics, where flocks of more than 50 individuals and daily watchsite counts of more than 600 birds have been reported (see Chapter 8 for details).

Several species of long-distance migrants begin to gather in flocks even before beginning their journeys. In late summer, Swallow-tailed Kites breeding in the southeastern United States assemble by the hundreds at nocturnal roosts in southern Florida before migrating across the Gulf of Mexico to South America (Millsap 1987), and Swainson's Hawks aggregate by the hundreds to the thousands across the grasslands of western North America while gorging on grasshoppers and other insects, before migrating to Argentina and elsewhere in South America (England et al. 1997) (see Chapter 9). In both instances, premigratory flocking appears to function, at least in part, to assemble migrants for massed long-distance travel in soaring flight along major flyways. Flocking seems to be particularly important in species in which first-year migrants follow experienced adults, and in which intergenerational learning helps maintain the geography of "traditional" flyways along *thermal corridors* (*sensu* Schüz et al. 1971) providing predictable soaring opportunities for migrants (Berthold 2001). Well-established regional *migration corridors* and intercontinental *migration flyways* often converge on narrow land bridges, including the Isthmus of Tehuantepec and Isthmus of Panama in the New World, and the Iberian, Sinai, Arabian, and Malay peninsulas in the Old World, and along island archipelagos, such as the Japanese, Ryu Kyu, and Philippine islands in the Far East, all of which extend the possible of "overland" travel. *Migration bottlenecks* such as these create major migration flyways, five of which are recognized globally: (1) the Trans-American Flyway, (2) the Western European–West African Flyway, (3) the Eurasian–East African Flyway, (4) the East-Asian Continental Flyway, and (5) the East-Asian Oceanic Flyway (see Figure 1) (Bildstein and Zalles 2005). All five flyways are chiefly north-south routes that extend for at least 5000 km. All but one (the Western European–West African Flyway) are transequatorial, and all but one (the East–Asian Oceanic Flyway) are almost entirely overland routes.

Major Raptor-Migration Flyways

Trans-American Flyway

Each autumn, as many as ten million raptors travel along this 10,000-km overland system of regional corridors that stretches from central Canada to southern South America (see Figure 1). The only major flyway in the New World, the Trans-American is far and away the world's most numerically important raptor-migration flyway. Four regional migration corridors join to form the flyway in North America.

1. The Eastern Corridor, which is dominated by Broad-winged Hawks, funnels large numbers of migrants along the Appalachian Mountains, the northern shorelines of lakes Ontario and Erie, and the northwestern shorelines of Lake Superior.
2. The Prairie Corridor, which is somewhat diffuse and little studied, funnels southbound Swainson's Hawks across Texas into northeastern Mexico.
3. The Rocky Mountain Corridor, which is dominated by accipiters and Golden Eagles, funnels migrants south into northern Mexico.
4. The Intermountain Corridor, which is dominated by accipiters and buteos in the east and by Turkey Vultures in the west, funnels birds from the Great Basin and elsewhere in far western North America.

Additional North American corridors not directly connected to the Trans-American Flyway include the Atlantic Coast Corridor, which stretches from New England to peninsular Florida and from there into the Caribbean and the Pacific Coast Corridor, along which western accipiters and buteos shuttle north and south within the continent (Zalles and Bildstein 2000; Hoffman and Smith 2003).

In northern Mexico the Eastern, Prairie, Rocky Mountain, and Inter-mountain corridors join to form the Mesoamerican Land Corridor, a 4000-km anastomosing route that extends from northern Mexico southeast into eastern Panama (see Figure 19). Here, the flight is made up of long- and short-distance movements of 32 species of North American and Central American raptors that include Ospreys, Turkey Vultures, three species of kites, three accipiters, eight buteos, and five falcons. Species migrating in the thousands include Turkey Vultures (2,000,000 [minimal estimate extrapo-lated from visual counts at full-season autumn hawkwatches in Mexico and Costa Rica]), Ospreys (5000), Swallow-tailed Kites (1000), Plumbeous Kites (1000), Mississippi Kites (300,000), Northern Harriers (1000), Sharp-shinned Hawks (5000, northern part only), Cooper's Hawks (2000, north-ern part only), Broad-winged Hawks (1,500,000), Swainson's Hawks (800,000), American Kestrels (3000, northern part only), Merlins (1000), and Peregrine Falcons (5000) (Bildstein and Zalles 2001).

During outbound migration, the flight-lines of the four most numerous migrants in the corridor (Turkey Vulture, Mississippi Kite, Broad-winged Hawk, Swainson's Hawk) converge in coastal Veracruz, Mexico, where be-tween three and six million raptors are counted in most years (see Veracruz River-of-Raptors, Chapter 9). South of Veracruz, most Turkey Vultures and Swainson's Hawks cross to the Pacific slope at Isthmus of Tehuantepec before entering Guatemala, whereas most of the Broad-winged Hawks continue east on the Caribbean slope across the Péten of Guatemala and into northwestern Honduras.

Visual counts of migrants are sporadic in El Salvador, Honduras, and Nicaragua, and the geography of the flight is less well understood there than elsewhere in the region. Satellite tracking of outbound Broad-winged Hawks and Swainson's Hawks, together with visual tracking of Turkey Vultures in Chiapas, Mexico, however, suggest that whereas large numbers of broad-wings travel along the Caribbean slope of the continental divide well into central Honduras, most Swainson's Hawks and vultures remain along the Pa-cific slope through this portion of the flyway (Tilly et al. 1990; Fuller et al. 1998; Haines et al. 2003). The two flight-lines join again in northwestern Nicaragua, and the combined movement proceeds southeast along the coastal Pacific coastal plain through southwestern Nicaragua.

Once the flight enters the lowlands of northwestern Costa Rica, most mi-grants turn east and track the foothills of the Caribbean slope into Panama. In central Panama most of the flight again crosses to the Pacific slope west of the Panama Canal before entering northwestern Colombia in South America. Falcons and Ospreys migrating coastally in Mesoamerica appear to join the main flight-line whenever it comes to within several kilometers of the coast.

Once the flyway reaches Colombia, the flight-line turns almost directly south, with most birds following the Magdalena Valley toward Tolima in central Colombia before entering the Amazon lowlands on their way to east-central Bolivia and, from there, the Pampas of northeastern Argentina. In addition, some of the migrants, including many Swallow-tailed Kites, travel through Colombia along the Pacific slopes of the Andes, thereafter crossing that range to the east near the border with Ecuador (K. Meyer, pers. comm.).

Broad-winged Hawks begin to drop out in large numbers and settle into wintering areas as far north as southern Nicaragua and northern Costa Rica, and most members of this species appear to have left the principal flight-line before it reaches southern Colombia, as, apparently, have most Turkey Vultures. Large numbers of Mississippi Kites and Swallow-tailed Kites continue along the flyway at least as far south as central Bolivia, and almost all Swainson's Hawks remain on it until the flyway ends in Argentina (Bildstein 2004; M. Bechard, C. Marquez, and K. Meyer, pers. comm.).

In spring, many Trans-American migrants retrace their outbound journeys. Even so, several differences are apparent. In Mesoamerica, for example, returning migrants are more likely to tract the Caribbean slope of central Panama (versus the Pacific in autumn), and the Pacific slope of Costa Rica (versus the Caribbean in autumn), most likely because of seasonal differences in the weather. And in North America, most returning Broad-winged Hawks migrate west of their principal outbound routes, presumably because of easterly wind drift encountered in northeastern Mexico and southern Texas (Skutch 1945; Smith 1985b; Kerlinger 1989).

In Canada and the United States, the geography of the Trans-American Flyway is as well understood as that of any major migration corridor, and recent field work in Mesoamerica is quickly closing gaps in our understanding in that part of the flyway as well (Zalles and Bildstein 2000). By comparison, the flyway is relatively little studied south of Mesoamerica. Significant hawkwatches along North American and Mesoamerican portions of this route include Hawk Mountain Sanctuary, in eastern Pennsylvania; Hawk Ridge, in northeastern Minnesota; Golden Gate Raptor Observatory, at the mouth of San Francisco Bay, California; Hazel Bazemore State Park, in Corpus Christi, Texas; Veracruz River-of-Raptors, in coastal Veracruz, Mexico; and the Kéköldi Indigenous Reserve, in coastal Talamanca, Costa Rica (Table 16) (see also Chapter 9).

Table 16. *Representative ≥ 10,000-migrant, full-seasonal hawkwatches along the five major migration flyways and associated corridors*

Hawkwatch and location	Average count and number of species of regular migrants
Trans-American Flyway	
Tadoussac Bird Observatory (Quebec, Canada)	20,000 (12)
Holiday Beach Migration Observatory (Ontario, Canada)	70,000 (15)
Quaker Ridge (Connecticut, United States)	20,000 (14)
Montclair Hawk Lookout (New Jersey, United States)	25,000 (13)
Hawk Mountain Sanctuary[a] (Pennsylvania, United States)	18,000 (16)
Hawk Ridge Nature Reserve[a] (Minnesota, United States)	60,000 (16)
Goshute Mountains (Nevada, United States)	11,000 (17)
Golden Gate Raptor Observatory (California, United States)	23,000 (19)
Corpus Christi Hawkwatch (Texas, United States)	800,000 (16)
Veracruz River-of-Raptors (Veracruz, Mexico)	>3,000,000 (15)
Kéköldi Indigenous Reserve[a] (Talamanca, Costa Rica)	>1,000,000 (15)
Concepción[a] (central Bolivia)	40,000 (13)
Western Europe–West African Flyway	
Falsterbo (southwestern Sweden)	30,000 (10)
Stevns Klint (northeastern Denmark)	18,000 (19)
Fort L'Ecluse (southeastern France)	16,000 (13)
Leucate (southern France)	>16,000 (17)
Organbidexka (southwestern France)	24,000 (17)
Straits of Messina (eastern Sicily)	18,000 (17)
Strait of Gibraltar[a] (southernmost Spain)	380,000 (19)
Rock of Gibraltar[a] (Gibraltar)	20,000 (17)
Cap Bon[b] (northern Tunisia)	10,000 (22)
Eurasian-East African Flyway	
Burgas (eastern Bulgaria)	>65,000 (30)
Chokpak Pass (southern Kazakhstan)	15,000 (28)
Bosporus[a] (northwestern Turkey)	75,000 (31)
Borçka (northeastern Turkey)	>210,000 (31)
Dana Wildlife Reserve[a] (west-central Jordan)	>10,000 (19)
Northern Valleys (north-central Israel)	470,000 (27)
Elat[b] (southernmost Israel)	830,000 (20)
Suez[a] (northeastern Egypt)	130,000 (34)
Bab-el-Mandeb Straits (northern Djibouti)	>240,000 (27)
East-Asia Continental Flyway	
Beidaihe (northeastern China)	12,000 (21)
Chumphon[a] (southern Thailand)	>20,000 (15)
Tanjung Tuan[a] (Cape Rachado)	>10,000 (6)
Teluk Terima (northwest Bali)	>11,000 (15)

Table 16, continued

Hawkwatch and location	Average count and number of species of regular migrants
East-Asian Oceanic Flyway	
Tsushima Island (Strait of Korea, Japan)	>400,000 (approx. 17)
Manchou (southern Taiwan)	14,500 (5)
Sheting (southern Taiwan)	46,000 (7)

Note: The hawkwatches listed represent a small subset of active >10,000-migrant migration watchsites. More complete lists of watchsites can be found in Heintzelman 1986, 2004, and Zalles and Bildstein 2000. The watchsites listed are typically active in autumn only unless noted otherwise. Except for spring-only watchsites average count and species numbers reflect autumn efforts.
[a] Active in both spring and autumn.
[b] Active in spring only.

Western European–West African Flyway

Each autumn, more than 400,000 raptors travel along the 5000-km overland system of corridors known as the Western European–West African Flyway. The flyway, which stretches from Scandinavia to coastal West Africa, is used by migrants from as far east as Finland, Germany, Switzerland, Italy, and, at least for Eurasian Griffons, Croatia (see Figure 1). The geography of raptor migration in Western Europe and North Africa is strongly influenced by the east-west orientation of the principal mountain ranges (Alps and Pyrenees) and seas (Baltic and Mediterranean) in the region, as well as by the Sahara Desert. Major flight-lines include a circum-Baltic, North Sea route dominated by Eurasian Sparrowhawks that migrate together with their songbird prey from northern Europe into continental France and Spain; and a Eurasian Griffon circum-northern Mediterranean route with origins in Croatia that passes east to west through northern Italy and southern France, and from there south into Spain. An additional corridor dominated by Black Kites and Eurasian Buzzards follows the foothills of the northern Alps and eastern slopes of the Jura Mountains southwest into France and Spain. The most significant passage in western Europe, however, in most areas is a diffuse, broad-frontal movement that begins in north-central Sweden and continues southwest to the Strait of Gibraltar at the western end of the Mediterranean, and from there south across the western Sahara and Sahel, into the tropical forests of equatorial West Africa.

At least 22 species of raptors, including Ospreys, Western Honey Buzzards, Black Kites, Egyptian Vultures, Eurasian Griffons, two harriers, Short-toed Snake Eagles, two accipiters, two buteos, Booted Eagles, and four falcons, migrate along this flyway and its principal corridors. Migration bottlenecks in the system include the world's oldest "northern" hawkwatch, Falsterbo, in southwestern Sweden (see Chapter 9); and one of the most stunning of all hawkwatches, Organbidexka, in the Pyrenees of southwestern France.

A Central Mediterranean Corridor that is not directly connected to the flyway funnels about 30,000 raptors through Italy into North Africa. The principal axis of the 17-species flight, which is dominated by Western Honey Buzzards, flows south through the Italian peninsula and onto the "toe" of southern Italy and from there into North Africa, via the Mediterranean islands of Sicily and Malta. A smaller branch of this corridor funnels migrants to the "heel" of the Italian peninsula and thereafter into western Greece, via the Strait of Otranto at the southern terminus of the Adriatic Sea.

Unfortunately, all of these routes are little studied south of the Mediterranean, and information regarding the geography of raptor movements in Africa is imprecise. Except for small numbers of Ospreys, harriers, and some falcons, trans-Saharan migration appears to occur mainly along the desert's western edge with many, if not most, Peregrine Falcons concentrating along the coast where migratory waders and waterfowl provide ready sources of prey. By the time migrants reach the scrublike Sahel south of the Sahara, most inland movements appear to be broad frontal.

As is true elsewhere, return migration along the Western European–West African Flyway is not as well known as outbound migration. The Strait of Gibraltar is the region's most significant bottleneck in spring as well as in autumn (Finlayson 1992; Zalles and Bildstein 2000). Cap Bon, in northeastern Tunisia, also records large numbers of northbound migrants presumably in route to Sicily across the 150-km wide Sicilian Channel. The Strait of Gibraltar, Organbidexka, and Falsterbo hawkwatches are described in Chapter 9. Additional watchsites in the region are listed in Table 16.

Eurasian–East African Flyway

Each autumn, more than a million and a half raptors migrate along the Eurasian-East African Flyway, a 10,000-km system of largely overland corridors that extends from eastern Scandinavia and western Siberia through the Middle East and into southern Africa (see Figure 1). From the Middle East and south, the flyway chiefly follows the course of the Great Rift Valley into and through East Africa. Principal over-water bottlenecks on the flyway include the Bosporus, Sinai Peninsula, and Bab el Mandeb strait.

The Eurasian–East African Flyway is both the most numerically significant and most species-diverse raptor-migration passageway in the Old World. Well over one million raptors, representing more than 40 species and including Western Honey Buzzard, Black Kite, three accipiters, three buteos, three *Aquila* eagles, and nine falcons, use the flyway at its most concentrated crossroads in the Middle East. Six species, Western Honey Buzzard (330,000 individuals), Black Kite (26,000), Levant Sparrowhawk (40,000), Steppe Buzzard (350,000), Lesser Spotted Eagle (82,000), and Steppe Eagle (24,000), comprise the bulk of the visible flight along this portion of the flyway (Shirihai et al. 2000). Additional long-distance migrants include Rough-legged Hawks (northern third of the flyway only), Lesser Kestrels, Red-footed Falcons, Amur Falcons (springtime only), Merlins, Northern Hobbies, and Peregrine Falcons.

Three regional corridors funneling raptors from breeding areas spanning nearly 90° of longitude from central Europe to eastern Asia join in the deserts east of the Mediterranean Sea to create the massive flight-line. The Via Pontica, or Western Black Sea Corridor, funnels approximately 100,000 raptors of 30 species, including large numbers of Western Honey Buzzards, Eurasian Buzzards, and Lesser Spotted Eagles, from central and eastern Europe through the Balkan Peninsula and across the Bosporus in northeastern Turkey. From there, the flight continues southeast through central Turkey before turning directly south at the Gulf of Iskenderun at the northeastern corner of the Mediterranean Sea.

The Trans-Caucasian Corridor funnels more than a quarter of a million migrants from eastern Russia and Ukraine through mountain passes in the Greater Caucasus Mountains, and from there south through Georgia, eastern Turkey, Armenia, and Azerbaijan into the Middle East, where migrants join the Via Pontica flight before proceeding south through the Jordan Valley of Palestine, Israel, and Jordan. Thereafter, the flight-line splits, with some birds entering Africa via the Sinai Peninsula, and others continuing south into the Arabian Peninsula, where migrants traveling from as far east as central Asia join the flight. The combined trans-desert passage proceeds to the southern tip of the Arabian Peninsula where the birds enter Africa at Djibouti via the <30-km Bab el Mandeb strait at the southern terminus of the Red Sea (see Figure 21).

Many of the migrants are counted on outbound migration at a 75-km-wide Northern Valleys "transect" hawkwatch in northern Israel, and again on return migration near Elat, in southernmost Israel. Other important count sites on the flyway include the Bosporus, in Istanbul, Turkey; Batumi, Georgia, on the eastern shoreline of the Black Sea; and Burgas, Bulgaria, on the western shoreline of the sea. Excepting Suez, Egypt, systematic counts are nonexistent in Africa, and knowledge of the flight farther south is scant. What is known suggests that the flight-line splits in East Africa, with some birds traveling along the eastern escarpment of the Great Rift Valley, and others along the western. Some migrants, including Steppe Buzzards (the northern, or *vulpinus* subspecies of the Eurasian Buzzard from Scandinavia and northern Russia) migrate as far as South Africa along the flyway.

The geography of the return flight differs from the outbound in two ways. First, the eastern escarpment of the Great Rift Valley is used more heavily and the western less heavily than in autumn. And second, most returning migrants depart Africa via Sinai at the northern end of the Red Sea rather than via the Bab el Mandeb strait at the southern end, which appears to occur on the outbound flight. Thereafter, however, the flight-line again splits into three corridors, with birds from western Europe retracing portions of the Via Pontica route across the Bosporus and into the Balkans, eastern European breeders following the Trans-Caucasian Corridor into western Russia, and many Asian populations following the Tian-Shan-Hindu-Kush Corridor through Iran and Afghanistan, and from there the northern fringes of the Tibetan Plateau.

The hawkwatch at Elat, Israel, is described in Chapter 9. Additional hawkwatches along the flyway are listed in Table 16.

East-Asian Continental and Oceanic Flyways

Raptor migration in East Asia is only now being studied in detail and only at a few sites. Presumably this will change as news of significant flights in the region spread within the ornithological and conservation communities. Because of this, my descriptions of the region's principal flyways and corridors are a bit sketchy and speculative.

With an average elevation of nearly 5000 meters, central Asia's Tibetan Plateau is the highest mountainous region on earth. This so-called roof of the world presents a formidable barrier to migrating raptors. Although a few migrants, including substantial numbers of Steppe Eagles and smaller numbers of at least ten other species, are known to trickle south along the slopes of the deep-mountain gorges that dissect the plateau (DeCandido et al. 2001), most raptors breeding north of this barrier circumnavigate it, either by traveling along its northern fringes via the Tian-Shan-Hindu-Kush Corridor en route to the Middle East and the Eurasian–East African Flyway or by traveling southeast along its eastern fringe via the East-Asian Inland Corridor into south central and southeastern Asia (Zalles and Bildstein 2000).

Farther east, more than one million raptors from eastern Siberia, Kamchatka, northern China, Korea, and Japan migrate south across eastern Asia and into Southeast Asia along the East-Asian Continental Flyway, a 7000-km, mostly overland system of corridors that stretches from eastern Siberia to Southeast Asia and onto the Indonesian Archipelago and that includes over-water journeys of up to 60 km at the Straits of Malacca, Sunda, Bali, and Lombok in Malaysia and Indonesia (see Figure 1). The route, which is used by at least 33 raptors, including four accipiters, three buteos, and seven falcons, is dominated by tens to hundreds of thousands of Crested Honey Buzzards, Grey-faced Buzzards, and Japanese and Chinese Sparrowhawks. Members of the northeast Asian *japonicus* subspecies of the Eurasian Buzzard migrate in large numbers in the northern half of the flyway. Additional long-distance migrants using the corridor include Rough-legged Hawks (northern third only), Amur Falcons, Merlins, Northern Hobbies, and Peregrine Falcons. The Beidaihe hawkwatch on the northern shore of the Bay of Bohai, 250 km east of Beijing, regularly reports movements of more than 20,000 migrants representing 21 species of raptors, including a flight of upward of 15,000 Pied Harriers that corresponds to more than half of the world population of this little-studied migrant (Williams 2000). Much farther south on the Malay Peninsula, the Tanjung Tuan (Cape Rachado) hawkwatch on the Strait of Malacca near Kuala Lumpur, Malaysia, and across from the Indonesian island of Sumatra, reports significant movements of at least six species of raptors, including large numbers of Crested Honey Buzzards (Zalles and Bildstein 2000).

Farther east still lies the region's second major migration route, the 5000-km-long, largely over-water East-Asian Oceanic Flyway, which stretches from northeastern Siberia and Kamchatka, through the Kuril Islands, eastern China, Korea, Japan, and the Ryu Kyu Islands, into Taiwan, the Philippines, and, for a few species, Borneo, Sulawesi, and the Moluccas. As many as half a million raptors representing 19 species travel along this, the world's only major oceanic raptor-migration flyway. The flight is dominated by large-scale movements of tens to hundreds of thousands of two long-distance, super-flocking, soaring migrants, the Chinese Sparrowhawk and the Grey-faced

Buzzard, which use *sea thermals* (see Chapter 4) to complete the many over-water passages encountered en route. Other long-distance migrants using this flyway include Rough-legged Hawks and Eurasian Buzzards (principally along the northern continental third of the flyway only), Merlins, Northern Hobbies, and Peregrine Falcons.

In addition to Tsushima Island in the Strait of Korea where more than 400,000 Chinese Sparrowhawks were counted in late September 1999, well-established hawkwatches on the flyway include Sheting and Manchou in southernmost Taiwan (see Table 16) (Zalles and Bildstein 2000).

Synthesis and Conclusions

1. Global raptor-migration geography is shaped by numerous extrinsic and intrinsic factors.
2. Extrinsic factors affecting migration geography include the seasonal nature of prey availability, and the distribution and juxtaposition of the world's continental landmasses.
3. Intrinsic factors affecting migration geography include the flight mechanics, body sizes, and metabolic rates of the birds themselves.
4. Most raptors are loath to undertake water crossings of more than 25 kilometers. Consequently, the overwhelming majority of regional migration corridors and all but one of the world's five major raptor-migration flyways are largely or exclusively overland routes.
5. Many island raptors, almost all of which are nonmigratory, likely evolved from migratory continental forms.
6. Within species of migratory raptors, populations that breed at high latitudes often migrate longer distances than populations that breed at lower latitudes, resulting in *leapfrog migration.*
7. Many migrants take different routes on outbound and return migration, resulting in *elliptical* or *loop migration.*
8. The migration behavior and ecology of many migrants differs substantially inside and outside of the tropics.
9. Some raptors migrate altitudinally, typically from high-mountain breeding sites to lower-elevation overwintering areas.
10. There are five major raptor migration flyways, one in the New World and four in the Old World. All but one of these, the Western European–West African, are transequatorial, and all but one, the East-Asian Oceanic Flyway, are largely overland routes.

—8—

Migration Life Histories

Ecology molds life-history patterns in predictable ways.

Frank Gill, 1990

The "rules" of raptor migration as laid out in the previous seven chapters are a bit misleading. Not because
they are wrong but because they tend to homogenize and overly distill the ex-
ceedingly diverse and extraordinarily wide-ranging phenomenon that is raptor migration.

In much the same way that each species of raptor differs from all others genetically and physically, each species also differs behaviorally. Furthermore, in
almost all cases, geographic populations *within* species also differ behaviorally, as do individuals living *within* those populations. Within species,
such variation is the raw material for evolution by natural selection. Across
species, it is part of what makes a species a species.

This chapter details the migration *life histories*, or "significant features of the life cycle through which an organism passes" (Lincoln et al. 1998), of eight species of partial and complete migratory raptors. These stories, which describe the geography, timing, and ecology of each species' flight, together with the amount of regional and individual variation therein, provide examples of the extent to which raptor migration differs both among and within species. The species whose life histories are described were chosen on the basis of world geography and migration type, as well as on the amount of information available. Tropical species and irruptive and local migrants are not represented, not because their stories are unimportant but because too little is known about their migrations to tell their full stories. Descriptions of their migration patterns await new studies in the discipline.

There are two main messages in this chapter. The first is that migration is a variable and profoundly adaptable characteristic that permits raptors to take advantage of geographically disjunct and ecologically unique habitats in ways that allow them to achieve and maintain far larger populations than would be possible otherwise. The second is that the geographic and ecological rules of raptor migration set forth earlier in this book do indeed hold, but that raptor diversity *in particular* and biological diversity *in general* allow them to be applied successfully in many different ways.

Species Life Histories

Turkey Vulture

Spanish: Zopilote cabecirrojo, Aura cabecirroja

German: Truthahngeier

French: Urubu à tête rouge

aka: Turkey Buzzard

Size: Length 68 cm; wingspan 170 cm; weight 1400–2400 grams

Estimated world population: >5,000,000; increasing

Type migrant: Partial; some migratory populations long-distance, transequatorial, and transcontinental

Most of the world's 22 species of vultures do not migrate. There are exceptions, however, and the world's most widely distributed avian scavenger, the Turkey Vulture, is one of them. Although many populations of Eurasian Griffons and, to an even greater extent, Egyptian Vultures, are intermediate-distance, latitudinal migrants, the Turkey Vulture is the world's only truly transequatorial, long-distance migratory vulture. No other species of vulture really comes close. Turkey Vultures, which are restricted to the Western Hemisphere, are extraordinarily widespread within it, ranging from 52° north in southern Canada to more than 52° south on the islands of Tierra del Fuego in southernmost South America. Turkey Vultures also occur across most of the West Indies, as well as on the south Atlantic Falkland Islands, approximately 500 km off the coast of Argentina. One of the smallest of all vultures, the species is an extraordinarily adept soaring machine that ravenously scavenges both small and large carcasses, as a well as human refuse, and readily adapts to human-modified landscapes. Throughout many portions of its range, the Turkey Vulture is the most common bird of prey (Kirk and Mossman 1998).

There are six recognized subspecies of Turkey Vultures, but only two are known to migrate regularly, both of which breed principally or entirely in North America. In eastern North America, the subspecies *septentrionalis* is a partial, intermediate-distance, leapfrog migrant whose northern populations retreat in winter into Mexico and the southeastern United States (Plate 9). In western North America, the slightly smaller and darker subspecies *meridionalis* is a mostly complete, long-distance, transequatorial migrant, most of whose populations overwinter in Central and South America (Ferguson-Lees and Christie 2001) (Plate 10).

Turkey Vultures belong to the family Cathartidae, a group of seven species of New World vultures that some specialists believe are more closely related to storks than to raptors. This, together with the fact that they are nonpredatory scavengers that lack the charismatic allure of "real" raptors, has meant that many hawkwatchers have not kept careful records of vulture migration. And, as if this were not problem enough, vultures routinely urinate on their legs, a decidedly socially unacceptable and as yet unexplained habit that has compromised banding efforts. Although many believe the birds engage in urohidrosis—the literal translation from ancient Greek is "sweat urine"—to evaporatively cool themselves in the heat of summer (Hatch 1970), that they do so in winter as well suggests an additional or alternative function as well. Turkey Vultures frequently stand on the carcasses they feed upon, which as they rot serve as ideal breeding grounds for flesh-eating microbes. Although the antiseptic nature of vulture urine remains to be tested, its chemical composition suggests that it may help keep a vulture's feet and legs free of infections that might otherwise develop in cuts and scratches. Whatever the reason, urohidrosis has the potential to hobble a vulture if urine "cements" to a leg band (Parmalee 1954), and for this reason, both Canada and the United States have prohibited the banding of vultures for decades.

Fortunately, wing-tags, satellite tracking, and the establishment of several million-bird hawkwatches in Mexico and Central America in the 1990s have rekindled an interest in Turkey Vulture migration, and we are beginning to understand the geographic scope, magnitude, and nature of this species' migratory journeys. The picture that is now emerging suggests that the Turkey Vulture's largely—if not entirely—food-free, long-distance trek between North and South America ranks among the most extraordinary of all raptor migrations.

Vultures, in general, tend to be social, gregarious birds, and Turkey Vultures are no exception. Most Turkey Vultures, for example, roost communally, year-round, often in the company of Black Vultures. Turkey Vultures also come together while migrating. On outbound migration, flocks of vultures build quickly from several individuals to several dozens of individuals, and soon thereafter swell to multihundred and multithousand bird aggregations along major corridors and flyways. The same occurs during return migration in spring.

In both eastern and western North America, Turkey Vultures begin to migrate in late August. The birds, however, spend quite a bit of time feeding early in the migrations, and the bulk of the flight occurs later, particularly in eastern North America, where overall distances traveled are much shorter than in the American West. At Hawk Mountain Sanctuary, for example, more than half of all migrating Turkey Vultures are counted after 20 October, and in many years the largest flights occur in November.

The most significant flight east of the Mississippi is in southern Ontario and southeastern Michigan, where in recent years more than 100,000 migrating vultures have concentrated along the northern shorelines of Lake Erie while being diverted southwest. Numbers in the region peak in mid-October, with daily counts exceeding thousands of birds in most years (Kielb 1994; Kirk and Mossman 1998; Zalles and Bildstein 2000).

The real action, however, takes place in the American West, where transequatorial *meridionalis* makes its appearance. Hints of a flight begin in mid-September in coastal British Columbia and in Washington State, where more than a thousand Canadian breeders travel across the 20-km Strait of Juan de Fuca from the southern tip of Vancouver Island in British Columbia to make landfall in northwestern Washington. Several weeks later, and approximately 1600 km farther south, the incipient torrent has built to 30,000 individuals at the southern tip of the Sierra Nevada in southern California. This and other vulture streams from farther east converge on one another as a growing queue of individuals flows southeast along the slopes of the Sierra Madre Occidental of northern Mexico. Somewhere south of Monterrey, the flight joins similarly swelling streams of outbound Broad-winged and Swainson's Hawks and, shortly thereafter, the three species converge north of the world's narrowest and most significant migration bottleneck near Cardel, in Veracruz, Mexico, where 1.5 million to more than 2 million southbound Turkey Vultures are counted each October.

Most individuals continue south across the Isthmus of Tehuantepec, before turning westward and following the foothills of the Pacific slopes of southern Mexico, Guatemala, El Salvador, Honduras, and Nicaragua. In northern Costa Rica, the birds cross the continental divide for a third time and soar above the Caribbean slopes of that country's Talamanca Mountains before entering Panama and, after that, northeastern Colombia (Bildstein and Zalles 2001).

The South American wintering grounds of western North America's more than two million Turkey Vultures remain something of a mystery. It almost seems as if the birds vanish upon reaching South America. Part of the mystery is due to the fact that South America's abundant resident Turkey Vultures make it difficult to determine where the migrants settle each autumn; another complication is that Turkey Vultures are not banded in North America, so there is no chance of band recoveries on the wintering grounds.

The lack of banding recoveries notwithstanding, anecdotal reports, including that of a wing-tagged individual from Saskatchewan sighted overwintering in Maracaibo, Venezuela, in January 2006, suggest that many North American Turkey Vultures overwinter in Panama, Colombia, and Venezuela, rather than continuing farther south into central South America. At least some are known to overwinter in the expansive freshwater wetlands or "Llanos" of central Venezuela, where researchers have observed them dominating the smaller resident, *ruficollis* subspecies. The migrants, who outcompete residents in more than 80 percent of aggressive encounters observed, replace the latter at their preferred feeding and roosting areas. Fortunately, the North American subspecies arrives at the onset of the dry season, a time when reptilian and mammalian mortality increase substantially, enhancing overall "prey" availability for both races of vultures (Kirk and Currall 1994). Even so, resident vultures in the area forgo breeding until after the migrants leave in spring, and competition between the two groups probably is substantial.

Although the geography of Turkey Vulture migration is reasonably well known, energy management during their journeys is not. One thing is clear: There is no evidence of significant feeding en route, at least not south of the United States. Indeed, with 80 percent of the outbound flight of more than one million Turkey Vultures passing southern Costa Rica in fewer than two weeks each autumn (i.e., at a rate approaching 100,000 individuals per day), it seems highly unlikely that individual birds could find and consume food while traveling in such close quarters. On the other hand, there is every indication that Turkey Vultures expend remarkably little energy while traveling long distances. My own observations, both in Pennsylvania and in Costa Rica, suggest that once vultures have been airborne for 5 to 10 minutes each morning (an initial period of flight in which an individual seeks and finds its first thermal or updraft), migrants travel solely via slope and thermal soaring for the remainder of the day, and rarely flap, until a few minutes prior to the end of the day's flight, when they descend to roost.

Smithsonian Tropical Research Institution researcher Neal Smith, who has studied the species' migrations in Panama, together with those of long-distance Broad-winged and Swainson's Hawk migrants, rated the vulture's soaring ability as "vastly superior" to that of the two buteos (Smith 1985b). Even so, Turkey Vultures arrive in Venezuela in November in "poor condition" and need to rebuild their body mass during their stay before returning north the following spring (Kirk and Gosler 1994). It seems that a combination of accumulated body fat, excellent flight skills, abundant solar energy in the form of near-continuous thermals, and a likely drop in core body temperature at night enable western North American populations of Turkey Vultures to successfully complete an approximately 14,000-km round-trip journey each year.

Where to watch the migration. Turkey Vultures are one of the easiest raptors to see on migration. Of the 129 North American watchsites in *Hawks Aloft Worldwide* (Zalles and Bildstein 2000), 118 report the species as outbound or return migrants or both; and two festivals, one in Hinckley, Ohio, in March, and one in Weldon, California, in September, celebrate the bird's return in spring and autumn, respectively. For really staggering numbers, visit the Veracruz River-of-Raptors watchsite in Chichicaxtle and Cardel, Mexico, in mid-October, where in 1998–2003 counts averaged 1,550,000 and peaked at 2,677,000; Kéköldi Indigenous Reserve watchsite in Talamanca, Costa Rica, in late October, where in 2000–2001 counts averaged 934,000 and peaked at 1,144,00; and Ancon Hill, in central Panama, where more than 300,000 vultures are seen in late October–early November in most years.

North American hotspots include Lake Erie Metropark near the mouth of the Detroit River in southern Michigan, where in 1996–2003 counts averaged 38,348 and peaked at 73,886 and where 104,538 vultures were seen in 2005; Tehachapi Valley, southeast of Bakersfield, California, where in 1999–2002 counts averaged 31,597 and peaked at 38,743; and Kern Valley, south of Weldon, California, where in 1994–2002 counts averaged 26,770 and peaked at 32,926.

Conservation concerns. Although considered by most to be "beneficial scavengers," or nature's sanitation engineers, more than 100,000 Turkey and Black Vultures were killed in the early to mid-1900s by Texas ranchers, both for "polluting" watering holes with their regurgitations and defecations and, mistakenly, for transmitting diseases including anthrax and hog cholera. (There is no evidence of disease transmission in the wild.) Fortunately, the species is now largely protected, abundant, and usually appreciated throughout most of its range. Even so, growing populations of vultures near airports, where the birds are said to threaten aircraft during takeoffs and landings, and instances of property damage by individuals and small groups of birds, have resulted in the federal government issuing depredation permits for the "taking" of dozens to hundreds of vultures. Lead poisoning, in areas where lead shot is used in hunting, also remains a threat to populations (Kirk and Mossman 1998).

Osprey

Spanish: Águila pescadora

German: Fischadler

French: Balbuzard pêcheur

aka: Fish Hawk

Size: Length 55–60 cm; wingspan 150–170 cm; weight 1200–2000 grams

Estimated world population: <100,000; increasing

Type migrant: Complete; long-distance and partially transequatorial

Eagle-sized, widespread, and conspicuous on migration, the nearly cosmopolitan Osprey is one of the most thoroughly studied and best known of all migratory raptors.

Ospreys breed across more than 25 million km² of the world's landmass, mainly in the Northern Hemisphere. The species nests north of the Arctic Circle in Alaska and Western Canada, as well as in the fiords of northernmost

Norway. Ospreys breed across most of coastal Australia south to southern Victoria, but not in Tasmania or New Zealand. Although Ospreys are widespread migrants in South America as far south as central Chile, and although first-year birds over-summer there as well, the species does not breed in South America. Nor does it breed in sub-Saharan Africa, although it overwinters there.

The Osprey is one of only two raptors, and one of only six birds overall, that occurs on six continents. Despite its widespread nature, however, Ospreys are truly abundant in only a handful of sites, and its population was recently estimated at less than 100,000 individuals (Ferguson Lees and Christie 2001), although this number seems substantially low in light of rates of recent increase in several well-studied populations.

Ospreys feed almost entirely on live fish, and seasonal changes in fish availability, including the freezing over of lakes, rivers, ponds, and streams, frequently force individuals to migrate. At the beginnings of its migrations, Ospreys usually travel alone or in small groups. And indeed, until recently, the largest reported flock of migrating Ospreys numbered 11 individuals. Overall, the species is decidedly less likely to follow leading lines than are other species of migrants, and at most watchsites Ospreys make up less than 4 percent of the overall flight (Zalles and Bildstein 2000).

The geography of Osprey migration is best known for North American and Western European breeders; regions in which tens of thousands of Ospreys have been banded during the past 75 years (Worth 1936), and where more than 100 individuals have been tracked with satellite telemetry (Kjellén et al. 1997; Martell et al. 2001, 2004). Australian breeders are said to be largely sedentary, although range extensions do occur seasonally and most individuals there forage over wider areas when they are not breeding (Marchant and Higgins 1993). North African breeders, too, appear to be largely sedentary. Asian populations are completely migratory in northern areas inland, and partially migratory or sedentary in coastal and southern areas.

Ospreys have been considered the quintessential "broad frontal migrant" ever since Sten Österlöf characterized them as such in 1951 and, outside of the tropics at least, the species only occasionally concentrates at migration bottlenecks. Fewer than 100 are counted among the 150,000 outbound migrants at the Strait of Gibraltar, for example. Coastlines, however, often serve to concentrate migrants, and a growing body of evidence suggests that the species avoids unnecessarily long over-water passages whenever possible. In North America, for example, banding returns and satellite-tracking data indicate that many central and most western Ospreys migrate overland along the Mesoamerican Land Corridor between North and South America each year and that up to 90 percent of the Eastern Seaboard population migrates overland along the lengths of peninsular Florida and, thereafter, Cuba before continuing south across the Caribbean Sea into South America each autumn. Similarly, many Ospreys breeding in Western Europe funnel through the Iberian Peninsula and reach Africa via water crossings at or near the Strait of Gibraltar, rather than following shorter, more direct routes across the more expansive western Mediterranean (Hake et al. 2001).

The extent to which Ospreys congregate on migration perhaps is best seen at La Gran Piedra watchsite in tropical Cuba. La Gran Piedra ("the big rock" in English), is a somewhat rectangular, small-office-building-sized boulder precariously perched atop the central spine of the Sierra Maestra of southeastern Cuba. The 1234-m promontory, 10 km inland from the Caribbean and 22 km east of Santiago de Cuba, offers spectacular views of the region's coastal and interior lowlands, including Guantánamo Bay, as well as of oncoming Ospreys (Figure 24). During 18 days of observation from 27 August to 17 October 2001, more than 1000 Ospreys were counted migrating along updrafts at the site. Making up an amazing 96 percent of all migrants at the

Figure 24. View to the west from La Gran Piedra raptor-migration watchsite in the Sierra Maestra of southeastern Cuba, 22 km east of Santiago de Cuba. Note the Caribbean Sea in the background. La Gran Piedra is along one of the world's most important migration corridors for Ospreys.

site, Ospreys passed at a rate of more than 18 birds per hour. The flight included a single-day record count of 279 individuals, and a single-hour record count of 171 birds during which a flock of 43 Ospreys and 10 Swallow-tailed Kites passed the watchsite. Ospreys traveling into and out of midday *adiabatic clouds* at the site frequently call to one another, suggesting that they are trying to stay together, presumably in an effort to find updrafts more efficiently, as well as to remain together for the oncoming 600-km trans-Caribbean water crossing.

Observations east of La Gran Piedra, together with satellite-tracking data, indicate that most Ospreys seen at the site depart Cuba for an over-water passage to South America either from Guantánamo Bay, 30 km southeast of the site, or from southwestern Haiti, after they have crossed the 100-km Windward Passage between eastern Cuba and western Hispaniola (Crouse and Keith 1999; Rodriguez Santana et al. 2003).

Overall, Ospreys appear to be one of the world's most versatile raptor migrants, both within and across geographic areas. Among North American breeders, males tend to migrate significantly shorter distances than females (Martell et al. 2001), possibly to be closer to their breeding grounds in spring. And in both North America and Europe, parental males depart their breeding areas 2 to 3 weeks later than their female counterparts. It is not clear why females leave earlier than males. Some believe they do so because they travel farther than males or because they are attempting to reduce competition for food with their young. Others believe that males *delay* their departures because they are more familiar with prey resources on the breeding grounds than are females and, hence, find it easier to lay down fat reserves there prior to migration. That males spend fewer days feeding at stopover sites on their outbound journeys than females supports the latter notion (Kjellén et al. 2001).

An extensive study of 74 satellite-tracked Ospreys from across North America demonstrates substantial differences in the migration routes of birds from different nesting areas. On outbound migration, most East Coast Ospreys follow the route described above with most crossing the Florida Straits into Cuba and from there traveling across the Caribbean Sea to South America. Midwestern Ospreys, by comparison, travel along one of three routes: (1) southeast into Florida and then along the route taken by East Coast birds, (2) south along the Mississippi drainage and directly across the Gulf of Mexico to the Yucatan Peninsula and thereafter southeast along the Mesoamerican Land Corridor into northwestern Colombia, South America, or (3) southsouthwest around the Gulf of Mexico and into northeastern Mexico, and thereafter along the Mesoamerican Land Corridor into South America. West Coast Ospreys tend to track south across a relatively broad front toward the Pacific and Gulf coasts of Mexico, en route to wintering areas that are north of most Midwestern and East Coast birds (Martell et al. 2001).

Even within regions, Ospreys often differ in their migrations. A study of 14 satellite-tracked breeders in subtropical Florida illustrates the extent of such variation (Martell et al. 2004). Seven of the birds tracked for one to two years overwintered in South America, four migrated after breeding but stayed within Florida, and two of the birds remained on their breeding grounds year-round. Individuals that migrated to South America migrated an average of 4100 km, whereas those that remained in Florida migrated an average of only 145 km. Overall, most of the birds were away from their breeding grounds for almost half a year. Individuals that were tracked for two seasons followed the same migratory paths and overwintered in the same areas. At the same time of the year that Florida breeders migrate, Ospreys from farther north migrate into and through the state. Although most of the latter continue on to overwintering areas in the Caribbean Basin and South America, a few overwinter in Florida. Northern migrants traveling to South America reach their wintering grounds after Florida migrants and remain there later in spring than their Florida counterparts. The extent to which these different populations interact behaviorally and competitively has yet to be examined.

Flexibility in migratory behavior, together with an ability to undertake long-distance over-water travel—Ospreys are "regular" vagrants to numerous oceanic islands including the Galapagos and Hawaiian archipelagos—are probably responsible for the species cosmopolitan range.

Where to watch the migration. Ospreys are reported as outbound or return migrants or both at 283 of 388 *Hawks Aloft Worldwide* migration watchsites, making them the most widely distributed of all migratory raptors (Zalles and Bildstein 2000). At most sites, annual counts range from several individuals to several hundreds of birds. Coastal and near coastal sites south of large breeding concentrations frequently report thousands of birds.

North American hotspots include Lighthouse Point, on the outskirts of New Haven, Connecticut, where in 1996–2002 counts averaged 1341 and peaked at 1811; Cape May Point, New Jersey, at the mouth of Delaware Bay, where in 1996–2003 counts averaged 3068 and peaked at 6734; Kiptopeke, Virginia, at the mouth of the Chesapeake Bay, where in 1996–2002 counts averaged 3305 and peaked at 5775; and Hilton Head Island, South Carolina, northeast of Savannah, Georgia, where in 1993–1996 counts averaged 1154 and peaked at 1562.

Eurasian hotspots include Falsterbo in southwesternmost Sweden, where in 1998–2003 counts averaged 299 and peaked at 413; Skagen, a spring-migration site at the northern tip of the Danish peninsula, where in 1972–1998 counts averaged 223 and peaked at 477; and Cape Emine, a peninsular watchsite near Burgas in Black Sea coastal Bulgaria, where in 1981 34 Ospreys were seen.

Conservation concerns. Until recently, Osprey–human interactions have had negative consequences for the birds. In Scotland, the species was eliminated by gamekeepers and egg collectors in the early twentieth century. Fortunately, the species has been successfully reintroduced into this part of its former range. The greatest human threat to Ospreys occurred during the "DDT era" of the mid-twentieth century, when global numbers dipped to as few as 25,000 to 30,000 pairs (Poole 1989; Chapter 10). All indications, however, suggest that numbers have rebounded substantially from these lows, particularly in North America. Current threats include indiscriminant shooting, especially in areas where overwintering birds aggregate at fish farms (Bechard and Márquez-Reyes 2003).

Ospreys readily adapt to nesting on human-constructed structures including channel markers and duck blinds in and around water, as well as to nesting platforms erected specifically for their use, and both are known to have significantly increased populations regionally. Overall, the species' ability to nest and overwinter successfully in areas of high human densities—so long as it is not shot or poisoned—bodes well for the Osprey's continued success.

Bald Eagle

Spanish: Águila calva

German: Weißkopf-Seeadler

French: Balbuzard pêcheur

aka: White-headed Eagle, Sea Eagle, American Eagle

Size: Length 70–95 cm; wingspan 170–245 cm; weight 3000–6300 grams

Estimated world population: >100,000; increasing

Type migrant: Partial

The national emblem of the United States of America, the Bald Eagle is the only New World member of the near-cosmopolitan genus *Haliaeetus*, an otherwise Old World assemblage of nine species of "fish or sea eagles."

Bald Eagles, which are endemic to North America, breed from above the Arctic Circle in the Brooks Range of Alaska, east across Canada to Labrador and northern Newfoundland, and south in large numbers to southern Florida; the species breeds in smaller numbers to about 23° north in Baja, Sonora, and Chihuahua, Mexico. Bald Eagles are common and sometimes abundant in many parts of its range, particularly in Alaska, western and maritime Canada, Maine, the Chesapeake Bay, and Florida (Palmer 1988; Buehler 2000). Together with the African Fish Eagle, the Bald Eagle ranks as the most common "sea eagle" in the world.

Bald Eagles are complete migrants in northern parts of their range, partial migrants at midlatitudes, and partial migrants or sedentary in the south. Juvenile and subadult eagles—individuals do not breed until they are about 5 years old—are far more migratory than adults, and most members of these age classes disperse or migrate, even in areas where adults are sedentary.

Although the species does not depend on fish to the same extent as do Ospreys—many Bald Eagles regularly take waterfowl and other species of birds, and most feed on carrion as well—their long-distance movements tend to be driven by the seasonal availability of this important food resource. In western North America, for example, many Bald Eagles time their movements to coincide with those of several species of migratory salmon (*Salmo* spp.), which form a keystone prey base for eagles in the region. In the Pacific Northwest, for example, large numbers of adult and subadult eagles migrate north along the coast to the Chilkat River in southeastern Alaska, where they congregate by the thousands to feed on enormous numbers of dead and dying recently spawned salmon. Farther north, Alaskan breeders similarly track salmon runs south along the coast. Eagles from breeding populations in Saskatchewan, Alberta, and the Northwest Territories of Canada migrate south along the Rockies, predictably interrupting their movements at traditional stopover sites for up to several weeks to feed on the carcasses of spent salmon. In the East, birds from the Great Lakes feed on fish while migrating along the Mississippi River (Buehler 2000).

At Hawk Mountain Sanctuary in eastern Pennsylvania, late autumn and early winter pulses of migrating eagles typically follow on the heels of cold spells that freeze bodies of water north of the watchsite, placing a proverbial lid on the region's essential fish resource.

One of the best examples of the extent to which shifts in fish availability affect the migration of Bald Eagles comes from Florida, where more than 1000 pairs of eagles now nest. Peninsular Florida is largely subtropical, and unlike eagles to the north, which breed in spring and summer, Florida Bald Eagles breed in midwinter. In Florida, nest building begins in late September, and many clutches are completed before the first of the year. Young fledge approximately 12 weeks later, with some eaglets leaving their nests in February. Most likely, wintertime breeding is linked to both the vertical and geographic migrations of the area's fishes.

A bit of fish biology explains the situation. Although some species, including salmon, migrate long distances geographically, many others migrate short distances vertically. In temperate regions, for example, fish begin to settle into deeper waters in autumn as warm surface waters start to cool and sink. In warmer climates, however, the reverse occurs: fish descend to cooler depths in summer to avoid overheated waters closer to the surface, and return to the surface only after relatively cooler temperatures again prevail in winter (Eckmann and Imbrock 1996). Although the distances involved in these "migrations" are often less than a meter, the ecological consequences of the movements, both for the fish and their predators, can be substantial. In Florida, for example, the migrations create a situation in which fish are decidedly more available to surface-feeding eagles in winter and less available in summer, which is exactly the opposite of what occurs farther north. Eagles shift the timing of their nesting in response to this phenomenon. In addition, in North Florida, the midwinter spawning migrations of American Shad, an anadromous fish that, like salmon, grows in salt water but spawns in fresh, also appears to play a role in the timing of Bald Eagle breeding, with pairs of eagles timing their reproductive efforts to take advantage of the shad's spawning runs (B. Watts, pers. comm.).

Although most of Florida's breeding adults over-summer near their nests—probably to maintain possession of their breeding territories and feeding areas for the following winter—most recently fledged and subadult eagles leave the state. The peninsular geography of Florida presents migrants with two choices: Fly south over water to over-summering areas in the tropical Caribbean and northern South America or fly north over land to over-summering areas in temperate North America.

Almost without exception, Florida's eagles choose the latter, most likely for two reasons: (1) overland travel across continental North America is far less expensive energetically for these soaring migrants than is over-water travel across the Caribbean, and (2) fish are more available north of Florida in summer than to the south. Although some individuals migrate only a few hundred miles into the Carolinas, most travel at least as far as the prey-rich Chesapeake Bay, and some journey more than 2000 km into Maine and eastern Canada. Studies of banded, color-marked, and radio-tracked eagles indicate some individuals take as long as three weeks to complete their journeys, whereas others travel more than 200 km per day and manage to reach their destinations in less than a week. First-year birds migrate farther and tend to remain in over-summering areas longer than their older counterparts, and many individuals return to the same over-summering areas in subsequent years (Broley 1947; Buehler et al. 1991; Wood 1992).

Although the migrations of Florida's Bald Eagles make sense ecologically, they are unique among raptors geographically. No other Northern Hemisphere raptor migrates north on its outbound migration and south on its return migration. Nor, for that matter, does any other Northern Hemisphere migrant undertake outbound movements in boreal spring and return movements in boreal autumn. Unusual in many ways, the migrations of Florida's eagles are "the exception that proves the rule" of prey availability as the principal driving force in raptor migration.

The migrations of Florida's Bald Eagles also create a unique opportunity for hawkwatchers to simultaneously count outbound and returning migrants at a single watchsite. At Hawk Mountain Sanctuary, the overlapping migrations of northern and southern populations of Bald Eagles create a somewhat bimodal or two-peaked pattern in the seasonal timing of the species flight, with the return movements of southern Bald Eagles peaking in early September and the outbound movements of northern Bald Eagles peaking in November and December (Figure 25). It is not clear if Bald Eagles nesting in southwestern North America (e.g., Arizona and northwestern Mexico) exhibit the same migratory peculiarities. These latter populations do, however,

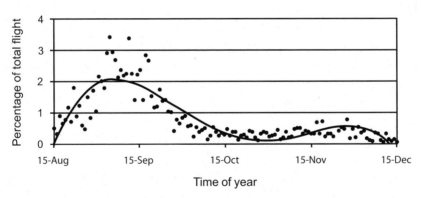

Figure 25. Seasonal timing of the autumn flight of Bald Eagles at Hawk Mountain Sanctuary, Pennsylvania. Note the major peak in early September and a far smaller, secondary peak in late November–early December. The first represents the return movements of Florida Bald Eagles, the second the outbound movements of eagles breeding north of the sanctuary.

breed during the winter, and the possibility that they, too, over-summer to the north seems reasonable.

Where to watch the migration. Bald Eagles are reported as outbound or return migrants or both at 121 of 129 *Hawks Aloft Worldwide* North American migration watchsites, making them one of the most widely distributed of all of North America's migratory raptors (Zalles and Bildstein 2000). Most hawkwatches report several birds to several dozen birds each season. Numbers at coastal and near-coastal watchsites south of large breeding concentrations and at watchsites in the Central Appalachians of eastern Pennsylvania often reach hundreds of eagles each year. Southern breeders are early migrants, with most of the passage occurring in August and September. Movements of northern breeders typically peak in November and December.

Bald Eagle migration hotspots include Windy Point in southwestern Alberta, where counts averaged 458 and peaked at 1229 between 1994 and 2002; Hawk Ridge Minnesota, on the outskirts of Duluth, where counts averaged 3079 and peaked at 4368 in 1994–2003; Eagle Valley, Wisconsin, along the Mississippi River near Cassville, where counts averaged 2317 and peaked at 4108 in 1996–2002; Cape Flattery, Washington, where 769 eagles were seen in 1992; Hitchcock Nature Area, southwestern Iowa, where counts averaged 620 and peaked at 908 in 1999–2003; and Kiptopeke, Virginia, at the mouth of the Chesapeake Bay, where counts averaged 277 and peaked at 410 in 1996–2002.

Conservation concerns. Historically, people have been the greatest threat to Bald Eagles. Native Americans trapped and killed the birds for their feathers. More recently in Alaska, descendants of European settlers placed bounties of fifty cents to two dollars on eagles for more than three decades in the first half of the twentieth century. More than 128,000 birds were bountied during this period, and it seems likely that thousands of others were shot and not claimed. Unfortunately, the species remains an occasional target throughout its range. As recently as the mid-1980s, human persecution remained the leading case of death for postfledgling Bald Eagles, with 200 to 300 eagles being shot in South Dakota alone (Bildstein et al. 1993). Bald Eagles have been fully protected by federal law since 1972.

Agricultural pesticides, including DDT and related organochlorines, significantly impacted the reproductive success of Bald Eagles in mid-twentieth-century North America, resulting in the extirpation of many breeding populations. Fortunately, the numbers of eagles rebounded substantially following bans on the widespread use of DDT in Canada and the United States in the early 1970s. Nevertheless, current populations probably represent a small fraction of what they were in advance of European settlement. Recently, many conservationists have proposed removing the Bald Eagle from the federal Endangered Species List, where it remains as of early 2006. The greatest current threats to Bald Eagles include both direct and indirect effects associated with increased densities of human populations throughout much of coastal North America, where many of the largest concentrations of Bald Eagles now breed (Palmer 1988; Buehler 2000).

Western Honey Buzzard

Spanish: Abejero Europeo

German: Wespenbussard

French: Bondrée apivore

aka: Honey Buzzard, Eurasian Honey Buzzard

Size: Length 50–60 cm; wingspan 120–145 cm; weight 450–1050 grams

Estimated world population: 1,000,000; apparently stable

Type migrant: Complete; long-distance and transequatorial

A buteo-like kite with a slender neck, tightly feathered pigeon-shaped head, and a long rounded tail, the Western Honey Buzzard is a widespread European and west Asian breeder that evacuates high- to midlatitude breeding grounds in late August–early September for tropical wintering areas in sub-Saharan Africa.

As its name suggests, the Western Honey Buzzard feeds extensively on bees and wasps. Its closet relative and East Asian counterpart, the Crested Honey Buzzard, is a partial migrant that breeds in northeastern China, eastern Russia, and Japan and overwinters in Southeast Asia, India, the Philippines, and Indonesia. A third member of the genus, the Barred Honey Buzzard, is a little-studied, nonmigratory species found only on the island of Sulawesi and in the Philippines. Sporadically common throughout its range, the Western Honey Buzzard is principally philopatric in Western Europe but frequently nomadic in Russia (Cramp and Simmons 1980; Kostrzewa 1998).

The species is a strong flyer, particularly among flocking and soaring migrants, and is capable of completing relatively long over-water journeys. A somewhat broad-frontal migrant at the beginnings and ends of its migrations—the flight is said to dissolve and disappear into the species' Afrotropical wintering grounds—Western Honey Buzzards are super-flocking migrants (see Table 11), and most individuals complete the bulk of their migrations while traveling in multihundred to multithousand bird groups along well-established corridors and flyways. Individuals from Western Europe travel to and from Africa mainly via the Strait of Gibraltar where more than 10,000 birds have been seen crossing on single days. The lightly wing-loaded species is regularly pushed laterally by winds at the crossing, and many birds, particularly juveniles, attempt crossings more than 100 kilometers east and west of the narrowest point along the strait. Most east European and Asian populations pass into Africa via the Middle East, with major concentrations transiting the Bosporus in northeastern Turkey and the Gulf of Iskenderun, at the northeastern corner of the Mediterranean. A third, and decidedly smaller, passage occurs through the central Mediterranean, where tens of thousands of individuals fly south along the Italian peninsula onto Sicily and, thereafter, either across the Sicilian Channel to Tunisia or via Malta to Libya.

Honey buzzards specialize on the larvae of bees and wasps, and their outbound migration from Europe tends to be earlier in autumn and later in spring than those of the region's long-distance migrants that depend upon less seasonal prey. The bulk of the outbound passage at 30° to 50° north occurs in late-August and early September. In spring the return flight peaks acutely in early May. At many sites most of the flight passes in less than a week, whereas at others, adults precede juveniles by as many as three weeks. Most honey buzzards spend but three months on their breeding grounds, and their nesting cycle is compressed accordingly, especially during courtship and nest construction (Brown 1976). Western Honey Buzzards are strong flyers that migrate rapidly even in adverse winds—nine satellite-tracked individuals averaged 170 km/day in Europe, 270 km/day across the Sahara, and 125 km/day farther south in Africa (Hake et al. 2003)—and stopovers are brief, suggesting that the species does not feed regularly once migration begins.

Adult and juvenile honey buzzards differ in both plumage and proportions, and in the field the two age classes are easily separated at close range in good light. Age-specific differences are many, but overall, adults have decidedly cleaner and more conspicuous markings than juveniles, and their body is smaller in relation to their wingspan than is that of shorter-winged first-year birds (Forsman 1999). As a result of such distinctions, we know that migration behavior of the two age classes differs substantially. Juveniles are less likely to detour along overland routes and are more likely to undertake overwater crossings than are adults, and most young birds remain in Africa during their entire second year and return to their breeding grounds in their third year of life (Cramp and Simmons 1980).

Counts at traditional hawkwatches in the central Mediterranean provide some of the best examples of the extent to which adult and juvenile buzzards differ in the timing and geography of their migrations. Adults migrate through southern Italy in late August–early September each year, typically following the Italian peninsula south to the toe before crossing the Straits of Messina into eastern Sicily, and from there west across the island, before flying across the narrowest part of the Sicilian Channel en route to Cape Bon, Tunisia. The return flight in spring largely retraces this route. First-year birds, which migrate through southern Italy later in September and generally do so across a broader front, track south (rather than west) once crossing onto Sicily, and undertake a far longer over-water passage to North Africa from southeastern Sicily through Malta, and from there on to Libya.

Although members of the two age classes sometimes commingle during their southbound journeys, in autumn most flocks are made up entirely of adults or juveniles. Presumably, juveniles require more time to acquire enough fat for their journeys than do adults, hence the delay in their flight. The broader frontal and seemingly more direct north-to-south route taken by juveniles suggests that the first-time migrants rely largely on compass orientation, whereas experienced adults are using true navigation and are detouring overland to bypass lengthy over-water passages (Agostini and Logozzo 1995; Agostini et al. 2002b). Movements of six adult and three juvenile honey buzzards tracked by satellite from breeding areas in Sweden to wintering grounds in Africa confirm this idea (Hake et al. 2003).

Satellite-tracked adults traveled more quickly on outbound migration than did juveniles, taking on average 42 days to complete their journeys, compared with 64 days for juveniles. Adults were more likely to detour around the western Mediterranean and cross into Africa at the Strait of Gibraltar than were juveniles, and, although juveniles initially set out more directly for their wintering grounds than adults, they subsequently showed greater "directional scatter" while migrating—possibly due to wind drift—thereby negating any shortcut effect, even while engaging in lengthy over-water travel.

Most likely, adults learn how to navigate on their initial outbound and return migrations; and those that do not are able to take advantage of the skills of more knowledgeable individuals by flocking with them. Inexperienced first-year birds, which leave the breeding grounds after adults have departed, are forced to depend on a hard-wired orientation capacity which, for Swedish birds, takes them on a southwesterly course toward, but not necessarily to, the Strait of Gibraltar. Wind drift spreads the juvenile flight more widely than that of experienced migrants, resulting in its greater broad-frontal nature.

The rudimentary direction-finding skills of juveniles are not without cost: a recent analysis of the population dynamics of Swedish birds indicates that second-year and adult honey buzzards have annual survival rates of rates of 86 percent, versus 49 percent in first-year birds. A poignant example of the consequences of navigational naïveté comes from a satellite-tracked first-year bird taken from a nest in Sweden and brought to Scotland as part of a reintroduction effort there. The bird in question was fitted with a satellite transmitter at its nest near Inverness, Scotland on 10 August 2002. On 15 September it began migrating south. One week later it was in southwestern England. Two days after that, it was flying downwind in a westerly direction over the North Atlantic more than 600 kilometer west of Land's End in southwesternmost England. The last signal was received on 4 October when the bird was at the latitude of the Strait of Gibraltar but more than 1000 kilometers west of it in the middle of the North Atlantic, obviously lost at sea (R. Dennis, pers. comm.).

The ability and willingness (at least among juveniles) of Western Honey Buzzards to fly long distances over water, their use of both soaring and flapping flight en route, and their tendency to continue migrating in adverse conditions allow the species to complete one of the most rapid of all long-distance migrations. Unfortunately, these same traits allow first-year birds to get into trouble quickly, which may explain why this migration strategy is relatively uncommon among raptors.

Where to watch the migration. Western Honey Buzzards are reported as outbound or return migrants or both at 132 *Hawks Aloft Worldwide* migration watchsites, principally in Europe and the Middle East (Zalles and Bildstein 2000). Although annual counts at most watchsites range from dozens of birds to hundreds of individuals, a handful of watchsites report flights of thousands to more than one-hundred thousand birds.

European hotspots include Falsterbo, in southwesternmost Sweden, where 10,000 honey buzzards were seen on a single day in early September 1971, and where counts averaged 5,200 and peaked at 22,110 in 1986–1997; Col de Bretolet in the Swiss Alps, where counts averaged 859 in 1980–1994; Organbidexka in the western Pyrenees, southern France, where counts averaged 11,740 and peaked at 21,500 in 1981–1994; Leucate, a spring hawkwatch on the Mediterranean Sea in southern France, where counts averaged 10,000 in 1982–1991; Tarifa, at the Strait of Gibraltar in southernmost Spain, where more than 40,000 were seen crossing to Morocco in 1997; the Straits of Messina in northeastern Sicily, where counts averaged 19,273 in 1989–1998, and where 5552 were seen on a single day in early May 1998; Burgas, a Black

Sea site in eastern Bulgaria, where counts averaged 23,000 in 1979–1996, and where 4740 were seen on a single day in late August 1993; and the Bosporus in northwestern Turkey, where counts average 9000, and where 25,745 were counted in 1971. Middle Eastern hotspots include the Northern Valleys, a transect watchsite in northern Israel where counts averaged 343,370 and peaked at 437,400 in 1988–1991; and Elat, a springtime watchsite in southern Israel, where counts averaged 363,200 in 1977–1988 and peaked at 851,600 in 1985 (Zalles and Bildstein 2000).

Conservation concerns. Western Honey Buzzards appear to have been little affected by pesticide misuse during the DDT Era. Land-use change, habitat loss (particularly that of rain forests in the species' West African breeding grounds), and shooting pose serious threats. The species continues to be shot on migration—both for sport and for use in private taxidermy collections— particularly in the Pyrenees, southern Italy and Sicily, southern Turkey, Lebanon, and Africa. In Malta, an archipelago nation in the central Mediterranean, individuals are shot while attempting to enter or leave Buskett Gardens, a small forested bird sanctuary and traditional roost site (Plates 11 and 12). In Sweden, adults and recently fledged young also are shot on their breeding grounds (Tjernberg and Ryttmann 1994). In areas where Northern Goshawks are heavily persecuted, nestling honey buzzards are sometimes killed when they are misidentified as the former (Kostrzewa 1998).

Honey buzzards are long-lived raptors with low reproductive rates, and, as such, shooting can be especially problematic. Although provisionally considered "secure" in Europe, overall the species is in significant decline in both Sweden and Finland (Birdlife International 2004), presumably at least in part because of persecution there. Sustained and, at times, ferocious antishooting campaigns in eastern Sicily have managed to reduce significant shooting there (Giordano et al. 1998), and the same technique is now being applied elsewhere. In time, such efforts, together with widespread education campaigns, offer the promise of eradicating this unfortunate problem.

Northern Harrier

Spanish: Aguilucho pálido, Gavilán rastrero, Gavilán sabanero

German: Kornweihe

French: Busard Saint-Martin

aka: Hen Harrier, Marsh Hawk

Size: Length 41–52 cm; wingspan 97–122 cm; weight 290–600 grams

Estimated world population: 100,000–250,000; generally declining

Type migrant: Partial; some migratory populations long-distance, a few individuals transcontinental

The Northern Harrier, which is known as the Hen Harrier in Great Britain, is a medium-sized, low-flying, slender raptor with a distinctive white rump. It occurs in a variety of open habitats across much of the northern temperate zone. The species is the most northerly distributed and the second most widespread of the world's 16 species of harriers, and it may be the most abundant harrier in the world.

The Northern Harrier nests on the ground, often in loose colonies. Individuals roost communally on the ground in winter as well. Harriers search for prey almost entirely on the wing, most often while coursing or quartering within a few meters of the ground. The species feeds primarily on small mammals, especially voles (*Microtus* spp.), as well as on birds, reptiles, amphibians, and insects (MacWhirter and Bildstein 1996; Ferguson-Lees and Christie 2001).

The Northern Harrier is a quintessential partial migrant. Most of its small-mammal prey becomes decidedly less available following the first significant snowfall in late autumn or winter, and its northernmost populations—the species nests above the Arctic Circle in both the Old and New World—are completely migratory. Populations that breed at low latitudes are partially migratory, with the extent of movement in any one year depending on snow cover and, to a lesser extent, temperature. Banding suggests that harriers are *leapfrog migrants,* with northern populations migrating earlier and across longer distances than populations at lower latitudes. Locations of winter communal roosts tend to be traditional, suggesting that at least some individuals return to the same wintering areas in successive years.

Unlike perch-hunting raptors and species that hunt while soaring high above the landscape, Northern Harriers spend about 30 percent of each day in semi-active hunting flight close to the vegetative canopy. As a result, harriers are strong flyers and, although they often soar while migrating, are far less deterred in their migratory efforts by weather than are most migrants and are well known for continuing their movements during periods of inclement weather. At Hawk Mountain, for example, harriers often migrate during periods of both intermittent and continuous rain, and although some individuals detour around local rain showers and snow squalls, others fly through such events. As a result, the magnitude of the species' flight is less affected by the passage of cold fronts than that of any other migrant at the Sanctuary (Allen et al. 1996; MacWhirter and Bildstein 1996).

Like many other migratory raptors, Northern Harriers regularly concentrate along regional *diversion lines* (e.g., coastlines) and at peninsular water crossings. Nevertheless, they are far less likely to track leading lines than are many other migratory birds of prey, and, consequently, usually compose a small (<5%), albeit consistent, portion of the flight at most watchsites. Although low percentages accurately reflect the species broad-frontal tendencies, small population size and the fact that the species frequently migrates at tree-top level below the "radar screen" of many hawkwatchers also may play a role in their relative low numbers on migration counts.

As a group, harriers are well known for their willingness to cross large bodies of water. Pacific Marsh Harriers for example, regularly migrate across the 160-km-wide Bass Strait that separates Tasmania from southeastern Australia, as well as across the 130-km Torres Strait between New Guinea and northeastern Australia; and many Pied Harriers breeding on continental Asia overwinter on the Pacific Islands of Taiwan, the Philippines, and Borneo. Northern Harriers are no exception in this regard. Small numbers regularly migrate across the 100-km Florida Strait between southern Florida and Cuba en route to overwintering grounds in Cuba, Hispaniola, and Puerto Rico; European breeders overwinter in Corsica and Sardinia in the western Mediterranean; and continental Asian breeders overwinter throughout the Japanese archipelago in the Far East. That the species has been recorded as a vagrant in both Iceland and Hawaii also suggests considerable over-water flight ability.

Ecologically, the migration behavior of Northern Harriers can best be thought of as "linearization" of the species daily hunting routine. Northern Harriers regularly hunt while migrating, and individuals sometimes interrupt their flight for days or even weeks to do so. This extensive feeding explains several of the distinctive features of the species' migration. Harriers are remarkably gregarious raptors both when nesting colonially during the breeding season and when roosting communally in winter; however, the species is not gregarious on migration. Indeed, unlike other broad-frontal migrants, including the Osprey and Peregrine Falcon, both of which often travel along major migration corridors in loose flocks of up to a dozen or more individuals, Northern Harriers rarely do so. This, together with the fact that the Northern Harrier has one of the most seasonally protracted of all migrations (Table 17), strongly suggests that individuals purposefully keep their distances while migrating, presumably to reduce competition for food en route.

Table 17. *Seasonal timing of outbound raptor migration at Hawk Mountain Sanctuary, 1936–1995*

Species	Days to complete middle	
	50% of the flight	75% of the flight
Osprey	19	31
Bald Eagle	30	55
Northern Harrier	**39**	**58**
Sharp-shinned Hawk	16	28
Cooper's Hawk	16	29
Northern Goshawk	24	38
Red-shouldered Hawk	19	32
Broad-winged Hawk	8	13
Red-tailed Hawk	19	32
Rough-legged Hawk	22	36
Golden Eagle	23	39
American Kestrel	25	38
Merlin	16	30
Peregrine Falcon	15	30

Note: Note the protracted seasonal progression of Northern Harriers at the site, which is typical for the species. The only species that approaches that of the Northern Harrier in terms of a protracted migration at the site is the Bald Eagle, whose autumnal movements include those of both outbound and return migrants (see Bald Eagle description for details).

Part of the Northern Harrier's seasonally prolonged migration is reflected in consistent sex- and age-specific differences in migration periodicity in the species. On outbound migrations in autumn, for example, the juvenile flight precedes the adult flight by as much as a month or more. Juvenile males tend to precede juvenile females by as much as a week, and adult females precede adult males by as much as three weeks. In spring, the progression is somewhat reversed with males preceding females and adults preceding juveniles (Bildstein et al. 1984; Bildstein 1988). Although explanations for the sex- and age-specific differences are often tied to differences in molt or to the idea that males migrate earlier in spring to gain breeding territories, the end result is that individual Northern Harriers are well spread out during migration, making the species one of the most solitary of all raptor migrants.

That said, not all species of harriers are solitary migrants. The long-distance and completely migratory Pied Harrier, a species that breeds in northwestern Asia and overwinters in southeastern Asia, India, and on several

Pacific archipelagos, frequently flocks on migration, at least at places such as Beidaihe, China, where close to 3000 individuals were seen on single days in early September 1986 (Zalles and Bildstein 2000). Presumably, this little-studied raptor fuels its journey by fattening prior to migration or by encountering concentrated food resources en route, neither of which occurs in the Northern Harrier.

Where to watch the migration. Northern Harriers are reported as outbound or return migrants or both at 243 of 388 *Hawks Aloft Worldwide* migration watchsites, making them one of the most widely distributed of all migratory birds of prey (Zalles and Bildstein 2000). At most watchsites, annual counts range from a few individuals to several hundreds of birds. At coastal and lakeside watchsites south of large breeding concentrations, numbers can grow to thousands of birds seasonally.

North American outbound hotspots include Holiday Beach Migration Observatory east of the mouth of the Detroit River on the northern shore of Lake Erie in southern Ontario, where counts averaged 918 and peaked at 1276 in 1998–2003; Hawk Cliff, on Lake Erie in southern Ontario, where counts averaged 827 and peaked at 1488 in 1996–2003; Hawk Ridge, on the outskirts of Duluth, Minnesota, at the western end of Lake Superior, where counts averaged 700 and peaked at 1373 in 1996–2003; Cape May, in peninsular southern New Jersey, where counts averaged 1752 and peaked at 2421 in 1996–2003; and Kiptopeke, Virginia, a peninsular watchsite at the mouth of the Chesapeake Bay where counts averaged 1080 and peaked at 1970 in 2002–2003. North American return migration hotspots include Braddock Bay near Rochester, New York, on the southern shoreline of Lake Ontario, where counts averaged 746 and peaked at 1022 in 2002–2003; and Derby Hill, on the southeastern shoreline of Lake Ontario, north of Syracuse, New York, where counts averaged 624 and peaked at 1554 in 1995–2003.

European outbound hotspots include Falsterbo in southwestern Sweden, where counts averaged 239 and peaked at 379 in 1998–2003. Return hotspots include Skagen, in northern peninsular Denmark, where counts averaged 201 and peaked at 548 in 1972–1998.

As mentioned above, Northern Harriers are protracted migrants, and most of the passage at between 30° and 40° north is spread thinly from mid-September through late November and beyond.

Conservation concerns. Although the species was never specifically targeted as a "chicken hawk" in North America, its conspicuous hunting behavior and tendency to roost communally at traditional winter roosts made it a frequent target of shooters in the early and mid-1900s. On the British Isles, where its common name is Hen Harrier, the species has been, and continues to be, fiercely persecuted as a predator on upland game including Red Grouse (Redpath and Thirgood 1997). Harrier populations declined dramatically in many areas of North America and Europe during the DDT era of the mid-twentieth century but have since rebounded in most locations. The continued loss of freshwater and estuarine wetlands across much of its range, together with the unintentional destruction of active nests during haying and grain harvest in agricultural areas, pose the greatest current threats to most populations. Overall, the species appears to be declining globally (del Hoyo et al. 1994; MacWhirter and Bildstein 1996).

Grey-faced Buzzard

Spanish: Busardo Carigrís

German: Kiefernteesa

French: Busautour à jouses grises

aka: Frog Hawk, Grey-faced Buzzard-Hawk, Grey-faced Buzzard Eagle

Size: Length 46 cm; wingspan 105 cm; weight 375–430 grams

Estimated world population: 100,000–1,000,000; apparently stable or declining

Type migrant: Complete; long-distance, and partially transequatorial

Together with the Eastern Honey Buzzard, Chinese Sparrowhawk, and Japanese Sparrowhawk, the Grey-faced Buzzard is one of four East Asian species that make up the bulk of raptor migration along the East-Asian Continental and Oceanic flyways (see Figure 1). It also is one of the least studied of all long-distance migrants.

The largely forest-dwelling raptor breeds in wooded and mountainous areas of southeasternmost Russia, southern Manchuria, northern China, and central and southern Japan. Grey-faced Buzzards overwinter in southeastern China, Southeast Asia, Taiwan, Indonesia, and the Philippines. The species feeds primarily on frogs, reptiles, and rodents (Brown and Amadon 1968; del Hoyo et al. 1994; Zalles and Bildstein 2000; Ferguson-Lees and Christie 2001).

Grey-faced Buzzards have long, slender, pointed wings and relatively long tails. As such the species is ideally suited to a flap-and-glide, accipiter-like flight while hunting for frogs and other small vertebrate prey. Little studied anywhere in its range, the species is believed to be in significant decline in

Russia. As recently as the 1990s, large numbers of Grey-faced Buzzards were shot on migration in southern Taiwan.

By far the most migratory of four species in an otherwise largely sedentary genus, Grey-faced Buzzards depart for their Southeast Asian and Pacific Island wintering grounds in late September and early October. Most travel in flocks ranging from several birds to well over a thousand individuals. Many migrate south along the East-Asian Continental Flyway and overwinter in eastern China and Southeast Asia, and the species is one of the most common migrating raptors in Thailand. Most of the world population, however, migrates south along the East-Asian Oceanic Flyway. Although some join the flyway in southern Japan after traveling south along the Korean Peninsula, many travel south across the Japanese archipelago, before island hopping along the Ryukyu Islands of the East China Sea. From there Grey-faced Buzzards travel onto and through Taiwan, and thereafter across the Bashi Channel and Luzon Strait, en route to the Philippines, Borneo, and northwestern Oceania. On Honshu, in central Japan, Grey-faced Buzzards migrate over both land and water, with many individuals ringing skyward before shortcutting across both broad and narrow bays rather than following the course of the region's highly dissected coast (Brazil and Hanawa 1991).

The over-water journeys of Grey-faced Buzzards, which include individual passages of more than 300 km, qualify the species as one of the most oceanic of all long-distance raptor migrants. And indeed only Amur Falcons, a species whose Indian Ocean travels are mentioned later in the chapter, and Chinese Sparrowhawks, which precede Grey-faced Buzzards on outbound migration in autumn along the same East-Asian Oceanic Flyway, regularly engage in as much over-water travel on their migrations.

Exactly how Grey-faced Buzzards manage to complete their long-distance over-water movements remains something of a mystery. Like other over-water migrants in the region, the species appears to time its flights to take advantage of regional tail winds, both on outbound and return migrations. In addition, much of the over-water portion of the journey occurs within the trade wind zone, a region in which predictable 24-hour *sea thermals* (see Chapter 4 for details), allow the birds to migrate day and night in low-cost soaring flight. The extent to which Grey-faced Buzzards lay down fat prior to their movements, although unstudied, is probably significant, as typhoons and other cyclonic storms sometimes suspend the flight for a week or more. The birds, which often travel in large flocks, are unlikely to find much in the way of food during such interruptions.

Although the energetic details of the Grey-faced Buzzard's unusual migration strategy remain largely speculative, the geography of the flight is well understood. One hundred and six of 2,486 southbound Grey-faced Buzzards that were banded in the Ryukyu archipelago in the 1960s were later shot in the Philippines. One of these individuals had traveled at least 1000 km in five days, another at least 1600 km in 19 days. Overall, 26 of the birds survived for at least five years, and one was recovered alive eight years after having been banded. Unfortunately, 60 percent had been killed by people before the next breeding season, indicating the extent to which survivorship in the species is influenced by human action (McClure 1998).

Where to watch the migration. Grey-faced Buzzards are reported as outbound or return migrants or both at 24 *Hawks Aloft Worldwide* watchsites, principally in Japan, Taiwan, and Southeast Asia (Zalles and Bildstein 2000). Miyako Island in the Ryukyus is a traditional stopover site for tens of thousands of outbound Grey-faced Buzzards that use the East-Asian Oceanic Flyway each autumn. "Shashiba," as they are called locally, approach the island from the north on seasonal "miinishi" tail winds in linear flocks, known as "hawk pillars." Farther south in southernmost Taiwan, Kenting National Park ranks as one of the best places to watch the outbound flight. More than 18,000 buzzards were counted at the peninsular watchsite in autumn 2001, as they headed out across the Bashi Channel and the Luzon Strait en route to the Philippines. Daily flights of more than 1000 birds are typical at the site in mid-October. Other concentration points include Kohyama-cho in Kagoshima, Japan, where an estimated 32,000 buzzards were seen during three weeks in late September–mid-October 1999.

Conservation concerns. Grey-faced Buzzards, along with Chinese Sparrowhawks, were once shot by the hundreds, at first for food and, more recently, for the taxidermy trade, both on the Ryukyus and Taiwan. This is no longer true, at least not in heavily populated areas and major roosts where conservationists have mounted campaigns to protect them (Severinghaus 1991). Nor are they kept as household pets as was once common on Miyako Island in the Ryukyus. On the other hand, timber production and farmland expansion continue to reduce breeding habitat in northeastern China (Deng et al. 2003).

Steppe Buzzard

Spanish: Busardo Estepario

German: Steppenbussard

French: Buse de la steppe

aka: Desert Buzzard, Foxy Buzzard

Size: Length 45 cm; wingspan 115 cm; weight 400–950 grams

Estimated world population: 500,000–1,000,000; apparently stable

Type migrant: Complete; long-distance, transequatorial, and transcontinental

The Old World "Steppe Buzzard" is the most migratory of the 11 subspecies of the Eurasian Buzzard, the most widely distributed and most common true "buzzard" in the world.

Smaller and with narrower wings than less migratory Eurasian Buzzards, the Steppe Buzzard is also more rufous (i.e., reddish), hence its subspecific name *vulpinus,* which means "foxy." Steppe Buzzards breed as far north as the Arctic Circle (66° 33' north) in eastern Scandinavia, west into the mountains and steppes of central Asia into Mongolia, and south to about 41° north in the northern Caucasus range. The most northern race of all Eurasian Buzzards, Steppe Buzzards leapfrog over their less migratory cousins and overwinter in sub-Saharan and southern Africa where they become one of the region's most common open-habitat raptors.

A quintessential land-based soaring migrant that avoids water crossings whenever possible, the Steppe Buzzard is particularly gregarious on migration and frequently travels in flocks of from hundreds to thousands of birds along well-established corridors with few water crossings (Cramp and Simmons 1980; Ferguson-Lees and Christie 2001).

One of the longest-distance migrants of all raptors, Steppe Buzzards travel up to 13,000 km one way between their Eurasian breeding grounds and East and South African wintering areas. One of southern Africa's most widespread raptors, Steppe Buzzards overwinter as far into the continent as the Cape of Good Hope (Figures 26 and 27). The species spends so much on migration (a period in which it does not molt) that individuals require more than a year to replace all of their flight feathers (Herremans 2000). The perils of long-distance migration apparently are substantial, especially for younger individuals, close to two-thirds of which die within 12 months of fledging (Brown 1976).

Steppe Buzzards feed principally on small mammals, both on their breeding grounds and in their wintering areas, and they often concentrate in agricultural landscapes while doing so. Although studies have shown that Steppe Buzzards lay down considerable fat prior to migration, the large numbers of migrants that have been captured with food-baited traps in the Middle East indicate that at least some individuals supplement stored fat by feeding en route (Gorney and Yom-Tov 1994).

Figure 26. Coastal Mediterranean-like Fynbos habitat on the Cape of Good Hope south of Cape Town, South Africa; typical overwintering habitat for migratory Steppe Buzzards. (Photo by the author)

Figure 27. The wine lands west of Cape Town. Migrating Steppe Buzzards that breed in subarctic Europe and Asia are the most common raptors in these habitats in austral summer. (Photo by the author)

Like most soaring migrants, Steppe Buzzards depend on weather, including thermals and favorable winds, to complete their long-distance journeys. In Africa, for example, many are assisted on both their south- and northbound flights by tailwinds associated with the *Intertropical Convergence Zone* (ITCZ), a regional weather pattern that oscillates seasonally north and south across the tropics of sub-Saharan Africa (Auburn 1994).

Steppe Buzzards are sometimes difficult to distinguish on migration from other races of Eurasian Buzzards, particularly when individuals pass high above in large flocks. Banding and trapping, however, confirm that the overwhelming majority of "buzzards" that pass through the Middle East each year are Steppe Buzzards, rather than the less migratory nominate Eurasian form that occurs at lower latitudes throughout much of Europe. The species follows an elliptical migration in the Middle East, with most of the southbound flight passing east of Israel in autumn and entering Africa at Djibouti across the Bab el Mandeb strait from Yemen in southernmost Arabia; whereas the bulk of the northbound flight follows the western shorelines of the Red Sea toward Sinai before entering southern Israel near Elat (Shirihai et al. 2000).

The species' migration is perhaps best studied at the northern end of the Gulf of Aqaba, in and around Elat, Israel, where close to half a million buzzards are counted each spring and more than 4500 birds have been banded since 1984 (Shirihai et al. 2000). Research at the site indicates that returning adults precede juveniles by several weeks, and that the former have significantly greater fat reserves than the latter while doing so (Gorney and Yom-Tov 1994). Surprisingly, investigators have not detected dehydration in the birds that they have handled, despite the fact that the migrants have just crossed a thousand or more kilometers of Saharan desert. Even so, close to 7 percent of the birds that are trapped at Elat have tarred or oiled feathers and feet, presumably the result of their misidentifying oil-field spills in North Africa as sources of freshwater en route (Clark and Gorney 1987; Yosef et al. 2002). Steppe Buzzards tracked with radar while flying across the deserts of southern Israel soared as high as 2000 m (or 2 km) while traveling cross-country at speeds of 30 to 40 km per hour (Spaar 1995).

Where to watch the migration. Eurasian Buzzards, including Steppe Buzzards, are reported as outbound or return migrants or both at 166 of 225 European, Asian, and African *Hawks Aloft Worldwide* watchsites (Zalles and Bildstein 2000). One of the best places to see large numbers of the species is several miles west of the city of Elat, in southern Israel, where large multi-thousand bird flocks pass in early April in most years. Other, albeit more remote, sites that count large numbers of Steppe Buzzards include Borçka in the Pontic Mountains of northeastern Turkey, where close to a quarter of a million buzzards are seen on outbound migration each autumn, and where as many as 80,000 individuals have been recorded on single days in late September; and Burgas, on the Black Sea Coast of eastern Bulgaria, where outbound counts average 30,000 birds. Conditions for soaring are likely to be good to excellent wherever the species appears regularly in large numbers. Spectacular flights tend to form quickly and rise to great heights with many birds appearing as "pepper specks" while passing. Overall, the outbound flight at 30° to 40° north peaks in mid- to late September.

Conservation concerns. The Steppe Buzzard subspecies of the Eurasian Buzzard does not appear to be threatened currently. The species dependence on small mammals in agricultural areas, however, suggests that habitat change and loss may pose a problem in the future.

Amur Falcon

Spanish: Cernicalo del Amur

German: Amurfalke

French: Faucon de l'Amour

aka: Eastern Red-footed Falcon, Manchurian Falcon

Size: Length 30 cm; wingspan 75 cm; weight 120–160 grams

Estimated world population: 250,000–500,000; apparently stable

Type migrant: Complete; long-distance, transequatorial, and transcontinental

If one species can claim the title for undertaking the most arduous of all raptor migrations, it is the Amur Falcon, a slender, long and pointed-winged, kestrel-sized falcon that breeds across 3.8 million km² of open and semi-open areas in northeastern Asia and overwinters in southern Africa (Plate 13).

Once considered an eastern subspecies of the Red-footed Falcon of Europe and western and central Asia—the breeding ranges of the two forms are separated by a gap near Lake Baikal in southern Siberia—its plumage and behavior differ sufficiently from its western counterpart, and raptor taxonomists now rank the Amur Falcon as a full species. In addition to the Red-footed Falcon, the species other close relatives include the Lesser Kestrel, Madagascar Kestrel, and American Kestrel (Cade 1982; Kemp and Crowe 1993; del Hoyo et al. 1994; Ferguson-Less and Christie 2001).

A true transcontinental, transequatorial, long-distance flocking migrant, the Amur Falcon's breeding and principal wintering ranges are separated by both 70° of latitude and longitude, and the species' approximately 22,000-km round-trip annual journey is one of the longest migrations of any raptor. What really distinguishes its migratory habits from those of all other raptors, however, is that more than 3000 km of its outbound journey occurs above the Indian Ocean, making its migration far and away the most oceanic of any bird of prey.

Much about the Amur Falcon remains enigmatic. Indeed, the species has yet to be studied in detail on its breeding grounds. What is known about this tiny falcon is that adults and juveniles gorge themselves on insects, including migratory locusts, and on small vertebrates before evacuating their east-Asian breeding in early autumn. Although some travel across the Himalayas of central Nepal, the majority of Amur Falcons, particularly adults, avoid this high-altitude passage by flying along the eastern edge of the Tibetan Plateau, before stopping for several months in northeastern India and Bangladesh. Once there, the birds again feed voraciously and fatten noticeably before embarking on a lengthy overland flight that bisects the Indian peninsula and, apparently immediately thereafter, an even longer over-water journey across the western Indian Ocean. The initial overland leg of travel presumably occurs only by day. The subsequent 3000-km over-water leg, however, by necessity involves both day- and nighttime flight. The timing of this second leg of the journey appears to be critical. More than a month of preflight fattening in northeastern India and Bangladesh delays the over-water southwest passage well into late November and early December. By then, northern or "boreal-winter" easterlies have established themselves across the region, and these tailwinds, together with sea thermals associated with the monsoonal weather, significantly reduce the metabolic needs of the migrants during the over-water portion of their journey. Even so, some Amur Falcons, particularly those with inadequate fat reserves or poor navigational skills, almost certainly fail to reach the equatorial African coasts of eastern Somalia and Kenya. That the migrants travel in enormous flocks rather than alone (Ali and Ripley 1978; de Roder 1989) no doubt enhances their likelihood of success.

The species' return journey, which begins in late February and early March, is less well understood. Amur Falcons appear to follow an elliptical course that takes the birds northwest of their outbound route, with flocks of thousands of falcons journeying overland north to the Horn of Africa and from there northwest into the Arabian Peninsula en route to Iran, Afghanistan, and Pakistan. Whether the birds pass north or south of the Tibetan

Plateau, or fly directly across it, awaits additional study. Springtime observations of migrants in northern Afghanistan, however, indicate that at least some of the flight detours north and around this formidable barrier (Ali and Ripley 1978).

The relatively small size and, consequently, high metabolic rate of the Amur Falcon, its gregarious nature during migration, the availability of a suitable staging area for intramigration fattening, and predictable tailwinds during a lengthy over-water passage, together with the falcon's predisposition for powered migratory flight, conspire to produce one of the most unusual and extreme forms of raptor migration anywhere.

Although the overwhelming majority of the world's more than 250,000 Amur Falcons overwinter in southern Africa each year, counts of more than 1000 migrants at the Beidaihe watchsite 250 km east of Beijing, China, in October 1993, together with reports of smaller numbers at the same site in late April; a report of a less-than-25-bird flight in Hong Kong in autumn 2003; and scattered sightings of individual birds in Southeast Asia in winter indicate that at least some Amur Falcons regularly migrate along the land-based East-Asian Continental Flyway as well. Whether such individuals represent a distinct geographic breeding population is unknown.

Where to watch the migration. Despite their large-scale movements, Amur Falcons are difficult to see on migration both because of the geography of their movements and the heights and speeds at which they travel. Indeed, as incredible as it seems, the species has not been reported in large numbers along its principal migration corridor in southwestern India since the late nineteenth century when a "huge flock numbering some thousands" was reported near Belgaum (15° 54' N, 74° 36' E) in late November and "immense scattered flocks" were reported in several years in late November–early December near Karwar (circa 14° 30' N) in coastal southwestern India (Ali and Ripley 1978). Although Amur Falcons are reported as outbound or return migrants at six Asian and seven African *Hawks Aloft Worldwide* (Zalles and Bildstein 2000) watchsites, the counts tend to be small and sightings somewhat unpredictable. One of the best places to see the species in large numbers is on its wintering grounds in South Africa, where individuals roost in trees by the thousands in the centers of small towns in eastern Cape Province and the Transvaal.

Conservation concerns. There no recent reports of declines—at least not regionally—anywhere in the species range. The Amur Falcon's need to refuel at least once while migrating, its gregarious nature en route as well as on the wintering grounds, and its seeming dependence on swarming insect prey (see

Chapter 10), suggest that pesticide misuse, together with the loss of grass-lands in Asia and Africa, pose the greatest threat to the species.

Final Thoughts

The eight raptors whose migration life histories are summarized above reveal the extent to which individual species have been able to employ various migration strategies and tactics to successfully complete long and, in some instances, not-so-long journeys. In a few species, including the Amur Falcon, almost all individuals behave the same way at the same time. In other more widespread species, such as the Eurasian Buzzard, virtually all individuals in some subspecies migrate, whereas most individuals in others do not. Some species, including the Northern Harrier, travel largely alone while migrating, whereas some, such as the Osprey, that do so in the temperate zone, tend to migrate in flocks in the tropics, at least when anticipating over-water journeys. Others, such as Grey-faced Buzzards, Steppe Buzzards, and Amur Falcons, almost always travel in large groups. Some species, including western North American populations of Turkey Vultures, forgo feeding en route, at least for most of their journey, whereas others, such as Northern Harriers, regularly stop to feed while migrating.

Although the take-home message initially seems confusing, viewed through the lens of biological diversity the many different ways that raptors migrate makes perfect sense. Each species uses those features of migration that best suit its ecological circumstances, and because the circumstances that each faces differ considerably, their migrations differ as well. And indeed, the flexible nature of raptor migration is one of the principal reasons that so many of the world's raptors migrate in the first place.

—9—

Great Hawkwatches

A bad day at Hawk Mountain Sanctuary is better
than a good day anywhere else.
Anonymous

One of the best ways to develop an appreciation for the
numerous rules and countless complexities of raptor
migration is to see migrants in action at a hawkwatch. Indeed, well-timed visits to established migration watchsites provide opportunities for seeing large
numbers of migrating birds of prey up close and in the company of experienced hawkwatchers who can help identify them.

The sport of hawkwatching has its deepest roots in the United States,
Canada, and Europe, and most of the world's famous watchsites are found
there. These areas, however, have no corner on the market, and any list of
hawkwatches that failed to include migration watchsites elsewhere would be
far from complete. Indeed, the real challenge in compiling the list of watch-

sites that follows has been to reduce to a dozen the number of "representative" sites described herein. Several of the watchsites mentioned were chosen largely for their history and conservation actions, others for their diversity of species or the incredible magnitude of their flights, and others still for their geographic settings and landscapes. Hundreds of additional great raptor migration watchsites are described in Heintzelman (1986, 2004) and in Zalles and Bildstein (2000).

Hawk Mountain Sanctuary, Pennsylvania, U.S.A.

Hawk Mountain Sanctuary, the world's first refuge for birds of prey, was founded in 1934 by conservationist Rosalie Edge, who wanted to stop the shooting of thousands of raptors migrating along the Kittatinny Ridge in the central Appalachian Mountains of eastern Pennsylvania. The Sanctuary is 40 kilometers west of Allentown, Pennsylvania, and 170 km west of New York City. Today, Hawk Mountain Sanctuary maintains the longest and most complete record of raptor migration in the world. In addition to its colorful conservation history, the Sanctuary offers magnificent views of 16 species of migrants, including regionally scarce and seldom-seen raptors such as Northern Goshawks and Golden Eagles, and panoramic views of Pennsylvania's central Appalachian countryside.

Modern weather and ancient orogeny are responsible for the large numbers of migrants that pass Hawk Mountain's lookouts each autumn. When they were formed 300 million years ago, the peaks of the Kittatinny and other central Appalachian ridges towered as high as those of the Alps. Millions of years of "mass wasting," however, have reduced the once-mighty range to the far more modest corduroy hills of Pennsylvania's Valley-and-Ridge Province, including the southeasternmost Kittatinny. The region's local relief—the vertical distance between a mountain's peak and the surrounding lowlands—rarely exceeds 300 meters, less than half of what geologists would call mountainous terrain. But what the ridges of the central Appalachians lack in height, they more than make up for in length. The Kittatinny Ridge alone extends across 400 kilometers northeast-to-southwest from southern New York State through northern New Jersey and into eastern Pennsylvania, almost as far as Maryland. The Appalachian Trail, which forms the Sanctuary's eastern boundary, is seven times as long, and the entire Appalachian range spans 20° of latitude, or almost one-fourth the distance from the equator to the North Pole. The range's exceptional length, together with its largely north-south orientation, creates the backdrop for one of the raptor world's great migration flight-lines. Hundreds of thousands of raptors use this *updraft corridor* each autumn. Northern breeders include Peregrine Falcons from Greenland and Labrador together with Ospreys, Sharp-shinned Hawks, and Broad-winged Hawks from Eastern Quebec. Southern breeders include Turkey Vultures, Cooper's Hawks, and Red-shouldered Hawks from New England and the Mid-Atlantic states.

Migration at Hawk Mountain is most pronounced when prevailing northwesterly winds strike the northeast-to-southwest oriented Kittatinny at right angles. Deflected up and over the ridges, the updrafts that result form an important corridor for soaring birds of prey that creates a leading line for thousands of outbound migrants each autumn.

A Storied Past

Hawk Mountain Sanctuary owes its origins to the irruptive movements of Northern Goshawks along the Kittatinny during the winters of 1926–1927 and 1927–1928. The Northern Goshawk was considered a vicious killer at the time, even by many conservationists (Bildstein and Compton 2000), and the species' "invasions" into Pennsylvania in the late 1920s were not welcome events. Rural residents reported the unappreciated irruptions to local game protectors, and they, in turn, alerted State Ornithologist George Miksch Sutton, who visited Hawk Mountain in October 1927. Sutton and his companions collected several shot raptors, including four goshawks. On a second trip three days later, and accompanied by several shooters, the group secured "in a remarkably short time" 90 Sharp-shinned Hawks, 11 Cooper's Hawks, 16 Northern Goshawks, 32 Red-tailed Hawks, and 2 Peregrine Falcons. No wonder local residents called the site "Hawk" Mountain.

Sutton published his findings in the *Wilson Bulletin*, a quarterly journal of ornithology, the following June (Sutton 1928a). The 12-page technical report had two diametrically opposed effects: First, the Pennsylvania Game Commission used the report to justify a five-dollar bounty on Northern Goshawks, second, it alerted conservationists to shooting at the site, setting into motion a series of events that resulted in the founding of Hawk Mountain Sanctuary. Shortly after the article appeared, two Philadelphia birdwatchers, Richard Pough and Henry Collins, visited the ridgetop shooting gallery and confirmed and expanded the initial report in accounts published in *Bird Lore* (Pough 1932) and *The Hawk and Owl Society Bulletin* (Collins 1933). In the autumn of 1933, Pough displayed photographs of the shooting at Hawk Mountain at a meeting of the Linnaean Society in New York City. Conservationist Rosalie

Figure 28. View to the northeast from Hawk Mountain Sanctuary's official long-term count site, the North Lookout. (Hawk Mountain Sanctuary archives)

Edge, founder and head of the Emergency Conservation Committee, was in the audience the evening Pough spoke. Outraged by what she saw, Edge sprang into action. Together with her son Peter, Edge toured Hawk Mountain in June of 1934. After her visit, Edge leased, and one year later purchased, the 565 hectares that was to become Hawk Mountain Sanctuary. That August, Edge hired a young Massachusetts birdwatcher, Maurice Broun, as "ornithologist-in-charge" of the new refuge.

Together with wife Irma, Broun arrived at the shambles of a Sanctuary in early September and spent most of that month posting "no-hunting" signs and informing the neighbors of the site's new status as the world's first refuge for birds of prey. On 30 September 1934 he began counting migrants from what was then called Observation Rocks, and what is now known as the North Lookout (Figure 28). Although Broun initiated the counts primarily to document the numbers of raptors that were being protected at the site, he quickly realized that a series of season-long counts would allow the Sanctuary to monitor regional populations of the birds. Indeed, by the second year of operation, autumn counts of migrants became the principal feature of Hawk Mountain Sanctuary's field work (Broun 1939).

Broun's reports of substantial flights of Golden Eagles at the site (39 birds in his first autumn), of the abrupt passage of Broad-winged Hawks in mid- to late September, and of the relationship between cold fronts and the magnitude of visible migration at the site rank among the Sanctuary's most significant contributions to ornithology (Bildstein and Compton 2000). By the mid-twentieth century, Hawk Mountain's long-term counts were being used by conservationists, including Rachel Carson, to document pesticide era population declines in several species of raptors, including Bald Eagles and Peregrine Falcons. By the end of the twentieth century, Hawk Mountain had established itself as a global information hub and training center for raptor conservationists with its successful international internship program, its authorship of *Raptor Watch: A Global Directory of Raptor Migration Sites* (Zalles and Bildstein 2000), and the construction of a world-class biological field station, The Acopian Center for Conservation Learning, for hosting visiting scientists.

The Flight

Each autumn, counters at Hawk Mountain record a visible passage of approximately 18,000 migrating birds of prey. Three species, Sharp-shinned Hawk, Broad-winged Hawk, and Red-tailed Hawk, make up more than 95 percent of the flight. The elliptical migrations of many migrants seen at the site in autumn result in a return flight that is less than 10 percent of the far more impressive outbound migration. Although some of the raptors migrating at Hawk Mountain appear as "pepper specks" hundreds of meters above the Sanctuary's 11 available lookouts, many are seen at close range as they slope soar within a few meters of the treetops of the Kittatinny's deciduous-coniferous forests. The passage rates of most species increase substantially shortly after cold fronts pass through the region, and many visitors time their visits to take advantage of this relationship.

The site's official long-term count is made at the North Lookout, a less than quarter-acre escarpment promontory, 1.5 kilometers from the Sanctuary's entrance gate. Other staffed lookouts include South Lookout and Appalachian Overlook. Activities at the lookouts include interpretation of the flight, scheduled and impromptu talks on raptor identification and cultural and natural history, and ongoing question-and-answer sessions on raptor migration and conservation. The South Lookout is 300 meters from the main parking lots and is wheelchair accessible. Altogether, 11 Sanctuary lookouts are open to the public.

Although the official autumn count begins on 15 August and concludes on 15 December, a few migrants, including southern Bald Eagles and American Kestrels, can be seen as early as late July, and in most years weather-related pulses of migrating Northern Bald Eagles, Northern Harriers, and Red-tailed Hawks occur well into December and January. The bulk of the outbound migration passes from mid-September through mid-October, with the largest movement occurring during the third week of September at the peak of the Broad-winged Hawk flight.

The official spring count begins 1 April and continues through 15 May. In most years the return flight peaks during the third week of April.

Hawk Mountain's Visitor Center houses raptor exhibits, including a gallery with life-size, in-flight models of all 16 of the Sanctuary's regular migrants, historical displays, a bookstore and gift shop, and restrooms. Hawk Mountain Sanctuary maintains a large and regularly updated website (http://www.hawkmountain.org) that includes directions to the site and information about restaurants and accommodations in the area, as well as news of the flight and other activities.

Three books have been written about Hawk Mountain Sanctuary: *The Mountain and the Migration* by Jim Brett (1991) serves as a useful guide to the site and a wonderful introduction to hawkwatching; *Hawks Aloft* by Maurice Broun (1949) is a captivating account of the Sanctuary's early years; *The View from Hawk Mountain* by Michael Harwood (1973) updates the history of the Sanctuary through the early 1970s and provides recollections of both hawkwatching and hawkwatchers there. *Racing with the Sun: The Forced Migration of the Broad-winged Hawk* (Bildstein 1999) describes the flight of Broad-winged Hawks at Hawk Mountain, and *Mountaintop Science: The History of Conservation Ornithology at Hawk Mountain Sanctuary* (Bildstein and Compton 2000) summarizes the watchsite's contributions to science and conservation.

Migration Specifics

Sixteen species are recorded as regular migrants at Hawk Mountain; two species are irregular migrants. Approximately 18,000 and 1000 migrants are seen in autumn and spring, respectively. The information below—average [and record] annual count, record one-day count, and peak period of passage for each species—is based on 67 years of autumn counts between 1934 and 2003.

Black Vulture (50 [80 in 1999], 21 on 15 Nov 1998, Nov); *Turkey Vulture*

(250 [367 in 1999], 80 on 24 Oct 1994, late Oct–Nov); *Osprey* (380 [869 in 1990], 175 on 23 Sep 1989, Sep–early Oct); *Bald Eagle* (60 [211 in 2003], 48 on 4 Sep 1948, late August–Sep); *Mississippi Kite* (vagrant); *Northern Harrier* (230 [475 in 1980], 36 on 30 Sep 1953 and 29 Oct 1955, mid-Sep–mid-Nov); *Sharp-shinned Hawk* (4350 [10,612 in 1977], 2475 on 8 Oct 1979, Sep–mid-Nov); *Cooper's Hawk* (350 [1,118 in 1998], 204 on 8 Oct 1981, mid-Sep–mid-Nov); *Northern Goshawk* (70 [347 in 1972], 64 on 10 Nov 1973, late Oct–mid-Dec); *Red-shouldered Hawk* (275 [468 in 1958], 148 on 19 Oct 1958, Oct–mid-Nov); *Broad-winged Hawk* (8230 [29,519 in 1978], 11,349 on 16 Sep 1948, 12-25 Sep); *Swainson's Hawk* (irregular, 13 total in 11 different years); *Red-tailed Hawk* (3310 [6208 in 1939], 1144 on 24 Oct 1939, Oct–Nov); *Rough-legged Hawk* (9 [31 in 1961], 7 on 11 Nov 1961, Nov); *Golden Eagle* (55 [159 in 2003], 31 on 20 Nov 2003, late Oct–Nov); *American Kestrel* (170 [835 in 1989], 168 on 3 Sep 1977, Sep–early Oct); *Merlin* (50 [176 in 2001], 36 on 10 Oct 1997, late Sep–Oct); *Gyrfalcon* (irregular, 6 total in 5 different years); *Peregrine Falcon* (25 [62 in 2002], 31 on 5 Oct 2002, late Sep–Oct).

Cape May Point, New Jersey, U.S.A.

With a record of serious hawkwatching dating from 1932 (Allen and Peterson 1936), Cape May Point is one of the oldest raptor-migration watchsites in the world. The sandy, coastal-plain peninsula in southernmost New Jersey also is a world-class birding hotspot where single-day record counts of thrushes and wood warblers regularly exceed 100,000 individuals, and where more than 1.5 million shorebirds arrive each spring to feast on hundreds of millions of recently laid horseshoe crab eggs. The official count is conducted from a wooden deck at the northeast corner of a parking lot at the foot of the famed Cape May Lighthouse, one sand dune in from the Atlantic surf (Figure 29).

The migration funnel that forms the northern lip of the entrance to Delaware Bay has deep ornithological roots. Dutch colonist Pieterson de Vries reported enormous flocks of Passenger Pigeons at the site in 1633 (Connor 1991); the "Father of American Ornithology," Alexander Wilson, first visited the area in the winter of 1811; and George Ord collected the type specimen of the Cape May Warbler in a maple swamp on the peninsula later that year (Hunter 1983). Late-eighteenth and early nineteenth century ornithologist Witmer Stone's classic two-volume work, *Bird Studies at Old Cape May* (1937) summarizes four decades of field work on the Cape. Not surpris-

Figure 29. View to the north of Cape May Bird Observatory's watchsite. The count at Cape May Point is conducted from an observation deck at the northern edge of the parking lot. (Photo by the author)

ingly, Stone (1922) was the first to recognize the significance of raptor migration in the region, stating that "the broad expanse of Delaware Bay, where it meets the ocean, forms a break in the coast line and the migrants seem to hesitate to cross during a gale for fear of being blown out to sea." Stone also was the first to comment on shooting at the site:

> Poles were formerly attached to the tops of the pine and cedar trees, and gunners stationed below slaughtered the [Northern] Flickers which were continually alighting on them, by the thousand. Since the killing of flickers has been stopped by law, local gunners have established the Sharp-shinned Hawk as a game bird and regularly resort to the point in automobiles to kill them during September and October. In one week in September 1920 no less than 1400 were known to have been killed, one man securing 60. Most of the gunners eat the birds and claim that they are quite palatable.

Roger Tory Peterson (1965), who at the time was fast becoming the dean of American birding, tested the shooters' claim in September 1935:

I watched 800 sharpshins try to cross the firing line. Each time a "sharpy" sailed over the tree tops it was met by a pattern of lead. . . . By noon 254 birds lay on the pavement. That evening, in a Cape May home, I sat down to a meal of hawks—twenty sharpshins, broiled like squabs, for a family of six. I tasted the birds, found them good, and wondered what my friends would say if they could see me. Like a spy breaking bread with the enemy, I felt uneasy. I could not tell my hosts I disapproved, for their consciences were clear—weren't they killing the hawks as edible game and at the same time saving all the little songbirds.

Witmer Stone's and other conservationists' concerns led the National Association of Audubon Societies to launch sporadic counts and anti-shooting campaigns at the site for seven years in the 1930s, the effect of which was to all but shut down gunning there. Additional hawkwatches were conducted in the autumns of 1965 and 1970, however, despite its rich ornithological and conservation history, few birders were aware of the magnitude of the site's hawk flight until birder extraordinaire, Pete Dunne, reported more than 48,000 migrants during the Point's first "full season" count in 1976. Season-long counts have occurred annually since then.

The Flight

In most autumns, counters from New Jersey Audubon's Cape May Bird Observatory record a visible passage in excess of 55,000 migrating birds of prey. Species composition of the flight at Cape May differs substantially from that of the region's inland sites in that *Buteos* make up a relatively small part of the passage. North America's smallest *Accipiter*, the Sharp-shinned Hawk, is the most common migrant at the site, followed by the continent's smallest falcon, the American Kestrel.

These two species make up more than 70 percent of the flight, with Sharp-shinned Hawks alone representing more than half of the passage. Broad-winged Hawks rank a distant third, and in most years pass in numbers that are not much greater than those of Ospreys, Northern Harriers, Cooper's Hawks, Merlins, and Peregrine Falcons.

Coastal breezes, wetlands, expansive tidal marshes, migrating shorebirds and songbirds, wind drift, and, in at least one case, juvenile inexperience, conspire to produce the characteristic seaside flavor of Cape May's raptor flight. Migrants fly decidedly lower on days when winds are out of the northwest quarter, and they are far less likely to continue across the bay at such times, making them more visible to observers. As at other latitudinally similar hawkwatches in eastern North America, many of each season's strongest flights coincide with the passage of strong cold fronts, particularly when the latter pass on the heels of a prolonged warm spell near the seasonal peak of one or more of the watchsite's predominant migrants. Return migrants are far less numerous at the site, and there is no official spring count (Sutton and Sutton 1982–1983).

Ospreys presumably are drawn to the flyway by feeding opportunities offered by the region's coastal wetlands, Northern Harriers by its expansive brackish and freshwater marshes, and Merlins and Peregrines by its abundant shorebirds and songbirds. All of these species are strong flyers that readily undertake short and intermediate over-water flights and that thrive on Cape May's onshore breezes. The prolific Sharp-shinned Hawk, however, is another story entirely.

By far the most common migrant at the hawkwatch—a record 61,167 were seen in 1984—the overwhelming majority of Sharp-shinned Hawks at Cape May are first-year birds (Clark 1985a). For more than a century, hawkwatchers have suggested that although most Sharp-shinned Hawks migrate inland through the region, wind-drifted birds regularly stack up along the Atlantic Seaboard (Trowbridge 1895; Allen and Peterson 1936; Mueller and Berger 1967b; but see Murray 1964) (Figure 30). That most of the Sharp-shinned Hawks seen at Cape May are juveniles, that adults are relatively more common inland regionally, and that juveniles banded at Cape May are more likely to be recaptured as adults inland than coastally (Clark 1985a; Viverette et al. 1996) suggests that a juvenile propensity for wind drift (see Chapter 4 for details) contributes significantly to the enormous numbers of these small accipiters at the site.

In addition to the strong migration there, the bayside region of southern New Jersey directly northwest of Cape May supports exceptional numbers of Black Vultures, Turkey Vultures, Bald Eagles, Northern Harrier, Cooper's Hawks, Sharp-shinned Hawks, Red-tailed Hawks, Rough-legged Hawks, and American Kestrels in winter, highlighting the area's importance to raptors, as well as to the birdwatchers that are interested in them (Sutton and Kerlinger 1997).

The site's official migration count begins 1 September and concludes 30 November. The bulk of the flight occurs between late September and mid-October, when well over half of the passage is counted. This also is the best time for viewing large numbers of Peregrine Falcons, with more than a thousand being counted in several recent years.

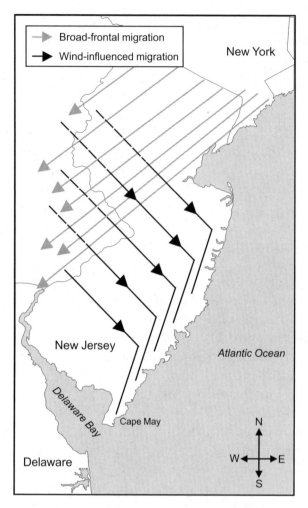

Figure 30. Schematic depicting how wind drift can result in large numbers of migrating Sharp-shinned Hawks and other raptors at Cape May Point, New Jersey (after Allen and Peterson 1936, 396).

Cape May Point Banding Station, a part of Cape May Bird Observatory, began operations in 1967. Between then and 1982, the station trapped more than 27,000 Sharp-shinned Hawks (Clark 1985a). Data from the station have been used to study age- and sex-related differences in over-wintering areas in the species, as well as the extent to which juveniles reuse the coastal corridor in subsequent years. Banded raptors are sometimes brought to the observation deck for viewing and release.

The Observatory's Northwood Center off of Sunset Boulevard at Lily Lake is open seven days a week. The Center offers travel, nature, and birding information, as well as a variety of books, gifts, and optical equipment. The Observatory also maintains a website (http://www.njaudubon.org/centers/CMBO) that includes seasonal totals for the site since 1976.

A number of books have been written about Cape May and its birds. Stone's 1937 classic *Bird Studies at Old Cape May* includes more than 60 pages on the area's raptors and their migrations. *The Birds of Cape May*, by David Sibley (1993), updates the status of raptors and other birds at the site and provides useful maps for birders. Jack Connor's colorful and informative narrative, *Season at the Point: The Birds and Birders of Cape May*, details the history of Cape May's modern count through the late 1980s. The book, which provides a hilarious account of the banders, birders, conservationists, and other colorful characters who have graced the Point over the years, is a must read for first-time visitors. Clay and Pat Sutton's (1982–1983) scholarly description of spring migration at the site also is worthwhile reading for those intending to visit the Point.

Migration Specifics

Sixteen species of raptors are recorded as regular migrants at Cape May Point, three species are irregular migrants, and two species are vagrants. Approximately 54,000 migrants are seen in autumn. The information below, including average [and record] annual count, record one-day count, and peak period of passage, is based on 28 years of autumn counts between 1976 and 2003.

Black Vulture (75 [370 in 1997], 41 on 2 Oct 2003, Nov); *Turkey Vulture* (1443 [6420 in 1996], 784 on 3 Nov 1996, Nov); *Osprey* (2495 [6734 in 1996], 1023 on 3 Oct 1989, late Sep–early Oct); *Mississippi Kite* (irregular, more common in spring); *Bald Eagle* (85 [284 in 1996], 24 on 19 Sep 1996, late Sep–early Oct); *Northern Harrier* (1757 [3115 in 1994], 278 on 12 Nov 1980, mid-Sep–mid-Nov); *Eurasian Sparrowhawk* (vagrant); *Sharp-shinned Hawk* (28,512 [61,167 in 1984], 11,096 on 4 Oct 1977, late Sep–Oct); *Cooper's Hawk* (2426 [5009 in 1995], 570 on 13 Oct 2003, Oct); *Northern Goshawk* (34 [89 in 1997], 13 [twice], late Oct–Nov), *Red-shouldered Hawk* (430 [872 in 1994], 165 on 10 Nov 1994, Nov); *Broad-winged Hawk* (2799 [13,918 in 1981], 9400 on 4 Oct 1977, late Sep–early Oct); *Swainson's Hawk* (irregular, 3 [10 in 1998], 3 on 2 dates, early Oct); *Red-tailed Hawk* (1952 [5135 in 1996], 1022 on 11 Nov 1994, late Oct–Nov); *Ferruginous*

Hawk (irregular); *Rough-legged Hawk* (4 [13 in 1999], 4 on 13 Nov 1983, Nov); *Golden Eagle* (12 [38 in 1996], 8 on 3 Nov 1996, Nov); *American Kestrel* (9980 [21,821 in 1981], 5038 on 30 Sep 1999, mid Sep–early Oct); *Common Kestrel* (vagrant); *Merlin* (1647 [2875 in 1985], 867 on 30 Sep 1999, late Sep–early Oct); *Peregrine Falcon* (636 [1793 in 1997], 298 on 5 Oct 2002 late Sep–early Oct).

Hawk Ridge Nature Reserve, Minnesota, U.S.A.

The open waters of the Great Lakes of North America, which together span 15° of longitude, create a formidable barrier for many of the continent's hydrophobic migrants. To the east, the Niagara Peninsula, separating Lake Huron from Lakes Erie and Ontario, funnels huge flights of raptors along the northern shorelines of the two easternmost lakes. Farther west, the main flight is similarly deflected by the northern shoreline of Lake Superior, which, together with the ancient Sawtooth Mountains at the lake's westernmost point, funnel large numbers of outbound migrants through the hillsides above the port city of Duluth, Minnesota (Figure 31).

Like its counterparts in eastern North America, Hawk Ridge Nature Re-

Figure 31. The Hawk Ridge watchsite, overlooking Lake Superior near Duluth, Minnesota. (Photo by the author)

serve owes its origins as a migration watchsite to an anti-shooting campaign. The story begins in the late 1940s when the Duluth Bird Club (now the Duluth Audubon Society) mobilized its forces to stop local gunners who were using raptors for target practice. Most shooting happened along the principal migration flight-line on the outskirts of town, which was known to the locals as "the hawk pass at Duluth." Newspaper accounts suggest that the recreational gunning of hawks was popular enough for several shooting blinds to have been erected along the route. Armed with legislation passed in 1945, which, on paper at least, forbade the shooting of all but 3 of the 20 species of Minnesota's raptors, the Duluth Bird Club publicized the illegal activity, and the prohibition against shooting was enforced within the city.

In 1951, the Duluth Bird Club began to count the migrants on somewhat ironically named "target days" in mid-September and early October. Once the magnitude of the flight became apparent, counts increased from just a handful of days to all-but-daily efforts from August through November. Systematic observations from the main overlook began in 1972, the same year that banding began at the site. Hawk Ridge also conducts spring counts several kilometers southwest of the reserve.

The Flight

Bolstered by an unprecedented flight of 200,000 migrants in 2003—the previous one-year record was 148,615 in 1993—the site now boasts a long-term average of 70,000 migrants a year. Three species, Broad-winged Hawks, Sharp-shinned Hawks, and Red-tailed Hawks, represent 90 percent of the flight. As is true at many sites where the flight is dominated by obligate soaring migrants, many birds pass high overhead. Many others, however, do not, and great looks at accipiters and falcons occur on most days between mid-September and mid-October. One notable feature of the site is that Broad-winged Hawks often roost in the woods at and around the reserve. Their massive liftoffs as thermals build the following morning, alone, are well worth a visit to the site.

The Hawk Ridge passage also includes exceptional flights of Bald Eagles and Northern Goshawks, both of which peak in late October through early November. Hawk Ridge also reports Swainson's Hawks, with as many as 34 individuals seen on a single day.

The banding station, which operates day and night between mid-August and late November, traps about 3000 owls and diurnal raptors each autumn. Sharp-shinned Hawks make up more than 60 percent of all raptors and owls

Figure 32. A crowd gathers around an educator at Hawk Ridge. Activities at the site include numerous weekend programs. (Photo by the author)

trapped at the site; Northern Saw-whet Owls make up another 19 percent. An astounding 7327 Northern Goshawks, or about 250 a year, have been trapped at the site. Data from the station have been used to study the timing and geography of Sharp-shinned Hawk migration, as well as mortality and exposure to organophosphate insecticides in the species (Rosenfield and Evans 1980; Evans and Rosenfield 1985).

Although there is no official visitor center at the reserve, there is an information display, as well as a bookstore and gift kiosk. Watchsite activities include help in raptor identification, demonstrations involving banded raptors, and a "Hawk Weekend" at the peak of the Broad-winged Hawk flight in September that features talks and other events (Figure 32). The site maintains a well-organized and frequently updated website (http://www.hawkridge.org).

The southwestern shoreline of Lake Superior offers a mirror-image diversion line for return migrants, and a spring count involving two observation points along West Skyline Drive, 11 and 19 kilometers southwest of the main overlook at Hawk Ridge, was initiated in 1997. Enger Tower, west of downtown Duluth, is used on most days. Thompson Hill, to the west, is used on days when easterly winds predominate and the birds adopt a more westerly flight-line around the Lake. The lack of a natural funnel results in a less concentrated movement in spring, but even so spring counts have averaged more than 25,000 birds since the second observation point was added in 2000. Spring flights are best on days with southern or southwesterly winds. Because the ground is still rather cold when most returning migrants pass through the region, thermals tend to be weaker in spring and most of the birds ride mountain updrafts, resulting in excellent opportunities for close looks.

Migration Specifics

Fourteen species are recorded as regular migrants at Hawk Ridge; seven species are irregular migrants. Approximately 70,000 migrants are seen in autumn. A spring hawkwatch conducted from one of two locations along West Skyline Drive, depending on the wind, reports an average 25,500 migrants annually. The information below, including average [and record] annual count, record one-day count, and peak period of passage, is based on 32 years of autumn counts between 1972 and 2003.

Black Vulture (irregular, 1 total); *Turkey Vulture* (899 [2119 in 2003], 799 on 29 Sep 1996, mid-Sep); *Osprey* (267 [575 in 1998], 68 on 12 Sep 2002, Sep–early Oct); *Bald Eagle* (1172 [4368 in 1994], 743 on 22 Nov 1994, late October); *Northern Harrier* (655 [1390 in 1994], 216 on 17 Sep 1994, mid-Sep); *Mississippi Kite* (irregular, 5 total); *Sharp-shinned Hawk* (14,356 [22,344 in 1997], 2034 on 8 Oct 2003, mid-Sep); *Cooper's Hawk* (130 [356 in 1993], 45 on 14 Sep 2000, mid-Sep); *Northern Goshawk* (1070 [5819 in 1982], 1229 on 15 Oct 1982, mid-Oct); *Red-shouldered Hawk* (irregular, 88 total); *Broad-winged Hawk* (40,905 [160,703 in 2003], 101,698 on 15 Sep 2003, 12–25 Sep; *Swainson's Hawk* (irregular, 178 total); *Red-tailed Hawk* (6412 [15,448 in 1994], 3,991 on 24 Oct 1994, mid-Oct); *Ferruginous Hawk* (irregular, 1 total); *Rough-legged Hawk* (431 [1011 in 1994], 204 on 10 Nov 1963, late Oct); *Golden Eagle* (57 [190 in 2001], 29 on 26 Oct 2001, late Oct); *American Kestrel* (1421 [3769 in 2002], 744 on 9 Sep 2002, mid-Sep); *Merlin* (162 [460 in 1997], 73 on 9 Oct 1998, mid-Sep); *Prairie Falcon* (irregular, 5 total); *Gyrfalcon* (irregular, 21 total); and *Peregrine Falcon* (37 [111 in 1997], 21 on 29 Sep 1997, late Sep).

Corpus Christi Hawk Watch, Texas, U.S.A.

Texans have long been known to claim that everything is bigger in the Lone Star State than elsewhere in the United States, and when it comes to counting raptors they are right on target. The Corpus Christi Hawk Watch at Hazel Bazemore

County Park in western Nueces County, Gulf Coast Texas, consistently reports the United States' largest flights of Broad-winged Hawks. With a record count of more than 970,000 of these small buteos in 1998, and a long-term average of approximately 700,000 birds, Corpus Christi ranks as the numerically most important watchsite anywhere in North America outside of Mexico.

The site owes the predictability of its enormous flight both to continental geography—Gulf Coast Texas is along the northeastern rim of North America's southern terminus—and to regional crosswinds, which push most of the passage close to the coast. A relatively hot coastal plain also helps. These factors, together with the fact that Corpus Christi sits at the junction of several important eastern migration corridors and at least one important western corridor, means that the site regularly reports counts that represent about half of the world's Broad-winged Hawks.

As is true of many newer watchsites, Corpus Christi Hawk Watch owes its origins to a small number of dedicated local volunteers who began counting migrants at Hazel Bazemore County Park and elsewhere in the area in the mid-1970s. Most of the early counts were episodic one-person events that depended on the combined availability of individual watchers and the likelihood of a spectacular movement. In 1988, John Economidy began 10-day counts at the Wood River Country Club outside Corpus Christi, and shortly after serious attempts were made to determine the regularity and locations of regional flight-lines. Based on these and other preliminary counts in the area, HawkWatch International conducted a full-season count at Hazel Bazemore County Park in the autumn of 1997 that reported a flight of 841,139 raptors representing 24 species (Smith et al. 2001).

The principal lookout, which sits atop a 28-meter "hill" on the southern bank of the Nueces River, represents the highest elevation in the region. The site has good visibility to the west and northeast. Three auxiliary count sites, first used in 1999, complement the primary lookout.

The Flight

Each autumn, counters at Hazel Bazemore County Park record a visible flight of approximately 730,000 migrants, 95 percent of which are Broad-winged Hawks. The next three most common migrants at the site, Turkey Vultures, Mississippi Kites, and Swainson's Hawks, together make up almost all of the remainder of the flight. Spring migration at the site, although potentially significant, has yet to be studied in detail. In autumn, most of the broadwing flight passes in a series of enormous flocks, frequently at considerable heights.

Kettles of more than 10,000 individuals are common, and single-day counts of 250,000 Broad-winged Hawks occur during the height of the species passage in late September. The largest single-day flight ever observed in the area occurred on the heels of a cold front in 1977, when 750,000 Broad-winged Hawks were estimated to have roosted near the site on the night of 4–5 October. Broadwing flight activity tends to peak at between 10 and 11 a.m. and again from 1 to 2 p.m. Other species exhibit different patterns.

Movements of Swallow-tailed Kites and Mississippi Kites peak in late August. Turkey Vultures and Swainson's Hawks peak in October. With average annual passages of close to 22,000 Turkey Vultures, and slightly more than 5000 Swainson's Hawks, Corpus Christi provides one of the better venues for these species north of Mexico.

The site also hosts small but predictable passages of White-tailed Hawks, Crested Caracaras, and Prairie Falcons and less-regular movements of Harris' Hawks, Zone-tailed Hawks, and Short-tailed Hawks, along with the passages of 11 species of more typical North American migrants.

The official count begins on 15 August and concludes on 15 November. There is a small admission fee to the 78-acre park, which is operated by the Nueces County Parks and Recreation Department. Camping is allowed in designated areas by permit. The site maintains an informative and humorous website (http://www.ccbirding.com/thw/) that includes directions and other useful information.

Migration specifics

Nineteen species are recorded as regular migrants at Hazel Bazemore County Park; 11 species are irregular migrants. Approximately 730,000 migrants are seen each autumn. The information below, including average [and record] annual counts, record one-day counts, and peak period of passage for each species, is based on seven years of counts between 1997 and 2003.

Black Vulture (484 [1398 in 1999], 254 on 1 Nov 1999, late Oct–early Nov); *Turkey Vulture* (21,894 [42,536 in 2002], 17,153 on 15 Oct 2002, Oct–early Nov); *Osprey* (141 [199 in 2003], 25 on 30 Sep 1999, Sep–early Oct); *Bald Eagle* (irregular, 10 total in five different years); *Northern Harrier* (161 [331 in 1999], 35 on 30 Sep 1999, late Sep–early Nov); *Hook-billed Kite* (irregular, 1 total); *Swallow-tailed Kite* (23 [57 in 2002], 16 on 20 Aug 2001, mid-Aug–early Sep); *White-tailed Kite* (irregular, 23 total in seven years); *Mississippi Kite* (6420 [10,155 in 2001], 2250 on 20 Aug 2001, mid-Aug–early Sep*); Sharp-shinned Hawk* (1169 [1869 in 2002], 221 on 7 Oct

1998 and 14 Oct 2003, late Sep–Oct); *Cooper's Hawk* (647 [1092 in 1999], 162 on 14 Oct 2003, late Sep–Oct); *Northern Goshawk* (irregular, 2 total in two different years); *Harris' Hawk* (11 [28 in 1999], 3 on 28 Oct 2001, mid-Sep–Oct); *Red-shouldered Hawk* (63 [92 in 2002], 12 on 24 Sep 2001, Sep–mid-Nov); *Broad-winged Hawk* (692,086 [970,025 in 1998], 446,200 on 26 Sep 2001, mid-Sep–late Sep); *Short-tailed Hawk* (irregular, 2 total in a single year); *Swainson's Hawk* (5461, [14,260 in 2001], 8756 on 14 Oct 2001, Oct–mid-Nov); *White-tailed Hawk* (6 [13 in 1999], 2 on 27 Sep 1999, 25 Sep 2001, and 14 Oct 2003, Sep–Oct); *Zone-tailed Hawk* (irregular, 18 total in five different years); *Red-tailed Hawk* (175 [282 in 1999], 58 on 9 Nov 2000, Oct–early Nov); *Ferruginous Hawk* (irregular, 20 total in six different years); *Rough-legged Hawk* (irregular, 5 total in two different years); *Common Black Hawk* (irregular, 1 total); *Golden Eagle* (irregular, 10 total in six different years); *Crested Caracara* (12 [21 in 2001 and 2003], 7 on 22 Oct 1999, Sep–Oct); *American Kestrel* (512 [860 in 2003], 184 on 14 Oct 2003, Sep–mid Oct); *Merlin* (31 [57 in 2003], 23 on 8 Oct 1999, Sep–mid Oct); *Prairie Falcon* (11 [33 in 1999], 5 on 23 Sep 1999, Sep–mid-Oct); *Peregrine Falcon* (143 [241 in 1999], 29 on 22 Sep 2003, Sep–mid Oct); *Aplomado Falcon* (irregular, 2 total in two different years).

Grassy Key, Florida, U.S.A.

The Florida Keys, a chain of sandy coralline islands that arches across more than 200 km of Caribbean Basin from peninsular Florida southwest along the northern side of the Straits of Florida, have been known to concentrate migrating raptors for well over a century. But although reports of the flight date from Audubon's time, it was not until the late 1980s, when a chapter of the National Audubon Society began sponsoring a single-day "All-Keys Hawkwatch" in October, that the true magnitude of the flight was at last recognized (Hoffman and Darrow 1992). The single-day counts, which scattered observers across eight sites from Key Largo to Key West in 1989, 1990, and 1991, documented flights of hundreds of raptors representing 13 species, including a then astounding one-day passage of 129 Peregrine Falcons on Boot Key on 13 October 1991.

The Flight

Sharp-shinned Hawks, American Kestrels, and Broad-winged Hawks, in that order, make up approximately 70 percent of the flight. Other numerically significant migrants at the site include Ospreys (6%), Northern Harriers (4%), Cooper's Hawks (3%), Merlins (4%), and Peregrine Falcons (10%). Indeed, with flights in excess of 2000 Peregrine Falcons in some years, Grassy Key, together with Kéköldi Indigenous Reserve (see below) in coastal Costa Rica at the other end of the Caribbean basin, ranks as one of the best watchsites for Peregrine Falcons anywhere. The site also is a great place to see an occasional Swallow-tailed Kite and Short-tailed Hawk, two migrants that are rarely counted elsewhere in North America, as well as small numbers of Swainson's Hawks, an uncommon migrant east of the Mississippi.

A noteworthy aspect of the flight is that of *reverse migration*, a phenomenon in which migrants that are first counted traveling south at the site reverse course upon reaching the southern terminus of the archipelago, and are re-counted traveling north. This turn-about migration, which is rare in most places, is common in the region, with at least some apparently lost or "misdirected" individuals retracing their flight paths well into peninsular Florida and, perhaps, beyond (Simons 1977; Darrow 1983). Counts of northbound migrants are subtracted from those of southbound migrants at the site to produce a "net" count each year.

The hawkwatch at Grassy Key is a partnership between HawkWatch International and the Florida Audubon Society. The site conducts official counts and offers guided visits and education programs on most days between 15 September and 13 November. There is an active raptor banding station near the lookout, and a wildlife and birding festival, "Broadwings on the Beach," is held in early October. The watchsite is halfway between Key Largo and Key West in Curry Hammock State Park, on the ocean side of U.S. Highway 1 at Mile Marker 56.1. Additional information about the hawkwatch can be found at http://www.hawkwatch.org/keysmigration/index.

Migration Specifics

Fourteen species are recorded as regular migrants at Grassy Key; one species is an irregular migrant. Approximately 15,400 migrants are seen each autumn. The information below, including peak period of passage, is based on 4 years of autumn counts between 1999 and 2002. Average [and record] annual counts are based on net annual counts (i.e., seasonal southbound counts minus northbound counts). Record one-day counts are based on single-day southbound highs.

Osprey (1098 [1657 in 2002], 284 on 26 Sep 2002, mid-Sep–early Oct); *Bald Eagle* (14 [21 in 2002], 4 on 3 Oct 2002, mid-Sep–early Oct); *Northern*

Harrier (613 [766 in 1999], 150 on 18 Oct 1999, Oct); *Swallow-tailed Kite* (9 [17 in 2001], 5 on 16 and 17 Sep 2001, mid-Sep–early Oct); *Mississippi Kite* (27 [57 in 2001], 23 on 16 Sep 2001, mid-Sep–early Oct); *Sharp-shinned Hawk* (3330 [4300 in 1999], 873 on 18 Oct 1999, Oct); *Cooper's Hawk* (402 [640 in 2000], 104 on 17 Oct 2000, Oct); *Red-shouldered Hawk* (12 [28 in 1999], 6 on 8 Oct 2000, Oct); *Broad-winged Hawk* (2958 [5194 in 2002], 883 on 4 Oct 2002, Oct); *Short-tailed Hawk* (26 [38 in 2001], 7 on 11 Nov 2001, mid-Oct–early Nov); *Swainson's Hawk* (43 [109 in 2001], 40 on 9 Nov 2001, late Oct–early Nov); *Red-tailed Hawk* (irregular, 8 total); *American Kestrel* (3113 [4338 in 2001], 966 on 1 Oct 2001, Oct); *Merlin* (566 [665 in 1999], 64 on 8 Oct 1999, late Sep–Oct); *Peregrine Falcon* (1645 [2001 in 2002], 333 on 5 Oct 2000, late Sep–mid Oct).

Golden Gate Raptor Observatory, California, U.S.A.

With a view overlooking the city of San Francisco, Golden Gate Raptor Observatory on the Marin Headlands, along San Francisco Bay, is one of the most attractive raptor migration watchsites in all of North America. The hawkwatch began in 1972, when Laurence Binford, having spent several years watching raptors migrating past his office window at the California Academy of Sciences Building at Golden Gate Park, decided to determine the extent of the regional flight. Binford situated his "official" watchsite on Bunker Hill, an old military installation above Point Diablo at the mouth of San Francisco Bay (the site is now called Hawk Hill). During his first six autumns of sporadic counts—the site was still being used by the military as a rifle range—Binford tallied close to 9000 hawks in fewer than 300 hours of observation, establishing the site as a bona fide coastal highway for migrating birds of prey.

The Flight

Red-tailed Hawks (33%), Turkey Vultures (30%), Sharp-shinned Hawks (15%), and Cooper's Hawks (10%) make up most of the 18-species, 30,000-bird flight. Northern Harriers, Red-shouldered Hawks, and American Kestrels round out most of the count. Migration is most pronounced on northwesterly winds. The heaviest flights occur during the second half of September. The flight remains strong through early November, however, and October is preferred by visitors that wish to avoid the fog that prevails in the season. Many migrants hesitate at the Headlands before crossing the mouth of San Francisco Bay, and there is ample opportunity to study many of the raptors that pass through. The site is a great place to see White-tailed Kites—a rare migrant at most North American watchsites—as well as the occasional western Broad-winged Hawk.

Golden Gate Raptor Observatory is a volunteer project of the Golden Gate National Parks Conservancy. The site maintains an attractive website (http://www.ggro.org) with daily updates of the flight, a raptor quiz, descriptions of past flights, and general information about the site. Counts are conducted most days between 20 August and 20 December. Weekend programs, including introductions to the basics of raptor migration and raptor identification, as well as banding demonstrations, are offered in September and October. The best hawkwatching is at Hawk Hill 1.8 miles up Conzelman Road from Highway 101.

Migration Specifics

Eighteen species are recorded as regular migrants at Golden Gate Raptor Observatory; two species are irregular migrants. Approximately 30,000 migrants are seen each autumn. The information below, including average [and record] annual count, and peak period of passage, is based on seven years of autumn counts between 1997 and 2003.

Turkey Vulture (9573 [11,046 in 2002], late Sep–Oct); *Osprey* (106 [138 in 2000], Sep); *Mississippi Kite* (irregular, 1 total); *White-tailed Kite* (61 [86 in 2001], Oct); *Bald Eagle* (5 [8 in 1997], Nov–Dec); *Northern Harrier* (847 [1369 in 1999], Oct–Nov); *Sharp-shinned Hawk* (4467 [6348 in 1999], mid-Sep–mid-Oct); *Cooper's Hawk* (2337 [3015 in 1999], mid-Sep–mid-Oct); *Northern Goshawk* (irregular, 12 total); *Red-shouldered Hawk* (401 [677 in 2002], Sep–mid-Oct); *Broad-winged Hawk* (123 [235 in 1999], mid-Sep–early Oct); *Swainson's Hawk* (5 [9 in 2002], Oct); *Red-tailed Hawk* (9278 [12,194 in 2002], mid-Oct–late Nov); *Ferruginous Hawk* (22 [34 in 2002], mid-Sep–Oct); *Rough-legged Hawk* (9 [19 in 1999], late Oct–Nov); *Golden Eagle* (20 [32 in 1997], Oct); *American Kestrel* (644 [728 in 1997], Sep–Oct); *Merlin* (161 [250 in 1998], mid-Oct–mid-Nov); *Peregrine Falcon* (149 [220 in 2003], late Sep–Nov); *Prairie Falcon* (6 [12 in 2002 and 2003], late Sep–Oct).

Kéköldi Indigenous Reserve, Costa Rica

Each autumn, millions of North American raptors travel along the Mesoamerican Land Corridor (see Chapter 7) on their way to overwintering areas in South America. At least half as many make the return journey each spring. The migrants include several million Turkey Vultures, close to two million Broad-winged Hawks, a million Swainson's Hawks, and hundreds of thousands of Mississippi Kites, along with thousands of Ospreys and Peregrines, and lesser numbers of up to a dozen other species of raptors. Kéköldi Indigenous Reserve in coastal Costa Rica—one of only three full-season watchsites in Mesoamerica—regularly reports more than one million migrants each autumn and about half that number each spring, ranking the site as one of only four million-bird watchsites globally.

Costa Rica has a rich ornithological history, and reports of significant and substantial raptor migration there date to the early twentieth century, when Carnegie Museum of Natural History Field Collector, Melvin A. Carricker, reported movements of large flocks of birds of prey west of Guacimo, Costa Rica, in the Caribbean lowlands (Carricker 1910). Another thirty years, however, would pass before the size and seasonal predictability of the flight was fully appreciated by ornithologists. Quintessential neotropical ornithologist Alexander Skutch (1945, 80) introduced the region's flight to his colleagues as follows:

> Except among the bird islands of Peru, I have never seen aggregations of birds so vast as those formed by the migrating Swainson's Hawks [in Costa Rica]. Perhaps now that the Passenger Pigeon has passed into oblivion, these are the most spectacular mass movements of birds to be seen on the North American continent. . . . Some of the flocks of Swainson's Hawks are so unbelievably vast the watcher receives the impression that practically the whole of the species must be represented in that one immense aggregation of migrating birds.

By the mid-1990s, the geography of the passage was well-enough understood (Hidalgo et al. 1995) that it made sense to prospect for full-season watchsites. Costa Rican nature photographer and migration specialist, Marco Saborío, and I did just that in the spring of 1999. During 28 hours on eight days in late March of that year, Marco and I counted close to 14,000 migrant raptors while scanning for flight-lines at 10 sites scattered across the country (Bildstein and Saborío 2000). Two of the more active sites, Bribri One and Bribri Two in the Fila Carbón (black hills) of Caribbean Coast Talamanca on the border with Panama, peaked our interest. Little did we know that a third site several kilometers north of Bribri One and Two would have the same effect on Nature Conservancy conservationist, Charles Duncan, and his Costa

Rican counterpart, Pablo Porras, later that autumn. Back in the United States, Duncan and I compared notes in December of that year, and Pablo Porras visited Hawk Mountain for four months of watchsite-development-and-management training the following spring. The plan was to establish a hilltop full-season watchsite in an indigenous reserve, where in October 1999 Duncan and Porras had witnessed an early morning movement they estimated to have been in excess of 100,000 raptors. The rest, as they say, is history.

Kékôldi Indigenous Reserve is an approximately 200-hectare homeland and protected area in the Fila Carbón above the region's Caribbean coastal plain, less than 20 km east of Cahuita National Park. The reserve teems with wildlife ranging from small Bullet Ants, dart poison frogs, and Eyelash Vipers to larger Kinkajous, Agoutis, and Three-toed Sloths, and just about everything in between. Kékôldi is home to several hundred indigenous Bribri people, all but a few of whom live in the site's lowlands. The 1.5-kilometer uphill walk to the lookout offers excellent birding opportunities as well as a fair chance to work off the previous evening's meal. Counts are conducted from a sturdy 10-meter canopy tower less than 3 kilometers from the beach. The first full-season count from 6 September through 15 December 2000 tallied more than 1.3 million raptors during 709 hours of observation, for an average passage rate of more than 1800 migrants per hour.

My field notes for the morning of 21 October 2000 during my first visit to the site provide a sense of place:

A Kékôldi Indian communal house protrudes from the forest on our left, and a small crowd has gathered atop a tiny wooden deck that juts out over a precipice to our right. Three individuals, a blonde Minnesotan and two dark-haired Costa Ricans, are gripping small metallic counters, while peering through binoculars into the distant coastal haze. Several small children clamor for attention at their feet. We approach the trio and are about to introduce ourselves when someone shouts: "Incoming raptors!" It is the largest flock of the day.

At once priorities shift, assignments are made, and before our eyes the three, actually the staff of the world's newest million-bird hawkwatch, spring into action. Half an hour later, more than five thousand birds of prey have been identified and counted before they sail southeast overhead into the Sixaola Valley en route to Panama, Colombia, and beyond.

By the end of the day, more than 50,000 raptors representing eight species had been tallied, raising the site's first-season's total to more than half a million migrants—a number that many temperate-zone watchsites would be happy to accomplish in a decade. In coastal Costa Rica, the number had been tallied in about seven weeks.

The Flight

The flight at Kékőldi begins considerably earlier in the morning than at temperate sites. Lift-off usually is well underway by 8 a.m., and the bulk of the passage occurs before noon on many days. Most migrants pass while soaring and gliding in a series of seemingly never-ending mixed-species "rivers-of-raptors." On most days the flight forms along the coast shortly after dawn and moves inland thereafter, passing directly overhead near midday. Although most migrants pass above a horizontal line-of-sight, many pass below the site's 10-meter tower. On rare occasions, portions of the flight pass so close that the occasional wing flaps of the individual migrants are clearly audible. Many raptors, most often flocks of Turkey Vultures and individual Broad-winged Hawks, are seen roosting in late afternoon.

As is true of hawkwatches elsewhere along the Mesoamerican Land Corridor, well over 98 percent of the flight consists of hundreds of thousands to millions of Turkey Vultures, Mississippi Kites, Broad-winged Hawks, and Swainson's Hawks. In both autumn and spring, Mississippi Kites are the first mega-migrants to pass, followed by Broad-winged Hawks, Swainson's Hawks, and Turkey Vultures, in that order. In most years, outbound and return migration peak during the last third of October and March, respectively. Given the magnitude of the autumn flight, it is almost impossible to have a slow day at the watchsite anytime between early October and early November, a period when the daily count almost always exceeds 5000.

Kékőldi is a great place to see migrating Peregrine Falcons, particularly in mid- to late October, when flocks of a dozen or more of the large falcons are common at close range. Millions of migrating swallows and swifts also migrate pass the site in autumn. Resident raptors regularly seen from the tower include King Vultures, Hook-billed Kites, Double-toothed Kites, Zone-tailed Hawks, White Hawks, Common Black Hawks, Short-tailed Hawks, Black Hawk-Eagles, and Bat Falcons.

The Kékőldi hawkwatch was the brainchild of Asociación ANAI, a Costa Rican nonprofit conservation organization headquartered in San Jose, and the local Kékőldi Wak ka Koneke Indigenous Association, which together organized the staff and volunteers that conducted the count through autumn

Figure 33. A young North American hawkwatcher introducing an even younger Bribri to raptor migration at the Kéköldi Indigenous Reserve, Costa Rica, during the site's first count season in autumn 2000. (Photo by the author)

2004 (Figures 33 and 34). Since then a new organization, Talamanca Raptors, has replaced Asociación ANAI. The hawkwatch operates from the tower in both spring and autumn, with counts occurring on most days between 1 March and 15 April, and on 1 September through 15 December. A website (http://www.talamancaraptors.org) provides information on the migration in the region and watchsite activities, as well as volunteer opportunities for interested participants. A full-color, waterproof observation guide to the watchsite, published in 2003, is sold at the site. Indigenous lunches can be arranged at the communal center at the hawkwatch. Those planning to visit the site should contact the Kéköldi Indigenous Reserve, Talamanca Raptors, or local tour-group operators in advance.

Migration Specifics

Fourteen species are recorded as regular migrants at Kéköldi Indigenous Reserve; one species is an irregular migrant. Approximately 800,000 and 1,950,000 migrants are seen in spring and autumn, respectively. The infor-

Figure 34. North and South American volunteers counting from the Kéköldi watch-site's 10-meter tower. (Photo by the author)

mation below, including average [and record] annual count, record one-day count, and peak period of passage, is based on four years of autumn counts between 2000 and 2003.

Turkey Vulture (911,659 [1,158,396 in 2001], 145,022 on 27 Oct 2003, Oct–Nov); *Osprey* (1201 [1698 in 2003], 150 on 1 Oct 2002, late Sep–Oct); *Northern Harrier* (irregular, 19 total); *Swallow-tailed Kite* (278 [427 in 2002], 204 on 27 Aug 2002, late Aug–early Sep); *Mississippi Kite* (75,190 [118,379 in 2001], 22,263 on 15 Sep 2001, Sep); *Plumbeous Kite* (583 [2245 in 2002], 2013 on 23 Sep 2002, Sep); *Sharp-shinned Hawk* (14 [22 in 2000], 7 on 22 Sep 2000, late Sep–Oct); *Cooper's Hawk* (15 [24 in 2000], 4 on 5 Nov 2000, mid-Oct–early Nov); *Broad-winged Hawk* (655,313 [847,584 in 2003], 221,906 on 10 Oct 2001, late Sep–Oct); *Swainson's Hawk* (293,432 [414,742 in 2003], 132,312 on 27 Oct 2003, mid-Oct–early Nov); *Zone-tailed Hawk* (15 [21 in 2003], 6 on 16 Oct 2003, Oct); *Red-tailed Hawk* (8 [20 in 2003], 3 on 3 Nov 2002 and 4 Dec 2003, mid-Oct–Nov); *American Kestrel* (6 [12 in 2000], 3 on 26 Sep 2000, late Sep–Oct); *Merlin* (67 [113 in 2003], 18 on 23 Oct 2001, Oct); *Peregrine Falcon* (1696 [2319 in 2003], 280 on 4 Oct 2003, Oct).

Veracruz River-of-Raptors, Mexico

With counts from two lookouts that together average more than five million raptors each autumn, the Veracruz River-of-Raptors watchsite in Veracruz, Mexico, ranks as the world's top hawkwatch in terms of overall numbers of migrants. The site takes its name from that fact that most birds of prey pass through the region in seemingly endless series of "rivers-of-raptors," a figure of speech Horace Loftin first used to describe the massive migrations of Turkey Vultures in Panama in the early 1960s (Loftin 1963). The dual-lookout watchsite operates simultaneous counts at the ends of an 11-km east–west transect, one each in the tiny village of Chichicaxtle and the considerably larger highway stopover town of Cardel. The latter is less than 15 kilometers northwest of La Antigua, Mexico, Hernán Cortez's initial head-quarters in the New World and the first Spanish settlement in the region. The site's concentrated flights result from its location directly south of where a spur of Mexico's eastern mountains, the Sierra Madre Oriental, pinch to within several kilometers of the Gulf of Mexico.

The history of the site's discovery by scientists typifies that of many "exotic" raptor migration watchsites. Museum collectors were the first to note the flight, principally remarking on its timing and geography, followed by a series of hawkwatch enthusiasts who scouted the area and made partial-season counts, and who, in turn, were followed by local conservationists who, at last, established a full-season hawkwatch. The series of events took most of the twentieth century to play out.

American Museum of Natural History Curator of Birds, Frank M. Chapman (1916), was arguably the first to describe—albeit in a decidedly under-stated fashion—hawk migration in coastal Veracruz: "In spring, on the eastern slope of the mountains of Vera Cruz, Mexico, I have seen flocks containing thousands of hawks migrating northward. Although closely massed they did not move onward in a solid body like a flock of blackbirds, but, like a swarm of bees, circled about and among each other in a most remarkable and confusing manner."

Chapman was followed almost three decades later by his Smithsonian Institution counterpart, Alexander Wetmore, who detailed a similar spring-time flight near Tres Zapotes (Wetmore 1943). The first anecdotal description of large-scale Turkey Vulture migration in the region is a 1967 report of a return flight south of Tecolutla (Bussjaeger et al. 1967). Detailed attempts to document the extent of the spring flight include efforts by Andrle (1968), Thiollay

(1980), Tilly (1985), and Tilly et al. (1990). The results of this series of episodic and partial-season counts left little doubt of major intercontinental, spring-time movements, with numbers approaching half a million or more migrants.

Confirmation of the flight came in the spring of 1991 when Mexican biologist, Ernesto Ruelas, organized the first transect count in an area along federal highway 140 between coastal La Antigua and Xalapa, approximately 50 km inland. A total of 408,555 raptors representing 16 species was seen during 1500 hours of observation between 15 March and 21 April. News of an even bigger flight, however, was still to come.

Globetrotting French raptor biologist Jean-Marc Thiollay (1977) was the first to report news of a massive outbound flight in the region. A decade later the raptor identification team of Bill Clark and Brian Wheeler confirmed the magnitude of this enormous autumn flight during a marathon road trip from southern Texas to central Veracruz in October 1989 (Wheeler 1990). These observations set the stage for Ruelas and his coworkers, who, in autumn 1992, initiated what was to become a series of full-season counts along a portion of the transect they had earlier used to count return migrants in spring. The first year's count of 2.5 million raptors, which included more than one million Turkey Vultures and nearly one million Broad-winged Hawks, shattered previous New World and Old World records set in the Canal Zone of central Panama and in Elat, Israel. The number also provided the foundation for substantially higher counts in more recent years—more than one million raptors, for example, were reported on a single day of counting in 1997 (see "Migration Specifics" below)—as the watchsite organizers honed the new skills needed to accurately document the enormous passage.

Counts from two lookouts, one on the roof of a six-storey hotel in the center of the town of Cardel, and the other atop a four-meter scaffold at the edge of a soccer field in the village of Chichicaxtle, 11 km to the west, are combined to produce the River-of-Raptors daily and seasonal totals. Three- and, sometimes, four-person count teams operate at the watchsite's two lookouts. The rooftop lookout, which features a full-service wet bar, functions as the principal venue for international visitors. The soccer field lookout provides the focal point for the watchsite's extensive outreach program in science education aimed at school children living along the flyway.

The Flight

The flight, which on many days passes in a series of gigantic sky-filling streams of migrants that give the site its name, is dominated by North American breeding populations of Turkey Vultures, Broad-winged Hawks, Swain-son's Hawks, and Mississippi Kites, in that order. The Turkey Vulture flight is drawn largely from western North American populations of this widespread and common New World species, and as such represents but a fraction of the species' overall continental population. The movements of Mississippi Kites, Broad-winged Hawks, and Swainson's Hawks, on the other hand, approxi-mate close to entire world populations of these species and, therefore, repre-sent annual updates of their conservation status.

In addition to offering visitors a chance to see more migrating raptors than anywhere else, the site also offers a unique opportunity to see hundreds of migrating "northern" populations of Hook-billed Kites, Grey Hawks, and Zone-tailed Hawks, three largely tropical species that are sedentary through-out much of their ranges farther south.

The River-of-Raptors watchsite is operated by Pronatura Veracruz, a Mexi-can conservation organization founded in 1981, with technical and logistical assistance from HawkWatch International and Hawk Mountain Sanctuary. In addition to the autumn transect-count, Pronatura operates a banding station in coastal La Mancha, 30 km north of Cardel, as well as a spring count at a municipal park in the colonial city of Xalapa. The organization's website (http://www.pronaturaveracruz.org) provides an excellent overview of the hawkwatches, recent count results, education activities built around the sites, and travel and accommodation information for international visitors. Several magazine articles, including two with the title *River of Raptors*, detail the count and associated conservation efforts, as well as local birding opportuni-ties in the area (Maxwell 1996; Sutton and Sutton 1999). Those planning to visit the count site should contact Pronatura Veracruz in advance.

Migration Specifics

Eighteen species are recorded as regular migrants at Veracruz River-of-Raptors; eleven species are irregular migrants. Approximately 625,000 and 5,200,000 migrants are seen in spring and autumn, respectively. The infor-mation below, including average [and record] annual count, record one-day count, and peak period of passage, is based on five years of autumn counts between 1999 and 2003.

Turkey Vulture (2,000,194 [2,677,355 in 2002], 707,798 on 17 Oct 2003, Oct–mid-Nov); *Osprey* (3256 [3727 in 2001], 700 on 26 Sep 2001, mid-Sep–mid-Oct); *Northern Harrier* (489 [859 in 2000], 116 on 27 Sep 2000, Nov); *Hook-billed Kite* (204 [302 in 2000], 51 on 18 Oct 2001, Oct); *Swallow-tailed*

Kite (195 [286 in 2001], 112 on 24 Aug 2001, late Aug–early Sep); *White-tailed Kite* (irregular, 7 total); *Mississippi Kite* (192,132 [306,274 in 2002], 95,989 on 1 Sep 2002, late Aug–mid-Sep); *Plumbeous Kite* (irregular, 16 total); *Snail Kite* (irregular, 7 total); *Sharp-shinned Hawk* (3870 [5937 in 1999], 731 on 14 Oct 1999, Oct); *Cooper's Hawk* (2716 [3764 in 2001], 918 on 15 Oct 2001, Oct); *Northern Goshawk* (irregular, 1 total); *Harris' Hawk* (6 [12 in 2003], 3 on 2 Oct 2000); *Grey Hawk* (323, [519 in 2001], 140 on 30 Oct 2001, Oct–Nov); *Red-shouldered Hawk* (9 [12 in 2001], 3 on 2 Oct 1999, Oct); *Broad-winged Hawk* (1,919,708 [2,389,232 in 2002], 775,760 on 28 Sep 2001, late Sep–early Oct); *Short-tailed Hawk* (irregular, 3 total); *Roadside Hawk* (irregular, 1 total); *Swainson's Hawk* (901,827 [1,197,850 in 2003], 782,653 on 17 Oct 2003, Oct); *White-tailed Hawk* (irregular, 2 total); *Zone-tailed Hawk* (140 [158 in 2001], 26 on 22 Sep 2002, late Sep–early Oct); *Red-tailed Hawk* (173 [201 in 2001], 16 on multiple dates and years, mid-Oct–Nov); *Ferruginous Hawk* (irregular, 3 total); *Common Black Hawk* (irregular, 20 total); *Golden Eagle* (irregular, 6 total); *Crested Caracara* (irregular, 3 total); *American Kestrel* (7322 [14,872 in 1999], 4511 on 7 Oct 1999, late Sep–Oct); *Merlin* (152 [261 in 1999], 56 on 1 Oct 1999, late Sep–Oct), *Peregrine Falcon* (767 [957 in 1999], 284 on 2 Oct 1999, late Sep–Oct).

Falsterbo Bird Observatory, Sweden

Located above 55° latitude, the Falsterbo Bird Observatory in Scania, in southwesternmost Sweden, ranks as the northernmost raptor-migration watchsite in the world. It also is one of the world's oldest continually active sites. The hammer-shaped, 7-km-long, flat and sandy peninsula that juts into the Baltic Sea, 24 km across the Öresund Strait from western Denmark, is a natural collecting point and major autumn migration bottleneck for many of western Scandinavia's land-restricted migrants (Grimmet and Jones 1989; Zalles and Bildstein 2000).

The site, which was first described as a migratory bottleneck in the early 1800s by zoologist Sven Nilsson's (Karlsson 2004), gained fame as a raptor-migration hotspot on the heels of Gustav Rudebeck's painstaking investigations of migration geography in the region in the 1930s and 1940s. Rudebeck, who was working on his doctoral dissertation at the time, backtracked, via bicycle, the paths of individual streams of migrants and mapped their movements toward the site through southwestern Sweden. His empirical approach allowed Rudebeck to develop a model for the concentrated nature and location of the flight that used a combination of regional coastal diversion lines, predominant winds, and a series of habitat-associated leading lines inland to explain each day's migration (Rudebeck 1950). His observations also laid the foundation for understanding the seasonal progression of the flight, starting with the acute passage of most of the site's Western Honey Buzzards over the course of several days in late August–early September, and concluding with the decidedly more protected passage of Northern Goshawks in October and early November.

Falsterbo has attracted the attention of numerous researchers over the years, and raptor migration has been as well-studied there as anywhere on earth. Rudebeck's (1950) pioneering study, although difficult to find, is essential reading for anyone planning a visit to the watchsite, as is the far-more-recent, color-illustrated, and informative account of activities there, *Wings over Falsterbo* (Karlsson 2004).

Ulfstrand et al. (1974) provides an additional useful overview of the site and update of visible migration there. More recently, animal ecologist Nils Kjellén has focused his attention on age and sex differences in the flight at Falsterbo, linking both annual fluctuations in age and sex ratios and age and sex differences in timing of the flight to critical aspects of the population biology and ecology of the species involved (Kjellén 1992, 1994, 1998). Kjellén (1997) also has compared the magnitude of migration at Falsterbo with published estimates of Swedish populations of migratory raptors to assess the degree to which the site serves as a regional bottleneck. His analysis suggests that, on average, Falsterbo records the movements of 38 percent of Sweden's Red Kites, 33 percent of its Western Honey Buzzards, and from 10 percent to 20 percent of its Western Marsh Harriers, Eurasian Sparrowhawks, Eurasian Buzzards, and Peregrine Falcons, confirming the site's count as a truly significant population monitoring effort.

The Flight

Two common and widespread European raptors, the Eurasian Sparrowhawk and the northern Steppe Buzzard subspecies of the Eurasian Buzzard, make up 55 percent and 30 percent of the flight, respectively. Other significant migrants include Western Honey Buzzards (8%), Red Kites (3%), Rough-legged Buzzards (:1%), and Common Kestrels (:1%). Together with several sites in neighboring Denmark—including Stevns Klint, directly across the Baltic Sea from Falsterbo, and Stigsæs on the southwest coast of Sjaelland (Zalles and Bildstein 2000)—Falsterbo offers the best opportunity for observing concentrated movements of raptors in all of Scandinavia.

Full-season counts have been conducted at the site by Skanes Ornitholo-
giska Forening (SOF; the Swedish Ornithological Society) since 1973.
Counts are made at Nabben at the southern end of the peninsula daily from
11 August through 20 November. SOF also operates the Falsterbo Bird Observatory in the town of Falsterbo on the peninsula, and the society maintains an active website (http://www.skof.se/fbo) that provides useful information about raptor migration and other ornithological events in the area.

Migration Specifics

Fourteen species are recorded as regular migrants at Falsterbo; thirteen
species are irregular migrants. Approximately 45,500 migrants are seen in autumn. The information below, including average [and record] annual count,
and peak period of passage, is based on six years of autumn counts between
1998 and 2003.

Western Honey Buzzard (3626 [5522 in 1999], late Aug–Sep); Black Kite
(irregular, 59 total); Red Kite (1199 [1445 in 2003], Sep–early Oct); White-
tailed Sea Eagle (22 [47 in 2003], Oct–Nov); Short-toed Snake Eagle (irregular, 1 total); Osprey (299 [413 in 1999], mid-Aug–late Sep); Western Marsh
Harrier (963 [1078 in 1999], mid-Aug–late Sep); Northern Harrier (239
[379 in 2003], Sep–Oct); Pallid Harrier (irregular, 27 total in 4 different
years); Montagu's Harrier (irregular, 35 total); Northern Goshawk (23 [44 in
2004], Nov); Eurasian Sparrowhawk (24,710 [30,072 in 1999], Sep–Oct);
Eurasian Buzzard (12,981 [18,502 in 1999], mid-Sep–Oct); Long-legged
Buzzard (irregular, 1 total); Rough-legged Buzzard (561 [1068 in 2001], mid-
Sep–mid-Oct); Lesser Spotted Eagle (irregular, 16 total); Greater Spotted Eagle
(irregular, 6 total); Steppe Eagle (irregular, 2 total); Imperial Eagle (irregular, 1
total); Golden Eagle (irregular, 10 total); Common Kestrel (586 [953 in 2003],
late Aug–Sep); Red-footed Falcon (irregular, 8 total); Merlin (249 [296 in
2001], Sep–early Oct); Northern Hobby (53 [71 in 2001], Sep); Eleonora's
Falcon (irregular, 1 total); Gyrfalcon (irregular, 2 total); Peregrine Falcon (43
[76 in 2003], late Aug–Sep).

Organbidexka Col Libre, France

Organbidexka Col Libre (literally "the free [from hunting] mountain pass at
Organbidexka") is one of a handful of migration watchsites in the Pyrenees
of southern France and northern Spain. The site offers spectacular views of
the northern Basque countryside, along with one of the best opportunities in

Europe for observing large numbers of both Red and Black kites. Like most watchsites in the region, Organbidexka owes its origins to the large-scale shooting of migratory birds, and in particular Wood Pigeons, that continues largely unabated elsewhere in the Pyrenees.

Although avian biologists have long speculated on the extent of visible migration in the Pyrenees, little had been published on the movements of birds through this sparsely populated part of Europe until the early 1950s when David and Elizabeth Lack reported the results of three autumns of migration "reconnaissance" (Lack and Lack 1952). Initially anticipating a concentrated coastal flight, the two biologists instead discovered extensive large-scale inland movements among the north-south *cols* (mountain passes) in the western Pyrenees that funneled raptors and other migratory species into concentrated streams of migrants. The Lacks also uncovered the ancient Basque pastime of "La chasse de la palombe" or Wood Pigeon hunting, in which teams of hunters hurling a series of *zimbelas* (small white wooden discs) below flocks of low-flying Wood Pigeons and Stock Pigeons (also known as Stock Doves), elicited an alighting response in the birds that caused them to descend, either into a series of nets or onto the ground, at which time a horn was sounded and the shooters "let fly in every direction." The so-called sport remains popular even today, and estimates of the annual kill range into the tens of thousands of pigeons and doves. The hunters are not selective in their targeting, and many raptors too are slaughtered in autumn.

This is the backdrop for Organbidexka Col Libre (OCL), which has been monitoring the movements of and protecting trans-Pyrenean migrants since it was founded in 1979. In addition to Organbidexka, which is located on the northern slopes of Pic d'Orhy halfway between Saint-Jean-Pied-de-Port and Tardets, France, OCL conducts counts and protects raptors at two other important watchsites in the western Pyrenees: Le Col de Lizarrieta, on the border with Spain, approximately 20 km south of Ascain; and Lindux, a Napoleonic fortification, 30 km south of Saint-Jean-Pied-de Port and several kilometers northwest of Col de Roncevaux, a historic site at which Roland of "The Song of Roland" fame was slain in 778 while conducting a rear-guard action for Charlemagne.

The Flight

Three species, Western Honey Buzzard (34% of the overall flight), Black Kite (55%), and Red Kite (6%), together make up 95 percent of all raptors seen.

Most migrants at the site fly relatively low while crossing the pass, making them easy to see and identify. Opportunities for seeing large numbers of migrants occur in August and early September during the peak movements of Black Kites and honey buzzards. Mid- to late September is the best time to see Red Kites, which are rare migrants elsewhere in Europe, as well as Booted Eagles, which are rare this far north. The most unusual aspect of the site is the late September–October flight of more than 100,000 Wood Pigeons and Stock Pigeons—both of which are legal game on migration. The autumn passage of these two species attracts thousands of hunters, many of which operate near the watchsite. Organbidexka is one of only a handful of raptor-migration watchsites that records the numbers of gunshots heard as well as the numbers of migrants seen, and the current single-day record of 25,360 shots heard on 28 October 1982 suggests the degree to which shooting, much of it indiscriminate, persists in the region.

Although all of OCL's watchsites are easy to find, the best place to begin a visit is at OCL headquarters at 11 Rue Bourgneuf F-64100 Bayonne, France.

Migration Specifics

Fourteen species are recorded as regular migrants at Organbidexka; seven species are irregular migrants. Approximately 31,000 migrants are seen in autumn. The information below, including average [and record] annual count, and peak period of passage, is based on three years of autumn counts between 2001 and 2003.

Osprey (138 [153 in 2002], mid-Sep–mid-Oct); *Western Honey Buzzard* (10,492 [12,354 in 2003], late Aug–early Sep); *Black Kite* (17,209 [23,510 in 2003], Aug); *Red Kite* (1721 [1943 in 2001], Oct); *Egyptian Vulture* (irregular, 5 total); *Short-toed Snake Eagle* (131 [142 in 2003], mid-Sep–early Oct); *Hen Harrier* (69 [82 in 2002], late Sep–Oct); *Montagu's Harrier* (86 [88 in 2003], late Aug–mid-Sep); *Western Marsh Harrier* (207 [237 in 2002], mid-Sep–mid-Oct); *Eurasian Sparrowhawk* (324 [418 in 2002], mid-Sep–mid-Oct); *Northern Goshawk* (irregular, 5 total); *Eurasian Buzzard* (91 [110 in 2003], Oct); *Steppe Buzzard* (irregular, 1 total); *Spanish Imperial Eagle* (irregular, 1 total); *Booted Eagle* (49 [54 in 2003], mid-Sep–mid-Oct); *Bonelli's Eagle* (irregular, 1 total); *Common Kestrel* (57 [89 in 2001], late Sep–mid-Oct); *Merlin* (27 [31 in 2003], early Oct–mid-Oct); *Northern Hobby* (41 [57 in 2001], late Sep–early Oct); *Eleonora's Falcon* (irregular, 3 total); *Peregrine Falcon* (irregular, 1 total).

Strait of Gibraltar, Spain

The narrow body of water that connects the western end of the Mediterranean Sea to the Atlantic Ocean is one of the most identifiable geographic features on Earth. The Strait of Gibraltar also is one of the world's most prominent *migration bottlenecks,* a 14-km-wide passageway through which hundreds of thousands of central and western European raptors travel en route to wintering areas in West Africa (Figure 35).

The Strait takes its name from Tariq ben Zaid, an eighth-century Berber who invaded southern Spain and fortified the 426-meter limestone promontory that now bears his name (The Rock "Gibraltar" is a European corruption of the Arabic *Jebel Tariq,* or Mount Tariq). Jebel Musa, the Rock of Gibraltar's mountain counterpart in northern Morocco, is the second "Pillar of Hercules" of Greek and Roman mythology.

That large numbers of raptors concentrate in southern Iberia before streaming into West Africa has been known since the late 1700s (Nisbet et al. 1961). British officer and ornithologist H. L. Irby was the first to detail the

Figure 35. A view across the Strait of Gibraltar from southern Spain west of Tarifa. The mountain in the distance is Jebel Musa in Morocco. (Photo by the author)

timing of the flight, as well as the role that crosswinds played in determining the likelihood and location of the passage (Irby 1875). It was not until the 1960s, however, that the magnitude of the flight became known to science (Evans and Lathbury 1973; Bernis 1980). Since then a number of researchers, most notably Gibraltar native Clive Finlayson (1992), have studied and reported on the flight.

The Flight

The 14-km-wide channel that separates Europe from Africa provides ample evidence for the extent to which raptors differ in their willingness to fly over water. Indeed, whereas the Strait appears to be a minor hindrance for some, it presents a formidable barrier for others. Ospreys, Western Honey Buzzards, harriers, Peregrine Falcons, and other migrants with powerful flapping flight regularly cross the passage almost immediately upon reaching land's end, whereas Eurasian Griffons, Black Kites, Booted Eagles, and other obligate soaring migrants spend up to a week or more milling about in southernmost Iberia waiting for the right weather. Although such species hydrophobia plays havoc with counting at the site, it also creates first-rate opportunities for birding there.

In general, migrants approach southernmost Spain and Gibraltar across a relatively broad front. With few exceptions, however, most eventually cross the Strait in *streams* during a series of narrow-frontal movements, with the exact point of departure along the length of the passageway depending on predominant winds. Movements tend to be greater overall and the flight heaviest at the eastern end of the Strait when Poniente or westerly crosswinds prevail, and lesser overall and heaviest toward the middle of the Strait when the far more dangerous Levante or easterly crosswinds prevail; the latter substantially increasing the likelihood of migrants being blown out into the Atlantic.

Black Kites (51% of the overall flight) and Western Honey Buzzards (18%), make up more than two-thirds of the overall flight. Five others—Booted Eagle (4%), Short-toed Snake Eagle (3%), Eurasian Griffon (3%), Egyptian Vulture (<1%), and Eurasian Sparrowhawk (<1%)—migrate by the thousands to tens of thousands. Aside from being a great place to see migrating Old World Vultures, the Strait of Gibraltar also is a great place to see three species of European harriers (Marsh, Hen, and Montagu's), as well as the occasional Lesser Kestrel, Common Kestrel, Northern Hobby, and Peregrine Falcon.

The late-summer and early-autumn movements of Black Kites and Western Honey Buzzards at the site are spectacular. Most kites pass in July and

August, whereas most honey buzzards do so during a brief period at the end of August and early September. Kites tend to cross along the central and western parts of the Strait, whereas honey buzzards, which typically approach along coastal Mediterranean flight-lines, are far more likely to depart from the Rock of Gibraltar at the eastern end of the Strait.

In addition to soaring raptors, tens of thousands of White Storks can be seen migrating in July and August, and thousands of Black Storks can be seen migrating in September and October.

Although systematic counts of spring migrants have yet to be made, similarly spectacular, albeit proportionately smaller, flights are known to reverse the crossing from Morocco on return migration.

The principal stream of migration shifts along the more than 20-km length of the Strait depending on the wind, and migration at the site is all-but-impossible to track from a single lookout. Consequently, counts are made from a series of watchsites, including the Rock of Gibraltar, in Gibraltar, as well as from a number of points in southern Spain between Punta del Carnero, south of Algeciras, west to Punta Marroquí, near Tarifa. The watchsite on the Rock of Gibraltar is operated by the Gibraltar Ornithological and Natural History Society; those in Spain are coordinated by Programa Migres (the Migration Program), a cooperative effort of Fundación Migres and the Government of Andalucía. Both organizations maintain active websites (http://www.gonhs.org; http://www.fundacionmigres.org). Programa Migres has produced a useful *Guide to the Common Birds of the Strait of Gibraltar*. The guide and maps of the watchsites are available at the Huerta Grande Visitor Center for Los Alcornocales National Park, in Pelayo, on the main coastal highway several miles west of Algeciras, which also is the best place to begin a visit to the site. An annual festival celebrating autumn migration is held in and around Algeciras in late September, at the time of maximum flight diversity. Clive Finlayson's *Birds of the Strait of Gibraltar* (1992) provides an excellent history of the site as well as useful details regarding the timing, ecology, and geography of each species' flight (Figure 36).

Migration Specifics

Twenty-five species are recorded as regular migrants at the Strait of Gibraltar; six species are irregular migrants. Approximately 1600 and 380,000 migrants are seen in spring and autumn, respectively. The information below, including average [and record] annual count, and peak period of passage, is based on autumn counts at the Programa Migres watchsites in 1997 and 1998.

Figure 36. Looking northwest from one of several migration-watchsite pavilions near Tarifa, Spain, at the Strait of Gibraltar. Note the wind turbines in the distance. (See Chapter 10 for details.) (Photos by the author)

Osprey (92 [119 in 1998], Sep); *Western Honey Buzzard* (70,918 [88,506 in 1998], late Aug–mid-Sep); *White-tailed Kite* (irregular, 3 total); *Black Kite* (253,667 [371,818 in 1998], late Aug); *Red Kite* (93 [110 in 1998], late Sep–early Oct); *Cinereous Vulture* (irregular, 5 total); *Eurasian Griffon* (16,455 [28,312 in 1998], late Oct); *Egyptian Vulture* (3307 [3402 in 1997], late Aug–Sep); *Bearded Vulture* (irregular, 2 total); *Ruppell's Griffon* (16 [27 in 1998], Oct); *Short-toed Snake Eagle* (17,337 [18,949 in 1997], mid-Sep–early Oct); *Hen Harrier* (114 [203 in 1998], late Jul); *Montagu's Harrier* (647 [710 in 1998], late Aug–early Sep); *Western Marsh Harrier* (261 [417 in 1998], early Oct); *Eurasian Sparrowhawk* (2687 [2753 in 1998], mid-Sep–mid-Oct); *Northern Goshawk* (53 [91 in 1997], Sep); *Eurasian Buzzard* (192 [221 in 1998], early Oct); *Lesser Spotted Eagle* (13 [25 in 1998], late Sep–early Oct); *Greater Spotted Eagle* (7 [12 in 1997], late Sep); *Spanish Imperial Eagle* (9 [13 in 1997], early Oct), *Golden Eagle* (7 [9 in 1997], early Oct), *Booted Eagle* (20,421 [20,835 in 1997], Sep–mid-Oct); *Bonelli's Eagle* (16 [23 in 1998], early Oct); *Lesser Kestrel* (105 [122 in 1998], Sep); *Common Kestrel* (227 [319 in 1998], early Oct); *Eleonora's Falcon* (11 [12 in 1997], late Aug); *Merlin* (irregular, 2 total); *Northern Hobby* (74 [94 in 1998], late

Sep–early Oct); *Lanner Falcon* (irregular, 4 total); *Saker Falcon* (irregular, 2 total); *Peregrine Falcon* (55 [74 in 1998], mid-Sep–early Oct).

Elat, Israel

Each spring, millions of birds of prey that have overwintered in Africa set out from that continent for breeding areas in Europe and Asia. Some leave Africa via the Strait of Gibraltar at the western end of the Mediterranean, others via the Sicilian Channel in the central Mediterranean. Most, however, do so via the Middle East, where the elliptical geography of the Eurasian–East African Flyway (see Chapter 7) usually positions the bulk of the flight over the outskirts of the coastal resort city of Elat, at the head of the Gulf of Aqaba in southernmost Israel.

One's first impression of the rugged, hard-scrabble mountains west of Elat is that this is not a place to watch migrating raptors. Aside from a blazing blue sky above, the Negev Desert landscape looks more lunar than earthly, and, indeed, Elat may be the only migration watchsite on earth where, while scanning for raptors, one can see more countries—four, including Israel, Jordan, Saudi Arabia, and Egypt—than trees (Figures 37 and 38). What Elat lacks in plant life, however, it more than makes up for in migrating raptors. The site is one of only three hawkwatches in the world that has counted more than a million raptors in a single season, and it has accomplished this in spring, during the inherently "thinner" return migration. With reports of 22 regular and 16 or more irregular or rare migrants, Elat also is one of the world's most biologically diverse hawkwatches.

Published accounts of raptor migration in the region date from Henry Baker Tristram's mid-nineteenth-century reports of large-scale movements in Palestine and Sinai (Tristram 1865–1868). Sporadic counts in and around Elat date from the late 1950s (Safriel 1968). Systematic, full-season counts date from 1977 when Steen Christensen and his coworkers reported more than 750,000 migrants at the site between February and May (Christensen et al. 1981).

The Flight

Two species, the Western Honey Buzzard and the Steppe Buzzard subspecies of the Eurasian Buzzard, together, make up about 85 percent of the flight. Other numerically significant migrants include the Black Kite (3%), Steppe Eagle (3%), and Levant Sparrowhawk (2%). Elat is one of the world's best

Figure 37. The view from the Elat, Israel, watchsite overlooking the Gulf of Aqaba. Jordan and Saudi Arabia are in the distance. (Photo by the author)

Figure 38. Official counters and hawkwatchers at the Elat watchsite. The only shade is provided by vehicles. (Photo by the author)

sites for viewing the latter, a small *Accipiter* whose migratory tactics, including obligate flocking and soaring migration, as well as nocturnal movements (see Chapter 8), belie its taxonomic affinities. It also is an excellent spot for viewing significant movements of the one of the world's largest long-distance migratory raptors, the Steppe Eagle, and for seeing migrating Egyptian Vultures and the Eurasian Griffons. Notable residents at the site include Verreaux's Eagles and the Barbary Falcon subspecies of the Peregrine Falcon. The return passage begins with Steppe Eagles in late February–early March; continues with Black Kites and Steppe Buzzards in late March and early April; and concludes with the decidedly more acute flights of Levant Sparrowhawks in late April–early May, and Western Honey Buzzards in early May. Although the flight can be high, on most days large numbers of the birds can be seen at close range, almost always in good light. Counts are conducted from a large gravel parking lot near Mount Loash, several kilometers west of Elat on the road to Egypt. A substantial, although far-less-studied autumn migration also occurs at the site (Shirihai and Christie 1992).

The most thorough description of migration at Elat is Hadoram Shirihai and David Christie's 1992 paper in *British Birds*. In addition, *Raptor Migration in Israel and the Middle East* provides a brilliant overview of 30 years of field work in the region (Shirihai et al. 2000). The International Birding and Research Center (IBRC) maintains an active banding station for raptors and other birds at and around its field station and headquarters north of Elat. IBRC organizes the counts, which, in most years, are made by one or more groups of volunteers. Those interested in visiting the site should contact the IBRC at Elat (http://www.arava.org/birds-eilat/).

Migration Specifics

Twenty-two species are recorded as regular migrants at Elat; 16 species are irregular or rare migrants. Approximately 827,000 and 17,000 migrants are seen in spring and autumn, respectively. The information below, including average [and record] annual count, and peak period of passage, is based on seven years of spring counts (1977, 1983, 1985–1988, 1994). Record one-day counts are based on counts in 1977, 1983, and 1985-1988.

Osprey (86 [130 in 1977], 30 on 5 Apr 1988, late Mar–mid-Apr); *Western Honey Buzzard* (389,270 [851,598 in 1985], 227,799 on 7 May 1985, early May); *Black-shouldered Kite* (rare, 2 total); *Black Kite* (26,462 [31,774 in 1988], 9956 on 29 Mar 1987, Mar); *White-tailed Sea Eagle* (rare, 2 total);

Egyptian Vulture (427 [802 in 1977], 42 in 1977, Mar–Apr); *Eurasian Griffon* (11 [22 in 1977], late Feb–early May); *Cinereous Vulture* (rare, 1 total); *Short-toed Snake Eagle* (162 [345 in 1985], 29 on 11 Mar 1985, late Feb–Mar); *Bateleur* (rare, 1 total); *Western Marsh Harrier* (170 [371 in 1983], 22 on 3 May 1985 and 28 Mar 1987, mid-Mar–early May); *Hen Harrier* (rare, 1 total); *Pallid Harrier* (57 [113 in 1985], 38 on 3 Apr 1983, mid-Mar–mid-Apr); *Montagu's Harrier* (17 [55 in 1983], 8 on 7 Apr 1983, mid-Apr); *Northern Goshawk* (irregular, 8 total); *Eurasian Sparrowhawk* (157 [456 in 1983], 31 on 17 Apr 1977, late Apr–early May); *Shikra* (rare, 1 total*);* *Levant Sparrowhawk* (20,316 [49,836 in 1987], 22,747 on 25 Apr 1987, late Apr); *Steppe Buzzard* (334,278 [465,827 in 1986], 130,000 on 2 Apr 1986, late Mar–early Apr); *Long-legged Buzzard* (48 [65 in 1994], 12 on 23 Mar 1985, late Mar); *Lesser Spotted Eagle* (56 [74 in 1985], 12 on 2 Apr 1986, late Mar–early Apr); *Greater Spotted Eagle* (6 [10 in 1983], mid-Mar–mid-Apr); *Steppe Eagle* (28,485 [75,053 in 1985], 14,164 on 6 Mar 1985, early Mar); *Imperial Eagle* (47 [95 in 1977], 11 on 25 Feb 1977, late Feb); *Golden Eagle* (irregular, 17 total); *Booted Eagle* (138 [175 in 1977], 30 on 5 Apr 1988, early Apr); *Bonelli's Eagle* (irregular, 27 total*);* *Lesser Kestrel* (36 [83 in 1994], early Apr); *Common Kestrel* (60 [190 in 1983], mid-Mar–mid-Apr); *Red-footed Falcon* (irregular, 20 total); *Merlin* (rare, 2 total); *Northern Hobby* (22 [54 in 1986], late Apr), *Eleonora's Falcon* (13 [21 in 1986], early May); *Sooty Falcon* (irregular, 8 total); *Lanner Falcon* (irregular,15 total); *Saker Falcon* (irregular, 2 total); *Peregrine Falcon* (irregular, 12 total); Barbary Falcon (irregular, 7 total).

Final Thoughts

This chapter provides a brief introduction to a dozen of the world's better known watchsites. Although many hawkwatchers spend most of their time at a single, favorite site, those who visit other watchsites regularly realize there is much to be learned in doing so. In addition to consulting the general references listed at the beginning of this chapter for information on other watchsites, those interested in learning more about North America's many other hawkwatches should visit the Hawk Migration Association of North America's website at http://www.hmana.org for details.

—10—

Protecting Migratory Raptors

The time to protect a species is while it is still common.
Emergency Conservation Committee, 1934

In the 300 or so years since the last Dodo was bludgeoned to death by a sailor on the Indian Ocean island of Mauritius, at least 92 species of birds have ceased to exist in any living form. By comparison, only 120 species had disappeared across the entire first 10,000 years of the Early Pleistocene, a time before humanity began to speed the rate of avian extinction (Temple 1986).

As a group, raptors have fared surprisingly well during the recent human onslaught. Only one bird of prey, the Guadalupe Caracara (aka the "Calalie"), has been lost completely. And that species was a small-island, sedentary form that had the misfortune of being shot and poisoned to extinction at the beginning of the twentieth century by an all-too-lethal combination of local shepherds and goatherds who feared for their animals and overzealous skin collectors who, toward the end, sought the bird because of its rarity (Greenway 1958; Flannery and Schouten 2001). And overall, not a single species of *migratory* raptor is known to have been lost at the hands of man. Even so, populations of many migratory birds of prey have been and remain threatened by a variety of human actions. At the time of this writing, 12 species of migratory raptors, including two complete migrants, six partial migrants, and four local and irregular migrants, are included among the 39 species of raptors that are currently listed as globally threatened (Stattersfield and Capper 2000) (Table 18).

It is against this background that I introduce several principles of human-related species endangerment, provide examples of how humanity has impacted raptors in the past, and conclude by suggesting which current threats pose the greatest dangers to migratory birds of prey. My theme throughout is that ecological knowledge and focused action are key to conservation success.

Principles of Species Endangerment

Largely as a result of increased human actions, populations of many of the world's birds, including those of many common species, are now in decline (BirdLife International 2004). Although the conservation story for each threatened species is unique, in most circumstances several principles, or general rules for endangerment, apply. Understanding these principles allows us to anticipate future endangerment and to forecast the likely success of specific conservation actions. These principles as applied to migratory raptors are described in turn below.

There are three general categories of human threats to raptors, and their effects are often additive. All wild birds, including raptors, are threatened by various human activities, the most pressing of which can be placed into one of three categories: (1) habitat degradation and habitat loss, (2) environmental contaminants, including pesticides and other agricultural chemicals, and (3) direct assault, including persecution and trapping for captive use. In the late 1990s, populations of more than half (52%) of all migratory raptors were threatened by habitat loss, 21% were threatened by environmental contaminants, and 31% were threatened by direct assault; 67% of all migratory raptors were threatened by at least one of these factors, 30% by at least two of these factors, and 8% by all three factors (Zalles and Bildstein 2000).

Human threats to raptors usually work additively. Direct persecution, for example, frequently forces raptors into areas far from human populations

Table 18. *The world's Critically Endangered, Endangered, and Vulnerable raptors*

Species	Type migrant	Continental distribution	Country distribution	Threats
Critically Endangered[a]				
California Condor	Local	North America	United States	Contaminants, Accidental death
White-collared Kite	Nonmigrant	South America	Brazil	Habitat loss
Cuban Kite[b]	Nonmigrant	North America	Cuba	Habitat loss, Persecution
Madagascar Fish Eagle	Nonmigrant	Africa	Madagascar	Habitat loss, Persecution, Exploitation
Indian White-backed Vulture	Partial migrant	Asia	Pakistan, India, Bangladesh, Nepal, Bhutan, Myanmar, Thailand, Malaysia, Laos, Cambodia, Vietnam, China	Contaminants
Long-billed Vulture[c]	Nonmigrant	Asia	Pakistan, India, Bangladesh, Nepal, Myanmar, Cambodia, Laos	Contaminants
Madagascar Serpent Eagle	Nonmigrant	Africa	Madagascar	Habitat loss
Ridgway's Hawk	Nonmigrant	North America	Haiti, Dominican Republic	Habitat loss, Persecution
Philippine Eagle	Nonmigrant	Pacific Islands	Philippines	Habitat loss, Contaminants, Persecution
Endangered[a]				
Réunion Harrier[d]	Nonmigrant	Africa	Réunion	Habitat loss, Contaminants (?), Persecution
Gundlach's Hawk	Nonmigrant	North America	Cuba	Habitat loss, Persecution
Grey-backed Hawk	Nonmigrant	South America	Ecuador, Peru	Habitat loss
Javan Hawk Eagle	Nonmigrant	Pacific Islands	Indonesia	Habitat loss, Exploitation

Table 18, continued

Species	Type migrant	Continental distribution	Country distribution	Threats
Vulnerable[a]				
New Britain Buzzard	Nonmigrant	Pacific Islands	Papua New Guinea	Habitat loss
Sanford's Sea Eagle	Nonmigrant	Pacific Islands	Papua New Guinea, Solomon Islands	Habitat loss
Pallas's Fish Eagle	Partial migrant	Asia	Kazakhstan, Russia, Tajikistan, India, Mongolia, China, Uzbekistan, Pakistan, Bhutan, Bangladesh, Myanmar, Nepal, Afghanistan	Habitat loss, Contaminants, Persecution
Steller's Sea Eagle	Partial migrant	Asia	Russia, Japan, China, North Korea, South Korea	Habitat loss, Contaminants
Cape Griffon	Local	Africa	South Africa, Lesotho, Swaziland, Mozambique, Botswana, Namibia, Zimbabwe	Habitat loss, Contaminants, Persecution, Accidental death
Lappet-faced Vulture	Partial migrant	Africa, Asia	Egypt, Senegal, Niger, Mali, Mauritania, Burkina Faso, Chad, Sudan, Ethiopia, Somalia, Rwanda, Congo, Kenya, Tanzania, Zambia, Malawi, Mozambique, Namibia, Botswana, Zimbabwe, Swaziland, South Africa, Saudi Arabia, Oman, United Arab Emirates, Yemen	Persecution, Accidental death

Table 18, continued

Species	Type migrant	Continental distribution	Country distribution	Threats
Kinabalu Serpent Eagle	Nonmigrant	Pacific Islands	Brunei, Malaysia, Indonesia	Habitat loss
Madagascar Marsh Harrier	Local	Africa	Madagascar, Comoro Islands	Habitat loss, Persecution, Exploitation
Black Harrier	Partial migrant	Africa	South Africa, Lesotho, Namibia	Habitat loss
Slaty-backed Goshawk	Nonmigrant	Pacific Islands	Papua New Guinea	Habitat loss
Imitator Sparrowhawk	Nonmigrant	Pacific Islands	Papua New Guinea, Solomon Islands	Habitat loss
New Britain Sparrowhawk	Nonmigrant	Pacific Islands	Papua New Guinea	Habitat loss
Red Goshawk	Nonmigrant	Australia	Australia	Habitat loss, Contaminants, Persecution
White-necked Hawk	Nonmigrant	South America	Brazil	Habitat loss
Crowned Solitary Eagle	Local (?)	South America	Brazil, Bolivia, Paraguay	Habitat loss
Galápagos Hawk	Nonmigrant	South America	Ecuador	Habitat loss Persecution
New Guinea Eagle	Nonmigrant	Pacific Islands	Indonesia, Papua New Guinea	Exploitation
Greater Spotted Eagle	Complete migrant	Africa, Asia, Europe	Finland, Latvia, Lithuania	Habitat loss, Persecution
Spanish Imperial Eagle	Nonmigrant	Europe	Spain	Habitat loss, Accidental death
Imperial Eagle	Partial migrant	Europe, Asia, Africa	Slovakia, Croatia, Yugoslavia, Greece, FYRO Macedonia, Hungary, Bulgaria, Turkey, Moldova, Ukraine, Russia, Georgia, Iran, Armenia, Azerbaijan, Turkmenistan, Uzbekistan, Kazakhstan, Mongolia, China	Habitat loss, Persecution, Accidental death
Philippine Hawk Eagle	Nonmigrant	Pacific Islands	Philippines	Habitat loss, Persecution

Table 18, continued

Species	Type migrant	Continental distribution	Country distribution	Threats
Wallace's Hawk Eagle	Nonmigrant	Asia, Pacific Islands	Myanmar, Thailand, Malaysia, Brunei, Indonesia	Habitat loss
Plumbeous Forest Falcon	Nonmigrant	South America	Colombia, Ecuador	Habitat loss
Lesser Kestrel	Complete migrant	Africa, Asia, Europe	Morocco, Algeria, Tunisia, Libya, Spain, Portugal, Gibraltar, France, Italy, Croatia, Bosnia-Herzegovina, Yugoslavia, FYRO Macedonia, Albania, Bulgaria, Romania, Greece, Turkey, Israel, Palestine, Jordan, Iran, Iraq, Armenia, Azerbaijan, Georgia, Russia, Moldova, Ukraine, Afghanistan, Uzbekistan, Kazakhstan, China, Mongolia	Habitat loss, Contaminants
Mauritius Kestrel	Nonmigrant	Africa	Mauritius	Introduced predators
Seychelles Kestrel	Nonmigrant	Africa	Seychelles	Habitat loss, Introduced predators

Source: Based on information in Stattersfield and Capper 2000.

[a] *Critically Endangered,* a species facing an extremely high risk of extinction in the wild in the immediate future; *Endangered,* a species facing a very high risk of extinction in the wild in the near future; *Vulnerable,* a species facing a high risk of extinction in the wild in the medium-term future (see Stattersfield and Capper 2000 for details).

[b] Considered by many to be a race of the Hook-billed Kite.

[c] Includes both the Long-billed (*Gyps indicus indicus*) and Slender-billed (*Gyps indicus tenuirostris*) forms.

[d] Considered by many to be a race of the Madagascar Marsh Harrier, the second race of which is listed as Vulnerable later in the table.

and activities where, eventually, they are threatened by habitat loss as such areas are developed. Similarly, agricultural development not only threatens raptors via habitat loss but also, in many cases, via exposure to environmental contaminants.

Habitat loss remains the principal threat of raptor endangerment. Habitat degradation and loss remains the greatest overall threat to raptors, particularly in the tropics (Bildstein et al. 1998). Recent global analyses of habitat degradation and loss suggest that the Indomalayan tropics of southeastern Asia and the Pacific Islands, and the African tropics, both of which in northern winter host many species of migratory raptors (Bildstein et al. 1998), are two of the most human-modified areas on earth (Hannah et al. 1994). And indeed, many tropical regions, including the West Indies, Madagascar, Java, and the Philippines, are dominated overwhelmingly by human landscapes.

More than two-thirds of all threatened and near-threatened tropical raptors are forest-dependent species (Bildstein et al. 1998), many of which require enormous tracts of contiguous forest for their survival (Thiollay 1989a, 1993). These and migratory species that depend on such tracts for wintering habitat are particularly vulnerable to habitat loss in the tropics. Because many tropical habitats are now threatened by increased and increasing levels of human disturbance and habitat loss, their degradation is likely to remain an important concern for some time.

Open-habitat migrants, including those that depend on superabundant prey associated with seasonally fluctuating wetlands (e.g., Snail Kites) or upon swarming locusts and other seasonally available upland prey (e.g., Montagu's Harriers, Swainson's Hawks, and Lesser Kestrels), also are vulnerable to habitat loss and degradation in the tropics. This is because many of these species are gregariously nomadic, and as such even local and restricted habitat loss—when the loss involves a seasonal concentration point for the species—can simultaneously affect regional and even entire continental populations of these species (Bucher 1992). The same can be true for single pesticide applications (Thiollay 1989b; Woodbridge et al. 1995). Furthermore, even when pesticide applications do not poison raptors "directly," the successful removal of agricultural pests that they engender can threaten raptors "indirectly" via reduced prey availability.

Rare raptors are at the highest risk of extinction. Species with small populations, particularly island- and restricted-range endemics, have a greater risk of extinction, not only because small populations provide little buffer against rapid environmental change but also because their smaller ranges tend to place most, if not all, members of the species in the same "ecological boat."

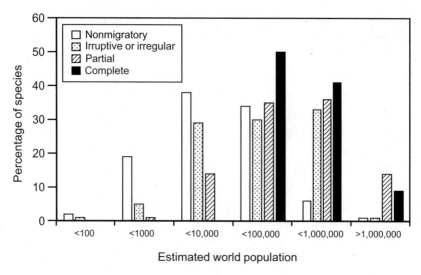

Figure 39. World populations of complete, partial, and irruptive and irregular migrants compared with those of nonmigratory species (from data in Ferguson-Lees and Christie 2001). Note that partial and complete migrants tend to have larger populations than irruptive and irregular migrants, and that migrants in general tend to have larger populations than nonmigrants.

An important corollary to this is that migratory raptors, which tend to have larger populations and larger ranges than do sedentary raptors (Figure 39), are less prone to extinction, overall. And indeed, whereas complete and partial migrants represent 41 percent of all raptor species, they represent only 21 percent of all globally endangered forms.

Migratory species face special risks. Although it is difficult to collect survival data on birds of prey during their migrations, the information that does exist suggests that migratory movements, and in particular long-distance movements, are one of the most difficult and dangerous activities birds undertake (Owen and Black 1991). Thus, whereas raptors may be at risk for many reasons, species that regularly migrate long distances often are especially vulnerable (Biber and Salathé 1991). Even though many migratory raptors reduce the energetic requirements of migration by soaring and gliding together within well-established updraft corridors, the concentrations of birds that result from narrow-front migration can create their own problems, including increased competition, the potential for the spread of disease, and the increased likelihood that a single local problem—human-induced or natural—will negatively impact a large part of a species' regional or, possibly, world population (Hunter et al. 1991; Zalles and Bildstein 2000).

Another threat unique to migrants arises as a result of *double endemism*. Several migratory raptors, including Levant Sparrowhawks, Amur Falcons, Eleonora's Falcons, and Sooty Falcons, breed and overwinter in geographically restricted ranges and as such are double endemics in that they coincidentally depend on the stability of not one but two small regions for survival. If either of these relatively small areas undergoes rapid ecological degradation, most, if not all, individuals in such species will face the problem simultaneously, increasing significantly the likelihood of specieswide endangerment. Other migrants, like the Swainson's Hawk and, to a lesser extent, the Northern Hobby, have large breeding ranges but far smaller overwintering ranges. Although such species are at lower intrinsic risk from endangerment than are so-called double endemics, they, too, face a greater risk of extinction than do species that have both large breeding *and* large wintering ranges.

A Brief History of Human Impacts on Migratory Raptors

There is considerable evidence that people have been affecting raptor populations for some time. Hunter-gatherers living along the shorelines of San Francisco Bay in western North America deposited the remains of at least nine species of migratory birds of prey, including both Bald Eagles and Peregrine Falcons, in shell middens dating back to 600 B.C. (Broughton 2004). Much the same is likely to have happened in other coastal areas wherever hunter-gatherers and migratory raptors co-occurred. Humanity's greatest prehistoric impacts, however, appear to have occurred on Pacific Islands that were settled by Polynesians and other seafarers. Species of eagles and hawks that were once major ecological features in Hawaii disappeared shortly after those islands were "peopled." Similarly, Haast's Eagle and Eyle's Harrier disappeared from New Zealand shortly after most of their lowland habitats were burned and hunted free of potential prey by the Maori colonists. That the latter's remains also have been found in local middens, suggests that hunting, too, may have played a role in its demise (Worthy and Holdaway 2002).

In sixteenth-century Europe, officials encouraged land owners to seek out and destroy raptors, not only to protect livestock but also to protect royal game. The indiscriminant extermination campaigns that followed targeted most species of birds of prey, and, as a result, many once-common raptors were extirpated from significant portions of their historical ranges. The Red Kite, for example, which earlier had been one of the most ordinary and widespread raptors in Great Britain—to the extent that it was said to have "thrived" on the streets of London in the first half of sixteenth-century England (Ratcliffe 1997)—was curtailed shortly thereafter to a single remnant population in a remote area of central Wales. Fortunately, efforts to bolster this small population, which have been underway for more than a century, have succeeded, and there are now self-sustaining populations of Red Kites in Scotland, England, and Wales. Even so, banding returns and direct observations indicate that the species still suffers from poisoning, shooting, and other forms of illegal persecution in many parts of Great Britain (Wernham et al. 2002; Carter et al. 2003).

The full impact of the direct human persecution in Europe will probably never be known, not only because most persecution was never "officially" documented but also because most of the mistreatment happened well before conservationists cared about the losses (Newton 1990; Bildstein 2001). What is known indicates that populations of many large raptors were substantially affected, that regional extirpations occurred in both urban and rural areas, that the primary habitats of many raptors shifted from open, human-dominated landscapes to remote, forest-dominated, high-elevation areas, and that despite more than 50 years of substantially reduced persecution in the latter twentieth and early twenty-first centuries, populations of many species have yet to return to pre-persecution levels of abundance.

Raptor Persecution in Pennsylvania

Some of the strongest evidence of human persecution of raptors comes from eastern North America, where game commissions in many states, including the Commonwealth of Pennsylvania, were once leading proponents of such activity. As was true of most places in the United States, raptors were unprotected in Pennsylvania throughout the eighteenth and nineteenth centuries, a time when episodic and largely unorganized raptor persecution was common. Organized and focused persecution increased substantially in the middle of the nineteenth century, with local newspaper accounts indicating that most rural residents considered the birds to be highly injurious to both game and livestock. By 1885, animosity for raptors within Pennsylvania reached a fevered pitch, and the state legislature placed a 50-cent bounty on the "heads" of all birds of prey, including owls. The so-called Scalp Act, which opinion polls indicate was supported by at least 90 percent of the general public, was actively embraced by many local residents. Over the course of the next two years, 180,000 raptor skins, or "scalps," were sent to the state capital in Harrisburg, by which time increased populations of destructive rodents and insects, along with many fraudulent claims that led to a drain on the state treasury, convinced the legislators to repeal what by then many, including the state veterinarian and author of *Diseases and Enemies of Poultry*, were calling unjust, uneconomic, foolish, and simply wrong-headed (Pearson 1897; Hornaday 1914).

Pennsylvania reinstated bounties on raptors in 1913, and in 1921, a year in which the state paid a total of $128,269 in predator bounties, its own employees killed at least 603 hawks and destroyed 41 nests (Kosak 1995). Birds of prey remained unprotected statewide until 1937 when, except for the three bird- and game-eating accipiters—Sharp-shinned Hawks, Cooper's Hawks, and Northern Goshawks—raptors, at long last, received legal protection (Plates 15 and 16) (Kosak 1995). Not surprisingly, the new "protective" measures were unpopular among farmers and hunters, and limited enforcement and misidentification continued to plague populations of legally protected species well into the 1960s. A specific bounty on Northern Goshawks established in 1929 was removed in 1951, but it was not until 1969 that the state granted full legal protection to all three bird-eating accipiters. Even then, the Great Horned Owl and Snowy Owl remained unprotected statewide until 1972, when the United States ratified an amendment to the Migratory Bird Treaty Act of 1918 that extended federal protection to all species of birds of prey.

Why did it take Pennsylvania so long to protect its birds of prey? Part of the answer lies within the conservation community of early twentieth-century North America (Bildstein 2001). Most of the conservationists who had opposed the so-called Scalp Act of 1885 took exception principally to its nonselective nature (i.e., that the American Kestrel was targeted along with the Northern Goshawk), rather than to the notion that some hawks needed to be destroyed (Hornaday 1913, 1914, 1931). And in fact, the latter half of the nineteenth century and the first half of the twentieth century was the age of "good" (i.e., rodent-eating) versus "bad" (bird- and game-eating) hawks (Fisher 1893) in conservation, where individual birds, and in some instances, entire species, were considered "chicken hawks" or "duck hawks" that needed to be controlled, whereas species that preyed on rodents and other agricultural pests, were not. Consider, for example the following passage from the autobiography of the father of modern North American conservation, John Muir (1913, 87):

When I went to the stable to feed the horses, I noticed a big white-breasted hawk [probably a Northern Goshawk or Red-tailed Hawk] on a tall oak tree in front of our chicken house, evidently waiting for a chicken breakfast . . . I ran to the house for a gun, and when I fired, he fell . . . then managed to stand erect. I fired again to put him out of pain. He flew off . . . but then died suddenly in the air, and dropped like a stone.

Although the event that Muir refers to took place when he was a young boy in 1850s Wisconsin, the founder of the Sierra Club expresses no remorse (other than finishing off the culprit quickly) when recalling the exploit more than 50 years later.

And John Muir was not alone. World-renowned conservationist, William T. Hornaday (1913, 225), the savior of the American Bison, Director of the New York Zoological Park, and founder of the Permanent Wildlife Protection Fund, had much the same view:

"[C]hicken hawk or hen hawk" are usually applied to the [Red-shouldered Hawk] or the [Red-tailed Hawk] species. Neither of these is really very destructive to poultry, but both are very destructive to mice, rats and other pestiferous creatures. . . . Neither of them should be destroyed—not even though they do once in a great while, take a chicken or wild bird, however [t]here are several species of birds that may at once be put under the sentence of death for their destructiveness of useful birds, without any extenuating circumstances worth mentioning. Four of these are Cooper's Hawk, the Sharp-shinned Hawk, [Merlin] and [Peregrine Falcon].

Hornaday's distinctions appear to be both moralistic and utilitarian: "The ethics of men and animals are thoroughly comparative. . . . Guilty animals, therefore, must be brought to justice" (Hornaday 1922).

By 1931, Hornaday had dropped the Merlin from his list of "bad hawks," presumably because of its increased rarity, but retained the others, along with the Great Horned Owl, Barred Owl, and, amazingly enough, the tiny Eastern Screech Owl.

Conservationists were not the only ones to think this way. The scientific and birdwatching communities of the time, too, were careful in selecting the raptors they were concerned about. In 1920, respected ornithologist and bird artist Louis Agassiz Fuertes, writing in the ever-popular *National Geographic* magazine, suggested, "The whole genus Accipiter, consisting of [Northern] Goshawk, Cooper's Hawk, and Sharp-shinned Hawk, are savage, bloodthirsty, and coldhearted slaughterers, and are responsible in large measure for the anathema that is portion to all hawks" (1920, 461). Pennsylvania's official state ornithologist, George Miksch Sutton, remarked in his *Introduction to the Birds of Pennsylvania* (1928, 59) that "[t]he sharpshin is the enemy of all small birds . . . [and that it] and [the] Cooper's Hawk, both bird killers, are fairly common and are rated as our most objectionable birds of prey. . . . They are not protected in Pennsylvania."

Even the venerable Mabel Osgood Wright, founding president of the Connecticut Audubon Society, recommended in her widely read *Birdcraft* (1936, 31) that one could help songbirds by "shooting some of their enemies," including several species of hawks. Boy Scouts, too, received instruction in the whys and wherefores of the existing raptor "conservation taxonomy." George E. Hix, a scoutmaster in Brooklyn, New York, writing in *Birds of Prey for Boy Scouts* (1933, 32) noted that "the beneficial hawks are the larger, slower species, [and that] the smaller swifter hawks are the ones which are destructive to wildlife. . . . [and that these include] the [Northern] Goshawk, Cooper's, Sharp-shinned, and Pigeon hawks [Merlin]."

Small wonder then that game- and bird-eating hawks were heavily persecuted during the first half of the twentieth century in North America. Moreover, because shooters often were unable or unwilling to distinguish the "bad hawks" from the "good hawks," all birds of prey were at risk (Broun 1949; Kosak 1995). The impact of the human onslaught was relatively little studied, except at raptor conservation hotspots like Hawk Mountain, Pennsylvania, and Cape May Point, New Jersey (see Table 4) and (see Chapter 8 for additional details), where estimates from the era suggest that thousands of hawks, eagles, and falcons were shot annually at single sites along major migration corridors in the northeastern United States. The overall impact appears to have been significant. Banding recoveries for one regularly targeted species, the Cooper's Hawk, indicate that first-year mortality from shooting ranged from 28 percent to 47 percent in 1929–1940, and from 12 percent to 21 percent in 1946–1957 (Henny and Wright 1972).

Long-term autumn migration counts of both Sharp-shinned Hawks and Cooper's Hawks suggest that by the early 1980s, populations of both species had largely rebounded from early- and midcentury declines caused initially by shooting and shortly thereafter by widespread misuse of organochlorine pesticides (Bednarz et al. 1990). Today both species appear to be doing well throughout their North American ranges (Rosenfield and Bielefeldt 1993; Bildstein and Meyer 2000). Although migration counts of the irruptive Northern Goshawk are less useful in documenting population change, this species, too, no longer appears to be threatened in most of its North American range (Squires and Reynolds 1997).

Even though raptors have been protected in Pennsylvania for more than 30 years, their current status remains controversial. In 1999, the Pennsylvania Game Commission, the agency that oversees hunting and wildlife management in the state, held a public hearing on a proposal from its president (commissioners are appointed by the state's governor) to "experimentally" control populations of Red-tailed Hawks and Great Horned Owls on several of its landholdings in an attempt to increase the survival of Ring-necked Pheasants there. Although the hearings revealed widespread opposition to the proposal, letters to the editors of many local newspapers indicated pockets of entrenched support for the proposal (Bildstein 2001).

Bald Eagles in Alaska

Regrettably, the conservation history of America's national emblem largely resembles that of America's accipiters. Colonial ornithologist Mark Catesby, writing in the *Natural History of Carolina, Florida, and the Bahama Islands* (1731–1743), praised the species' "great strength and spirit" (Feduccia 1985, 34) but also pointed to its tendency to prey upon pigs, the latter being something that Catesby's ornithological successors, Alexander Wilson (1808–1814) and John James Audubon (1840, 59 and 63), would repeat in the early 1800s. But whereas Wilson went on to suggest that the eagle had been inappropriately vilified by others, Audubon characterized it as "exhibit[ing] a great degree of cowardice," and he concluded his account by "griev[ing]" that it had been selected as the national emblem and agreeing with colonial statesman Benjamin Franklin who had earlier stated that, "For my part, I wish the Bald Eagle had not been chosen as the representative of our country; he is a bird of bad moral character. . . . [and] a rank coward" (Franklin, 1987).

In light of such comments, it is probably not surprising that by the beginning of the twentieth century, Bald Eagle numbers were low enough that William Hornaday, writing in *Thirty Years War for Wild Life* (1931, 66 and 67), was able to declare: "[W]ill someone tell me of a spot in the United States where the [Bald] Eagle is a 'pest'? Can any man this side of the Pacific Northwest Coast go out and find a pair of these birds in less than a week of diligent search?" Actually there was such a place, and the great conservationist was all-too-willing to point it out and recommend a solution: "The [Bald] Eagle is, in a few places in Alaska, too numerous; and there it should be thinned out." And thinned out it was.

From 1917 to 1952, the territory of Alaska paid bounties of from 50 cents to two dollars a head on 128,000 Bald Eagles. This translates to an average take of slightly more than 10 birds a day, every day, for 35 years. Unfortunately, Alaska was not the only place that eagles were shot in large numbers during the first half of the twentieth century. Retired bank manager Charles Broley started banding nestling Bald Eagles in central Florida in the late 1930s, and continued to do so into the late 1940s. Forty-eight of the 814 nestlings that Broley banded between 1939 and 1946 were later recovered in 13 states and four Canadian provinces. More than half had been shot or otherwise killed by humans (Beans 1996). And shooting—some of it from airplanes—was not the only way that Bald Eagles were persecuted. In the 1920s and 1930s, poultry farmers in southern New Jersey regularly cut down potential nesting trees for eagles whenever they came upon them (Stone 1937). By the mid-twentieth century, direct human persecution of the Bald Eagle, assisted by the growing use of DDT, appears to have had its intended effect.

Concerned that the species was on the verge of extirpation outside of Alaska, Congress enacted the Bald Eagle Protection Act of 1940 to save it. The Act, which initially excluded Alaska from its provisions, was amended in 1959 to include it. The Bald Eagle Protection Act was further amended in 1962 to extend protection to Golden Eagles because of their resemblance to juvenile Bald Eagles. The Bald Eagle, which was first listed as federally endangered in 1967 (Bean 1983), remained on the list as "threatened" in the lower 48 states in early 2006. That said, midwinter surveys of the eagles in the conterminous United States suggest that populations increased at 2 percent annually between 1986 and 2000 (K. Steenhof, pers. comm.), and all indications are that the species has rebounded from its persecution- and pesticide-era lows. Whether or not Bald Eagles will be able to sustain current population levels in America's increasingly peopled coastlines and inland waterways, however, remains to be seen.

Current Human Threats

Habitat Loss

The footprint of human civilization continues to impact migratory raptors in many ways. Historically, the advent of cultivated crops and, soon after, large-scale row-crop agriculture, increased the rate at which humans co-opted the primary productivity of the natural habitats they inhabited. Initially, the

growth of these human-dominated landscapes reduced both prey populations and nesting habitat for raptors. More recently, the development of
modern agriculture has resulted in the additional threat of pesticides (Hickey
1969).

Currently, the greatest rates of habitat loss are happening in the tropics. In
addition to forested landscapes, which are being cut for their wood and to
make way for housing and agriculture, tropical grasslands increasingly are
coming under the plow. In addition, both coastal and freshwater wetlands are
being drained for agriculture and modified for aquaculture and flood control
(Hannah et al. 1994). Habitat degradation in the tropics is particularly problematic for migratory raptors whose tropical wintering ranges already are far
smaller than their temperate breeding ranges, and even small losses in the former can impact large portions of world populations (Bildstein et al.1998).

Overall, habitat loss threatens more Old World raptors than New World
raptors. In Africa, for example, 52 percent of all migrants are threatened by
habitat loss, in Europe 61 percent, and in Australasia and the Pacific Islands
58 percent. By comparison 41 percent of all migrants are threatened by habitat loss in North America and the neotropics (Zalles and Bildstein 2000). As
use of the primary productivity of African grasslands and savannas shifts
from natural grazing to a combination of row-crop agriculture and wild-
game ranching, populations of migratory raptors, especially those that depend heavily on seasonally abundant insects, such as Lesser Spotted Eagles,
Steppe Eagles, and Lesser Kestrels, and double endemics, such as Levant
Sparrowhawks, are likely to suffer, particularly if pesticides are used to control insects on the newly planted row crops. Similarly, the accelerated development of Africa's closed canopy tropical forests promises to threaten Western Honey Buzzards, almost all of which overwinter there. In Australasia,
extensive habitat loss in the Indomalayan and Australasian tropics threatens
several migratory species, including the Black Baza and the Crested Honey
Buzzard, along with many of the region's island endemics (Bildstein et al.
1998; Thiollay 1998). In Europe, agricultural practices including shifts from
low-impact pastoral farming to high-impact agroindustry typified by the European Union's Common Agricultural Policy, are affecting many birds of
prey, including the region's vultures, which depend on the carcasses of large
mammals, as well as harriers and small falcons, which depend on natural
grasslands for nesting and feeding (Tucker and Heath 1994).

Although threats to neotropical forests have attracted the attention of conservationists for many years (Myers 1984), and although such losses continue
to threaten several of the region's sedentary endemics (Bierregaard 1998),

land-use changes in neotropical savannas and semi-open woodlands pose a greater threat to many of the region's short- and long-distance migrants, including Turkey Vultures, Swallow-tailed Kites, Snail Kites, Plumbeous Kites, Mississippi Kites, and Swainson's Hawks. Finally, in North America, habitat loss poses the greatest threat to recently rebounded populations of Bald Eagles, particularly in the heavily populated eastern United States, where increasing human populations near and within coastal and inland wetlands threaten both feeding and nesting sites.

Unfortunately, the somewhat idiosyncratic, species-specific nature of raptor migration (see Chapter 8 for details) makes it difficult to generalize about habitat loss. Consider for example, the following scenarios, which represent but a few of the situations that currently exist:

1. In species in which population size is currently regulated by events on the breeding grounds, habitat loss on the wintering grounds may have little, if any, effect on population size; whereas, habitat loss on the breeding grounds can have a major impact on population size.
2. In species in which breeders from different areas converge on a single wintering area, habitat loss in one breeding area, followed by a decline in the breeding population from that area, actually may improve breeding success in other breeding areas as a result of reduced competition on the wintering grounds.
3. In species that feed en route while migrating, habitat loss at one or more migration stopover sites can reduce population size, even if breeding habitats and wintering habitats remain intact.
4. Migratory species that compete for food with sedentary species on the wintering grounds actually may benefit from habitat degradation on the wintering grounds that acts to reduce the nesting habitat, but not the feeding habitat, of the competing sedentary species.

The complexity of potential scenarios increases considerably, both for partial migrants and for species that show age- or sex-differences in winter-habitat use. In partial migrants, for example, a species can shift from being mainly migratory to mainly or even entirely sedentary if habitat loss disproportionately affects migratory populations. The reverse is possible if habitat loss disproportionately affects sedentary populations. And in species that segregate by age or sex in winter, habitat loss on the wintering grounds can potentially affect some segments of the population but not others.

The examples above highlight the importance of understanding the details of the migration ecology of individual species. Without such knowledge it is all but impossible to predict how habitat loss will affect populations.

Finally, environmental change, including habitat loss, is inevitable. That most species of migratory raptors are *partial* rather than *complete* migrants suggests that members of this group are capable of modifying and adapting their migratory habits in light of local circumstances. Indeed, migration itself is an adaptive response to seasonal "habitat loss." That said, it is reasonable to assume that many migratory raptors will be able to reduce the potential impacts of habitat loss by modifying their migration strategies (Dolman and Sutherland 1994). Even so, some migrants may not be able to do so because of inherent constraints, because they lack appropriate alternative habitats, or because the loss of habitat is too large or too rapid to permit an adaptive response.

Environmental Contaminants

Humanity continues to contaminate ecosystems with numerous natural and synthetic substances, many of which threaten populations of migratory raptors. Because raptors are predators and scavengers, they are especially vulnerable to such threats because they are likely to come into contact with contaminants that have been biologically accumulated and magnified by the prey and carcasses on which they feed.

In most instances, the negative effects of such contamination have been both unintended and unanticipated. Even so, environmental contaminants have extirpated regional populations of raptors, and the costs of their cleanup and reversing population declines have been significant and substantial. Despite a history of unexpected effects, an overwhelming lack of foresight and learning continues to plague attempts to reduce this major and largely unnecessary threat to raptors, which continues to plague 21 percent of all migratory populations globally (Zalles and Bildstein 2000).

Pesticides. Much of the threat from environmental contaminants stems from the systematic misuse of agricultural pesticides, which impacts raptors both *indirectly* when birds of prey feed on poisoned pests and other organisms targeted by the pesticides and *directly* when they consume pesticides themselves as nontarget species. The most widely known example of the former involves the misuse of DDT (dichloro-diphenyl-trichloroethane), a synthetic organochlorine pesticide that came into widespread use across much of Canada, the United States, and Europe in the late 1940s and early 1950s. An inexpensive, broad-spectrum (i.e., it could be used against many insect and other invertebrate pests), and long-lasting pesticide that was far less toxic to vertebrates than the inorganic biocides it replaced, DDT earned its developer and chief proponent, Paul Müller, a Nobel Prize in Physiology or Medicine in 1948. Although this "wonder chemical's" widespread and often indiscriminate use began to raise alarms among conservationists as early as the late 1940s (Gabrielson et al. 1950), it and other organochlorine pesticides quickly established themselves as the insecticidal agents of choice in the agricultural world of the 1950s and 1960s.

Biologists began to notice regional declines in the reproductive success of Bald Eagles as early as the late 1940s (Broley 1950), but it was not until the late 1950s that anyone began to link the declines to the new generation of organochlorine pesticides (Broley 1958). Rachel Carson's best-selling book, *Silent Spring*, placed the pesticide problem in the hearts and minds of the American people in the early 1960s (Carson 1962), and in 1965 a group of concerned scientists and raptor aficionados met at the University of Wisconsin in Madison to discuss the situation. By then, populations of Peregrine Falcons and other raptors had been in free fall across much of eastern North America and western Europe for almost a quarter of a century (Ratcliffe 1993). The extent of the decline was mind-numbing.

In 1964, a careful survey of 133 traditional Peregrine Falcon breeding sites across the eastern United States failed to locate a single parental bird (Hickey 1969). In addition to the speed with which it had occurred, what was striking about the unprecedented decline was that the Peregrine Falcon was a widespread, near cosmopolitan, generalist predator, with a long-standing reputation for population stability. If the Peregrine Falcon could disappear so quickly, what bird of prey could survive?

The scientists that met in Wisconsin in the summer of 1965 focused their attention on the growing misuse of modern synthetic "biocides" in pest control and the ability of these new chemicals to be magnified biologically (i.e., increase in concentration) in organisms along food chains. High levels of several of the biocides in Peregrine Falcons suggested a link. This, together with an increase in eggshell breakage (Ratcliffe 1958), suggested a mechanism for reproductive failure.

With science on the case, things began to happen quickly. British falcon specialist, Derek Ratcliffe, published a benchmark analysis that tied the timing of eggshell thinning in British Peregrine Falcons to the widespread use of DDT (Ratcliffe 1967). Two years later, a carefully controlled experimental study involving captive American Kestrels conclusively demonstrated a "smoking gun" or cause-and-effect relationship between the two phenomena (Wiemeyer and Porter 1969; Porter and Wiemeyer 1969), a connection that

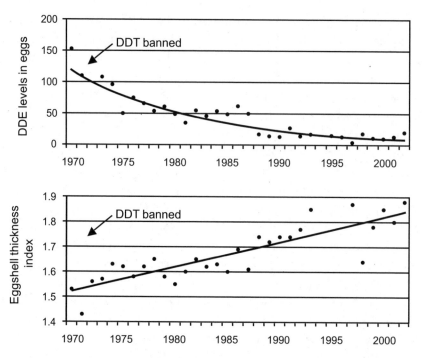

Figure 40. DDE levels in eggs (above) and eggshell thickness indexes (below) for Peregrine Falcons nesting in Baden-Württemberg, western Germany, 1970–2002. The widespread use of DDT was banned in the area in 1972. The numbers of territorial pairs in the region increased from 30 to 280 after the ban. (DDE is a metabolite of DDT. The eggshell index is calculated according to Ratcliffe [1967]) (after Wegner et al. 2005).

correlational studies in nature continue to confirm today (Wegner et al. 2005). Armed with this new information, conservationists successfully promulgated bans on the widespread use of DDT and other organochlorine pesticides across most of North America and western Europe in the early 1970s.

In most instances, the bans quickly led to reductions in contaminant levels and a reversal in eggshell thinning (Figure 40) (Wegner et al. 2005). Soon after, most populations that had suffered through pesticide-era lows began to rebound. In several notable instances, natural increases were assisted by reintroduction efforts (Beans 1996; Cade and Burnham 2003). And the by the mid-1980s, many recoveries were well underway (Cade et al. 1988; Bednarz et al. 1990).

One of the more instructive aspects of this saga involves the declines and recoveries of European populations of Peregrine Falcons in former West and

East Germany at the height of the Cold War (Wagner et al. 2005). Although both the Federal Republic of Germany (West Germany) and the German Democratic Republic (East Germany) banned DDT in 1972, the pesticide continued to be used in the latter for an additional 17 years. Not surprisingly, whereas West German populations of Peregrine Falcons turned the corner and began to rebound shortly after the official ban, the once-ubiquitous tree-nesting population of East Germany continued to decline through the mid-1970s and was extirpated later in that decade, almost certainly because of its protracted exposure to the contaminant (Wegner et al. 2005).

Although widespread use of DDT and many other organochlorine pesticides, including the far more toxic cyclodienes, aldrin and dieldrin, ceased in North America and Western Europe in the early 1970s, these broad-spectrum, persistent pesticides continue to pose a real threat to many populations of migratory raptors in less-developed areas in the tropics and southern hemisphere, where even local use of these pesticides can impact large numbers of individuals that concentrate on their wintering grounds while feeding on agricultural pests.

As luck would have it, the chemicals that have replaced organochlorine pesticides in areas where the latter have been banned create their own set of significant problems for raptors. Organophosphate pesticides came into use 1960s and 1970s, largely in response to growing concerns regarding the persistent nature of nature of organochlorine pesticides, some of which, including DDT, had half-lives of up to 15 years (i.e., 15 years after it is applied, half of the original DDT is still active, and 15 years later one quarter of the original DDT is still active). The good news about these newer pesticides, which include malathion, parathion, monocrotophos, and fenthion, is that because they have half-lives of a few hours to a few days, they are far less persistent environmentally than the organochlorines they replaced. The bad news is that organophosphates kill insects by inhibiting cholinesterase, an enzyme that turns off the principal neurotransmitter, acetylcholine, in the nervous systems of both vertebrates and insects, and as such are acutely toxic to both groups of animals.

Developed as part of nerve gas research in the Second World War, organophosphate pesticides are 10 to 100 times as toxic to vertebrates, including birds, as are the organochlorine pesticides they replaced. A second popular class of organochlorine replacements, carbamates, or urethanes (e.g., sevin, aldicarb, carbofuran, and mirax), share many of the properties of organophosphates, including enhanced vertebrate toxicity via anticholinesterase action. Unlike their predecessors, whose greatest threat was environmental persistence

Table 19. *Documented instances of secondary poisoning of raptors resulting from the use of cholinesterase-inhibiting liquid insecticidal sprays*

Insecticide used	Crop	Primary vertebrates killed	Raptors killed
Carbofuran	Grapes	Songbirds, small mammals	Northern Harrier Sharp-shinned Hawk, Red-tailed Hawk
	Corn, alfalfa	Songbirds, rabbits	White-tailed Kite, Northern Harrier
Parathion	Pastures	Songbirds	Red Kite
Monocrotophos	Alfalfa	Voles	Hen Harrier, Pallid Harrier, Long-legged Buzzard, Eurasian Buzzard, Greater Spotted Eagle, Lesser Spotted Eagle, Imperial Eagle, Common Kestrel

Source: After Mineau et al. 1999.

and eventual accumulation in the fatty body tissues of birds of prey, the new pesticides pose their greatest threat acutely and immediately whenever they are used in ways that allow raptors to contact them in undegraded form. Moreover, because these pesticides can be absorbed through the skin and lungs, as well as through the gastrointestinal tract, virtually any contact with them either indirectly as a result of eating recently poisoned prey, or directly, as a nontarget species, poses a considerable threat (Table 19).

Regrettably, there are many examples of this more recent pesticide threat, particularly as a result of so-called off-label or illegal use of these biocides. In England, where organophosphates and carbamates have been used illegally to control mammalian predators and to protect racing pigeons, 87 percent of 136 raptor kills reported between 1985 and 1994 were attributed to the use of these poisons (Mineau et al. 1999). In the eastern Mediterranean, where the highly toxic carbamate pesticide, Lannate, is used to protect grapes from vineyard moths, 150 Eleonora's Falcons were killed in 1999 (Ristow and Xirouchakis 2000; Tsatsakis et al. 2001). That this latter die-off occurred in the species' geographic stronghold, where most of the world's 7000 pairs of

Eleonora's Falcons are known to breed, highlights the sometimes disastrous consequences of even local pesticide use. The most striking example of how organophosphates can kill large numbers of raptors, however, involves New World Swainson's Hawks.

In the winter of 1995–1996, an estimated 6000 to 20,000 of these so-called locust hawks were killed by the organophosphates, monocrotophos and dimethoate, on their Argentine wintering grounds. Forensic analyses at the time indicated that monocrotophos alone poisoned more than 4000 hawks at six different sites. First-hand accounts indicate that the hawks died immediately upon being sprayed with the pesticides while hunting grass-hoppers in alfalfa and sunflower fields, or several days after eating poisoned insects. Neither of the pesticides involved had been approved for use in con-trolling grasshoppers on any crop in the region (England et al. 1997; Gold-stein et al. 1999a).

Subsequent meetings between conservation groups and the chemical com-pany producing monocrotophos resulted in the removal of the existing stock of the pesticide from the area in which the birds had been killed (Goldstein et al. 1999b). Although the problem appears to have been solved in Argentina, the pesticide continues to be used elsewhere in South America, as well as in many places in the Old World.

Other Contaminants. Unfortunately, pesticides are not the only agricul-tural chemicals that threaten raptors. The most recent large-scale raptor kill attributed to environmental contaminants involved a seemingly benign vet-erinary drug. The story begins on the Indian subcontinent, where in the mid-1990s Indian ornithologist Vibhu Prakash noted dramatic declines in popu-lations of several species of common and widespread vultures in a former vulture stronghold, Keoladeo National Park in Rajasthan, India (Prakash 1999). The birds in question included several species of *Gyps* vultures, five of which occur in India.

Gyps (the genus name is ancient Greek for "vulture") are large and highly social vultures that nest colonially and that often commingle while feeding on the soft body tissues of decaying large mammals. In areas where carcasses and potential nest sites are abundant, the density of *Gyps* vultures can greatly exceed that typically associated with birds of prey. In the 1970s and early 1980s, for example, the Indian White-backed Vulture, one of the species cur-rently in decline at Keoladeo and a bird that regularly associates with hu-mans, was nesting within the city of Delhi at densities of approximately three pairs per km^2 (or nine pairs per square mile) (Galushin 1971), and at four times that density in Keoladeo National Park (Prakash 1989). Given that the Indian White-backed Vulture ranges throughout most of the Indian subcontinent, as well as throughout much of southeast Asia, experts at the time suggested that this species quite possibly was the most abundant large raptor on earth (Houston 1985). Within 15 years of that assessment, however, the Indian White-backed Vulture, together with two close relatives, the Long-billed Vulture and the Slender-billed Vulture, was ranked among the most threatened of all birds of prey (BirdLife International 2000).

The coincidental and catastrophic declines of three populations of once common raptors alarmed the conservation community for two reasons. First, with minimum estimated declines in the 1990s of 96 percent for Indian White-backed Vultures and 92 percent for Long-billed and Slender-billed vultures, the rapidity with which these three species were disappearing was unprecedented. By comparison, although regional populations of the cosmopolitan Peregrine Falcon had undergone similar declines during the DDT Era, the fate of that entire species was never in doubt. This was not the case for these three species of vultures, all of which were in precipitous decline throughout their ranges. Second, and perhaps more troubling was that no one could explain why the populations were declining. The "usual suspects," habitat loss, pesticides, and direct persecution, offered little in the way of answers.

Biologists had known for some time that the increased and largely uncontrolled hunting of wild ungulates in southeast Asia had decimated the food base for vultures there, but carcasses remained readily available in India and Pakistan, and vulture populations had crashed there as well. Although a few conservationists pointed to direct persecution as the culprit—an argument intuitively supported by the region's high human densities—vultures were declining throughout their ranges, including in India where all three species were valued for their role as environmental scavengers and where, in certain parts of society, they were held in cultural and religious esteem (Pain et al. 2003). Pesticide or heavy-metal poisoning, initially, was thought likely, but exhaustive toxicological analyses of carcasses failed to detect clinical levels of these environmental contaminants (Oaks et al. 2001). In light of these dead ends, the conservation community began to focus on the possibility that an unknown pathogen was killing the birds.

The argument for a novel infectious disease to which the vultures were "immunologically naïve" made sense. After all, many of the birds looked sick. Neck drooping and lethargy were typical prior to death, and not one "affected" breeding colony had recovered once high mortality set in. Autopsied carcasses from India and Pakistan revealed renal malfunction and visceral gout in most individuals, along with a high frequency of enteritis, conditions that are often reflective of infectious diseases. Consequently, as recently as 2003, most conservation scientists believed that an epidemic disease, probably viral, was their most promising lead (Cunningham et al. 2003; Pain et al. 2003).

At about the same time, however, Lindsay Oaks, an avian pathologist at Washington State University, had reached a different conclusion. Oaks, whose earlier analyses of vulture tissues had eliminated the widespread use of pesticides and heavy metals as the problem (Oaks et al. 2001), had turned to analyzing fresh carcasses for signs of fragile viruses and bacteria. Finding none, by late 2002, Oaks had concluded that an epidemic disease was not likely. Frustrated, but determined to find an explanation for the ongoing ecological tragedy, Oaks began to focus on a series of less likely contaminants, including several veterinary drugs that had recently come into widespread use in livestock in the region. In early 2003, the new work paid off. Tests revealed that all 25 vultures Oaks examined that had died of renal failure had been exposed to diclofenac, a nonsteriodal anti-inflammatory painkiller that had come into use in India and Pakistan in the 1990s. On the other hand, none of the 13 vultures that Oaks examined that had succumbed from other causes showed any exposure to the drug. In addition, four nonreleasable vultures that had been given single oral doses of diclofenac, either at the normal mammalian dosage (2 individuals) or at one-tenth of that dosage (2 individuals), had died of renal failure within two days (Oaks et al. 2004). Additional analyses of carcasses from much larger areas of India and Nepal revealed high residues of the drug in dead vultures there as well (Shultz et al. 2004). A more recent simulation model of vulture demography indicates that diclofenac exposure rates as low as 1-in-760 available livestock carcasses could have produced the massive die-off (Green et al. 2004).

The population declines, which continued throughout the region into 2004, led conservationists to call for an immediate ban on the drug where it was in use and the maintenance of restrictions in areas where it was not in use. In early 2005 the Indian government decided to enact a six-month phaseout of diclofenac, and farmers there have been asked to replace the drug with alternatives that are believed to be less toxic to the birds (Bagla 2005). Because diclofenac already is widely distributed throughout the region and is likely to remain in use for some time even as new sales are banned, and because population modeling indicates the likelihood of extinction or at least extirpation throughout most of the ranges of the three affected species, prudence dictated that an adequate number of vultures be removed from the wild as soon as possible and that efforts begin to captively breed these birds, not only to ensure the long-term survival of these species but also to serve as breeding stock for future release efforts once the diclofenac has been "ecologically" removed (Green et al. 2004). That the latter approach helped quicken the restoration of Peregrine Falcons in several portions of their ranges following bans on DDT and other organochlorines (Cade and Burnham 2003) and that reintroduction also appears to be working for California Condors in the western United States (Moir 2005), suggests that in time populations of southern Asia's vultures, too, may rebound. That said, this episode demonstrates just how easy it is for human actions to eliminate functional populations of common raptors in ways that remain frustratingly difficult to predict.

Finally, although agricultural chemicals currently rank as the most significant and widespread environmental-contaminant threat, heavy metals, and in particular lead, also continue to threaten many populations of birds of prey. Lead poisoning, via the ingestion of contaminated prey and carcasses is problematic in areas where lead shot and lead pellets are used in sport and subsistence hunting. In North America, Red-tailed Hawks, Rough-legged Hawks, Golden Eagles, Prairie Falcons, and Peregrine Falcons have been diagnosed with lead poisoning (McBride et al. 2004). And in Spain, eight species, including Eurasian Griffon, Red Kite, Black Kite, and Western Marsh Harrier, have been similarly diagnosed (Mateo et al. 2003). Scavengers and species that are likely to feed upon hunter-injured waterfowl and upland game are at increased risk. Although the extent to which lead poisoning affects entire populations of raptors remains relatively little studied, the unintended poisoning of California Condors, presumably via ingestion of lead shot and fragments in consumed carcasses, almost certainly contributed to the decline of this currently critically endangered species in mid-twentieth century North America (Stattersfield and Capper 2000). The continued availability of lead-tainted carcasses in areas into which captive-bred condors are being released as part of an ongoing reintroduction effort may threaten the success of that program (Meretsky et al. 2000). A lead-awareness campaign for hunters, many of whom who are ignorant of the problem in condors, is currently underway, with the aim of having hunters bury entrails and other carcass remains in the field as well as having them switch to more benign shot, including copper and composites made of tin, tungsten, and bismuth (Moir 2005).

Other Human Threats to Raptors

In addition to the threats mentioned above, other human activities continue to threaten raptors. Although most of these threats are local or regional,
several have the potential to affect entire species of raptors.

Distribution of electrical energy. One area of human activity that continues
to place raptors at risk is the generation and distribution of electrical energy.
Despite numerous attempts to reduce raptor deaths along distribution
routes, power-line collisions and electrocution remain significant threats to
raptors, the former at migratory bottlenecks and other points of migration
concentration (Plate 14), and the latter in treeless areas, where power-line
poles frequently provide the only available elevated hunting perches for birds
of prey.

Large raptors are more vulnerable to electrocution because their broad
wingspans allow them to contact conducting and ground wires simultaneously while they are perched on utility poles. Although much of the mortality, especially among recently fledged juveniles, may be compensatory, there
is growing evidence that in some instances power-line electrocutions reduce
raptor populations locally. One example of this is a decline in the numbers of
vulnerable Spanish Imperial Eagles (see Table 18) in Doñana National Park
in southern Spain where, in the 1980s, 69 percent of all known eagle deaths
were attributed to electrocution (Ferrer et al. 1991). In the United States,
electrocutions were responsible for 25 percent of all Golden Eagle deaths reported by the National Wildlife Health Center in Madison, Wisconsin in the
early 1960s through the mid-1990s (Franson et al. 1995). Other species
whose populations have declined locally as a result of power-line electrocutions include Cape Griffons, Eurasian Griffons, Egyptian Vultures, and
Bonelli's Eagles (Lehman 2001; Harness, in press). Although some utility
companies have redesigned and retrofitted power lines to reduce the threat of
electrocution, and whereas some have procedures in place to monitor mortality, many do not. Even in developed countries, the overwhelming majority of
transmission poles fail to meet established standards for raptor safety
(Lehman 2001). Deregulation of the power industry in the United States and
elsewhere, together with an increased focus on competition and cost-cutting,
suggest that power-line electrocutions will continue to threaten birds of prey
for some time.

Wind farms. The generation of electricity at wind farms also poses a potential threat to raptors, particularly as the number of such installations
grows. Wind farms can affect raptors two ways: (1) via collisions with the tur-

bines themselves and (2) via habitat disturbance brought about by their construction and maintenance. All wind turbines are not equal. First-generation turbines, many of which remain in use today, were mounted on 60- to 80-foot open lattice-work towers, had 50- to 60-foot rotors, and turned at rates of 60 to 80 times per minute. Newer turbines are mounted on taller 200- to 260-foot tubular towers, have larger 150- to 260-foot rotors, and turn at slower rates of 11 to 28 times per minute. The new turbines, which produce considerably more energy per unit, are spaced more widely apart than the older units. Bird strikes at wind farms were first studied at an installation of more than 5000 old-style turbines installed at Altamont Pass, California. Raptors appeared to be at higher relative risk at the site than were other species of birds, at least in part because they often perched on and hunted from the turbines' lattice-work support structures.

Two recent publications based on work conducted in and around Tarifa, Spain—a major concentration point for raptors migrating between western Europe and Africa across the Strait of Gibraltar, where 700 old and new turbines are currently in use—provide insights into the extent of the threat. Both studies measured mortality at the installations and the factors responsible for it.

The first investigation found that (1) resident raptors, particularly Eurasian Griffons and Common Kestrels, were more likely to be killed by turbines than were migrating raptors, (2) Eurasian Griffons were most vulnerable in autumn and winter when a lack of thermals forced the vultures to slope soar closer to the ridgetop arrays of turbines, and (3) migrants were most vulnerable in summer when they were most abundant there and were attracted to preferred hunting habitats at one of the wind farms. Based on the numbers of carcasses found, and correcting for the removal of carcasses by scavengers between inspections, the authors of this study concluded that annual vulture and kestrel mortality approximated 0.12 and 0.14 individuals per turbine, respectively, or approximately 30 vulture kills and 36 kestrel kills per year at two wind farms with a combined total of 250 turbines. Because most of the collisions occurred at a small number of turbines and during predictable wind conditions, the authors recommended suspending operations of specific turbines during high-risk situations (Barrios and Rodríguez 2004).

The second study, which reported that most raptors noticeably avoided approaching active turbines, found evidence of only two collisions (a juvenile Eurasian Griffon and an adult Short-toed Snake Eagle) during 14 months of study, or an annual mortality of approximately 0.03 birds per turbine, and concluded that the 66-turbine wind farm in question was of low risk, most likely because migrants in the area were flying well above the height of the blades (de Lucas et al. 2004).

Studies of wind power–bird interactions continue to grow as the number of operational turbines increases. Two major themes appear to be emerging from these studies. First, older turbines kill more raptors than newer turbines. And second, regardless of the type of turbine, improperly sited and inappropriately managed wind farms can and almost certainly will cause problems for raptors, including migratory species. Key factors in reducing the potential impact of wind farms include (1) situating them away from high-density raptor populations and known migration corridors and bottlenecks, (2) avoiding sites that will displace existing populations from important nesting and feeding areas, and (3) using on-off cycles to reduce the likelihood of collisions during periods of peak raptor migration (Percival 2005).

Nuclear power. Nuclear power plants, too, may pose threats to migratory raptors. Although nuclear power does not inherently threaten birds of prey, the accidental release of radionuclides from malfunctioning generation sites has the potential for exposing raptors to dangerous radionuclides both directly via airborne plumes and indirectly via contaminated prey (Brisbin 1991). The unpredictable nature of this threat precludes detailed before-and-after studies. Even so, abrupt declines in the numbers of migrating Lesser Spotted Eagles in Israel following the Chernobyl nuclear accident of 1986, together with coincidental declines in the age ratios of migrating Levant Sparrowhawks and Steppe Eagles there, have led some researchers to suggest a cause-and-effect relationship (Yosef and Fornasari 2004; D. Alon, pers. comm.).

Global warming. One factor associated with the generation of energy that is likely to affect migratory raptors on a large scale is global climate change. Should the changes that are currently envisioned by climatologists occur, raptor migration can be expected to respond in several significant ways (Berthold 2001). Milder winters in the temperate zone should result in greater survivorship among resident species there, as well as an increased tendency for year-round residency among current populations of partial migrants. As sedentary populations of raptors increase, long-distance migrants overwintering in tropical areas could face increased competition on the breeding grounds, and those overwintering in temperate areas farther south would face increased competition on both the breeding and wintering grounds. The extent to which these migrants would survive as evolutionary units would depend on their ability to shorten their migratory journeys, which, in turn, could allow them to compete more successfully with nonmigrants by departing later in the autumn and returning earlier in the spring. Whether or not such species survived in the long term, the overall outcome would be much the same: a substantial shift from migratory behavior, particularly that of long-distance migration, toward increased sedentary behavior in raptor communities throughout much of the temperate zone. Exceptions would include subtropical regions where predicted increases in episodic droughts are likely to lead to increased nomadism and short-distance movements in some species, and coastal areas, where anticipated sea level rise would eliminate lowland breeding areas for many species. Although individual scenarios remain speculative, the overall impression of a warmer planet is one in which migratory raptors are far less common than now.

The Future

The examples above indicate that human activities have threatened and continue to threaten migratory raptors in many ways. The extent to which they will continue to do so depends both on the kinds of activities that society continues to engage in and the rate at which human populations continue to grow. There is every indication that land-use change and habitat loss will continue to be the main anthropogenic threat. Cultivated landscapes—areas in which a third or more of the land is in crops, aquaculture, or livestock production—now cover a quarter of the earth's land surface. Humanity's demand for food is expected to double in the next 45 years. Exactly how human populations will meet this challenge is unclear. What is clear is that an increased portion of the world's primary productivity will be given over to feeding people, and that this will leave less for other species, including raptors. Agricultural growth, acting through the loss of natural habitats, environmental contamination, and, in some instances, direct persecution, already poses the greatest threat to migratory raptors, many of which depend on the same seasonally productive open landscapes humans prize for farmlands. It is likely to do so into the future as well (Green et al. 2005). Intensified farming and modern forestry, particularly the widespread use of new chemicals, both to grow farm and forestry products more "efficiently" and to protect them from nonhuman users, almost certainly will produce new and, in many instances, unanticipated threats to raptors, and it is inevitable that at least some populations of birds of prey will decline as a result.

Although it would be easy to grow increasingly pessimistic in light of all of this, my own experiences with migratory raptors and the problems they face lead me in a different, more optimistic direction. My growing optimism for raptors in a human-dominated world is fueled by several factors. First, advances in our understanding of the environmental needs of raptors strengthen our ability to protect them. Knowledge is "the key to the realm" in on-the-ground conservation, and we are adding to our knowledge base faster than ever before. Second, a new generation of raptor biologists is growing by leaps and bounds, not only in North America and Europe but also in Asia, Australia, Africa, and Latin America, where many raptor migrants overwinter. More adequately prepared and better connected than their predecessors, this new cadre of conservationists is well positioned to protect migratory raptors throughout their intercontinental journeys.

Third, the recent push to engage local human populations in raptor protection and to incorporate the needs of migrating raptors into regional and continental management schemes for other natural resources promise to help ensure a future for migratory birds of prey. And fourth, and perhaps most important, the birds themselves have proved to be far more resilient than many conservationists have given them credit for. The fact that Alaskan populations of Bald Eagles were able to withstand more than one-third of a century of incessant bounty hunting, together with this and other species' ability to rebound from pesticide era lows of mid-twentieth-century North America, suggest that, so long as the threat is eventually reversed and is not so swift as to overwhelm the birds entirely, raptors are capable of withstanding the onslaught of intentional and unintentional human insults. Although it is impossible to overstate the irreversible nature of species extinction and the many problems that raptors currently face, it is equally impossible to overstate the resourceful nature of these birds.

If my optimism is tempered at all, it is only by the concern that we will fail to learn from the past. If we choose to build on our existing and growing body of knowledge and continue to study and learn more about how birds of prey function in natural and human-dominated landscapes, adult and juvenile migratory raptors will be traveling long distances in large numbers well into the future.

Synthesis and Conclusions

1. Only one raptor, the sedentary Guadalupe Caracara, has become extinct in the last 300 years.
2. Even so, 12 species of migratory raptors remain threatened globally, and populations of more than 100 species remain threatened in many parts the world.

3. The principal threats to migratory raptors are habitat degradation and loss; environmental contaminants, including pesticides and other agricultural chemicals; and direct assault, including persecution and trapping for captive use. Of these, habitat loss remains the greatest threat overall, particularly in the tropics.

4. Migratory raptors face special problems because many are *double endemics* whose livelihoods depend on the maintenance of not one but two disjunct habitats.

5. Human activities, including direct persecution for sport, predator control, and subsistence hunting, have affected migratory raptors since prehistoric times.

6. Direct persecution increased significantly once raptors were viewed as threats to domestic and game animals.

7. The misuse of agricultural pesticides reduced many populations of raptors in the mid-twentieth century and continues to do so, sporadically, today.

8. The large-scale generation of electrical energy for human use has and will continue to impact populations of raptors in many ways.

9. Learning from previous mistakes, a growing understanding of the ecological needs of migratory raptors, and an appreciation for the resilience of the birds themselves all are important aspects of successful raptor conservation.

APPENDIX: RAPTORS, OTHER BIRDS, AND OTHER ANIMALS MENTIONED IN THE TEXT

Raptors

Common Name	Scientific Name
African Cuckoo Hawk	*Aviceda cuculoides*
African Fish Eagle	*Haliaeetus vocifer*
African Goshawk	*Accipiter tachiro*
African Harrier Hawk	*Polyboroides typus*
African Hawk Eagle	*Hieraaetus spilogaster*
African Hobby	*Falco cuvierii*
African Little Sparrowhawk	*Accipiter minullus*
African Marsh Harrier	*Circus ranivorus*
African White-backed Vulture	*Gyps africanus*
American Kestrel	*Falco sparverius*
Amur Falcon	*Falco amurensis*
Andaman Serpent Eagle	*Spilornis elgini*
Andean Condor	*Vultur gryphus*
Aplomado Falcon	*Falco femoralis*
Archer's Buzzard	*Buteo archeri*
Augur Buzzard	*Buteo augur*
Australasian Goshawk	*Accipiter fasciatus*
Australian Black-shouldered Kite	*Elanus axillaris*
Australian Hobby	*Falco longipennis*
Australian Kestrel	*Falco cenchroides*
Ayres' Hawk Eagle	*Hieraaetus ayresii*
Bald Eagle	*Haliaeetus leucocephalus*
Banded Kestrel	*Falco zoniventris*
Banded Snake Eagle	*Circaetus cinerascens*
Barbary Falcon	*Falco peregrinus pelegrinoides*
Barred Forest Falcon	*Micrastur ruficollis*
Barred Hawk	*Leucopternis princeps*
Barred Honey Buzzard	*Pernis celebensis*
Bat Falcon	*Falco rufigularis*
Bat Hawk	*Macheiramphus alcinus*
Bateleur	*Terathopius ecaudatus*

Bearded Vulture	*Gypaetus barbatus*
Beaudouin's Snake Eagle	*Circaetus beaudouini*
Besra	*Accipiter virgatus*
Bicolored Hawk	*Accipiter bicolor*
Black Baza	*Aviceda leuphotes*
Black Caracara	*Daptrius ater*
Black Falcon	*Falco subniger*
Black Harrier	*Circus maurus*
Black Hawk Eagle	*Spizaetus tyrannus*
Black Kite	*Milvus migrans*
Black Solitary Eagle	*Harpyhaliaetus solitarius*
Black Sparrowhawk	*Accipiter melanoleucus*
Black Vulture	*Coragyps atratus*
Black-and-chestnut Eagle	*Oroaetus isidori*
Black-and-white Hawk Eagle	*Spizastur melanoleucus*
Black-breasted Buzzard	*Hamirostra melanosternon*
Black-breasted Snake Eagle	*Circaetus pectoralis*
Black-chested Buzzard Eagle	*Geranoaetus melanoleucus*
Black-collared Hawk	*Busarellus nigricollis*
Black-faced Hawk	*Leucopternis melanops*
Black-mantled Goshawk	*Accipiter melanochlamys*
Black-shouldered Kite	*Elanus caeruleus*
Black-thighed Falconet	*Microhierax fringillarius*
Blyth's Hawk Eagle	*Spizaetus alboniger*
Bonelli's Eagle	*Hieraaetus fasciatus*
Booted Eagle	*Hieraaetus pennatus*
Brahminy Kite	*Haliastur indus*
Broad-winged Hawk	*Buteo platypterus*
Brown Falcon	*Falco berigora*
Brown Snake Eagle	*Circaetus cinereus*
Buckley's Forest Falcon	*Micrastur buckleyi*
California Condor	*Gymnogyps californianus*
Cape Griffon	*Gyps coprotheres*
Carunculated Caracara	*Phalcoboenus carunculatus*
Cassin's Hawk Eagle	*Spizaetus africanus*
Changeable Hawk Eagle	*Spizaetus cirrhatus*
Chestnut-flanked Sparrowhawk	*Accipiter castanilius*
Chestnut-shouldered Goshawk	*Erythrotriorchis buergersi*
Chilean Hawk	*Accipiter chilensis*
Chimango Caracara	*Milvago chimango*
Chinese Sparrowhawk	*Accipiter soloensis*
Cinereous Harrier	*Circus cinereus*
Cinereous Vulture	*Aegypius monachus*
Collared Falconet	*Microhierax caerulescens*
Collared Forest Falcon	*Micrastur semitorquatus*

Collared Sparrowhawk	*Accipiter cirrhocephalus*
Common Black Hawk	*Buteogallus anthracinus*
Common Kestrel	*Falco tinnunculus*
Congo Serpent Eagle	*Dryotriorchis spectabilis*
Cooper's Hawk	*Accipiter cooperii*
Crane Hawk	*Geranospiza caerulescens*
Crested Caracara	*Caracara plancus*
Crested Goshawk	*Accipiter trivirgatus*
Crested Honey Buzzard	*Pernis ptilorhynchus*
Crested Serpent Eagle	*Spilornis cheela*
Crowned Hawk Eagle	*Stephanoaetus coronatus*
Crowned Solitary Eagle	*Harpyhaliaetus coronatus*
Cuban Kite	*Chondrohierax uncinatus wilsonii*
Dark Chanting Goshawk	*Melierax metabates*
Dickinson's Kestrel	*Falco dickinsoni*
Doria's Goshawk	*Megatriorchis doriae*
Double-toothed Kite	*Harpagus bidentatus*
East African Snake Eagle	*Circaetus fasciolatus*
Eastern Chanting Goshawk	*Melierax poliopterus*
Eastern Marsh Harrier	*Circus spilonotus*
Egyptian Vulture	*Neophron percnopterus*
Eleonora's Falcon	*Falco eleonorae*
Eyle's Harrier	*Circus eylesi (extinct)*
Eurasian Buzzard	*Buteo buteo*
Eurasian Griffon	*Gyps fulvus*
Eurasian Sparrowhawk	*Accipiter nisus*
Ferruginous Hawk	*Buteo regalis*
Fiji Goshawk	*Accipiter rufitorques*
Fox Kestrel	*Falco alopex*
Frances's Sparrowhawk	*Accipiter francesii*
Gabar Goshawk	*Micronisus gabar*
Galapagos Hawk	*Buteo galapagoensis*
Golden Eagle	*Aquila chrysaetos*
Grasshopper Buzzard	*Butastur rufipennis*
Great Black Hawk	*Buteogallus urubitinga*
Great Nicobar Serpent Eagle	*Spilornis klossi*
Greater Fishing Eagle	*Ichthyophaga ichthyaetus*
Greater Kestrel	*Falco rupicoloides*
Greater Spotted Eagle	*Aquila clanga*
Greater Yellow-headed Vulture	*Cathartes melambrotus*
Grey Falcon	*Falco hypoleucos*
Grey Hawk	*Buteo nitidus*
Grey Kestrel	*Falco ardosiaceus*
Grey-backed Hawk	*Leucopternis occidentalis*
Grey-bellied Goshawk	*Accipiter poliogaster*

Grey-faced Buzzard	*Butastur indicus*
Grey-headed Goshawk	*Accipiter poliocephalus*
Grey-headed Kite	*Leptodon cayanensis*
Guadalupe Caracara	*Polyborus lutosus* (extinct*)*
Guiana Crested Eagle	*Morphnus guianensis*
Gundlach's Hawk	*Accipiter gundlachi*
Gurney's Eagle	*Aquila gurneyi*
Gyrfalcon	*Falco rusticolus*
Haast's Eagle	*Harpagornis* sp. (extinct)
Harpy Eagle	*Harpia harpyja*
Harris' Hawk	*Parabuteo unicinctus*
Hawaiian Hawk	*Buteo solitarius*
Hen Harrier (Old World)	*Circus cyaneus*
Henst's Goshawk	*Accipiter henstii*
Himalayan Griffon	*Gyps himalayensis*
Hooded Vulture	*Necrosyrtes monachus*
Hook-billed Kite	*Chondrohierax uncinatus*
Imitator Sparrowhawk	*Accipiter imitator*
Imperial Eagle	*Aquila heliaca*
Indian Black Eagle	*Ictinaetus malayensis*
Indian White-backed Vulture	*Gyps bengalensis*
Jackal Buzzard	*Buteo rufofuscus*
Japanese Sparrowhawk	*Accipiter gularis*
Javan Hawk Eagle	*Spizaetus bartelsi*
Jerdon's Baza	*Aviceda jerdoni*
Kinabalu Serpent Eagle	*Spilornis kinabaluensis*
King Vulture	*Sarcoramphus papa*
Laggar Falcon	*Falco jugger*
Lanner Falcon	*Falco biarmicus*
Lappet-faced Vulture	*Aegypius tracheliotus*
Laughing Falcon	*Herpetotheres cachinnans*
Lesser Fishing Eagle	*Ichthyophaga humilis*
Lesser Kestrel	*Falco naumanni*
Lesser Spotted Eagle	*Aquila pomarina*
Lesser Yellow-headed Vulture	*Cathartes burrovianus*
Letter-winged Kite	*Elanus scriptus*
Levant Sparrowhawk	*Accipiter brevipes*
Lined Forest Falcon	*Micrastur gilvicollis*
Little Eagle	*Hieraaetus morphnoides*
Lizard Buzzard	*Kaupifalco monogrammicus*
Long-billed Vulture	*Gyps indicus indicus*
Long-crested Eagle	*Lophaetus occipitalis*
Long-legged Buzzard	*Buteo rufinus*
Long-tailed Buzzard	*Henicopernis longicauda*
Long-tailed Hawk	*Urotriorchis macrourus*

Long-winged Harrier	*Circus buffoni*
Madagascar Buzzard	*Buteo brachypterus*
Madagascar Cuckoo Hawk	*Aviceda madagascariensis*
Madagascar Fish Eagle	*Haliaeetus vociferoides*
Madagascar Harrier Hawk	*Polyboroides radiatus*
Madagascar Kestrel	*Falco newtoni*
Madagascar Marsh Harrier	*Circus maillardi*
Madagascar Serpent Eagle	*Eutriorchis astur*
Madagascar Sparrowhawk	*Accipiter madagascariensis*
Mangrove Black Hawk	*Buteogallus subtilis*
Mantled Hawk	*Leucopternis polionota*
Martial Eagle	*Polemaetus bellicosus*
Mauritius Kestrel	*Falco punctatus*
Merlin	*Falco columbarius*
Meyer's Goshawk	*Accipiter meyerianus*
Mississippi Kite	*Ictinia mississippiensis*
Moluccan Goshawk	*Accipiter henicogrammus*
Montagu's Harrier	*Circus pygargus*
Mountain Buzzard	*Buteo oreophilus*
Mountain Caracara	*Phalcoboenus megalopterus*
Mountain Hawk Eagle	*Spizaetus nipalensis*
New Britain Buzzard	*Henicopernis infuscata*
New Britain Goshawk	*Accipiter princeps*
New Britain Sparrowhawk	*Accipiter brachyurus*
New Caledonia Sparrowhawk	*Accipiter haplochrous*
New Guinea Eagle	*Harpyopsis novaeguineae*
New Zealand Falcon	*Falco novaeseelandiae*
Nicobar Sparrowhawk	*Accipiter butleri*
Northern Goshawk	*Accipiter gentilis*
Northern Harrier (New World)	*Circus cyaneus*
Northern Hobby	*Falco subbuteo*
Orange-breasted Falcon	*Falco deiroleucus*
Oriental Hobby	*Falco severus*
Ornate Hawk Eagle	*Spizaetus ornatus*
Osprey	*Pandion haliaetus*
Ovambo Sparrowhawk	*Accipiter ovampensis*
Pacific Baza	*Aviceda subcristata*
Pacific Marsh Harrier	*Circus approximans*
Pale Chanting Goshawk	*Melierax canorus*
Pallas's Fish Eagle	*Haliaeetus leucoryphus*
Pallid Harrier	*Circus macrourus*
Palmnut Vulture	*Gypohierax angolensis*
Pearl Kite	*Gampsonyx swainsonii*
Peregrine Falcon	*Falco peregrinus*
Philippine Eagle	*Pithecophaga jefferyi*

Philippine Falconet	*Microhierax erythrogenys*
Philippine Hawk Eagle	*Spizaetus philippensis*
Philippine Serpent Eagle	*Spilornis holospilus*
Pied Falconet	*Microhierax melanoleucus*
Pied Goshawk	*Accipiter albogularis*
Pied Harrier	*Circus melanoleucos*
Plain-breasted Hawk	*Accipiter ventralis*
Plumbeous Hawk	*Leucopternis plumbea*
Plumbeous Kite	*Ictinia plumbea*
Plumbeous Forest Falcon	*Micrastur plumbeus*
Prairie Falcon	*Falco mexicanus*
Puna Hawk	*Buteo poecilochrous*
Red Goshawk	*Erythrotriorchis radiatus*
Red Kite	*Milvus milvus*
Red-backed Hawk	*Buteo polyosoma*
Red-chested Goshawk	*Accipiter toussenelii*
Red-footed Falcon	*Falco vespertinus*
Red-headed Vulture	*Aegypius calvus*
Red-necked Buzzard	*Buteo auguralis*
Red-necked Falcon	*Falco chicquera*
Red-shouldered Hawk	*Buteo lineatus*
Red-tailed Hawk	*Buteo jamaicensis*
Red-thighed Sparrowhawk	*Accipiter erythropus*
Red-throated Caracara	*Daptrius americanus*
Réunion Marsh Harrier	*Circus maillardi maillardi*
Richardson's Merlin	*Falco columbarius richardsoni*
Ridgway's Hawk	*Buteo ridgwayi*
Roadside Hawk	*Buteo magnirostris*
Rough-legged Buzzard (Old World)	*Buteo lagopus*
Rough-legged Hawk (New World)	*Buteo lagopus*
Rufous-bellied Eagle	*Hieraaetus kienerii*
Rufous-breasted Sparrowhawk	*Accipiter rufiventris*
Rufous-necked Sparrowhawk	*Accipiter erythrauchen*
Rufous-tailed Hawk	*Buteo ventralis*
Rufous-thighed Hawk	*Accipiter erythronemius*
Rufous-thighed Kite	*Harpagus diodon*
Rufous-winged Buzzard	*Butastur liventer*
Rüppell's Griffon	*Gyps rueppellii*
Saker Falcon	*Falco cherrug*
Sanford's Sea Eagle	*Haliaeetus sanfordi*
Savanna Hawk	*Buteogallus meridionalis*
Scissor-tailed Kite	*Chelictinia riocourii*
Secretarybird	*Sagittarius serpentarius*
Semicollared Hawk	*Accipiter collaris*
Semiplumbeous Hawk	*Leucopternis semiplumbea*

Seychelles Kestrel	*Falco araea*
Sharp-shinned Hawk	*Accipiter striatus*
Shikra	*Accipiter badius*
Short-tailed Hawk	*Buteo brachyurus*
Short-toed Snake Eagle	*Circaetus gallicus*
Slatecolored Hawk	*Leucopternis schistacea*
Slaty-backed Forest Falcon	*Micrastur mirandollei*
Slaty-backed Goshawk	*Accipiter luteoschistaceus*
Slender-billed Kite	*Rostrhamus hamatus*
Slender-billed Vulture	*Gyps indicus tenuirostris*
Snail Kite	*Rostrhamus sociabilis*
Sooty Falcon	*Falco concolor*
Spanish Imperial Eagle	*Aquila adalberti*
Spot-tailed Sparrowhawk	*Accipiter trinotatus*
Spotted Harrier	*Circus assimilis*
Spotted Kestrel	*Falco moluccensis*
Spot-winged Falconet	*Spiziapteryx circumcinctus*
Square-tailed Kite	*Lophoictinia isura*
Steller's Sea Eagle	*Haliaeetus pelagicus*
Steppe Eagle	*Aquila nipalensis*
Steppe Buzzard	*Buteo buteo vulpinus*
Striated Caracara	*Phalcoboenus australis*
Sulawesi Dwarf Sparrowhawk	*Accipiter nanus*
Sulawesi Goshawk	*Accipiter griseiceps*
Sulawesi Hawk Eagle	*Spizaetus lanceolatus*
Sulawesi Serpent Eagle	*Spilornis rufipectus*
Swainson's Hawk	*Buteo swainsoni*
Swallow-tailed Kite	*Elanoides forficatus*
Taita Falcon	*Falco fasciinucha*
Tawny Eagle	*Aquila rapax*
Tiny Hawk	*Accipiter superciliosus*
Turkey Vulture	*Cathartes aura*
Upland Buzzard	*Buteo hemilasius*
Variable Goshawk	*Accipiter novaehollandiae*
Verreaux's Eagle	*Aquila verreauxii*
Vinous-breasted Sparrowhawk	*Accipiter rhodogaster*
Wahlberg's Eagle	*Aquila wahlbergi*
Wallace's Hawk Eagle	*Spizaetus nanus*
Wedge-tailed Eagle	*Aquila audax*
Western Honey Buzzard	*Pernis apivorus*
Western Marsh Harrier	*Circus aeruginosus*
Whistling Kite	*Haliastur sphenurus*
White Hawk	*Leucopternis albicollis*
White-bellied Sea Eagle	*Haliaeetus leucogaster*
White-breasted Hawk	*Accipiter chionogaster*

White-browed Hawk	*Leucopternis kuhli*
White-collared Kite	*Leptodon forbesi*
White-eyed Buzzard	*Butastur teesa*
White-fronted Falconet	*Microhierax latifrons*
White-headed Vulture	*Aegypius occipitalis*
White-necked Hawk	*Leucopternis lacernulata*
White-rumped Hawk	*Buteo leucorrhous*
White-tailed Hawk	*Buteo albicaudatus*
White-tailed Kite	*Elanus leucurus*
White-tailed Sea Eagle	*Haliaeetus albicilla*
White-throated Caracara	*Phalcoboenus albogularis*
White-throated Hawk	*Buteo albigula*
Yellow-headed Caracara	*Milvago chimachima*
Zone-tailed Hawk	*Buteo albonotatus*

Other Birds

Arctic Tern	*Sterna paradisaea*
Black Stork	*Ciconia nigra*
Blackcap	*Sylvia atricapilla*
Cape May Warbler	*Dendroica tigrina*
Cedar Waxwing	*Bombycilla garrulus*
Dodo	*Raphus cucullatus* (extinct)
Eurasian Starling	*Sturnus vulgaris*
Great Horned Owl	*Bubo virginianus*
Homing Pigeon	*Columba livia*
Hooded Crow	*Corvus corone*
House Sparrow	*Passer domesticus*
Indigo Bunting	*Passerina cyanea*
Magnificent Frigatebird	*Fregata magnificens*
Magpie	*Pica pica*
Northern Flicker	*Colaptes auratus*
Northern Saw-whet Owl	*Aegolius acadicus*
Passenger Pigeon	*Ectopistes migratorius* (extinct)
Raven	*Corvus corax*
Red Grouse	*Lagopus lagopus scoticus*
Red Knot	*Calidris canutus*
Ring-necked Pheasant	*Phasianus colchicus*
Rock Pigeon	*Columba livia*
Ruffed Grouse	*Bonasa umbellus*
Ruby-throated Hummingbird	*Archilochus colubris*
shorebirds	Order Charadriiformes
Stock Pigeon	*Columba oenas*
thrushes	Family Turdidae
White Stork	*Ciconia ciconia*

Wood Pigeon	*Columba palumbus*
Wood Warblers	Family Parulidae
Yellow-legged Gull	*Larus cachinnans*

Other Animals

Agouti	*Dasyprocta punctata*
American Shad	*Alosa sapidissima*
Apple Snails	*Pomacea* spp.
Bullet Ant	*Paraponera clavata*
Blue Whale	*Balaenoptera musculus*
Dart Poison Frogs	*Dendrobates* spp.
Desert Locust	*Schistocerca gregaria*
Domestic Cat	*Felis silvestris domesticus*
Eyelash Viper	*Bothrops schlegelii*
grasshoppers	Order Orthoptera
Green Turtle	*Chelonia mydas*
Horseshoe Crab	*Limulus polyphemus*
Human	*Homo sapiens*
Kinkajou	*Potos flavus*
Kokanee Salmon	*Oncorhynchus nerka*
lemmings	*Lemmus* spp.
locusts	Order Orthoptera
Monarch butterfly	*Danaus plexippus*
Opossum Shrimp	*Mysis relicta*
Reindeer	*Rangifer tarandus*
salmon	*Salmo* spp.
Snowshoe Hare	*Lepus americanus*
Three-toed Sloth	*Bradypus variegatus*
Vineyard moth	*Lobesia botrana*
voles	*Microtus* spp.

GLOSSARY

Accipiter A genus of approximately 50 largely forest-dwelling species of diurnal raptors, most of which have short, rounded wings and long tails. The genus belongs to the family Accipitridae, a group of approximately 240 species of small to large diurnal raptors that includes the kites, harriers, hawks, and eagles of the world.

Adaptive wind drift Voluntary wind drift that enables migrants to complete their journeys at lower costs than if they had attempted to compensate completely for wind drift en route. Adaptive wind drift is more likely early in migration than later on.

Adiabatic clouds Cumuliform clouds that form when moist air in mountain updrafts or thermals cools to the dew point and begins to condense into water droplets.

Albedo A measure of surface reflectivity. The fraction of electromagnetic radiation reflected by a surface expressed as a percentage.

Altitudinal migration Occurs when migrants shuttle between high-altitude breeding areas and low-altitude wintering areas.

Aspect ratio Most commonly measured as wingspan divided by wing width. Raptors with high aspect ratios have long and relatively slender wings; those with low aspect ratios have short and relatively broad wings.

Breeding range The geographic area where a species is known to reproduce.

Broad-front migration Occurs when dispersed migrants travel without deviating from their preferred directions (i.e., are largely unaffected by geographic features such as mountain ranges and coastlines, or by the company, or lack thereof, of conspecifics).

Buteo A genus of 28 species of largely open-habitat diurnal raptors with long, broad wings and short tails. Most members of this genus soar considerably while migrating.

Calendar migrant A species whose migrations are triggered and largely driven by day of year, rather than by weather, prey availability, or body condition; an obligate migrant. Calendar migrants typically flock when migrating. Compare with *weather migrant*.

Canalization Occurs when strong diversion lines or leading lines act to concentrate broad-frontal migrants along traditional regional corridors or continental flyways.

Chain migration Occurs when migratory populations that breed at high latitudes migrate approximately the same distance as those that breed at lower latitudes, thereby maintaining their latitudinal relationship between seasons. Compare with *leapfrog migration*.

Circle soaring Soaring in circles. Raptors often circle soar to remain within thermals.

Cold front A large-scale, synoptic weather event in which cold, dense air passes through an area. In eastern North America, such movements are typically from northwest to southeast and are accompanied by northwesterly winds. In autumn, some of the best hawk flights occur following the passage of a cold front.

Compass orientation Directed movement along a specific compass bearing.

Complete migrant Species or regional populations in which at least 90 percent of all individuals regularly migrate. A species or population, not an individual, characteristic. Compare with *irruptive migrant* and *partial migrant.*

Continental island An island that was once part of a continental landmass (e.g., Madagascar).

Coriolis force A deflecting force resulting from the earth's daily rotation that causes winds, oceanic currents, and migrating birds to be "deflected" to the right in the northern hemisphere and to the left in the southern hemisphere. The effect of the Coriolis force is greater poleward.

Cosmopolitan species A species that occurs worldwide or, in the case of birds, on all continents and most oceanic areas, except Antarctica.

Crosswinds Winds that intersect the preferred direction of migratory travel at perpendicular or near perpendicular angles, and that often alter the direction of travel via a process called *wind drift.*

DDT The synthetic organochlorine pesticide **d**ichloro-**d**iphenyl-**t**richloroethane. First synthesized by Othmar Zeidler in 1874 and first tested for its insecticidal abilities by Paul Müller in the late 1930s, this inexpensive, persistent (DDT has a half life of 15 years [i.e., 15 years after it is applied, half of the original DDT is still active]), broad-spectrum (i.e., it can be used to control many species of insect pests), fat-soluble pesticide came into widespread use in agriculture in Europe and North America at the end of the Second World War. DDT was banned in many countries in the early 1970s when it was found to be a widespread contaminant in human body tissue and in natural ecosystems globally. The pesticide is still used by public health organizations to control malarial mosquitoes. DDT negatively affects the reproductive success of birds, including raptors, by disrupting the female's ability to produce sufficient eggshell material for her eggs.

DDT Era The period from the mid-1940s to the early 1970s of widespread agricultural use of the organochlorine pesticide **d**ichloro-**d**iphenyl-**t**richloroethane (DDT) in North America and Western Europe. See *DDT* above.

Deflection updrafts Pockets of rising air created when horizontal winds encounter and deflect up and over mountains, ridges, escarpments, buildings, and even tall vegetation.

Delayed maturation Occurs when individuals that are physiologically capable of reproduction forgo doing so until older, presumably because reproduction at an earlier age is less likely to be successful than later on and because attempts to reproduce early would reduce lifetime fitness overall. In raptors, large species are more likely to delay reproduction than are smaller species.

Delayed return migration Occurs when juvenile raptors remain on their wintering grounds during their entire second and, in some instances, third year before returning to the breeding grounds in their third or fourth year. Delayed return migration often occurs in species with *delayed maturation.* The phenomenon is believed to save subadults the expense of migration and to eliminate competition with adults during the breeding season.

Differential migration Age- or sex-related differences in one or more aspects of migration behavior such as direction or speed of travel, distance traveled, and timing of departure.

Dihedral Flight profile of species that soar and glide with their wings held at an angle above the horizontal plane in a shallow V. Turkey Vultures have a classic dihedral flight profile.

Dispersal Purposeful movement away from population centers that acts to separate members of populations. Often undertaken by recently fledged individuals, dispersal acts to increase population ranges and to reduce population densities overall.

Diversion lines Geographic features, including mountain ranges, bodies of water, coastlines, deserts, and large unbroken forested or open areas that raptors avoid traveling across and that deflect migrants from their preferred directions of travel and serve to concentrate them.

Double endemic A migratory species that is native to and restricted to relatively small breeding and wintering areas that are geographically separated from each other.

Drag A force that resists the motion of a body through a gas or liquid. Birds encounter three types of drag when flying: *induced drag* created by trailing vortexes, *parasite drag* created by the outline of a bird's body, and *profile drag* created by the bird's flapping wings. Induced drag decreases as speed increases, parasite drag starts at zero and increases as a cube of speed, and profile drag is constant across speeds.

Dynamic soaring Soaring that takes advantage of the vertical wind gradient that occurs close to a flat surface, when friction slows the layer of air in contact with the surface. Birds engaged in dynamic soaring alternately soar upward into increasing headwinds to gain altitude and then turn and glide downwind to gain airspeed, before turning again into the headwind and using the kinetic energy gained on the downwind leg to gain altitude on the upwind leg. Albatrosses and other pelagic seabirds are believed to use dynamic soaring while soaring at sea.

Elliptical migration See *Loop migration.*

Falconidae A family of approximately 150 species of small- to medium-sized diurnal raptors that includes caracaras, forest-falcons, and falcons.

Flex gliding High-speed gliding during which a bird reduces its wingspan, wing slotting, and overall flight surface by flexing or partly folding its wings inward and toward its body. Flex gliding increases aerodynamic performance during high-speed gliding flight.

Flock A group of birds resulting from social attraction among the individuals involved.

Flocking Joining together in groups as a result of social attractions. Flocks differ from aggregations in that the latter result when birds are attracted to locations by physical or ecological factors alone.

Gliding Descending, nonflapping flight on fully or partly outstretched wings, during which lift is generated as air is deflected over the wings. Gliding often occurs alternately with soaring.

Headwinds Winds aligned against the preferred direction of travel, which hinder migrants by "holding" them back and slowing their ground speed.

Hyperphagia Excessive eating undertaken by some migrants in the weeks preceding migration as they attempt to lay down additional fat for the journey.

Intertropical Convergence Zone (ITCZ) The meteorological equator, or doldrums. Sandwiched between the northern and southern trade wind zones, and extending from approximately 5° north to 5° south, the ITCZ generally lacks horizontal winds and is characterized by intense solar heating, warm and moist rising air, and heavy rains. The zone shifts northward in boreal summer and southward in austral summer, and is largely responsible for tropical wet and dry seasons.

Intratropical migrants Wholly or mainly tropical species that migrate entirely within the tropics, usually in response to seasonal differences in prey availability driven by wet-dry seasonality. See also *rains migrants.*

Irruptive migrant Species or regional populations in which the extent of migratory movement varies annually, typically due to among-year shifts in prey abundance, and whose migrations are less regular than those of partial and complete migrants. A species or population, not an individual, characteristic. Compare with *complete migrant* and *partial migrant.*

Island hopping Migrating along archipelagos, presumably to reduce the risk of being lost at sea.

Kettle Hawkwatching term, particularly in North America, that refers to a group of raptors circling in a thermal. Raptors in such groups are said to be "kettling" (see Chapter 3).

Leading lines Geographic features, including mountain ranges and river systems, that serve to attract and channel migrants during their migrations.

Leapfrog migration Occurs when migratory populations that breed at high latitudes migrate substantially farther than and "leap over" migratory and nonmigratory populations breeding at lower latitudes, thereby reversing their latitudinal relationship between seasons. Compare with *chain migration.*

Lee waves Oscillating airstreams of various amplitudes that form on the lee, or downwind sides, of mountain ranges under specific wind and temperature conditions. Lee waves form most readily when horizontal winds are deflected over steep, high barriers. Higher barriers create lee waves with greater amplitudes, and amplitudes are sometimes enhanced when winds are deflected over a series of parallel ridges.

Linear soaring Long-distance, straight-line soaring in thermal streets, a phenomenon more typical of tropical than temperate regions.

Local migrant Species in which most populations, except those at the latitudinal periphery of the range, do not migrate.

Log transformation Statisticians frequently transform variables they analyze to meet the assumptions of their statistical tests. Log transformation involves converting variates to their common logarithms either when means are positively correlated with the variance or when frequency distributions are skewed to the right.

Long-distance migrant A species in which at least 20 percent of all individuals (sometimes entire subspecies) regularly migrate more than 1500 kilometers.

Loop migration Occurs when outbound and return migrations differ latitudinally with longitude. In the northern hemisphere, loop migration typically produces clockwise movements, with returning migrants traveling west of where they had traveled south during outbound migration. Loop or elliptical migration often results from greater wind drift during the early stages of outbound and return migration, together with greater compensatory movements later in the journey.

Meme From the ancient Greek *mime* (mimic). The cultural transmission of information via transgenerational imitation of behavioral patterns, including those associated with migration. Memes are believed to evolve by natural selection in much the same way as genes, with cultures that best improve a novice individual's chances of survival and reproduction thriving and spreading, and those that do not withering and dying. Memetic transfer is likely to be particularly important in long-distance migrants that follow complicated migration routes.

Migration Directed movements from one location to another, recurring seasonally and alternating in direction.

Migration bottleneck A site where migration corridors converge and subsequently diverge, and at which large numbers of migrants concentrate. Mountain passes, isthmuses, and narrow coastal plains and water crossings, including the Isthmus of Panama, the Strait of Gibraltar, and the Bosporus, are examples of migration bottlenecks. Major migration bottlenecks create "funnel shaped" *migration flyways.*

Migration corridor (or **migration flyway**) Pathway of travel along which raptors concentrate while migrating.

Migration-dosing speciation A series of events in which "doses" of diverted long-distance migrants arrive in areas tangential to or beyond their major migration flyways, remain there the following breeding season rather than returning to traditional breeding areas, breed, and eventually diverge, genetically, from parental stock in geographic isolation.

Migratory restlessness (or *Zugunruhe*). The increased rate of to-and-fro hopping and flitting movements and wing fluttering in caged birds during the species' periods of migration.

Narrow-front migration Migration in which dispersed migrants deviate from their initial directions, either because they are attracted to or are avoiding certain geographic features such as mountain ranges, river systems, and coastlines or because they seek out and join conspecifics en route. Narrow-front migration results in concentrated movements of migrants.

Navigation Movement toward a goal that often requires reorientation en route and includes knowledge of the distance between the present location and the goal.

New World North America, Central America, South America, and associated islands including Greenland. Also known as the Western Hemisphere. Compare with *Old World.*

Nomadic A roaming or wandering lifestyle. In birds, refers to species that move widely and episodically across their ranges in response to changing conditions.

Noonday lull A midday low point in the numbers of raptors counted at a migration watchsite. Often attributed to raptors flying at higher altitudes near midday than at other times.

Obligate migrant A species whose movements are triggered by day of year (see *calendar migrant*) and that migrates while soaring in large flocks. Also called obligate flocking or soaring migrant.

Obligate soaring migrants Species that soar in flocks while migrating to conserve energy and complete their journeys more efficiently. Most obligate soaring migrants are *long-distance complete migrants.*

Oceanic island An island formed from coral reefs or volcanic activity that has not been connected to a continental landmass (e.g., the Hawaiian Islands).

Old World Europe, Asia, Africa, Australia, and associated islands. Also known as the Eastern Hemisphere. Compare with *New World.*

Orientation Directed movement, typically along a single compass direction.

Outbound (or outward) **migration** Occurs when migrants move from breeding areas to nonbreeding areas.

Partial migrant Species or regional populations in which fewer than 90 percent of all individuals regularly migrate. A species or population, not an individual, characteristic. Compare with *complete migrant* and *irruptive migrant.*

Peninsular effect The tendency for many migrants to concentrate at the tip of a peninsula before initiating a water crossing, or to make landfall at the tip a peninsula, presumably because doing so shortens over-water travel.

Philopatry In ancient Greek, literally "love of the fatherland." In migratory species, the tendency to return to one's birthplace for breeding or to return to an initial breeding area in subsequent years. *Winter philopatry* is a tendency to return to one's initial wintering area.

Principal axis of migration A straight compass heading or rhumb line between a bird's breeding and wintering area. The principal axis of migration is the shortest route between breeding and winter areas only when those areas fall along a direct north-south axis. In all other cases a "great-circle route," in which a series of different regional principal axes of migration occurs, is the shortest path.

Rains migrants Species that migrate in response to rains and rainy seasons and whose breeding biology often is tied to these events, particularly in the tropics. (See also *intratropical migrants.*)

Return migration Occurs when migrants travel from nonbreeding areas to breeding areas.

Reverse migration Occurs in migrants that return early to high-latitude breeding grounds, when individuals reverse their direction of travel on return migration and "backtrack" when they confront unusually cold weather or storms en route. Not common in raptors.

River of raptors A large number of raptors moving in the same direction. Rivers of raptors, which are most common in the tropics, sometimes extend for miles and includes tens-of-thousands or more birds.

Sea thermals Updrafts of warm rising air that form above tropical and subtropical oceans and seas 5° to 30° north and south of the equator in regions that are dominated by easterly *trade winds*. Within these latitude belts, predominant northeasterly winds in the northern hemisphere and southeasterly winds in the southern hemisphere blow relatively cool, subtropical surface air toward the equator. As they do, the increasingly warmer surface waters of the equatorial zone heat the cooler air and in doing so produce sea thermals. Because the temperature differential between the cool winds and the warmer sea exists both day and night, sea thermals are generated 24 hours a day.

Sensu Latin, meaning "in the sense of."

Short-stopping A phenomenon, first described in migratory waterfowl, that occurs when migrants shorten the lengths of their outbound movements to take advantage of newly available wintering areas that are closer to their breeding grounds than are traditional sites.

Slope soaring Soaring in mechanical updrafts created when horizontal winds strike and are deflected over mountains and mountain ridges.

Soaring Level or ascending nonflapping flight on outstretched wings in which upward air movements are equal to or greater than the bird's rate of descent in a glide.

Stopover sites Sites along migration routes at which individuals interrupt their movements and aggregate to feed for up to a week or more, often in anticipation of migration across inhospitable habitats. Many stopover sites are traditional.

Streaming Movements by groups or "streams" of raptors in largely linear or, at least, single-direction flocks, from one updraft toward another updraft or within *thermal streets,* usually along the region's *principal axis of migration.* Streams of large numbers of raptors are sometimes called *rivers of raptors.*

Super-flocking migrants Long-distance, typically transequatorial migrants that travel in large flocks of hundreds to tens of thousands of birds, particularly in the tropics and subtropics.

Tailwinds Winds aligned with the preferred direction of travel. Tailwinds help migrants by increasing their ground speed and "carrying" them forward in the preferred direction of travel.

Thermal A pocket of warm, rising air created by the differential heating of the earth's surface.

Thermal corridors (or pathways) Migration routes that provide predictable thermals for soaring migrants.

Thermal soaring Soaring flight in thermals. Birds often soar in circles in thermals to remain within them.

Thermal streets Linear arrays of thermals that often are aligned with prevailing winds. When thermal streets are oriented along the region's *principal axis of migration* they enable migrants to soar linearly within them in much the same way as migrants *slope soar.*

Thermal strength The speed at which air rises in a thermal.

Trade winds Predominant northeasterly and southeasterly subtropical and tropical oceanic winds that encircle the globe 5° to 30° north and south of the equator. Thermal convection produced by these winds creates *sea thermals.*

Updraft corridors (or pathways) Migration routes that provide predictable updrafts for soaring migrants.

Vagrants Individuals or groups of raptors that appear in an area where they do not breed, overwinter, or regularly migrate through.

Weather migrant A species whose migrations are triggered and largely driven by weather conditions and prey availability, rather than by day of year; a facultative migrant. Weather migrants usually do not form large flocks on migration.

Wind drift Occurs when migrants encountering crosswinds are pushed off their intended course even while maintaining the proper heading.

Wing loading A bird's mass divided by the combined area of its outstretched wings. Species with "low wing loading" have relatively large wings for their body mass, whereas those with "high wing loading" have relatively small wings.

Wing slotting Occurs when the distal ends of the outermost primaries of a bird's wing are separated horizontally and vertically in flight, thereby creating separate aerodynamic surfaces. Wing slotting is enhanced in some species by the presence of emarginate, or notched, outermost primaries. Wing theory suggests that wing slotting increases the "aerodynamic wingspan" of a bird and reduces wing-tip drag at low speeds.

Wintering range The geographic area where a species is known to "overwinter" during the nonbreeding season.

Zugunruhe (or *migratory restlessness*) German. The increased rate of to-and-fro hopping and flitting movements and wing fluttering in caged birds during the species' periods of migration.

REFERENCES

Able, K. P. 1985. Radar methods of the study of hawk migration. In *Proceedings of Hawk Migration Conference IV,* ed. M. Harwood. 347–354. Lynchburg, VA: Hawk Migration Association of North America.

——. 1995. Orientation and navigation: A perspective on fifty years of research. *Condor* 97:592–604.

Agostini, N., and D. Logozzo. 1995. Autumn migration of Honey Buzzards in southern Italy. *J. Raptor Res.* 29:275–277.

Agostini, N., L. Baghino, C. Coleiro, F. Corbi, and G. Premuda. 2002a. Circuitous autumn migration in the Short-toed Eagle (*Circaetus gallicus*). *J. Raptor Res.* 36:111–114.

Agostini, N., C. Coleiro, F. Corbi, G. Di Lieto, F. Pinos, and M. Panuccio. 2002b. Water-crossing tendency of juvenile Honey Buzzards during migration. *Avocetta* 26:41–43.

Alerstam, T. 1990. *Bird migration.* Cambridge: Cambridge University Press.

Alexander, R. McN. 2003. *Principles of animal locomotion.* Princeton: Princeton University Press.

Ali, S., and S. D. Ripley. 1978. *Handbook of the birds of India and Pakistan,* 2nd ed. Vol. 1. Delhi: Oxford University Press.

Allen, P. E., L. J. Goodrich, and K. L. Bildstein. 1996. Within- and among-year effects of cold fronts on migrating raptors at Hawk Mountain, Pennsylvania, 1934–1991. *Auk* 113:329–338.

Allen, R. P., and R. T. Peterson. 1936. The hawk migrations at Cape May Point, New Jersey. *Auk* 53:393–404.

Alvarez-Cordero, E. 1996. Biology and conservation of the Harpy Eagle in Venezuela and Panama. Ph.D. diss., University of Florida.

Amadon, D. 1948. Continental drift and bird migration. *Science* 108:705–707.

Andrle, R. F. 1968. Raptors and other North American migrants in Mexico. *Condor* 70:393–395.

Arroyo, B. E., J. T. Garcia, and V. Bretagnolle. 2002. Conservation of Montagu's Harrier *Circus pygargus* in agricultural areas. *Anim. Conserv.* 5:283–290.

Asociación ANAI. 2003. *Rapaces migratorias: guía de observación.* San José, Costa Rica: Asoc. ANAI.

Auburn, J. 1994. Climatic influences on the movements of Palaearctic raptors. *Gabar* 9:8–12.

Audubon, J. J. 1840. *The birds of America,* vol. 1. Philadephia: J. B. Chevalier.

Augstein, E. 1980. The atmospheric boundary layer over tropical oceans. In *Meteorology over tropical oceans,* ed. D. B. Shaw. 73–104. Bracknell, UK: Royal Meteorological Society.

Bagla, P. 2005. India to outlaw animal drug. *Science* 307:1851.

Bahat, O. 1985. Hunting termites by Black Kites while on migration in the Arava region. *Torgos* 10:89–92. (In Hebrew.)

Baker, R. R. 1978. *The evolutionary ecology of animal migration.* New York: Holmes & Meier.

Barrios, L., and A. Rodríguez. 2004. Behavioural and environmental correlates of soaring-bird mortality at on-shore wind turbines. *J. Appl. Ecol.* 41:72–81.

Baughman, J. L. 1947. A very early notice of hawk migration. *Auk* 64:304.

Beaman, M., and C. Galea. 1974. The visible migration of raptors over the Maltese Islands. *Ibis* 116:420–431.

Bean, M. J. 1983. *The evolution of national wildlife law.* New York: Praeger.

Beans, B. E. 1996. *Eagle's plume.* Lincoln, NE: University of Nebraska Press.

Bechard, M. J., and Cesar Marquez-Reyes. 2003. Mortality of wintering Ospreys and other birds at aquaculture facilities in Colombia. *J. Raptor Res.* 37:292–298.

Bednarz, J. C., and P. Kerlinger. 1989. Monitoring hawk populations by counting migrants. In *Proceedings of the Northeast Raptor Management Symposium and Workshop.* Washington, DC: National Wildlife Federation.

Bednarz, J. C., D. Klem Jr., L. J. Goodrich, and S. E. Senner. 1990. Migration counts of raptors at Hawk Mountain, Pennsylvania, as indicators of population trends, 1934–1986. *Auk* 107:96–109.

Behrensmeyer, A. K., J. D. Damuth, W. A. DiMichele, R. Potts, H.D. Sues, and S. L. Wing, eds. 1992. *Terrestrial ecosystems through time.* Chicago: University of Chicago Press.

Bell, C. P. 2000. Process in the evolution of bird migration and pattern in avian ecogeography. *J. Avian Biol.* 31:258–265.

Bent, A. C. 1938. *Life histories of North American birds of prey,* pt. 2. New York: Dover.

Berger, D. D., and H. C. Mueller. 1959. The bal-chatri: A trap for the birds of prey. *Bird-Banding* 30:18–26.

Bernis, F. 1980. *La migración de las aves en el estrecho de Gibraltar.* vol. 1, *Aves planeadors.* Madrid: Univ. Computense de Madrid.

Berthold, P. 1999. A comprehensive theory of the evolution, control and adaptability of avian migration. *Ostrich* 70:1–11.

——. 2001. *Bird migration: A general study.* 2nd ed. Oxford: Oxford University Press.

Berthold, P., J. Griesinger, E. Nowak, and U. Querner. 1991. Satelliten-Telemetrie eines Gänsegeiers (*Gyps fulvus*) in Spanien. *J. für Ornithol.* 133:327–329.

Biber, J.-P., and T. Salathé. 1991. Threats to migratory birds. In *Conserving migratory birds,* ed. T. Salathé. 17–36. Cambridge: International Council for Bird Preservation.

Bierregaard, R. O., Jr. 1998. Conservation status of birds of prey in the South American tropics. *J. Raptor Res.* 32:19–27.

Bijlsma, R. G. 1987. Bottleneck areas for migratory birds in the Mediterranean region: an assessment of the problems and recommendations for action. Cambridge: International Council for Bird Preservation.

Bildstein, K. L. 1987. Behavioral ecology of Red-tailed Hawks (*Buteo jamaicensis*), Rough-legged Hawks (*Buteo lagopus*), Northern Harriers (*Circus cyaneus*), and American Kestrels (*Falco sparverius*) in south central Ohio. *Ohio Biol. Surv.* 18:1–53.

——. 1988. Northern Harrier *circus cyaneus.* In *Handbook of North American birds,* vol. 4, ed. R. S. Palmer. 251–303. New Haven: Yale University Press.

——. 1998. Long-term counts of migrating raptors: A role for volunteers in wildlife research. *J. Wildl. Manage.* 62:535–445.

——. 1999. Racing with the Sun: The forced migration of the Broad-winged Hawk. In *Gatherings of angels: Migrating birds and their ecology,* ed. K. P. Able. 79–102. Ithaca: Cornell University Press.

———. 2001. Raptors as vermin: a history of human attitudes towards Pennsylvania's birds of prey. *Endangered Species Update* 18:124–128.

———. 2004. Raptor migration in the Neotropics: patterns, processes, and evolutionary consequences. *Ornitol. Neotrop.* 15 (Suppl.):83–99.

Bildstein, K. L., and R. A. Compton. 2000. Mountaintop science: The history of conservation ornithology at Hawk Mountain Sanctuary. In *Contributions to the History of North American Ornithology,* ed. W. E. Davis, Jr. and J. A. Jackson. 153–181. Cambridge, MA: Nuttall Ornithol. Cl.

Bildstein, K. L., and D. Klem, Jr., eds. 2001. Hawkwatching in the Americas. North Wales, PA: Hawk Migration Association of North America.

Bildstein, K. L., and K. Meyer. 2000. Sharp-shinned Hawk. In *The birds of North America,* no. 482, ed. A. Poole and F. Gill. Philadelphia: Birds of North America.

Bildstein, K. L., and M. Saborío. 2000. Spring migration counts of raptors and New World Vultures in Costa Rica. *Ornitol. Neotrop.* 11:197–205.

Bildstein, K. L., and J. Zalles. 2001. Raptor migration along the Mesoamerican Land Corridor. In *Hawkwatching in the Americas,* ed. K. L. Bildstein and D. Klem, Jr. 119–141. North Wales, PA: Hawk Migration Association of North America.

Bildstein, K. L., and J. I. Zalles. 2005. Old World versus New World long-distance migration in accipiters, buteos, and falcons: The interplay of migration ability and global biogeography. In *Birds of two worlds: The ecology and evolution of migratory birds,* ed. R. Greenberg, and P. Marra. 154–167. Baltimore: Johns Hopkins University Press.

Bildstein, K. L., J. Brett, L. Goodrich, and C. Viverette. 1993. Shooting galleries: migrating raptors in jeopardy. *Am. Birds* 47:38–43.

Bildstein, K. L., W. S. Clark, D. L. Evans, M. Field, and L. Soucy. 1984. Sex and age differences in fall migration of Northern Harriers. *J. Field Ornithol.* 55:143–150.

Bildstein, K. L., W. Schelsky, J. Zalles, and S. Ellis. 1998. Conservation status of tropical raptors. *J. Raptor Res.* 32:3–18.

BirdLife International. 2000. Threatened birds of Asia: The BirdLife International red data book. Cambridge, UK: BirdLife International.

———. 2004. State of the world's birds 2004: Indicators for our changing world. Cambridge, UK: BirdLife International.

Blem, C. R. 1980. The energetics of migration. In *Animal migration, orientation, and navigation,* ed. S. A. Gauthreaux, Jr. 175–224. New York: Academic Press.

Bögel, R. 1990. Measuring flight altitudes of Griffon Vultures by radio telemetry. *Internatl. Ornithol. Congr.* 20:489–490.

Brazil, M. A., and S. Hanawa. 1991. The status and distribution of diurnal raptors in Japan. *Birds of Prey Bull.* 4:175–238.

Brett, J. 1991. The mountain and the migration. Ithaca: Cornell University Press.

———. 1995. Migration of lesser kestrels in the Serengeti National Park, Tanzania. *J. Afr. Raptor Biol.* 10:63.

Brisbin I. L. 1991. Avian radioecology. *Curr. Ornithol.* 8:69–140.

Britten, M. W., P. L. Kennedy, and S. Ambrose. 1999. Performance and accuracy of small satellite transmitters. *J. Wildl. Manage.* 63:1349–1358.

Brodeur, S., R. Décarie, D.M. Bird, and M. Fuller. 1996. Complete migration cycle of Golden Eagles breeding in Northern Quebec. *Condor* 98:293–299.

Broekhuysen, G. R., and W. R. Siegfried. 1970. Age and molt in the Steppe Buzzard in southern Africa. *Ostrich Suppl.* 8:223–237.

Broley, C. L. 1947. Migration and nesting of Florida Bald Eagles. *Wilson Bull.* 59:3–20.

——. 1950. Florida Bald Eagle threat growing. *Audubon Mag.* 52:139,141.

——. 1958. The plight of the American Bald Eagle. *Audubon Mag.* 60:162–163.

Broughton, J. M. 2004. Prehistoric human impacts on California birds: Evidence from the Emeryville Shellmound avifauna. *Ornithol. Monogr.* 56.

Broun, M. 1935. The hawk migration during the fall of 1934, along the Kittatinny Ridge in Pennsylvania. *Auk* 52:233–248.

——. 1939. Fall migration of hawks at Hawk Mountain, Pennsylvania, 1934–1938. *Auk* 56:429–441.

——. 1949. *Hawks aloft: The story of Hawk Mountain.* Cornwall, NY: Cornwall Press.

——. 1952. Curator's report. *Hawk Mountain Assoc. News Letter to Members* 21:3–7.

Brown, L. 1970. *African birds of prey.* London: Collins.

——. 1976. *British birds of prey.* London: Collins.

Brown, L., and D. Amadon. 1968. *Eagles, hawks and falcons of the World.* New York: McGraw-Hill.

Brown, L. H., E. K. Urban, and K. Newman. 1982. *The birds of Africa,* vol. 1. London: Academic Press.

Bub, H. 1978. *Bird trapping and bird banding.* Ithaca: Cornell University Press.

Bucher, E. H. 1992. The causes of extinction of the Passenger Pigeon. *Curr. Ornithol.* 9:1–36.

Buehler, D. A. 2000. Bald Eagle. In *The birds of North America,* no. 506, ed. A. Poole and F. Gill. Philadelphia: Birds of North America.

Buehler, D. A., T. J. Mersmann, J. D. Fraser, and J. K. D. Seegar. 1991. Differences in distribution of breeding, nonbreeding, and migrant Bald Eagles on the northern Chesapeake Bay. *Condor* 93:399–408.

Bullock, J. M., R. E. Kenward, and R. S. Hails, eds. 2002. *Dispersal ecology.* Malden, MA: Blackwell.

Burns, F. L. 1911. A monograph of the Broad-winged Hawk (*Buteo platypterus*). *Wilson Bull.* 23:143–320.

Busche, G., H. Bruns, and P. Todt. 1998. Zunahme rastender Wanderfalken (*Falco peregrinus*) im Western Schelswig-Holsteins ab 1980. *Vogelwarte* 39:183–189.

Bussjaeger, L. J., C. C. Carpenter, H. L. Cleveland, and D. L. Marcellini. 1967. Turkey Vulture migration in Veracruz, Mexico. *Condor* 69:425–426.

Cade, T. 1960. Ecology of the Peregrine and Gyrfalcon populations in Alaska. *U. Calif. Publ. Zool.* 63:151–290.

Cade, T. J. 1982. *The falcons of the world.* Ithaca: Cornell University Press.

Cade, T. J., and W. Burnham. 2003. *Return of the Peregrine.* Boise, ID: The Peregrine Fund.

Cade, T. J., and L. Greenwald. 1966. Nasal salt secretion in Falconiform birds. *Condor* 68:338–350.

Cade, T. J., J. H. Enderson, Carl G. Thelander, and C. M. White. 1988. *Peregrine Falcon populations; their management and recovery.* Boise, ID: The Peregrine Fund.

Campbell, B., and E. Lack. 1985. *A dictionary of birds.* Vermillion, SD: Buteo Books.

Candler, G. L., and P. L. Kennedy. 1995. Flight strategies of migrating Osprey: Fasting vs. foraging. *J. Raptor Res.* 29:85–92.

Carricker, M. A. 1910. An annotated list of the birds of Costa Rica, including Cocos Island. *Ann. Carnegie Mus. Nat. Hist.* 6:314–915.

Carson, R. 1962. *Silent spring.* Boston: Houghton Mifflin.

Carter, I., A. V. Cross, A. Douse, K. Duffy, B. Etheridge, P. V. Grice, P. Newbery, D. C. Orr-

Ewing, O'Toole, D. Simpson, and N. Snell. 2003. Re-introduction and conservation of the Red kite (*Milvus milvus*) in Britain: Current threats and prospects for future range expansion. In *Birds of prey in a changing environment,* ed. D. B. A. Thompson, S. M. Redpath, A. H. Fielding, M. Marquiss, and C. A. Galbraith. 407–416. Edinburgh: Stationary Office.

Catesby, M. 1731–1743. *The natural history of Carolina, Florida, and the Bahama Islands.* 2 vols. London.

Chapman, F. M. 1916. *The travels of birds.* New York: Appleton.

Christensen, S., O. Lou, M. Müller, and H. Wohlmuth. 1981. The spring migration of raptors in southern Israel and Sinai. *Sandgrouse* 3:1–42.

Clark, J. A., D. E. Balmer, J. R. Blackburn, L. J. Milne, R. A. Robinson, C. V. Wernham, S. Y. Adams, and B. M. Griffin. 2002. Bird ringing in Britain and Ireland in 2000. *Ringing & Migr.* 21:25–61.

Clark, R. J. 1975. A field study of the Short-eared Owl *Asio flammeus* (Pontoppidan) in North America. *Wildl. Monogr.* 47:1–67.

Clark, W. S. 1981. A modified dho-gaza trap for use at a raptor banding station. *J. Wildl. Manage.* 45:1043–1044.

———. 1985a. The migrating Sharp-shinned Hawk at Cape May Point: Banding and recovery results. In *Proceedings of Hawk Migration Conference IV,* ed. M. Harwood. 137–148. Lynchburg, VA: Hawk Migration Association of North America.

———. 1985b. Migration of the Merlin along the coast of New Jersey. *J. Raptor Res.* 19:85–93.

Clark, W. S., and E. Gorney. 1987. Oil contamination of raptors migrating along the Red *Sea. Environ. Pollut.* 46:307–313.

Clarke, W. E. 1912. *Studies in bird migration.* Edinburgh: Gurney and Jackson.

Cochran, W. W. 1972. A few days of fall migration of a Sharp-shinned Hawk. *Hawk Chalk* 11:39–44.

———. 1975. Following a migrating peregrine from Wisconsin to Mexico. *Hawk Chalk* 14:28–37.

———. 1985. Ocean migration of Peregrine Falcons: Is the adult male pelagic? In *Proceedings of Hawk Migration Conference IV,* ed. M. Harwood. 223–238. Lynchburg, VA: Hawk Migration Association of North America.

Collins, H. H., Jr. 1933. Hawk slaughter at Drehersville. *Ann. Rep. Hawk and Owl Soc. Bull.* 3:10–18.

Connor, J. 1991. *Season at the point: The birds and birders of Cape May.* New York: Atlantic Monthly Press.

Cooper, B. A., and R. J. Ritchie. 1995. The altitude of bird migration in east-central Alaska: A radar and visual study. *J. Field Ornithol.* 66:590–608.

Corso, A., and C. Cardelli. 2004. The migration of Pallid Harrier across the central Mediterranean: with particular reference to the Strait of Messina. *Brit. Birds* 97:238–246.

Cox, G. W. 1968. The role of competition in the evolution of migration. *Evol.* 22:180–192.

———. 1985. The evolution of avian migration systems between temperate and tropical regions of the New World. *Am. Nat.* 126:451–474.

Craighead, J. J., and F. C. Craighead. 1956. *Hawks, owls and wildlife.* Harrisburg, PA: Stackpole.

Cramp, S., and K. E. L. Simmons. 1979. Handbook of the birds of Europe, the Middle East, and North Africa: The birds of the Western Palearctic. Vol. 2, Hawks to buzzards. Oxford: Oxford University Press.

Crouse, D. G., and A. R. Keith. 1999. A remarkable Osprey flight and first record of Swallow-tailed Kite for Hispaniola. *El Pitirre* 12:91.

Cunningham, A. A., V. Prakash, D. Pain, G. R. Ghalsasi, G. A. H. Wells, G. N. Kolte, P. Nighot, M. S. Goudar, S. Kshirsagar, and A. Rahmani. 2003. Indian vultures: Victims of an infectious disease epidemic? *Anim. Conserv.* 6:198–197.

Darrow, H. N. 1983. Late fall movements of Turkey Vultures and hawks in the Florida Keys. *Fla. Field Nat.* 11:35–39.

Dawkins, R. 1976. *The selfish gene.* Oxford: Oxford University Press.

de Lucas, M., G. F. E. Janss, and M. Ferrer. 2004. The effect of wind farms on birds in a migration point: the Strait of Gibraltar. *Biodivers. Conserv.* 13:395–407.

de Roder, F. E. 1989. The migration of raptors south of Annapurna, Nepal, autumn 1985. *Forktail* 4:9–17.

DeCandido, R., D. Allen, and K. L. Bildstein. 2001. The migration of Steppe Eagles (*Aquila nipalensis*) and other raptors in central Nepal, autumn 1999. *J. Raptor Res.* 35:35–39.

Dekker, D. 1980. Hunting success rates, foraging habits, and prey selection of Peregrine Falcons migrating through Central Alberta. *Can. Field-Nat.* 94:371–382.

del Hoyo, J. A., A. Elliot, and J. Sargatal. 1994. *Handbook of the birds of the world.* Vol. 2. Barcelona: Lynx Ed.

DeLong, J. P., and S. W. Hoffman. 2004. Fat stores of migrant Sharp-shinned and Cooper's Hawks in New Mexico. *J. Raptor Res.* 38:163–168.

Deng, W.H., G. Wei, and Z. Guang-Mei. 2003. Nest and roost habitat characteristics of the Grey-faced Buzzard in northeastern China. *J. Raptor Res.* 37:228–235.

Devisse, J.-S. 2000. Organbidexka Col Libre et al chasse aux migrateurs au Pays Basque en guise de conclusión. In *Oiseaux migrateurs chassés en mauvais état de conservation et "points chauds" européens.* 109–112. Bayonne: Organbidexka Col Libre.

Dixon, C. 1895. *The migration of birds.* London: Chapman and Hall.

Dobzhansky, T. 1973. Nothing in biology makes sense except in light of evolution. *Am. Biol. Teacher* 35:125–129.

Dolman, P. M., and W. J. Sutherland. 1994. The response of bird populations to habitat loss. *Ibis* 137:S38–46.

Donázar, J. A., J. J. Negro, and F. Hiraldo. 1993. Foraging habitat selection, land-use changes and population decline in the lesser kestrel *Falco naumanni*. *J. Appl. Ecol.* 30:515–522.

Dorst, J. 1962. *The migrations of birds.* Boston: Houghton Mifflin.

Drost, R. 1938. Über den Einfluss von Verfrachtungen zur Herbstzugzeit auf den Sperber Accipiter nisus (L.). Zugleich ein Beitrag zur Frage nach der Orientierung der Vögel auf dem Zuge ins Winterquartier. *Proc. Int. Ornithol. Congr* 9:503–521.

Duncan, B. W. 1982. Sharp-shinned Hawks banded at Hawk Cliff, Ontario, 1971–1980. *Ontario Bird Band.* 15:24–38.

Duncan, C. D. 1996. Changes in the winter abundance of Sharp-shinned Hawks, *Accipiter striatus,* in New England. *J. Field Ornithol.* 67:254–262.

Dunn, E. H., and D. J. T. Hussell. 1995. Using migration counts to monitor landbird populations: review and evaluation of status. *Curr. Ornithol.* 12:43–88.

Dunn, E. H., and D. L. Tessaglia. 1994. Predation of birds at feeders in winter. *J. Field Ornithol.* 65:8–16.

Dupuy, A. 1969. *Catalogue ornithologique du Sahara Algerien. Osieau* 39:140–160.

Eastham, C. 1998. Satellite tagging of Sakers in the Russian Altai. *Falco* 12:10–12.

Eastwood, E. 1967. *Radar ornithology.* London: Methuen.

Eckmann, R., and F. Imbrock. 1996. Distribution and diel vertical migration of Eurasian perch (*Perca fluviatilis* L.) during winter. *Ann. Zool. Fennici* 33:679–686.

Edge, R. 1941. *Third annual report 1940–41.* Publ. No. 4. Drehersville, PA: Hawk Mountain Sanctuary.

Ellis, D. H., S. L. Moon, and J. W. Robinson. 2001. Annual movements of a Steppe Eagle (*Aquila nipalensis*) summering in Mongolia and wintering in Tibet. *J. Bombay Nat. Hist. Soc.* 98:335–340.

Elton, C. 1927. *Animal ecology.* London: Sidgwick & Jackson.

Emergency Conservation Committee. 1934. *Report for the calendar year 1933.* New York: Emergency Conserv. Comm.

Emlen, S. T. 1967. Migratory orientation in the Indigo Bunting, *Passerina cyanea. Auk* 84:309–342, 463–489.

Enderson, J. H. 1964. A study of the Prairie Falcon in the central Rocky Mountain region. *Auk* 81:332–352.

England, A. S., M. J. Bechard, and C. S. Houston. 1997. Swainson's Hawk (*Buteo swainsoni*). In *The birds of North America,* no. 265, ed. A. Poole and F. Gills. Philadelphia: Birds of North America.

Evans, D. L., and R. N. Rosenfield. 1985. Migration and mortality of Sharp-shinned Hawks ringed at Duluth, Minnesota, U.S.A. In *Conservation studies on raptors,* ed. I. Newton and R. D. Chancellor. Cambridge: Internatl. Coun. Bird Preserv.

Evans, P. R., and G. W. Lathbury. 1973. Raptor migration across the Straits of Gibraltar. *Ibis* 115:572–585.

Feduccia, A. 1985. *Catesby's birds of colonial America.* Chapel Hill: University of North Carolina Press.

———. 1996. *The origin and evolution of birds.* New Haven: Yale University Press.

Fenech, N. 1992. *Fatal flight: The Maltese obsession with killing birds.* London: Quiller Press.

Ferguson, A. L., and H. L. Ferguson. 1922. The fall migration of hawks as observed at Fishers Island, N. Y. *Auk* 39:488–496.

Ferguson-Lees, J., and D. A. Christie. 2001. *Raptors of the world.* Boston: Houghton Mifflin.

Ferrer, M. 2001. *The Spanish Imperial Eagle.* Barcelona: Lynx Edicions.

Ferrer, M., M. de la Riva, and J. Castroviejo. 1991. Electrocution of raptors on power lines in southwestern Spain. *J. Field Ornithol.* 62:181–190.

Fingerhood, E. D. 2001. Possible origin of the term 'kettle.' *Cassinia* 68:61–64.

Finlayson, C. 1992. *Birds of the Strait of Gibraltar.* London: T & AD Poyser.

Fischer, D. L. 1985. Piracy behavior of wintering Bald Eagles. *Condor* 87:246–251.

Fisher, A. K. 1893. Hawks and owls of the United States in relation to agriculture. Washington, DC: USDA Div. Ornithol. Mammal.

Fiuczynski, D. 1978. Zur populationsökologie des Baumfalken (Falcon subbuteo L., 1758). *Zool. Jb. Syst. Bd.* 105:193–257.

Flannery, T., and P. Schouten. 2001. *A gap in nature: Discovering the world's extinct animals.* New York: Atlantic Monthly Press.

Forsman, D. 1999. The raptors of Europe and the Middle East. London: Poyser.

Franklin, B. 1987. *Writings.* New York: The Library of America.

Franson, J. C., L. Siloe, and J. J. Thomas. 1995. Causes of eagle deaths. In *Our living resources: A report to the nation on the distribution, abundance, and health of U.S. plants, animals and ecosystems,* ed. E. T. LaRoe, G. S. Farris, C. E. Puckett, and P. D. Doran. Washington, DC: National Biological Survey.

Frey, E. S. 1940. Hawk notes from Sterrett's Gap, Pennsylvania. *Auk* 57:247–250.

Friedrich II, Emperor of Germany, 1194–1250. 1943. The art of falconry, being De arte venandi cum avibus of Frederick II of Hohenstaufen. Stanford: Stanford University Press.

Fuertes, L. A. 1920. American birds of prey—A review of their value. *Natl. Geogr.* 38:460–467.

Fuller, M. R., W. S. Seegar, and P. W. Howey. 1995. The use of satellite systems for the study of bird migration. *Israel J. Zool.* 41:243–252.

Fuller, M. R., W. S. Seegar, and L. S. Schueck. 1998. Routes and travel rates of migrating Peregrine Falcons *Falco peregrinus* and Swainson's Hawks *Buteo swainsoni* in the Western Hemisphere. *J. Avian Biol.* 29:433–440.

Gabrielson, I. N., R. P. Allen, I. McTaggart Cowan, P. A. Dumont, R. H. Pough, G. A. Swanson. 1950. Report of the A.O.U. Committee on bird protection, 1949. *Auk* 67:316–324.

Galushin, V. M. 1971. A huge urban population of birds of prey in Delhi, India. *Ibis* 113:522.

Garrison, B. A., and P. H. Bloom. 1993. Natal origins and winter site fidelity of Rough-legged Hawks wintering in California. *J. Raptor Res.* 27:116–118.

Gauthreaux, S. A., Jr. 1982. The ecology and evolution of avian migration systems. In *Avian biology*, vol. 6, ed. D. S. Farner, J. R. King, and K. C. Parkes. 93–168. New York: Academic Press.

Gauthreaux, S. A., C. G. Belser, and A. Farnsworth. 2001. How to use Doppler weather surveillance radar to study hawk migration. In *Hawkwatching in the Americas*, ed. K. L. Bildstein and D. Klem, Jr. 149–160. North Wales, PA: Hawk Migration Association of North America.

Geller, G. A., and S. A. Temple. 1983. Seasonal trends in body condition of juvenile Red-tailed hawks during autumn migration. *Wilson Bull.* 95:492–495.

Gensbol, B. 1984. *Collins guide to the birds of prey of Britain and Europe, North Africa, and The Middle East.* London: Collins.

Geyr von Schweppenburg, H. F. 1963. Zut Terminologie und Theorie der Leitlinie. *J. für Ornithol.* 104:191–204.

Gill, F. B. 1990. *Ornithology.* New York: Freeman.

Giordano, A., D. Ricciardi, S. Celeste, G. Candiano, and A. Irrera. 1998. Anti-poaching on the Straits of Messina: Results after 15 years of activities. *In Holarctic birds of prey*, ed. R. D. Chancellor, B.-U. Meyburg, and J. J. Ferrero. 623–630. Berlin: World Working Group on Birds of Prey and Owls.

Giron Pendleton, B. A., B. A. Millsap, K. W. Cline, and D. M. Bird, eds. 1987. Raptor management techniques manual. Washington, DC: National Wildlife Federation.

Goldman, H. 1970. Wings over Brattleboro. *Yankee* 3(10):100–105.

Goldstein, M. I., P. Bloom, J. I. Sarasola, and T. E. Lacher. 1999. Post-migration weight gain of Swainson's Hawks in Argentina. *Wilson Bull.* 111:428–432.

Goldstein, M. I., T. E. Lacher, Jr., B. Woodbridge, M. J. Bechard, S. B. Canavelli, M. E. Zaccagnini, G. P. Cobb, E. J. Scollon, R. Tribolet, and M. J. Hooper. 1999a. Monocrotophos-induced mass mortality of Swainson's Hawks in Argentina, 1995–96. *Ecotoxicol.* 8:201–214.

Goldstein, M. I., T. E. Lacher, M. E. Zaccagnini, M. L. Parker, and M. J. Hooper. 1999b. Monitoring and assessment of Swainson's Hawks in Argentina following restrictions on monocrotophos use, 1996–97. *Ecotoxicol.* 8:215–224.

Gorney, E., and Y. Yom-Tov. 1994. Fat, hydration condition, and moult of Steppe Buzzards *Buteo buteo vulpinus* on spring migration. *Ibis* 136:185–192.

Green, R. E., S. J. Cornell, J. P. W. Scharlemann, and A. Balmford. 2005. Farming and the fate of the world. *Science* 307:550–555.

Green, R. E., I. Newton, S. Schultz, A. A. Cunningham, M. Gilbert, D. J. Pain, and V. Prakash. 2004. Diclofenac poisoning as a cause of vulture population declines across the Indian subcontinent. *J. Appl. Ecol.* 41:793–800.

Greenway, J. C., Jr. 1958. Extinct and vanishing birds of the world. Special publication No. 13. New York: American Committee for International Wild Life Protection.

Griesinger, J., P. Berthold, U. Querner, C. Pedrocchi, and E. Nowak. 1992. Satellite tracking of a young Griffon Vulture in the north of Spain. In *Wildlife telemetry,* ed. I. G. Pride and S. M. Swift. 199–200. New York: Ellis Horwood.

Griffin, D. R., and R. J. Houk. 1948. Experiments on bird navigation. *Science* 107:347–349.

Grimmet, R. F., and T. A. Jones. 1989. *Important bird areas in Europe.* Cambridge: International Council for Bird Protection.

Grubb, T. G., W. W. Bowerman, and P. H. Howey. 1994. Tracking local and seasonal movements of wintering Bald Eagles *Haliaeetus leucocephalus,* from Arizona and Michigan with satellite telemetry. In *Raptor conservation today,* ed. B.-U. Meyburg and R. D. Chancellor. 347–358. Saskatchewan: Pica Press.

Hagar, J. A. 1988. Broad-winged Hawk migration. In *Handbook of North American birds,* vol. 5, ed. R. S. Palmer. 3–33. New Haven: Yale University Press.

Haines, A. M., M. J. McGrady, M. S. Martell, B. J. Dayton, M. B. Henke, and W. S. Seegar. 2003. Migration routes and wintering locations of Broad-winged Hawks tracked by satellite telemetry. *Wilson Bull.* 115:166–169.

Hake, M., N. Kjellén, and T. Alerstam. 2001. Satellite tracking of Swedish Ospreys *Pandion haliaetus*: Autumn migration routes and orientation. *J. Avian Biol.* 32:47–56.

Hake, M., N. Kjellén, and T. Alerstam. 2003. Age-dependent migration strategy in Honey Buzzards *Pernis apivorus* tracked by satellite. *Oikos* 103:385–396.

Hamerstrom, F. 1969. A harrier population study. In *Peregrine Falcon populations: Their biology and decline,* ed. J. J. Hickey. Madison: University of Wisconsin Press.

Hankin, E. H. 1913. *Animal flight: A record of observation.* London: Illiffe.

Hannah, L., D. Lohse, C. Hutchinson, J. L. Carr, and A. Lankerani. 1994. A preliminary inventory of human disturbance of world ecosystems. *Ambio* 23:246–250.

Harden, S. M. 1993. Fat content of American Kestrels (*Falco sparverius*) and Sharp-shinned Hawks (*Accipiter striatus*) estimated by total body electrical conductivity. Master's thesis, Utah State University.

Harmata, A. R. 1984. Bald Eagles in the San Luis Valley, Colorado: Their winter ecology and spring migration. Ph.D. diss., Montana State University.

———. 2002. Vernal migration of Bald eagles from a southern Colorado wintering area. *J. Raptor Res.* 36:256–264.

Harness, R. E. In press. Impacts and mitigation techniques. In *Raptor management and techniques manual,* ed. D. M. Bird and K. L. Bildstein. 2nd ed. Hastings, MN: Raptor Research Foundation.

Harwood, M. 1973. *The view from Hawk Mountain.* New York: Scribner's.

———, ed. 1975. *Proceedings of the Hawk Migration Conference 1974.* Washington Depot, CT: Hawk Migration Association of North America.

———, ed. 1985. *Proceedings of the Hawk Migration Conference IV.* Lynchburg, VA: Hawk Migration Association of North America.

Hatch, D. E. 1970. Energy conserving and heat dissipating mechanisms of the Turkey Vulture. *Auk* 87:111–124.

Haugh, J. R. 1972. A study of hawk migration in eastern North America. *Search* 2:1–60.

Hawk, S., N. A. Chingiz kizi, J. Musina, and K. McCarty. 2002. Ridge adherence in Bald Eagles migrating along the Kittatinny Ridge between Bake Oven Knob and Hawk Mountain Sanctuary, Pennsylvania, 1998–2001. *Am. Hawkwatcher* 28:11–17.

Hedenstrom, A. 1993. Migration by soaring or flapping flight in birds: the relative importance of energy cost and speed. *Phil. Trans. R. Soc. Lond. B* 342:353–361.

Heiling, A. M., M. E. Herberstein, and L. Chittka. 2003. Frigates ride high on thermals. *Nature* 421:333–334.

Heintzelman, D. S. 1975. Autumn hawk flights: the migration in eastern North America. New Brunswick, NJ: Rutgers University Press.

——. 1979. *A guide to hawk watching in North America.* University Park, PA: Keystone Books.

——. 1982. Variation in utilization of the Kittatinny Ridge in eastern Pennsylvania in autumn by migrating Golden Eagles and Bald Eagles. *Am. Hawkwatcher* 3:1–4.

——. 1986. *The migrations of hawks.* Bloomington: Indiana University Press.

——. 2004. *Guide to hawk watching in North America.* Guilford, CT: Globe Pequot Press.

Helbig, A. J. 2003. Evolution of bird migration: A phylogenetic and biogeographic approach. In *Avian migration,* ed. P. Berthold, E. Gwinner, and E. Sonnenschein. Berlin: Springer-Verlag.

Henny, C. J. 1977. Birds of prey, DDT, and tussock moths in the Pacific Northwest. *Trans. 42nd North Am. Wildl. Nat. Res. Conf.* 1977:397–411.

Henny, C. J., and H. M. Wright. 1972. Population ecology and environmental pollution: Red-tailed and cooper's hawks. In *Population ecology of migratory birds.* Wildl. Res. Rep. 2. Washington, DC: U.S. Fish & Wildlife Serv.

Herremans, M. 2000. The 'chaotic' flight feather moult of the Steppe Buzzard *Buteo buteo vulpinus. Bird Study* 47:332–343.

Hickey, J. J. ed. 1969. Peregrine Falcons: Their biology and decline. Madison: University of Wisconsin Press.

Hidalgo, C., J. Sánchez, C. Sánchez, and M. T. Saborío. 1995. Migración de falconiformes en Costa Rica. *HMANA Hawk Migr. Stud.* 21(1):10–13.

Hiebl, I., and G. Braunitzer. 1988. Anpassungen der Hämoglobine von Streifengans (*Anser idicus*), Andengans (*Chloephaga melatoptera*) und Sperbergeier (*Gyps rueppellii*) an Bedingungen. *J. für Ornithol.* 129:217–226.

Hix, G. E. 1933. *The birds of prey for Boy Scouts.* Brooklyn, NY: Privately published.

Hobson, K. A. 2002. Incredible journeys. *Science* 295:981–983.

Hoffman, S. W. 1985. Autumn Cooper's Hawk migration through northern Utah and northeastern Nevada, 1977–1982. In *Proceedings of the Hawk Migration Conference IV* (M. Harwood. ed.). Lynchburg (VA): Hawk Migration Association of North America.

Hoffman, S. W., and J. P. Smith. 2003. Population trends of migratory raptors in western North America, 1977–2001. *Condor* 105:397–419.

Hoffman, S. W., J. P. Smith, and T. D. Meehan. 2002. Breeding grounds, winter ranges, and migratory routes in the mountain West. *J. Raptor Res.* 36:97–110.

Hoffman, W., and H. Darrow. 1992. Migration of diurnal raptors from the Florida Keys into the West Indies. *HMANA Hawk Migr. Stud.* 17(2):7–14.

Hofslund, P. B. 1966. Hawk migration over the western tip of Lake Superior. *Wilson Bull.* 78:79–87.

Holmgren, N., and S. Lundberg. 1993. Despotic behaviour and the evolution of migration patterns in birds. *Ornis Scand.* 24:103–109.

Holroyd, G., and J. Duxbury. 1999. Travels of Peregrine Falcon #5735. *Blue Jay* 57:146–149.

Hornaday, W. T. 1913. *Our vanishing wild life.* New York: New York Zool. Soc.

———. 1914. *Wild life conservation in theory and practice.* New Haven: Yale University Press.

———. 1922. *The minds and manners of wild animals.* New York: C. Scribner's Son.

———. 1931. *Thirty years war for wild life.* New York: C. Scribner's Son.

Houston, D. C. 1985. Indian white-backed vulture (*G. bengalensis*). In *Conservation studies on raptors,* ed. I. Newton and R. D. Chancellor. Cambridge: International Council for Bird Preservation.

Hudson, W. H. 1920. *Birds of La Plata,* vol. 2. New York: Dent and Sons.

Hunt, W. G., R. R. Rogers, and D. J. Stowe. 1975. Migratory and foraging behavior of Peregrine Falcons on the Texas coast. *Can. Field-Nat.* 89:111–123.

Hunter, C., ed. 1983. *The life and letters of Alexander Wilson.* Philadelphia: American Philosophical Society.

Hunter, L., P. Caenevari, J. P. Myers, L. X. Payne. 1991. Shorebird and wetland conservation in the western Hemisphere. In *Conserving migratory birds,* ed. T. Salathé. Cambridge: International Council for Bird Preservation.

Inoue, K. 1993. Spring Accipiter migration in north-west Shikoku. *Strix* 12:85–92.

Irby, L. H. 1875. *The ornithology of the Straits of Gibraltar.* London: R. H. Porter.

Izhaki, I., and A. Maitav. 1998. Blackcaps *Sylvia atricapilla* stopping over at the desert edge; physiological state and flight-range estimates. *Ibis* 140:223–233.

Jacobs, E. A. 1996. A mechanical owl as a trapping lure for raptors. *J. Raptor Res.* 30:31–32.

Janis, C. 1993. Victors by default. In *The book of life, ed.* S. J. Gould. New York: Norton.

Jaramillo, A. P. 1993. Wintering Swainson's Hawks in Argentina: food and age segregation. *Condor* 95:475–479.

Jespersen, P., and Å. V. Tåning, eds. 1950. *Studies in bird migration: Being the collected papers of H. Chr. C. Mortensen.* Copenhagen: Munksgaard.

Johnson, C. G., L. A. Nickerson, and M. J. Bechard. 1987. Grasshopper consumption and summer flocks of nonbreeding Swainson's Hawks. *Condor* 89:676–678.

Jorde, D. G., and G. R. Lingle. 1988. Kleptoparasitism by Bald Eagles wintering in south-Karr, central Nebraska. *J. Field Ornithol.* 59:183–188.

Karlsson, L. 2004. *Wings over Falsterbo.* Falsterbo, Sweden: Falsterbo Bird Observatory.

Karr, J. R. 1976. On the relative abundances of north temperate migrants in tropical habitats. *Wilson Bull.* 88:433–458.

Kastner, J. 1986. *A world of watchers.* New York: Alfred A. Knopf.

Kemp, A., and T. Crowe. 1993. A morphometric analysis of *Falco* species. In *Biology and conservation of small falcons,* ed. M. K. Nicholls and R. Clarke. 223–232. London: Hawk and Owl Trust.

Kenward, R. E., S. S. Walls, K. H. Hodder, M. Pahkala, S. N. Freeman, and V. R. Simpson. 2000. The prevalence of non-breeders in raptor populations: evidence from rings, radio-tags and transect surveys. *Oikos* 91:271–279.

Kerlinger, P. 1984. Flight behaviour of Sharp-shinned Hawks during migration. 2. Over water. *Anim. Behav.* 32:1029–1034.

———. 1985. Water-crossing behavior of raptors during migration. *Wilson Bull.* 97:109–113.

———. 1989. *Flight strategies of migrating hawks.* Chicago: University of Chicago Press.

Kerlinger, P., and S. A. Gauthreaux. 1984. Flight behaviour of Sharp-shinned Hawks during migration. 1. Over land. *Anim. Behav.* 32:1021–1028.

——. 1985a. Flight behavior of raptors during spring migration in south Texas studied with radar and visual observations. *J. Field Ornithol.* 56:394–402.

——. 1985b. Seasonal timing, geographic distribution, and flight behavior of Broad-winged Hawks during spring migration in south Texas: A radar and visual study. *Auk* 102:735–743.

Kerlinger, P., V. P. Bingman, and K. P. Able. 1985. Comparative flight behaviour of migrating hawks studied with tracking radar during autumn in central New York. *Can. J. Zool.* 63:755–761.

Kielb, M. 1994. Turkey Vulture. In *The birds of Michigan,* ed. J. Granlund, G. A. McPeek, R. J. Adams, P. C. Chu, J. Rienoehl, C. Nelson, R. Schinkel. 55–56. Bloomington: Indiana University Press.

Kirk, D. A., and J. E. P. Currall. 1994. Habitat associations of migrant and resident vultures in central Venezuela. *J. Avian Biol.* 25:327–337.

Kirk, D. A., and A. G. Gosler. 1994. Body condition varies with migration and competition in migrant and resident South American vultures. *Auk* 111:933–944.

Kirk, D. A., and M. J. Mossman. 1998. Turkey Vulture (*Cathartes aura*). In *The birds of North America,* no. 339, ed. A. Poole and F. Gill. Philadelphia: Birds of North America.

Kirkley, J. S. 1991. Do migrant Swainson's Hawks fast en route to Argentina? *J. Raptor Res.* 25:82–86.

Kjellén, N. 1990. Sex and age ratios in migrating and wintering raptors in Skåne, southern Sweden. *Vår Fagelvärld* 49:211–220.

——. 1992. Differential timing of autumn migration between sex and age groups in raptors at Falsterbo, Sweden. *Ornis Scand.* 23:420–434.

——. 1994. Differences in age and sex ratio among migrating and wintering raptors in southern Sweden. *Auk* 111:274–284.

——. 1997. Importance of a bird migration hot spot: Proportion of the Swedish population of various raptors observed on autumn migration at Falsterbo 1986–1995 and population changes reflected by the migration figures. *Ornis Svecica* 7:21–34.

——. 1998. Annual variation in numbers, age and sex ratios among migrating raptors at Falsterbo, Sweden from 1986–1995. *J. für Ornithol.* 139:157–171.

Kjellén, N., M. Hake, and T. Alerstam. 1997. Strategies of two Ospreys *Pandion haliaetus* migrating between Sweden and tropical Africa as revealed by satellite tracking. *J. Avian Biol.* 28:15–23.

——. 2001. Timing and speed of migration in male, female and juvenile Ospreys *Pandion haliaetus* between Sweden and Africa as revealed by field observation, radar and satellite tracking. *J. Avian Biol.* 32:57–67.

Klem, D., Jr., B. S. Hillegass, and D. A. Peters. 1985. Raptors killing raptors. *Wilson Bull.* 97:230–231.

Klem, D., Jr., B. Hillgass, D. A. Peters, J. A. Villa, and K. Kranick. 1985. Analysis of individual flight patterns of migrating raptors at a break in the Kittatinny Ridge: Lehigh Gap, Pennsylvania. In *Proceedings of the Hawk Migration Conference IV,* ed. M. Harwood. 1–12. Lynchburg, VA: Hawk Migration Association of North America.

Koester, F. 1982. Observations on migratory Turkey Vultures and Lesser Yellow-headed Vultures in northern Colombia. *Auk* 99:372–375.

Kokko, H. 1999. Competition for early arrival in migratory birds. *J. Anim. Ecol.* 68:940–950.

Kosak, J. 1995. The Pennsylvania Game Commission 1895–1995. Harrisburg, PA: Pennsylvania Game Comm.

Kostrzewa, A. 1998. *Pernis apivorus* Honey Buzzard. *BWP Update* 2:107–120.

Kramer, G. 1952. Experiments on bird orientation. *Ibis* 94:265–285.

Lack, D. 1946. Competition for food by birds of prey. *J. Anim. Ecol.* 15:123–129.

Lack, D., and E. Lack. 1953. Visible migration through the Pyrenees: An autumn reconnaissance. *Ibis* 95:271–309.

Lank, D. B., R. W. Butler, J. Ireland, and R. Ydenberg. 2003. Effects of predation danger on migration strategies of sandpipers. *Oikos* 103:303–319.

Laybourne, R. C. 1974. Collision between a vulture and an aircraft at an altitude of 37,000 feet. *Wilson Bull.* 86:461–462.

Layne, J. N. 1982. Analysis of Florida-related banding data for the American Kestrel. *N. Am Bird Band.* 7:94–99.

Lehman, R. N. 2001. Raptor electrocution on power lines: current issues and outlook. *Wildl. Soc. Bull.* 29:804–813.

Leshem, Y., and Y. Yom-Tov. 1996. The magnitude and timing of migration by soaring raptors, pelicans and storks over Israel. *Ibis* 138:188–203.

Liechti, F., D. Ehrich, and B. Bruderer. 1996. Flight behavior of White Storks *Ciconia ciconia* on their migration over southern Israel. *Ardea* 84:3–13.

Lin, W. H., and L. L. Severinghaus. 1998. Raptor migration and conservation in Taiwan. In *Holarctic birds of prey*, ed. R. D. Chancellor, B.-U. Meyburg, and J. J. Ferrero. Berlin: World Working Group on Birds of Prey and Owls.

Lincoln, F. C. 1936. Recoveries of banded birds of prey. *Bird-Band.* 7:38–45.

Lincoln, R., G. Boxshall, and P. Clark. 1998. *A dictionary of ecology, evolution and systematics.* 2nd ed. Cambridge: Cambridge University Press.

Lindström, Å., and M. Klassen. 2003. High basal metabolic rates of shorebirds while in the Arctic: A circumpolar view. *Condor* 105:420–427.

Loftin, H. 1963. Notes on autumn bird migrants in Panama. *Caribbean J. Sci.* 3:63–68.

Lowther, P. E., and C. L. Cink. 1992. House Sparrow. *The birds of North America,* no. 12, ed. A. Poole and F. Gill. Philadelphia: Birds of North America.

Mac Arthur, R. H., and E. O. Wilson. 1968. *The theory of island biogeography.* Princeton: Princeton University Press.

MacCready, P. B., Jr., 1976. Soaring bird aerodynamics—clues for hang gliding. *Ground Skimmer* 45:17–19.

MacCurdy, E. 1938. *The notebooks of Leonardo Da Vinci.* Vol. 1. London: J. Cape.

MacWhirter, R. B., and K. L. Bildstein. 1996. Northern Harrier. *In The birds of North America,* no. 210, ed. A. Poole and F. Gill. Philadelphia: Birds of North America.

Maransky, B. P., and K. L. Bildstein. 2001. Follow your elders: Age-related differences in the migration behavior of Broad-winged Hawks at Hawk Mountain Sanctuary, Pennsylvania. *Wilson Bull.* 113:350–353.

Maransky, B., L. Goodrich, and K. Bildstein. 1997. Seasonal shifts in the effects of weather on the visible migration of Red-tailed Hawks at Hawk Mountain, Pennsylvania, 1992–1994. *Wilson Bull.* 109:246–252.

Marchant, S., and P. J. Higgins, eds. 1993. *Handbook of Australian, New Zealand & Antarctic birds.* Vol. 2. Melbourne: Oxford University Press.

Martell, M. S., C. J. Henny, P. E. Nye, and M. J. Solensky. 2001. Fall migration routes, timing, and wintering sites of north American Ospreys as determined by satellite telemetry. *Condor* 103:715–724.

Martell, M. S., M. A. McMillan, M. J. Solensky, and B. K. Mealey. 2004. Partial migration and wintering use of Florida by Ospreys. *J. Raptor Res.* 38:55–61.

Martell, M. S., S. Willey, and J. Schadweiler. 1998. Nesting and migration of Swainson's Hawks in Minnesota. *Loon* 70:72–81.

Martin, B. P. 1992. *Birds of prey of the British Isles.* Newton Abbot, UK: England David & Charles.

Mateo, R., M. Taggart, and A. A. Meharg. 2003. Lead and arsenic in bones of birds of prey from Spain. *Environ. Pollut.* 126:107–114.

Matray, P. F. 1974. Broad-winged Hawk nesting and ecology. *Auk* 91:307–324.

Matthews, G. V. T. 1968. *Bird navigation.* Cambridge: Cambridge University Press.

Maxwell, J. 1996. River of raptors. *Nat. Hist.* 105:50–55.

McBride, T. J., J. P. Smith, H. P. Gross, and M. J. Hooper. 2004. Blood-lead and ALAD activity levels of Cooper's Hawks (*Accipiter cooperii*) migrating through the southern Rocky Mountains. *J. Raptor Res.* 38:118–124.

McCanch, N. V. 1997. Sparrowhawk *Accipiter nisus* passage through the Calf of Man 1959–1993. *Ringing & Migr.* 18:1–13.

McCarty, K., K. Arnold, J. Ottinger, and K. L. Bildstein. 2000. HMANA data at Hawk Mountain Sanctuary: an update through January 2000. *HMANA Hawk Migr. Stud.* 25(2):30–39.

McClelland, B. R., L. S. Young, P. T. McClelland, J. G. Crenshaw, H. L. Allen, and D. S. Shea. 1994. Migration ecology of Bald Eagles from autumn concentrations in Glacier National Park. *Wildl. Monogr.* 125:1–61.

McClure, H. E. 1998. *Migration and survival of the birds of Asia.* Bangkok: White Lotus Press.

McNabb, B. K. 2002. *The physiological ecology of vertebrates.* Ithaca: Cornell University Press.

Mead, C. J. 1973. Movements of British raptors. *Bird Study* 20:259–286.

Mearns, R. 1982. Winter occupancy of breeding territory and winter diet of Peregrines in south Scotland. *Ornis Scand.* 13:79–83.

Medawar, P. 1984. *The limits of science.* Oxford: Oxford University Press.

Meehan, T. D., C. A. Lott, Z. D. Sharp, R. B. Smith, R, N. Rosenfield, A. C. Stewart, and R. K. Murphy. 2001. Using hydrogen isotope geochemistry to estimate the natal latitudes of immature Cooper's Hawks migrating through the Florida Keys. *Condor* 103:11–20.

Meinertzhagen, R. 1959. *Pirates and predators.* Edinburgh: Oliver and Boyd.

Meredith, R. L. 1999. *American falconry in the twentieth century.* Boise, ID: Archives Amer. Falconry.

Meretsky, V. J., N. F. R. Snyder, S. R. Beissinger, D. A. Clendenen, and J. W. Wiley. 2000. Demography of the California Condor: Implications for reestablishment. *Conserv. Biol.* 99:957–967.

Merriam, C. H. 1877. A review of the birds of Connecticut with remarks on their habits. *Trans. Conn. Acad.* 4:1–50.

Meyburg, B.-U., and E.G. Lobkov. 1994. Satellite tracking of a juvenile Steller's Sea Eagle *Haliaeetus pelagicus. Ibis* 136:105–106.

Meyburg, B.-U., and C. Meyburg. 2002. Monitoring raptors by means of satellite telemetry. In *Raptors in the new millennium,* ed. R. Yosef, M. L. Millar, and D. Pepler. Elat, Israel: International Birding & Research Center.

Meyburg, B.-U., T. Blohm, C. Meyburg, I. Börner, and P. Sömmer. 1994. Satelliten- und Bodentelemetrie bei einem jungen Seeadler *Haliaeetus albicilla* in der Uckermark: Wiedereingliederung in den Familienverband, Bettelflug, Familienauflösung, Dispersion und Überwinterung. *Vogelwelt* 115:115–120.

Meyburg, B.-U., X. Eichaker, C. Meyburg, and, P. Paillat. 1995b. Migrations of an adult Spotted Eagle tracked by satellite. *Brit. Birds* 88:357–361.

Meyburg, B.-U., L. Hatraszthy, C. Meyburg, and L. Viszlo. 1995c. Satelliten- und Bodentelemetrie bei einem jungen Kaiseradler *Aquila heliaca*: Familienauflosung und Dispersion. *Vogelwelt* 116:153–157.

Meyburg, B.-U., J. Matthes, and C. Meyburg. 2002. Satellite-tracked Lesser Spotted Eagle avoids crossing water at the Gulf of Suez. *Brit. Birds* 95:372–376.

Meyburg, B.-U., J.M. Mendelson, D.H. Ellis, D.G. Smith, C. Meyburg, and A.C. Kemp. 1995d. Year-round movements of a Wahlberg's Eagle *Aquila wahlbergi* tracked by satellite. *Ostrich* 66:135–140.

Meyburg, B.-U., C. Meyburg, and J. C. Barbraud. 1998. Migration strategies of an adult Short-toed Eagle *Circaetus gallicus* tracked by satellite. *Alauda* 66:39–48.

Meyburg, B.-U., C. Meyburg, W. Scheller, and P. Paillat. 1996. Satellite tracking of eagles: Method, technical progress and first personal experiences. In *Eagle studies,* ed. B.-U. Meyburg and R. D. Chancellor. 529–549. Berlin: World Work. Grp. Birds of Prey.

Meyburg, B.-U., P. Paillat, and C. Meyburg. 2003. Migration routes of Steppe Eagles between Asia and Africa: A study by means of satellite telemetry. *Condor* 105:219–227.

Meyburg, B.-U., W. Scheller, and C. Meyburg. 1995a. Migration and wintering of the Lesser Spotted Eagle (*Aquila pomarina*): A study by means of satellite telemetry. (Zug und Uberwintering des Schreiadlers *Aquila pomarina*: Satellitentelemetrishce Untersuchungen.) *J. für Ornithol.* 136:401–422.

Millsap, B. A. 1987. Summer concentration of American Swallow-tailed Kites at Lake Okeechobee, Florida, with comments on post-breeding movements. *Fla. Field Nat.* 15:85–112.

Mineau, P., M. R. Fletcher, L. C. Glaser, N. J. Thomas, C. Brassard, L. K. Wilson, J. E. Elliott, L. A. Lyon, C. J. Henny, T. Bollinger, and S. L. Porter. 1999. Poisoning of raptors with organophosphorous and carbamate pesticides with emphasis on Canada, U.S. and U.K. *J. Raptor Res.* 33:1–35.

Moir, J. 2005. Bringing back the condor: Adaptive management guides the recovery effort. *Birding* 37:44–50.

Moreau, R. E. 1972. *The Palaearctic-African bird migration systems.* New York: Academic Press.

Morel, G., and F. Roux. 1966. Les migrateurs paléarctiques en Sénégal 1—Les nonpassereaux. *Terre et Vie* 20:19–72.

Moritz, D., and G. Vauk. 1976. Der Zug de Sperbers (*Accipiter nisus*) auf Helgoland. *J. für Ornithol.* 117:317–328.

Morton, M. L., and M. E. Pereyra. 1994. Autumnal migration departure schedules in mountain White-crowned Sparrows. *Condor* 96:1020–1029.

Mueller, H. C., and D. D. Berger. 1967a. Fall migration of Sharp-shinned Hawks. *Wilson Bull.* 79:397–415.

——. 1967b. Wind-drift, leading lines, and diurnal migration. *Wilson Bull.* 79:50–63.

——. 1969. Navigation by hawks migrating in spring. *Auk* 86:35–40.

Mueller, H. C., D. D. Berger, and G. Allez. 1977. The periodic invasions of Goshawks. *Auk* 95:652–663.

Mueller, H. C., D. D. Berger, and N. S. Mueller. 2003. Age and sex diferences in the timing of spring migration of hawks and falcons. *Wilson Bull.* 115:321–324.

Mueller, H. C., N. S. Mueller, D. D. Berger, G. Allez, W. Robichaud, and J. L. Kaspar. 2000.

Age and sex differences in the timing of fall migration of hawks and falcons. *Wilson Bull.* 112:214–224.

Muir, J. 1913. *The story of my boyhood and youth.* Boston: Houghton Mifflin.

Mundy, P., D. Butchart, J. Ledger, and S. Piper. 1992. *The vultures of Africa.* London: Academic Press.

Murray, B. G., Jr. 1964. A review of Sharp-shinned Hawk migration along the northeastern coast of the United States. *Wilson Bull.* 76:257–264.

Myers, J. P. 1981. A test of three hypotheses for latitudinal segregation of the sexes in wintering birds. *Can. J. Zool.* 59:1527–1534.

Myers, N. 1984. *The primary source.* London: Norton.

Nagy, A. 1970. Curator's report. *Hawk Mtn. News* 42:4–12.

——. 1979. Miracle day. *Hawk Mtn. News* 50:25–29.

Nakazawa, Y., A. T. Peterson, E. Martinez-Meyer, and A. G. Navarro-Sigüena. 2004. Seasonal niches of Nearctic-Neotropical migratory birds: Implications for the evolution of migration. *Auk* 121:610–618.

Nebel, S., D. B. Lank, P. D. O'Hara, G. Fernandez, B. Haase, F. Delgado, F. A. Estela, L. J. Evans Ogden, B. Harrington, B. E. Kus, J. E. Lyons, F. Mercier, B. Ortego, J. Y. Takekawa, N. Warnock, and S. E. H Warnock. 2002. Western Sandpipers (*Calidris mauri*) during the nonbreeding season: Spatial segregation on a hemispheric scale. *Auk* 119:922–928.

Newton, I. 1975. Movements and mortality of British Sparrowhawks. *Bird Study* 22:35–43.

——. 1976. Population limitation in diurnal raptors. *Can. Field-Nat.* 90:274–300.

——. 1979. *Population ecology of raptors.* Vermillion, SD: Buteo Books.

——. 1986. *The sparrowhawk.* Calton, UK: T&AD Poyser.

——. 1990. Human impacts on raptors. In *Birds of prey*, ed. I. Newton. 190–207. New York: Fact on File.

——. 1995. Relationship between breeding and wintering ranges in Palaearctic-African migrants. *Ibis* 137:241–249.

——. 1998. Migration patterns in West Palaearctic raptors. In *Holarctic birds of prey*, ed. R. D. Chancellor, B.-U. Meyburg, and J. J. Ferrero. 603–612. Berlin: World Working Group on Birds of Prey and Owls.

——. 2003. *The speciation and biogeography of birds.* Amsterdam: Academic Press.

——. 2004. Population limitation in migrants. *Ibis* 146:197–226.

Newton, I., E. Meek, and B. Little. 1978. Breeding ecology of the Merlin in Northumberland. *Brit. Birds* 71:376–398.

Nice, M. M. 1937. Studies in the life history of the Song Sparrow. Vol. 1. *Trans. Linnean Soc. NY* 4:1–246.

Nicoletti, F. J. 1997. American Kestrel and Merlin migration correlated with Green Darner movements at Hawk Ridge. *Loon* 68:216–220.

Niles, L. J., J. Burger, and K. E. Clark. 1996. The influence of weather, geography, and habitat on migrating raptors on Cape May Peninsula. *Condor* 98:382–394.

Nisbet, I. C. T., and T. C. Smout. 1957. Autumn observations on the Bosphorus and Dardanelles. *Ibis* 99:483–499.

Nisbet, I. C. T., P. R. Evans, and P. P. Feeny. 1961. Migration from Morocco into southwest Spain in relation to weather. *Ibis* 103a:349–372.

O'Reilly, K. M., and J. C. Wingfield. 1995. Spring and autumn migration in shorebirds: same distance, different strategies. *Am. Zool.* 35:222–233.

Oaks, J. L., M. Gilbert, M. Z. Virani, R. T. Watson, C. U. Meteyer, B. A. Rideout, H. L. Shivaprasad, S. Ahmed, M. J. I. Chaudhry, M. Arshad, S. Mahmood, A. Ali, and A. A. Khan. 2004. Diclofenac residues as the cause of vulture population decline in Pakistan. *Nature* 427:630–633.

Oaks, L., B. A. Rideout, M. Gilbert, R. Watson, M. Virani, and A. A. Khan. 2001. Summary of diagnostic investigation into vulture mortality: Punjab Province, Pakistan, 2000–2001. In *Reports from the workshop on Indian Gyps vultures,* ed. T. Katzner and J. Parry-Jones. Gloucestershire, UK: Natl. Centre Birds of Prey.

Odum, E. P. 1993. *Ecology and our endangered life-support systems.* 2nd ed. Sunderland, MA: Sinauer.

Olsen, P. 1995. *Australian birds of prey.* Baltimore: Johns Hopkins University Press.

Olson, C. V., and D. P. Arsenault. 2000. Differential winter distribution of Rough-legged Hawks (*Buteo lagopus*) by sex in western North America. *J. Raptor Res.* 34:157–166.

Olson, S. L. 1985. The fossil record of birds. *Avian Biol.* 9:79–238.

Österlöf, S. 1951. The migration of Swedish Ospreys (*Pandion haliaetus*) (L.). *Vår Fågelvårld* 10:1–15. (In Swedish.)

Owen, M., and J. M. Black. 1991. The importance of migration mortality in non-passerine birds. In *Bird population studies,* ed. C. M. Perrins, J.-D. Lebreton, and G. J. M. Hirons. 360–370. Oxford: Oxford University Press.

Pain, D., A. A. Cunningham, P. F. Donald, J. W. Duckworth, D. C. Houston, T. Katzner, J. Parry-Jones, C. Poole, V. Prakash, P. Round, and R. Timms. 2003. Causes and effects of temporospatial declines of *Gyps* vultures in Asia. *Conserv. Biol.* 17:661–671.

Palmer, R. S., ed. 1988. *Handbook of North American birds.* Vols. 4 and 5. New Haven: Yale University Press.

Parmalee, P. W. 1954. The vultures: Their movements, economic status, and control in Texas. *Auk* 71:443–453.

Pearson, L. 1897. *Diseases and enemies of poultry.* Harrisburg, PA: C. M. Busch.

Pennycuick, C. J. 1969. The mechanics of bird migration. *Ibis* 111:525–556.

———. 1971. Gliding flight of the White-backed Vulture *Gyps africanus. J. Exp. Biol.* 55:13–38.

———. 1972. *Animal flight.* London: Edward Arnold.

———. 1983. Thermal soaring compared in three dissimilar tropical bird species: *Fregata magnificens, Pelecanus occidentalis* and *Coragyps atratus. J. Exp. Biol.* 102:307–325.

Percival, S. 2005. Birds and windfarms: What are the real issues? *Brit. Birds* 98:194–204.

Peterson, R. T. 1934. *A field guide to the birds.* Boston: Houghton Mifflin.

———. 1965. Introduction to the Dover Edition. In *Bird studies at Old Cape May,* vol. 1, W. Stone. vii–xiii. New York: Dover.

Pienaar, H. 1996. Piracy by Eastern Red-footed Falcons on Lesser Kestrels. *J. Afr. Raptor Biol.* 11:20–21.

Pienkowski, M. W., and P. R. Evans. 1985. The role of migration in the population dynamics of birds. In *Behavioural ecology: Ecological consequences of adaptive behaviour,* ed. R. M. Sibly and R. H. Smith. 331–352. Oxford: Blackwell.

Place, J., R. Kaiser-Antonowich, E. Henckel, and J. Henckel. 2001. Movements of marked and radio-tagged Turkey Vultures in and around northwestern New Jersey, USA. In *Hawkwatching in the Americas,* ed. K. L. Bildstein and D. Klem, Jr. North Wales, PA: Hawk Migration Association of North America.

Platt, J. B. 1976. Gyrfalcon nest site selection and winter activity in the western Canadian Arctic. *Can. Field-Nat.* 90:338–345.

Poole, A. F. 1989. *Ospreys: A natural and unnatural history.* Cambridge: Cambridge University Press.

Poole, A., and F. Gill, eds. 1992–2002. *The birds of North America.* Philadelphia: Birds of North America.

Porras-Peñaranda, L. Robichaud, and F. Branch. 2004. New full-season count sites for raptor migration in Talamanca, Costa Rica. *Ornitol. Neotrop.* 15 (Suppl.):267–278.

Porter, R. D., and S. N. Wiemeyer. 1969. Dieldrin and DDT: Effects on Sparrow Hawk eggshells and reproduction. *Science* 165:199–200.

Potapov, E., N. Fox, D. Sumya, B. Gombobaatar, F. Launay, O. Combreau, C. Eastham. 2001. The Mongolian Saker Falcon: Migratory, nomadic or sedentary? *Argos Newsl.* 58:11.

Pough, R. H. 1932. Wholesale killing of hawks in Pennsylvania. *Bird-Lore* 34:429–430.

Prakash, V. 1989. The general ecology of raptors in Keoladeo National Park, Bharatpur. Ph.D. diss., Bombay University, Mumbai.

———. 1999. Status of vultures in Keoladeo National Park, Bharatpur, Rajasthan, with special reference to population crash in *Gyps* species. *J. Bombay Nat. Hist. Soc.* 96:365–378.

Prévost, Y. A. 1979. Osprey-Bald Eagle interactions at a common feeding site. *Auk* 96:413–414.

———. 1982. The wintering ecology of Ospreys in Senegambia. Ph.D. diss., University of Edinburgh.

Pulliam, H. R. 1988. Sources, sinks, and population regulation. *Am. Nat.* 132:652–661.

Rafanomezantsoa, S., R. T. Watson, and R. Thorstrom. 2002. Juvenile dispersal of Madagascar Fish-Eagles tracked by satellite telemetry. *J. Raptor Res.* 36:309–314.

Rappole, J. H. 1995. *The ecology of migrant birds: A Neotropical perspective.* Washington, DC: Smithsonian Institution Press.

Ratcliffe, D. 1958. Broken eggs in peregrine eyries. *Brit. Birds* 51:23–26.

———. 1967. Decrease in eggshell weight in certain birds of prey. *Nature* 215:208–210.

———. 1993. *The Peregrine Falcon.* 2nd ed. London: T. & A. D. Poyser.

———. 1997. *The Raven.* London: T. & A. D. Poyser.

Redpath, S. M., and S. J. Thirgood. 1997. *Birds of prey and Red Grouse.* London: Stationary Office.

Richardson, W. J. 1975. Autumn hawk migration in Ontario studied with radar. In *Proceedings of the North American hawk migration conference, 1974,* ed. M. Harwood. 47–58. Washington Depot, CT: Shiver Mountain Press.

Riesing, M. J., L. Kurckenhauser, A. Gamauf, and E. Haring. 2003. Molecular phylogeny of the genus *Buteo* (Aves: Accipitridae) based on mitochondrial marker sequences. *Mol. Phylogenet. Evol.* 27:328–342.

Ristow, D., and S. Xirouchakis. 2000. What is killing Eleonora's Falcons? *World Birdwatch* 22(1):14–15.

Robbins, C. S. 1975. A history of North American hawkwatching. In *Proceedings of the North American hawk migration conference, ed.* M. Harwood. Washington Depot, CT: Hawk Migration Association of North America.

Robinson, W. 1950. Montagu's Harriers. *Bird Notes* 24:103–114.

Rodriguez Santana, F., L. M. Hernández, M. Martell, and K. L. Bildstein. 2003. Cuban raptor-migration counts in 2001. *J. Raptor Res.* 37:330–333.

Rosenfield, R. N., and J. Bielefeldt. 1993. Cooper's Hawk. In *The Birds of North America,* no. 75, ed. A. Poole and F. Gill. Philadelphia: Birds of North America.

Rosenfield, R. N, and D. L. Evans. 1980. Migration incidence and sequence of age and sex classes of the Sharp-shinned Hawk. *Loon* 52:66–69.

Rudebeck, G. 1950. Studies on bird migration based on field studies in southern Sweden. *Vår Fågelvårld,* Suppl. 1:5–49, 74–85, 147–148.

Russell, R. W. 1991. Nocturnal flight by migrant "diurnal" raptors. *J. Field Ornithol.* 62:505–508.

Safriel, U. 1968. Bird migration at Elat Israel. *Ibis* 110:283–320.

Sammut, M., and E. Bonavia. 2004. Autumn raptor migration over Buskett, Malta. *Brit. Birds* 97:318–322.

Schifferli, A. 1967. Vom Zug schweizerischer Schwarzer Milane *Milvus migrans* nach Ringfunden. *Ornith. Beob.* 64:34–51.

Schmid, H. 2000. Separate routes: Autumn migration of juvenile and adult European Honeybuzzards *Pernis apivorus*—a synthesis. *Ornith. Beob.* 97:191–222.

Schmidt-Nielson, K. 1972. Locomotion: Energy cost of swimming, running and flying. *Science* 177:272–228.

Schmutz, J. K. 1992. Molt of flight feathers in Ferruginous and Swainson's Hawks. *J. Raptor Res.* 26:124–135.

Schüz, E., P. Berthold, E. Gwinner, and H. Oelke. 1971. *Grundriß der Vogelzugskunde.* Berlin: Parey.

Seegar, W.S., P. N. Cutchis, M. R. Fuller, J. J. Suter, V. Bhatnagar, and J. G. Wall. 1996. Fifteen years of satellite tracking development and application to wildlife research and conservation. *Johns Hopkins APL Tech. Dig.* 17:401–411.

Serrano, D., J. L. Tella, M. G. Forero, and J. A. Donázar. 2001. Factors affecting breeding dispersal in the facultatively colonial Lesser Kestrel: Individual experience vs. conspecific cues. *J. Anim. Ecol.* 70:568–578.

Severinghaus, L. L. 1991. The status and conservation of Grey-faced Buzzard-eagles and Brown Shrikes migrating through Taiwan. In *Conserving migratory birds,* ed. T. Salathé. 203–223. Cambridge: International Council for Bird Preservation.

Shelley, E., and S. Benz. 1985. Observations of aerial hunting, food carrying and crop size of migrant raptors. In *Conservation studies on raptors,* ed. I. Newton and R. D. Chancellor. 299–301. Cambridge: Intnational Council for Bird Preservation.

Sherrod, S. K., C. M. White, and F. S. L. Williamson. 1976. Biology of the Bald Eagle (*Haliaeetus leucocephalus alascanus*) on Amchitka Island, Alaska. *Living Bird* 15:143–183.

Shirihai, H., and D. A. Christie. 1992. Raptor migration at Eilat. *Brit. Birds* 85:141–186.

Shirihai, H., R. Yosef, D. Alon, G. M. Kirwin, and R. Spaar. 2000. *Raptor migration in Israel and the Middle East.* Elat, Israel: International Birding and Research Center; Tel Aviv: Society for the Protection of Nature in Israel.

Shoemaker, V. H. 1972. Osmoregulation and excretion in birds. In *Avian biology,* vol. 2, ed. D. S. Farmer and J. R. King. 527–574. New York: Academic Press.

Shultz, S. H. S. Baral, S. Charman, A. A. Cunningham, D. Das, G. R. Ghalsasi, M. S. Goudar, R. E. Green, A. Jones, P. Nighot, D. J. Pain, and V. Prakash. 2004. Diclofenac poisoning is widespread in declining vulture populations across the Indian subcontinent. *Proc. R. Soc. Lond. B.* (Suppl.) DOI 10.1098/rsbl.2004.0223.

Sibley, D. 1993. *The birds of Cape May.* Cape May Point, NJ: Cape May Bird Observatory.

Simons, M. M. 1977. Reverse migration of Sharp-shinned Hawks on the west coast of Florida. *Fl. Field Nat.* 5:43–44.

Skutch, A. F. 1945. The migration of Swainson's and Broad-winged Hawks through Costa Rica. *Northwest Sci.* 19:80–89.

Smallwood J. A., and D. M. Bird. 2002. American Kestrel (*Falco sparverius*). In *The birds of North America,* no. 602, ed. A. Poole and F. Gill. Philadelphia: Birds of North America.

Smeenk, C. 1974. Comparative ecological studies of some East African birds of prey. *Ardea* 62:1–197.

Smith, D. G., C. R. Wilson, and H. H. Frost. 1972. The biology of the American Kestrel in central Utah. *Southwest. Nat.* 17:73–83.

Smith, J. P., J. Simon, S. W. Hoffman, and C. Riley. 2001. New full-season autumn Hawk-watches in coastal Texas. In *Hawkwatching in the Americas,* ed. K. L. Bildstein and D. Klem, Jr. 67–91. North Wales, PA: Hawk Migration Association of North America.

Smith, N. G. 1980. Hawk and vulture migrations in the Neotropics. In *Migrant birds in the Neotropics,* ed. A. Keast and E. Morton. 51–66. Washington, DC: Smithsonian Institution Press.

——. 1985a. Thermals, cloud streets, trade winds, and tropical storms: How migrating raptors make the most of atmospheric energy in Central America. In *Proceedings of the hawk migration conference IV,* ed. M. Harwood. 51–66. Lynchburg, VA: Hawk Migration Association of North America.

——. 1985b. Dynamics of trans-isthmian migration of raptors between Central and South America. In *Conservation studies on raptors,* ed. I. Newton and R. C. Chancellor. 271–290. Cambridge: Internatl. Council Bird Preserv.

Smith, N. G., D. L. Goldstein, and G. A Bartholomew. 1986. Is long-distance migration possible for soaring hawks using only stored fat? *Auk* 103:607–611.

Smith, R. B., T. D. Meehan, and B. O. Wolf. 2003. Assessing migration patterns of Sharp-shinned Hawks *Accipiter striatus* using stable-isotope and band encounter analysis. *J. Avian Biol.* 34:387–394.

Snow, D. W. 1978. Relationships between the European and African avifaunas. *Bird Stud.* 25:134–148.

Snyder, J. P. 1993. *Flattening the earth: Two thousand years of map projections.* Chicago: University of Chicago Press.

Sodhi, N. S., and L. W. Oliphant. 1993. Prey selection by urban-breeding Merlins. *Auk* 110:727–735.

Sodhi, N. S., L. W. Oliphant, P. C. James, and I. G. Warkentin. 1993. Merlin. In *The birds of North America,* no. 44, ed A. Poole and F. Gill. Philadelphia: Birds of North America.

Spaar, R. 1995. Flight behavior of Steppe Buzzards (*Buteo buteo vulpinus*) during spring migration in southern Israel: A tracking radar study. *Israel J. Zool.* 41:489–500.

——. 1997. Flight strategies of migrating raptors: A comparative study of interspecific variation in flight characteristics. *Ibis* 523–535.

Spaar, R., and B. Bruderer. 1996. Soaring migration of Steppe Eagles *Aquila nipalensis* in southern Israel: Flight behaviour under various wind and thermal condition. *J. Avian Biol.* 27:289–301.

——. 1997. Optimal flight behavior of soaring migrants: A case study of migrating Steppe Buzzards, *Buteo buteo vulpinus. Behav. Ecol.* 8:288–297.

Spaar, R., H. Stark, and F. Liechti. 1998. Migratory strategies of Levant Sparrowhawks: Time or energy minimization? *Anim. Behav.* 56:1185–1197.

Spencer, C. N., B. R. McClelland, and J. A. Stanford. 1991. Shrimp stocking, salmon collapse, and eagle displacement. *BioScience* 41:14–21.

Squires, J. R., and R. T. Reynolds. 1997. Northern Goshawk. In *The birds of North America,* no. 298, ed A. Poole and F. Gill. Philadelphia: Birds of North America.

Stark, H., and F. Liechti. 1993. Do Levant Sparrowhawks *Accipiter brevipes* also migrate at night? *Ibis* 138:233–236.

Stattersfield, A. J., and D. R. Capper. 2000. *Threatened birds of the world*. Barcelona and Cambridge: Lynx Ediciones and Birdlife International.

Steyn, P. 1982. *Birds of prey of Southern Africa*. Cape Town: David Philip.

Stine, E. S. 1989. *Pennsylvania German dictionary*. Birdsboro, PA: Pa. German Soc.

Stone, W. 1922. Hawk flights at Cape May Point, N. J. *Auk* 39:567–568.

———. 1937. *Bird Studies at Old Cape May*, vols. 1 & 2. Philadelphia: Delaware Valley Ornithological Club.

Stotz, N. G., and L. J. Goodrich. 1989. Sexual differences in timing of American Kestrel migration at Hawk Mountain Sanctuary, PA. *J. Raptor Res.* 23:167–177.

Sutton, C., and P. Kerlinger. 1997. The Delaware bayshore of New Jersey: A raptor migration and wintering site of hemispheric significance. *J. Raptor Res.* 31:54–58.

Sutton, C., and P. Sutton. 1982–1983. The spring hawk migration at Cape May, New Jersey. *Cassinia* 60:5–18.

———. 1999. River of raptors: Exploring and enjoying Pronatura's raptor conservation project. *Birding* 31:229–236.

Sutton, G. M. 1928a. Notes on a collection of hawks from Schuylkill County, Pennsylvania. *Wilson Bull.* 40:84–95.

———. 1928b. An introduction to the birds of Pennsylvania. Harrisburg, PA: McFarland.

———. 1945. Behavior of birds during a Florida hurricane. *Auk* 62:603–606.

Tabb, E. C. 1973. A study of wintering Broad-winged Hawks in southeastern Florida, 1986–1973. *E. Bird Band. Assoc. News Suppl.* 36:11–29.

———. 1977. Winter returns of American Kestrels in southern Florida. *N. Am. Bird Band.* 2:163.

———. 1979. Winter recoveries in Guatemala and southern Mexico of Broad-winged Hawks banded in south Florida. *North Am. Bird Band.* 4:60.

Tabor, S. P., and C. T. McAllister. 1988. Nocturnal flight by Turkey Vultures (*Cathartes aura*) in southcentral Texas. *J. Raptor Res.* 22:91.

Temeles, E. J., and T. I. Wellicome. 1992. Weather-dependent kleptoparasitism and aggression in a raptor guild. *Auk* 109:920–923.

Temple S. A. 1986. The problem of avian extinctions. In *Current ornithology*, vol. 3, ed. R. F. Johnston. New York: Plenum Press.

Thake, M. A. 1980. Gregarious behaviour among migrating Honey Buzzards (*Pernis apivorus*). *Ibis* 122:500–505.

Thiollay, J.-M. 1971. L'exploitation des feux de brousse par les oiseaux en Afrique Occidentale. *Alauda* 39:54–72.

———. 1977. La migration d'automne sur la côte orientale du Mexique. *Alauda* 45:344–346.

———. 1980. Spring hawk migration in eastern Mexico. *J. Raptor Res.* 14:13–20.

———. 1989a. Area requirements for the conservation of rainforest raptors and game birds in French Guiana. *Conserv. Biol.* 3:128–137.

———. 1989b. Distribution and ecology of Palearctic birds of prey wintering in West and Central Africa. In *Raptors in the modern world*, ed. B.-U. Meyburg and R. D. Chancellor. London: World Work. Grp. Birds of Prey and Owls.

———. 1993. Response of a raptor community to shrinking area and degradation of tropical rainforest in the south west Ghâts (IN). *Ecography* 16:97–110.

———. 1998. Current status and conservation of Falconiformes in tropical Asia. *J. Raptor Res.* 32:40–55.

Thomson, A. L. 1926. *Problems of bird migration*. London: H. F. & G. Witherby.

Thompson, D. B. A., S. M. Redpath, A. H. Fielding, M. Marquiss, and C. A. Galbraith. (eds.). 2003. *Birds of prey in a changing environment.* Edinburgh: Stationary Office.

Thorup, K., T. Alerstam, M. Hake, and N. Kjellen. 2003. Bird orientation: Compensation for wind drift in migrating raptors is age dependent. *Proc. R. Soc. Lond. B (Suppl.) Letter* 7:1–4.

Tilly, F. 1985. Spring raptor migration in eastern Mexico, 1984. *HMANA Hawk Migr. Newsl.* 11(1):16–17.

Tilly, F. C., S. W. Hoffman, and C. R. Tilly. 1990. Spring hawk migration in southern Mexico, 1989. *HMANA Hawk Migr. Stud.*15:21–29.

Titus, K., M. R. Fuller, and D. Jacobs. 1990. Detecting trends in hawk migration count data. In *Survey designs and statistical methods for the estimation of avian population trends,* ed. J. R. Sauer and S. Droege. Washington, DC: U.S. Fish & Wildlife Service.

Tjernberg, M., and H. Ryttmann. 1994. Bivakens *Pernis apivorus* överlevnad och bestandsutveckling i Sverige. *Ornis Svecia* 4:133–139.

Tristram, H. B. 1865–1868. Notes on the ornithology of Palestine. *Ibis* 1:67–83, 241–263; 2:59–88, 280–292; 3:73–97,360–371; 4:204–215, 321–335.

Trowbridge, C. C. 1895. Hawk flights in Connecticut. *Auk* 12:259–270.

———. 1902. The relation of wind to bird migration. *Am. Nat.* 36:735–753.

Tsatsakis, A., M. Christakis-Hampas, S. Xirouchakis, F. Baum, and D. Ristow. 2001. Whodunnit? The case of the disappearing Eleonora's Falcons. *World Birdwatch* 23:25–27.

Tucker, G. M., and M. F. Heath. 1994. *Birds in Europe: Their conservation status.* Cambridge: Birdlife International.

Tucker, V. A. 1993. Gliding birds: Reduction of induced drag by wing tip slots between primary feathers. *J. Exp. Biol.* 180:285–300.

Ueta, M., and H. Higuchi. 2002. Difference in migration pattern between adult and immature birds using satellites. *Auk* 119:832–835.

Ueta, M., and V. V. Ryabtsev. 2001. Migration routes of four juvenile Imperial Eagles *Aquila heliaca* from the Baikal region of eastern Russia. *Bird Conserv. Internatl.* 11:93–99.

Ueta, M., F. Sato, E. G. Lobkov and N. Mita. 1998. Migration route of White-tailed Sea Eagles *Haliaeetus albicilla* in northeastern Asia. *Ibis* 140:684–686.

Ueta, M., F. Sato, H. Nakagawa, and N. Mita. 2000. Migration routes and differences of migration schedule between adult and young Steller's Sea Eagles *Haliaeetus pelagicus. Ibis* 142:35–39.

Ulfstrand, S., G. Roos. T. Alerstam, and L. Österdahl. 1974. Visible bird migration at Falsterbo, Sweden. *Vår Fågelvårld,* Suppl. 8:1–245.

Van Fleet, P. K. 2001. Geography of diurnal raptors migrating through the Valley-and-Ridge Province of central Pennsylvania. In *Hawkwatching in the Americas,* ed. K. L. Bildstein and D. Klem. North Wales, PA: Hawk Migration Association of North America.

Van Maanen, E., I. Goradze, A. Gavashelishvili, and R. Goradze. 2001. Trapping and hunting of migratory raptors in western Georgia. *Bird Conserv. Internatl.* 11:77–92.

van Manen, W. 2004. Why do Northern Goshawks *Accipiter gentiles* in Białowieża National Park (East-Poland) only breed in coniferous forests? *De Takkeling* 12:76–80.

Verner, W. 1909. *My life among the wild birds in Spain.* London: John Bale Sons and Danielsson.

Viverette, C. B., S. Struve, L. J. Goodrich, and K. L. Bildstein. 1996. Decreases in migrating Sharp-shinned Hawks (*Accipiter striatus*) at traditional raptor-migration watch sites in eastern North America. *Auk* 113:32–40.

Von Haartman, L. 1968. The evolution of resident versus migratory habitats in birds. Some considerations. *Ornis Fennica* 45:1–7.

Wallin. K., M. L. Wallin, T. Jaras, and P. Standvik. 1987. Leap-frog migration in the Swedish Kestrel *Falco tinnunculus* population. *Proc. 5th Nordic Ornithol. Congr.* 1985:213–222.

Walls, S. S., S. Mañosa, R. M. Fuller, K. H. Hoddwer, and R. E. Kenward. 1999. Is early dispersal enterprise or exile? Evidence from radio-tagged buzzards. *J. Avian Biol.* 30:407–415.

Ward, F. P., and R. B. Berry. 1972. Autumn migration of Peregrine Falcons on Assateague Island, 1970–1971. *J. Wildl. Manage.* 36:484–492.

Warkentin, I. G., P. C. James, and L. W. Oliphant. 1990. Body morphometrics, age structure, and partial migration of urban Merlins. *Auk* 107:25–34.

Wasser, J. S. 1986. The relationship of energetics of falconiform birds to body mass and climate. *Condor* 88:57–62.

Weathers, W. W. 1979. Climatic adaptation in avian standard metabolic rate. *Oecologia* 42:81–89.

Wegner, P., G. Kleinstäuber, F. Baum, and F. Schilling. 2005. Long-term investigation of the degree of exposure of German Peregrine Falcons (*Falco peregrinus*) to damaging chemicals from the environment. *J. Ornithol.* 146:34–54.

Welch, W. A. 1975. Inflight hawk migration study. *J. Hawk Migr. Assoc. N. Am.* 1:14–22.

Wernham, C. V., M. P. Toms, J. H. Marchant, J. A. Clark, G. M. Siriwardena, and S. R. Baillie, S. R., eds. 2002. *Migration atlas: Movements of the birds of Britain and Ireland.* London: T. & A. D. Poyser.

Wetmore, A. 1943. The birds of southern Veracruz, Mexico. *Proc. U.S. Natl. Mus.* 93:215–340.

Wheeler, B. K. 1990. Mexico region. *HMANA Hawk Migr. Stud.* 16(1):86.

Whiteman, C. D. 2000. *Mountain meteorology.* Oxford: Oxford University Press.

Wiemeyer, S. N., and R. D. Porter. 1969. DDE thins eggshells of captive American Kestrels. *Nature* 227:737–738.

Wilkerson, J. K. 1980. Man's eighty centuries in Veracruz. *Natl. Geogr.* 158:202–231.

Williams, M. 2000. Autumn bird migration at Beidaihe, China, 1986–1990. Hong Kong: Beidaihe International Birdwatching Society.

Willoughby, E. J., and T. J. Cade. 1964. Breeding behavior of the American Kestrel (Sparrow Hawk). *Living Bird* 3:75–96.

Wilson, A. 1808–1814. *American ornithology.* 9 vols. Philadelphia: Bradford and Inskeep.

Wing, S. L., H.-D. Sues, R. Potts, W. A. DiMichele, and A. K. Behrensmeyer. 1992. Evolutionary paleoecology. In *Terrestrial ecosystems through time,* ed. A. K. Behrensmeyer, J. D. Damuth, W. A. DiMichele, R. Potts, H.D. Sues, and S. L. Wing. 1–14. Chicago: Chicago University Press.

Woffinden, N. D. 1986. Notes on the Swainson's Hawk in central Utah: Insectivory, premigratory aggregations, and kleptoparasitism. *Great Basin Natur.* 46:302–304.

Wolfson, A. 1948. Bird migration and the concept of continental drift. *Science* 108:23–30.

Wood, C. A., and F. M. Fyfe, eds. 1943. *The art of falconry, being De arte venandi cum avibus of Frederick II of Hohenstaufen.* Stanford: Stanford University Press.

Wood, P. B. 1992. Habitat use, movements, migration patterns, and survival rates of subadult Bald Eagles in north Florida. Ph.D. diss., University of Florida.

Woodbridge, B., K. K. Finley, and S. T. Seager. 1995. An investigation of the Swainson's Hawk in Argentina. *J. Raptor Res.* 29:202–204.

Worth, C. B. 1936. Summary and analysis of some records of banded Ospreys. *Bird-Band.* 7:156–160.

Worthy, T. H., and R. N. Holdaway. 2002. *The lost world of the Moa.* Bloomington: Indiana University Press.

Wright, M. O. 1936. *Birdcraft.* 9th ed. London: Macmillan.

Yosef, R. 1996. Raptors feeding on migration at Eilat, Israel: Opportunistic behavior or migratory strategy? *J. Raptor Res.* 30:242–245.

Yosef, R., and D. Alon. 1997. Do immature Palaearctic Egyptian Vultures *Neophron percnopterus* remain in Africa during the northern summer? *Vogelwart* 118:285–289.

Yosef, R., and L. Fornasari. 2004. Simultaneous decline in Steppe Eagle (*Aquila nipalensis*) and Levant Sparrowhawk (*Accipiter brevipes*) reproductive success: Coincidence or Chernobyl legacy? *Ostrich* 75:20–24.

Yosef, R., L. Fornasari, P. Tryjanowski, M. J. Bechard, G. S. Kaltenecker, and K. Bildstein. 2003. Differential spring migration of adult and juvenile Levant Sparrowhawks *Accipiter brevipes* through Eilat, Israel. *J. Raptor Res.* 37:31–36.

Yosef, R., P. Tryjanowski, and K. Bildstein. 2002. Spring migration of adult and immature buzzards (*Buteo buteo*) through Eilat, Israel: Timing and body size. *J. Raptor Res.* 36:115–120.

Young, L. S., and M. N. Kochert. 1987. Marking techniques. In Raptor management techniques manual, ed. B. A. Giron Pendleton, B. A. Millsap, K. W. Cline, and D. M. Bird. 125–156. Washington, DC: National Wildlife Federation.

Zalles, J. I., and K. L. Bildstein. 2000. *Raptor watch: A global directory of raptor migration sites.* Cambridge, UK: BirdLife International; Kempton, PA: Hawk Mountain Sanctuary.

INDEX